INTERNATIONAL COURTS AND TRIBUNALS SERIES

General Editors: PHILIPPE SANDS, RUTH MACKENZIE, and CESARE P.R. ROMANO

Professional Ethics at the International Bar

INTERNATIONAL COURTS AND TRIBUNALS SERIES

A distinctive feature of modern international society is the increase in the number of international judicial bodies and dispute settlement and implementation control bodies; in their case-loads; and in the range and importance of the issues they are called upon to address. These factors reflect a new stage in the delivery of international justice. The International Courts and Tribunals series has been established to encourage the publication of independent and scholarly works which address, in critical and analytical fashion, the legal and policy aspects of the functioning of international courts and tribunals, including their institutional, substantive, and procedural aspects.

Professional Ethics at the International Bar

ARMAN SARVARIAN

OXFORD
UNIVERSITY PRESS

OXFORD
UNIVERSITY PRESS

Great Clarendon Street, Oxford, OX2 6DP,
United Kingdom

Oxford University press is a department of the University of Oxford.
It furthers the Universitys objective of excellence in research, scholarship,
and education by publishing worldwide. Oxford is a registered trade mark of
Oxford University Press in the UK and in certain other countries

First Edition published in 2013

Impression: 1

Published in the United States of America by Oxford University Press
198 Madison Avenue, New York, NY 10016, United States of America

British Library Cataloguing in Publication Data
Data available

Library of Congress Control Number: 2013943481

ISBN 978–0–19–967946–1

Printed and bound in Great Britain by
CPI Group (UK) Ltd, Croydon, CR0 4YY

Preface

The aim of this work is to inquire into the problem of divergent ethical standards applicable to counsel appearing before international courts and tribunals. The question is increasingly topical with the greater frequency and importance of ethical issues in general in the international judicial system, particularly those concerning the role of counsel. As a first effort to comprehensively examine the problem across the system, it brings original research and analysis to bear, including little-known material that can enrich the emerging debate about counsel ethics in the international law community.

The work comprises the culmination of a project spanning four years and based upon my doctoral thesis completed at the University College London Faculty of Laws. I thank my primary supervisor, Professor Philippe Sands, for his rigorous and invaluable supervision throughout the course of the project and for his assistance in its realization in myriad ways. I thank my secondary supervisor, Dr Douglas Guilfoyle, for his constant readiness to provide close scrutiny and a fresh perspective even in the most busy of times. I thank the University College London Faculty of Laws and the *Modern Law Review* for their financial support.

I thank the interviewees who participated in this study for their generous participation. I thank numerous librarians, court officials, and others who have assisted in facilitating the practical tasks that are vital to the success of a research project. Most importantly, I thank my family for its unfailing support throughout the project. Any errors contained in the work are entirely my own.

Arman Sarvarian

London, United Kingdom

Contents

List of Abbreviations

AEHRY	All-European Human Rights Yearbook
AFdDI	Annuaire Français de Droit International
AUJILP	American University Journal of International Law and Policy
AJIL	American Journal of International Law
ALQ	Arab Law Quarterly
ASILP	American Society of International Law Proceedings
BJILP	Berkeley Journal of International Law Publicist
BJIL	Berkeley Journal of International Law
BYIL	British Yearbook of International Law
CAHDI	Committee of Legal Advisers on Public International Law
CJR	Comparative Judicial Review
CLF	Criminal Law Forum
CLJ	Cambridge Law Journal
CLP	China Law & Practice
CLR	Canterbury Law Review
CMLR	Common Market Law Reports
CQ	The China Quarterly
CLP	Current Legal Problems
CMLR	Common Market Law Review
DJCIL	Duke Journal of Comparative and International Law
DLJ	Duke Law Journal
DLR	DePaul Law Review
DRI	Dispute Resolution International
DRJ	Dispute Resolution Journal
DSJ	Dispute Settlement Journal
ECR	European Court Reports
EEHRR	East European Human Rights Review
EHRLR	European Human Rights Law Review
EIPR	European Intellectual Property Review
EJIL	European Journal of International Law
EPIL	Encyclopaedia of Public International Law
ELR	European Law Review
ETMR	European Trade Marks Reports
FILJ	Fordham International Law Journal
GJLE	Georgetown Journal of Legal Ethics
GLJ	Georgetown Law Journal
GYIL	German Yearbook of International Law
HLR	Harvard Law Review
HaLR	Hamline Law Review
ICLQ	International and Comparative Law Quarterly
ICLR	International Criminal Law Review
ICSID Rev.-FILJ	ICSID Review Foreign Investment Law Journal
IJIL	Indian Journal of International Law
IJLI	International Journal of Legal Information

ILQ	International Law Quarterly
ILR	Israel Law Review
IRIPCL	International Review of Intellectual Property and Competition Law
Ir-USCTR	Iran-US Claims Tribunal Reports
JCL	Journal of Chinese Law
JHIL	Journal of the History of International Law
JIA	Journal of Investment Arbitration
JIC	Journal of Interprofessional Care
JICJ	Journal of International Criminal Justice
JJLS	The Journal of Japanese Legal Studies
JSCL	Journal of the Society of Comparative Legislation
LPICT	Law and Practice of International Courts and Tribunals
LSPI	Legal Services Policy Institute
MIAR	Mealey's International Arbitration Report
MLJ	McGill Law Journal
MLR	Michigan Law Review
MoLR	Modern Law Review
MPEPIL	Max Planck Encyclopaedia of Public International Law
MPYUNL	Max Planck Yearbook of United Nations Law
NCLR	New Criminal Law Review
NILQ	Northern Ireland Legal Quarterly
NJIL	Nordic Journal of International Law
NJW	Neue Juristische Wochenschrift
NQHR	Netherlands Quarterly of Human Rights
NUJIHR	Northwestern University Journal of International Human Rights
NYUJILP	New York University Journal of International Law and Politics
OJEU	Official Journal of the European Union
PILR	Pace International Law Review
QB	Queen's Bench
RdC	Recueil des Cours
RdDI	Revue de Droit International
RDP	Revue du Droit Public et de la Science Politique
RGdDIP	Revue Générale de Droit International Public
Rtdb	Annales de droit: revue trimestrielle de droit belge
RTDE	Revue Trimistrielle de Droit Européenne
SCLR	Santa Clara Law Review
SFDI	Société française pour le droit international
SULR	Suffolk University Law Review
TDM	Transnational Dispute Management
TGS	Transactions of the Grotius Society
TIL	The International Lawyer
TILJ	Texas International Law Journal
TxLR	Texas Law Review
TLR	Tulane Law Review
UNCIO	United Nations Conference on International Organization
UNGAOR	United Nations General Assembly Official Records
UNRIAA	United Nations Reports of International Arbitral Awards
UPILR	University of Pennsylvania International Law Review
VJIL	Virginia Journal of International Law

YEL	Yearbook of European Law
YLJ	Yale Law Journal
YJIL	Yale Journal of International Law

Table of Cases

*Arranged by jurisdiction in alphabetical order.

INTERNATIONAL CASES

Ad hoc Inter-State Arbitration

Commercial Arbitration

European Court of Human Rights

European Court of Justice, General Court of the European Union and European Free Trade Area Court

International Centre for the Settlement of Investment Disputes (including NAFTA)

International Court of Justice

International Criminal Tribunal for Rwanda

International Criminal Tribunal for the Former Yugoslavia

International Labour Organisation Administrative Tribunal

International Tribunal for the Law of the Sea

Iran-US Claims Tribunal

Permanent Court of International Justice

Special Court for Sierra Leone

World Trade Organisation

NATIONAL CASES

United States

United Kingdom

Table of Treaties and Other International Instruments

*Arranged by jurisdiction in alphabetical order. Dates denote either year of adoption or of most recent version, as appropriate.

International Codes of Conduct

International Criminal Tribunal for the Former Yugoslavia

Nuremberg International Military Tribunal

Permanent Court of International Justice

United Nations

World Trade Organisation

Table of National Legislation and Codes of Conduct

*Arranged by jurisdiction in alphabetical order. Dates denote either year of adoption or of most recent version, as appropriate.

UNITED STATES OF AMERICA

Introduction

The practice of public international law has been evolving over the past thirty years.[1] International litigation, once a rarefied field confined to insiders at traditional institutions such as the ICJ, has expanded greatly. This has been prompted by two major trends, namely an increase in the number of international courts and tribunals[2] ('international courts') and the revitalization of older courts. As parties have shown a greater propensity to litigate, older institutions like the PCA and ICJ have seen a resurgence of business and new courts have been created in growth areas like international criminal law and international investment law.

Moreover, the subject matter of international litigation has diversified. Once largely confined to areas such as territorial disputes and the law of the sea, it now covers a wider range of politically sensitive areas such as the use of force, trade, investment, and criminality. International law in general has correspondingly acquired a higher profile in the consciousness of societies throughout the world due to the expansion of the international judicial system. Whether in a war crimes trial at the ICC, trade disputes at WTO dispute settlement panels, or inter-State disputes at the ICJ, outsiders to international litigation have a growing interest in it.

One of the consequences of this expansion for the international judicial system is a greater focus on procedural matters. As parties resort to international litigation more often and in more sensitive areas and societies acquire a greater awareness of international courts, expectations of the judicial process can be expected to rise accordingly. Not only are new procedural issues such as jurisdictional conflicts between international courts emerging but longstanding matters like the independence of the judiciary have renewed importance.

Amidst these historical trends, this book examines the problem of common ethical standards for counsel appearing before international courts. As an emerging procedural issue, the regulation of advocacy in international litigation is increasingly important as the quantity and quality of litigation continues to grow and diversify. Traditionally considered to be a minor matter that was the exclusive prerogative of parties,[3] the conduct of counsel in international litigation has become increasingly topical.[4] In investment arbitration, procedural objections concerning the conduct of counsel and applications for their disqualification have become more commonplace

[1] Eg, Buergenthal, 'Proliferation of International Courts and Tribunals: Is it Good or Bad?', 14 *LJIL* (2001), 267–75; Guillaume, 'Advantages and Risks of Proliferation: A Blueprint for Action', 2 *JICJ* (2004), 300–3; Pocar, 'The Proliferation of International Criminal Courts and Tribunals: A Necessity in the Current International Community' 2 *JICJ* (2004), 304–8.

[2] For definition, see Chapter 1.

[3] Historically, 'parties' were only States—see Chapter 4. Today, parties are far more diverse.

[4] Eg, Vagts, 'The International Legal Profession: A Need for More Governance?' 90 *AJIL* (1996), 250–61; Mendelson, 'The International Lawyer in Domestic Law' in Wickremasinghe, *The International Lawyer as Practitioner* (2000), 163–84, 180–3; Cot, 'Appearing "For" or "On Behalf Of" a State: The

and there is ongoing debate concerning the feasibility of common ethical standards for counsel. The conduct of counsel appearing before other courts such as the ICJ and ITLOS has also been scrutinized. Prosecutors, defence counsel, and judges at the international criminal tribunals have encountered a variety of problems in creating a common culture designed to promote the integrity of the international judicial process.

As the parties in international litigation have greatly diversified, so too has the profile of the counsel who represent them. Whilst the group of primarily European professors and practitioners who have traditionally dominated the ICJ bar remains pre-eminent, the volume and variety of international litigation has nevertheless opened access to the international judicial system for counsel from other national and professional backgrounds. Those counsel bring with them a greater diversity of cultural traditions, standards, and preconceptions concerning the role of advocacy. The college of international lawyers has become increasingly aware of the propensity of these cultures to conflict, creating important procedural problems.

In the latter half of the twentieth century, there was a trend towards codification of ethical standards amongst national jurisdictions.[5] Wider developments such as the advent of the European Economic Community prompted efforts to identify common ethical standards amongst national jurisdictions for transnational work.[6] These include the International Bar Association (IBA) International Code of Ethics 1956, the Council of Bars and Law Societies of Europe (CCBE) Code of Conduct for European Lawyers 1988, the UN Basic Principles on the Role of Lawyers 1990 and the *Union Internationale des Avocats* Turin Principles of Professional Conduct for the Legal Profession in the Twenty-first Century 2002. In addition, codes of conduct were prescribed by the international criminal tribunals created at the turn of the twentieth century.[7] However, these articulated standards were not intended to address the specific problems arising for counsel from diverse national jurisdictions appearing before international courts.

Role of Private Counsel Before International Tribunals' in Ando, McWhinney, and Wolfrum, *Liber Amicorum Judge Shigeru Oda* (2002), 835–47; Jennings, 'The Work of the International Bar' in Vohrah et al, *Man's Inhumanity to Man* (2003), 443–66; Benson, 'Can Professional Ethics Wait: The Need for Transparency in International Arbitration', 3 *Dispute Resolution International* (2009), 78; Mosk, 'Attorney Ethics in International Arbitration', 5 *Berkeley Journal of International Law Publicist* (2010), 32–7; Higgins, 'Ethics and International Law' 23(2) *LJIL* (2010), 277–89, 288–9; Rogers, 'The Ethics of Advocacy in International Arbitration' in Bishop and Kehoe, *The Art of Advocacy in International Arbitration* (2010), 49–66; Crawford, 'Advocacy Before the International Court of Justice and Other International Tribunals in State-to-State Cases' in Bishop and Kehoe, *The Art of Advocacy*, 303–30, 304; Sands, 'Interaction between Counsel and International Courts and Arbitral Tribunals: Ethical Standards for Counsel' in Wolfrum and Gätzschmann (eds), *International Dispute Settlement: Room for Innovations?* (2010), 127–36; Sthoeger and Wood, 'The International Bar', in Romano, Alter, and Shany (eds), *The Oxford Handbook of International Adjudication* (2013). *Confer* the view that 'no legal rule governs the profession of Counsel before the ICJ'—Pellet, 'The Role of the International Lawyer in International Litigation' in Wickremasinghe, *The International Lawyer as Practitioner*, 147–62, 149.

[5] See Chapter 2.

[6] For background, see Rogers, 'The Ethics of Advocacy in International Arbitration' in Bishop and Kehoe, *The Art of Advocacy*, 49–68.

[7] See Chapter 8.

As a reaction to the perceived need for common ethical standards for counsel focusing upon international litigation senior members of the informal college of international lawyers have begun to address the problem. In 2001, the ILA created its 'Study Group on International Courts and Tribunals' tasked with, inter alia, examining ethics at the international Bench and Bar. In 2004, the Study Group published its 'Burgh House Principles on the Independence of the International Judiciary'. In 2010, this was followed by the 'Hague Principles on Ethical Standards for Counsel Appearing before International Courts and Tribunals'. In 2010, the IBA Arbitration Committee created a 'Task Force on Counsel Ethics in International Arbitration' to investigate whether the lack of international guidelines and conflicting norms in counsel ethics undermines the fundamental protections of fairness, equality, and the integrity of international arbitration proceedings. Also in 2010, the CCBE also created a working group to examine much the same territory.

Amidst the emerging debate concerning the need for professionalization of advocacy before international courts, there is limited scholarship on the subject. Although there is a growing awareness amongst practitioners concerning the problems emanating from divergent ethical standards, the causes and consequences of such conflicts have not been explored. The existing literature has drawn attention to specific problems (eg conflicts of interest) arising in the practice of particular courts but there is no work that comprehensively examines the subject from the perspective of the international judicial system as a whole. Whilst identifying particular problems (eg 'double deontology'[8]) concerning the prescription of common ethical standards, the scholarship has not hitherto comprehensively analysed the professionalization of advocacy.

Against this background, this book examines whether the professionalization of international advocacy through the articulation of common ethical standards for counsel is desirable and feasible. In addressing this question, the book has three objectives aimed at filling the gap in the scholarship in order to inform the debate concerning professionalization. The first objective is empirical, whereby it is intended to provide original research concerning hitherto little-known problems of international advocacy. As nascent initiatives to articulate common ethical standards and problems concerning counsel continue, the book is designed to provide judges, practitioners, and academics interested in the subject with a comprehensive analysis. Thus, the debate can be assisted by the original research contained in the book.

The second objective is practical, in that the book is aimed at providing judges and practitioners with a resource that can assist in the resolution of procedural problems arising from divergent ethical standards. Judges, arbitrators, registrars, and counsel who need to address challenges to the participation of counsel, allegations of professional misconduct, or other ethical issues connected to counsel would be able to refer to this book as a resource. The book can also assist in explaining points of divergence between national standards of advocacy.

The third objective is normative, whereby the book advocates the professionalization of advocacy. In this respect, the book is aimed widely at all persons (specialists,

[8] For explanation, see Chapter 2.

lawyers, or non-lawyers alike) who are interested in the conduct and integrity of the international judicial process. In seeking to persuade its readers of the potential benefits of professionalization, the book is intended to stimulate the process and thereby encourage the progressive development of international judicial procedure and the creation of an international judicial culture.

The book addresses divergences amongst ethical standards of counsel appearing before international courts. Accordingly, its scope is restricted to the practice of international advocacy connected with litigation. This necessarily excludes issues such as the advisory functions of legal advisers to governments, diplomatic functions exercised in international negotiations, and non-litigious dispute settlement. Whilst the book engages in comparative analysis of national ethics, it is also not concerned with transnational advocacy involving counsel appearing before various national courts.

Whilst select reference is made to various international courts, the book focuses upon the practice of advocacy before the ICJ, the ECJ, and the ICC. These courts were selected due to their different histories, jurisdictions and cultures. Whereas the ICJ is a traditional inter-State court, the ECJ is a regional court with a review-based jurisdiction for States, EU organs, and individuals and companies and the ICC is a criminal court hearing the Prosecutor (representing the States Parties and victims) and individual defendants. Thus, their commonalities (eg all three are permanent courts) and differences (eg different parties) provide a basis for comparison concerning the problems of advocacy in the international judicial system.

In considering the role of counsel, the book adopts a functional definition whereby it considers those who appear as counsel before international courts regardless of their professional or national backgrounds. This enables not only the identification of divergent standards in practice according to backgrounds but also the analysis of the efficacy of qualification requirements that already exist and additional requirements that could be imposed. Finally, it provides consideration of the functions of representatives (eg agents and counsel) before courts without preconceptions.

The material of the book comes from three categories of sources. The first category consists of primary research on treaties, cases, rules of procedure, national legislation and codes of conduct, international codes of conduct, and other instruments. The sources for this category comprise archival research, commentaries written by drafters and other key actors as well as biographical research into the protagonists. Thus, the book seeks not only to describe the cases and instruments but also to contextualize and interpret them in light of the participants' national and professional backgrounds.

The second category entails secondary sources, including commentaries concerning the practice and procedure of international litigation. In addition to the standard sources of published books and journal articles, the book draws upon electronic and other resources (particularly in constructing biographical information). The comparative analyses of national ethical standards rely upon national legislation, codes of conduct, and secondary commentaries by legal scholars and anthropologists upon the historical development of the legal professions.

The third category comprises 23 interviews with judges, registrars, and counsel from various international courts. These have been invaluable not only in informing the research and strengthening the analysis but also in illustrating the issues that are of particular concern to practitioners. The interviews are cited where permission has been given by the interviewee pursuant to approved drafts on file with the author. Where remarks have been provided on condition of anonymity, no attribution to the source has been made. Materials confidentially provided have similarly not been attributed but are noted as being on file with the author.

The book adopts a broadly historical structure which also accords with the division of the book into the two research questions of the desirability and feasibility of professionalization. Chapter 1 identifies the conceptual issues engaged by the topic and the arguments for and against the professionalization of advocacy. In particular, it focuses upon the role of advocacy within the international judicial system and its connection to the integrity of the international judicial process. It defines the key concepts and breaks the research question into its component parts.

Chapter 2 explores the historical origins of professional advocacy in key national jurisdictions and compares them in order to determine their commonalities and differences concerning the role and ethical standards of the professional advocate. In explaining the ethical standards and professional cultures that counsel bring with them to international courts, it provides the context in which international advocacy can be examined. Chapter 3 examines the historical development of international advocacy from the nineteenth century until the PCIJ, focusing upon the functions of representation in international judicial procedure and the issues arising in historical cases. This historical narrative identifies the origins of the modern procedural system of representation and brings hitherto unknown historical examples of arbitral tribunals and the PCIJ considering the professional regulation of counsel.

Chapters 4 to 8 examine certain aspects of the practice of advocacy before the ICJ, ECJ, and ICC. This continues the historical approach in moving from the oldest to the newest court. The structure of each chapter is broadly similar. First, it sets out the historical background to the creation of the court. Secondly, it analyses the relevant provisions concerning advocacy in its statute and rules of procedure. Thirdly, it examines the requirements laid down by the court for the admission of counsel to practise before it. Fourthly, it scrutinizes the problems that have arisen in practice in connection with the professional conduct of counsel. Finally, it addresses the disciplinary regime available at each court to address matters arising in practice concerning the conduct of agents and counsel.

Chapters 9 and 10 concern the current and future professionalization of advocacy before international courts. Chapter 9 examines the legal and practical challenges to international courts exercising regulatory jurisdiction over counsel as well as the nascent efforts made by practitioners to articulate common ethical standards. As indicated in Chapter 2, this is because international courts are considered by practitioners to be the principal candidates to regulate counsel in the event of professionalization in the absence of an international bar authority. Chapter 10 considers the possibility of creating such an authority as a long-term project as well as the potential consequences of professionalization for the international judicial system. The concluding section of this book summarizes its findings and offers final thoughts concerning the prospects for professionalization of advocacy before international courts and tribunals.

The central thesis of this book is that the professionalization of advocacy before international courts—the articulation of common, fundamental ethical standards regulating counsel appearing before international courts—is both desirable and feasible as a means of protecting the integrity of the international judicial process and thereby promoting the legitimacy of international courts. In arguing that professionalization is desirable, the book refers not only to its practical necessity as a means of solving existing problems and precluding potential ones but also as a means of raising standards in order to enhance the image of the international judicial system. In arguing that professionalization is feasible, the book refers both to the legal and practical challenges to its realization. In particular, it addresses the jurisdictional issues concerning the regulatory powers of international courts as well as the resources necessary for that jurisdiction to be exercised fairly and in harmony with national bars.

In proposing its central thesis, the book also offers arguments concerning the various sub-issues. A key argument concerning the articulation of common ethical standards is that conflicts amongst national standards should be resolved through selection where compromise and hybridization are impossible. This selectivity should be generally in favour of a stricter standard in the interest of procedural integrity. The book proposes a related argument that the ideological foundation of the international bar should be based upon the professional values of justice, independence, and the rule of law. Whilst these values are not shared by authoritarian judicial systems, they are nevertheless espoused as the core values of professional advocacy both by historical legacy and by moral necessity.

This subject is concerned with the creation of an 'international judicial culture'[9] within the procedural laws of international courts and tribunals. This necessarily entails the articulation of uniform professional values and the inculcation of those values into the practice of international advocacy. Whilst this endeavour is much broader than the role of counsel, the professionalization of advocacy is a part of that wider process. Professionalization is but one step in the continuous journey towards a comprehensively developed international judicial system that is equipped to handle the full spectrum of procedural issues connected to the judicial and arbitral settlement of international disputes.

[9] Harhoff, 'It is All in the Process: Reflections on the Relation Between International Criminal Tribunals and International Humanitarian Law' 78(4) *NJIL* (2009), 469–80.

1

The Role of Counsel Ethics in International Litigation

You are a Belgian professor retained as counsel in an ICJ case concerning a territorial dispute. Your client, without your prior involvement, annexes to its memorial 'historical documents' previously unknown to historians and emanating from its own archives to substantiate its claim. The veracity of those documents is challenged by the opposing party, following which your client admits that they are false and withdraws them. Your client instructs you to construct a new argument in the counter-memorial to replace the one undermined by the withdrawal of the false documents.

You are an English barrister in an ICSID arbitration concerning lucrative mineral rights. During proceedings, your client informs you that four private meetings have recently taken place between its representatives and a senior member of the legal team for the opposing party. In those meetings, the latter disclosed confidential information concerning his client's legal strategy and proposed a corrupt bargain whereby he would persuade his client to accept a settlement favourable to your client in exchange for a bribe. Your client insists that you keep your knowledge of them confidential.

You are a Gambian lawyer employed as an ICC Prosecutor. During a trial concerning a charge of forcibly conscripting child soldiers, your first witness abruptly recants in the witness box and accuses intermediaries you employed to gather evidence of bribing him to commit perjury. The Trial Chamber orders you to disclose the names of the intermediaries. The ICC Prosecutor instructs you to disregard the order on the ground that he has a higher duty under the ICC Statute to protect the safety of the intermediaries in a war zone.

These three scenarios are based upon real cases, for which all of the international courts concerned have not prescribed ethical standards applicable to the counsel concerned. All three individuals differ by nationality and vocation: the Dutch professor is bound by no professional standard, the English barrister is bound by the 'international practice rules' of the English Code and the Gambian lawyer has no code of conduct prescribed by the Gambian Bar Association. All three situations pose complex ethical problems upon which national standards diverge. All three problems threaten the integrity of the international judicial process.

This chapter outlines the central question of this book, namely, whether the professionalization of advocacy before international courts and tribunals through the articulation of common ethical standards for counsel is desirable and feasible. Whilst this question is highly practical, it also engages underlying questions of principle concerning the nature of international litigation and the role of counsel. These questions illustrate the complexity of professionalization and the consequent need for a nuanced approach.

Section 1.1 of the chapter sets out the principal function of the international judicial system. Contextualization of advocacy within the system is important because its professionalization could greatly affect the dynamics of litigation. Section 1.2 identifies the role of professional advocacy within international litigation. It analyses two distinct concepts, namely, professionalization as the *process* of creating a profession and professionalism as its *outcome*. Sections 1.3 and 1.4 consider the arguments for and against professionalization. The issues that arise concerning professionalization are based upon three central questions, namely: (1) its feasibility; (2) its desirability; and (3) its consequences. The arguments regarding these respective questions engage not only basic principles underpinning litigation but also tangible interests of the various actors involved, which define the emerging debate concerning professionalization. Section 1.5 summarizes the main themes of the research question.

1.1 The Function of the International Judicial System

To contextualize the role of representatives and professionalism within the international judicial system, it is necessary first to identify the function of that system. *Sensu stricto*, it is arguable that there is no 'system'[1] at all due to the absence of formal links between most international courts. However, such links may be informal (eg academia, personnel, or cross-fertilization). According to Brown:

> The emergence of a common law of international adjudication is significant for reasons other than its practical effects, for it might inform answers to broader questions concerning the systemic coherence of the international legal order... international courts are not created as part of a formal system. Several international tribunals have expressly stated that they consider themselves to be self-contained regimes without any links to other international courts. Yet the emergence of common standards in the procedure and remedies applied in international adjudication permits the suggestion to be made that despite the absence of formal institutional connections, international courts are beginning to operate as if they formed part of the same system.[2]

[1] '1. An organized or connected group of objects. 1.a. A set or assemblage of things connected, associated or interdependent, so as to form a complex unity; a whole composed of parts in orderly arrangement according to some scheme or plan'—'system *n.*', *Oxford English Dictionary* (1989), online: <http://www.oed.com/view/Entry/196665?redirectedFrom=system#eid> (Accessed: 6 June 2011).

[2] Brown, *A Common Law of International Adjudication* (2007), 255.

Thus, in this book the term 'international judicial system' is used loosely to describe a system with informal links amongst international courts.

Having asserted the existence of an informal system, the next step is to define an international court or tribunal. Whilst the term has become standard in the jurisprudence, it has yet to be definitively defined.[3] A useful, minimal definition employed for the purposes of this book is a permanent court or temporary tribunal created by an international instrument and vested with jurisdiction to adjudicate or arbitrate disputes between parties of which at least one is a State or international organization.[4] Although this circumvents definitional problems, it is useful for the purposes of this book because it encapsulates the issue of international adjudication with representatives from multiple national jurisdictions.

If the international judicial system can be described as an informal one, the next question is to identify its purpose. There are considerable jurisdictional and cultural differences amongst the respective courts. Nonetheless, the common feature to all international courts is the resolution of international disputes through judicial or arbitral procedure. Despite their considerable procedural differences, investment arbitral tribunals and criminal tribunals are both concerned with the common feature within the international judicial system, namely, the settlement of international disputes by arbitral or judicial means.

Two main schools of thought exist concerning the functional purpose of international litigation.[5] The first school asserts that international courts perform a private function in that they settle disputes between the parties and 'do justice' to them. The second school argues that international litigation also serves a public function beyond dispute settlement to develop the law and the wider legal system. The dividing line between these schools appears to be the degree of activism appropriate to the international judiciary in performing their duties.

If litigation[6] is the principal function of the international judicial system, the next question is whether there exist core standards of fairness by which litigation is conducted. This question, upon which no comprehensive study has been done, is vital in order to identify the elements of fair trial that are fundamental to all international courts. Whilst the scope of this book precludes a comprehensive examination of this important question, tentative observations are made in order to illustrate the connection between the integrity of judicial proceedings ('procedural integrity') and ethical standards for counsel.

In this book, procedural integrity entails fair trial principles connected to advocacy: (1) the equality of the parties; (2) the right to a fair hearing; (3) the right to counsel; and (4) an independent and impartial judiciary. Within these principles,

[3] Romano, 'The Proliferation of International Judicial Bodies: The Pieces of the Puzzle' 31 *NYUJILP* (1998–1999), 709–52, 712.

[4] Romano, 'The Proliferation of International Judicial Bodies', 713–15. *Confer* ILA Hague Principles, Principle 1.2.

[5] Brown, *A Common Law of International Adjudication*, 72–4.

[6] '1. The taking of legal action by a litigant; 2. The field of law that is concerned with all contentious matters'—*Oxford Dictionary of Law* (2009), online: <http://www.oxfordreference.com> (Accessed: 9 February 2011).

there are a number of sub-issues such as equality of arms, competent counsel and the submission of evidence. Whilst some of these principles are more obviously affected by counsel's conduct than others, professionalization is directly linked to the interests of the parties and the court to preserve procedural integrity. Lower standards of integrity endanger the confidence of the parties and the wider international community. Since the legitimacy of the system depends upon, inter alia, its procedural integrity, there is a manifest interest for judges, registrars and practitioners to promote it.

As the function of counsel is to represent parties before the court, his conduct not only concerns the parties' legal interests but also the international court's ability to effectively discharge its judicial duties. For example, admission standards for counsel clearly impact upon the right of parties to competent representation. Counsel's handling of evidence affects the parties' right to adduce evidence as well as the court's evaluation of it. Relations between bench and bar bear upon party equality and the independence and impartiality of the judiciary. Thus, there are clear links between the conduct of counsel, procedural integrity, and the legitimacy of the court.

There are three potential sources of law for procedural integrity within the international judicial system: (1) treaty law; (2) general principles of law; and (3) peremptory norms. Treaty law may be generally disregarded because there are few standards of procedural integrity common to international courts' statutes.[7] The criminal courts have statutory provisions[8] setting out extensive fair trial duties. The principles of procedural integrity common to the 'civil' courts appear to comprise party equality alongside judicial independence and impartiality.[9] The right to counsel is also prescribed in most statutes.[10]

There consequently appear to be two standards of procedural integrity in criminal courts and civil courts. The statutory duties imposed upon the criminal courts are more detailed and stringent whereas civil courts operate under more flexible and generic rules. This difference may be attributable to historical and cultural reasons (eg the 'diplomatic tradition' of classical inter-State arbitration) and the especially grave consequences of criminal trials for individual liberty. As explained below, aspects of fair trial that are connected to the prohibitions upon torture, inhumane treatment, and extrajudicial executions are considered to be peremptory norms. Thus, though it is possible to identify principles of procedural integrity that are common to all international courts, there exist different standards for criminal and civil litigation.

[7] Whilst each court's statute is central to its own proceedings, it rarely impacts upon other courts. Whilst the human rights treaties may create a universal standard applicable in national jurisdictions, these are generally inapplicable to international courts.

[8] Eg ICTY Statute, Art 21; ICC Statute, Arts 64, 67.

[9] Eg ILC Model Rules on Arbitral Procedure 1957, Preamble, OP5; ICJ Statute, Arts 2, 20, 35(2); ITLOS Statute, Arts 2(1), 11; AU Court of Justice Protocol, Arts 4, 9, 13, 15, 18(2); ECHR, Art 21(3); ECJ Statute, Arts 2, 4, 49; IACtHR Statute, Art 11(1), 18(1)(c). See also Rosenne, *The Law and Practice of the International Court 1920–2004* (2005), Vol III, 1036–9, 1048–52.

[10] Eg ICJ Statute, Art 42; ECJ Statute, Art 19; ICC Statute, Art 67. This was not allowed in the WTO dispute settlement body until 1997—*Bananas*, paras 4–12.

The second potential source of law for procedural integrity is as a 'general principle of law recognised by civilized nations'.[11] This entails its recognition as a duty of national courts within municipal legal systems, transposed to the international level. In both common law and civil law jurisdictions, it is axiomatic that courts must judge cases in accordance with core standards of procedural integrity. These are often enshrined in national constitutions and international human rights treaties, as refined by the jurisprudence of constitutional and international human rights courts.[12]

The third potential source of law for procedural integrity is the category of *jus cogens* or 'peremptory norms'. There is no clear consensus concerning their jurisprudential nature. One potential explanation is that they are natural law applied as international public policy[13] through international judicial practice, codifying bodies such as the International Law Commission and academia. As Orakhelashvili explains:

> ...it may be suggested that *jus cogens* is based on an autonomous body of superior rules, independent of any source of international law. This suggestion is intended not to provoke a discussion on the relationship between natural and positive law, but to emphasize the special character of peremptory norms. Also, the affirmation that peremptory norms can be created through an autonomous source does not necessarily operate to the exclusion of the relevance of other sources in the same process. It is only meant to address the question of possible lack of relevance of the traditional sources of law in giving rise to peremptory norms, and suggest the viable alternatives of comprehending the international public order in the context of the process of international law-making.[14]

The naturalist explanation for peremptory norms is historically accurate[15] and explains their doctrinal inconsistency with the *grundnorm* of consent,[16] both in their prescription and their superiority. One possibility is that they are subsumed as general principles of law recognized at the international level, not necessarily by States.[17]

An alternative explanation is that peremptory norms are an enhanced form of custom.[18] This, however, may be criticized as an attempt to artificially reconcile a non-consensual communal norm with the orthodoxy of consent.[19] Doctrinally,

[11] Brown, *A Common Law of International Adjudication*, 53–5.

[12] Eg Clayton and Tomlinson, *The Law of Human Rights* (2009), 11.425.

[13] Orakhelashvili, *Peremptory Norms in International Law* (2006), 36–8. Eg *Reservations to the Convention on the Prevention and Punishment of the Crime of Genocide*, [1951] *ICJ Rep* 15, 23. See also *Application of the Convention on the Prevention and Punishment of the Crime of Genocide (Bosnia and Herzegovina v Serbia and Montenegro)(Provisional Measures)*, 13 September 1993, Sep Op Judge Lauterpacht, 440 (para 100).

[14] Orakhelashvili, *Peremptory Norms in International Law*,109.

[15] Whewell, *Hugonis Grotii de jure belli et pacis libri tres* (1853) (Vol I), 9 (IX.2).

[16] Byers, 'Conceptualising the Relationship between *Jus Cogens* and *Erga Omnes* Rules', 66 *NJIL* (1997), 211–39, 230–1; Orakhelashvili, *Peremptory Norms in International Law*, 268–70, 518–27; Tams, *Enforcing Obligations Erga Omnes in International Law* (2005), 139–57.

[17] Orakhelashvili, *Peremptory Norms in International Law*, 126.

[18] Eg Byers, 'Conceptualising the Relationship between Jus Cogens and Erga Omnes Rules'.

[19] Orakhelashvili, *Peremptory Norms in International Law*, 125.

empirically, and historically the basis of custom is doubtful.[20] Not only is *jus cogens* the historical successor to *jus naturale* but there is scant evidentiary support of States for specific peremptory norms[21] alongside challenges to the existence of the category itself. Although there is no settled view concerning the creation of peremptory norms, the rationale of international public policy founded upon natural law through a combination of judicial and academic opinion seems more persuasive.

Having set out the difficulty of identifying the creation of a peremptory norm, the next question is whether procedural integrity is such a norm. Whilst it has been suggested that non-derogable elements within fair trial (eg judicial review of a criminal conviction) are peremptory norms,[22] the point is contested.[23] There is some judicial practice supporting that assertion but with scant reasoning.[24] The most recent authority is *Kadi*,[25] in which the EU General Court implicitly held that the right to be heard is a peremptory norm. However, the Court did not expressly endorse the applicant's argument on peremptory status but rather asserted that *all* 'fundamental human rights' are peremptory[26] and indirectly reviewed a UNSC resolution on the basis of fair hearing.[27]

Though dated, the most comprehensive study of fair trial remains the Chernichenko and Treat Report to the UN Commission on Human Rights of 1994.[28] The Special Rapporteurs concluded that fair trial had not been recognized as non-derogable in its entirety but only elements relating to criminal trials, including the right to counsel and to an independent and impartial tribunal.[29] They wrote:

> Therefore, while the right to a fair trial has not been recognized as a non-derogable right in article 4 of the International Covenant on Civil and Political Rights, [other treaties] indicate that aspects of the right to a fair trial have been accepted as non-derogable. Moreover, the broad framework of international standards related to fair trial which are not in the form of treaties, such as... the Basic Principles on the Independence of the Judiciary... the Basic Principles on the Role of Lawyers, and the Guidelines on the Role of Prosecutors, are intended to apply at all times... it is essential that the draft third optional protocol to the International Covenant on Civil and Political Rights be adopted. This optional Protocol, if adopted, would make the provisions of the International Covenant on Civil and Political Rights guaranteeing a fair trial and a remedy non-derogable in all situations.[30]

No such Protocol has since been adopted, suggesting that the Special Rapporteurs' conclusions remain broadly valid.

[20] Orakhelashvili, *Peremptory Norms in International Law*, 126–7.

[21] Orakhelashvili, *Peremptory Norms in International* Law, 114.

[22] Orakhelashvili, *Peremptory Norms in International Law*, 60 (note 138).

[23] Zappala, *Human Rights in International Criminal Proceedings* (2003), 9, 154.

[24] *Tadić* (Allegations of Contempt), p 3.

[25] *Kadi*. See also the related *Yusuf* (General Court) case. Although the judgment was set aside on appeal, the ECJ did not address the CFI findings on *jus cogens*—*Yusuf* (ECJ), paras 327–30.

[26] *Kadi*, paras 228–30.

[27] *Kadi*, paras 253–92.

[28] UN Commission on Human Rights, 'The right to a fair trial: Current recognition and measures necessary for its strengthening', UN Doc E/CN.1/Sub.2/1991/21 (3 June 1991).

[29] UN Commission on Human Rights, 'The right to a fair trial', paras 127–40.

[30] UN Commission on Human Rights, 'The right to a fair trial', para 140.

Thus, whilst fair trial is a derogable human right, elements of it are peremptory.[31] It may be suggested that there exists a 'core, irreducible minimum'[32] of fairness that is absolutely fundamental to judicial procedure. The Chernichenko and Treat Report suggests that, in the national context, core standards have hitherto focused upon criminal trials. Similarly, the jurisprudence at the international level (with the exception of the *Kadi* cases) recognizing peremptory elements of fair trial derives almost entirely from criminal tribunals. The explanation for this stricter standard lies in the gravity of criminal sanctions; in particular, the potential deprivation of personal liberty for convicts.[33]

1.2 The Role of Professional Advocacy in International Litigation

In considering the role of professional advocacy, the crucial question is whether professionalization would assist the international judicial system in discharging its principal function of adjudication. Efficiency and integrity are the rationales for professionalism: in exchange for creating a privileged class of advocates through a bar of admission, the system would benefit from strict standards of integrity and competence through ethical standards backed by disciplinary sanctions.

Societies throughout the world[34] have followed Shakespeare's tongue-in-cheek advice to revolutionaries to firstly 'kill all the lawyers'[35] by creating judicial systems that specifically excluded professional counsel as a privileged and corrupt class. These historical examples suggest that the downfall of professionalism has been intimately linked to the legitimacy of the profession. As Lord Bingham wrote:

> Few would choose to set foot in a court at any time in their lives if they could avoid it, perhaps echoing an Italian author's description of courtrooms as 'gray hospitals of human corruption'. As for the judges, the public entertain a range of views, not all consistent... although often unfavourable. But belief in the rule of law does not import unqualified admiration of the law, or the legal profession, or the courts, or the judges....The hallmarks of a regime which flouts the rule of law are, alas, all too familiar: the midnight knock on the door, the sudden disappearance, the show trial....The list is endless. Better to put up with some choleric judges and greedy lawyers.[36]

Thus, professionalism is predicated upon its ability to dedicate counsel to the service of justice and the rule of law with the tradeoff of an elite with a monopoly over rights of hearing and correspondingly reduced public accessibility to the courts. Ironically, this requires counsel to represent deeply unpopular clients (eg an alleged perpetrator of genocide or a 'pariah State'). Although international courts are more

[31] Orakhelashvili, *Peremptory Norms in International Law*, 59.

[32] *Per* Lord Bingham of Cornhill, *Secretary of State for the Home Department v MB (FC)* [2008] 1 AC 440, 479 (para 34), 482 (para 43).

[33] UN Commission on Human Rights, 'The right to a fair trial', para 129.

[34] Eg ancient China and Japan, pre-Georgian England, Saudi Arabia, the Massachusetts Bay Colony as well as revolutionary France, Russia, Iran, and the United States. See Chapter 2.

[35] *Henry the Sixth*, Act IV, Scene II.

[36] Bingham, *The Rule of Law* (2010), 9.

detached from the public eye, their public image is an important factor in their relevance to dockets.

1.2.1 Professionalism

If professional advocates have a class interest in the integrity and legitimacy of the judicial system upon which they depend for their existence, this begs the question of what public function this class serves thereby.[37] Since it is theoretically possible to construct judicial systems without professional counsel (as indeed is most of the international judicial system), it must be shown why professionalism is better than the alternatives. The most convincing rationale is that professionalism, in requiring moral behaviour from counsel through collective ethics and discipline, is a better safeguard for the integrity and competence of the international judicial system than the alternatives of general self-representation or amateur representation.

Professional ethics are a collective set of moral rules governing the provision of a service. They are, of course, not the only potential motivation for professional conduct. Others include personal morality and pressures from other collective entities whether from clients, the wider State law, the legal services markets, family, community, religion, and so on. What differentiates professional ethics from other sources of collective moral rules is their narrow application to select occupations as well as their endorsement by the State. This description of the status of professional ethics at the national level, however, does not explain why professionalism exists. The concept is of historically recent origin as a response to corruption by compelling advocates to behave morally. Architectural reforms in France, the UK, and elsewhere to liberalize the legal professions and promote a 'competitive ethos' have challenged this traditional ideology.

If the overarching rationale of professionalism is to promote the fundamental norm of procedural integrity within the international judicial system, the concept has still to be defined to identify its features. Three distinct criteria are necessary for the existence of a professional system of representation: (1) qualification requirements for the admission of representatives to advocacy; (2) ethical rules governing representatives' professional conduct; and (3) a disciplinary regime that investigates and enforces alleged professional misconduct. The function of admission requirements is to ensure a minimal threshold of competence and training in the art of forensic advocacy. Professional ethics guide advocates by defining their duties, particularly in difficult situations. A disciplinary regime exists to investigate and sanction professional misconduct with expertise and procedural fairness.

Prescription is an important, perhaps even an indispensable, part of professional ethics. It provides corporealness and precision to ethereal custom and etiquette. This is particularly important in moving beyond ethereal principles to address specific, nuanced dilemma. Although ethical principles appeared in statutes from the

[37] Do lawyers have a concordat with society to do 'good works' as the price for their independence—Abel, 'Revisioning Lawyers' in Abel and Lewis, *Lawyers in Society: An Overview* (1995), 1–38, 16.

Middle Ages, professional ethics primarily existed in custom through rulings by self-regulating professional bodies until the twentieth century. This may be responsible for the subconscious perception of ethics in some quarters as cultural rather than legal principles. Thus, codification of ethics is not only a matter of articulating common principles but also of enhancing their authority to compel advocates to respect those principles in practice. Crucial to their authoritativeness is the content of the principles themselves in striking the right balance between a disregard for the benefits of consensus amongst practitioners and a failure to address controversial issues that demand normativity.

1.2.2 Professionalization

Advocacy has primarily been a self-regulating profession within the European jurisdictions whence it originated. Gradually, the professions organized into bar associations to which individual advocates are professionally accountable. Two principal justifications may be offered for this approach: (1) professional independence, particularly to preserve freedom from client pressure; and (2) competence in forensic advocacy, in that non-professionals cannot presume to judge what they have not themselves done.

However, self-regulation is not a requirement for the existence of a profession. It should not be assumed that self-regulation is necessarily the end-goal of professionalization or that it is the ideal or only form which a profession can take. It is arguable that professionalism stems not from institutions but from culture. A profession formally regulated by the State may be substantively independent whilst one formally self-regulating may in reality be subservient. Moreover, it is arguable that expertise in the ethics of advocacy may be attained from study and not only from experience against the common wisdom that only those who have been practitioners can judge practitioners.

An additional objection to self-regulation is the existence of an incentive to promote collective interests as perceived by the profession. Paradoxically, institutions comprising professionals may not be the most trustworthy to uphold professionalism. A variety of motives may corrupt professional discipline and begin the process of de-legitimization and decay of the profession itself. Although the survival of professional advocacy is linked to its reputation amongst the wider public, professionalization is arguably self-defeating by creating a corporate interest of professionals that replaces the altruistic interests of justice that they are intended to serve.

Professionalization is employed in this book to denote the transition from an unregulated system of advocacy to one regulated by professionalism.[38] The two traditional sociological theories are the 'trait' approach and 'functionalist' approach.[39] The former is concerned with identifying key attributes of professionalism and assessing whether a given occupation possesses them to qualify as

[38] Johnson, *Professions and Power* (1972), 22.
[39] Johnson, *Professions and Power*, 27–38.

a profession. The latter is a reaction to the former by contextualizing the occupation within the wider society to which it belongs rather than accepting the image that professionals have of themselves. Although other theories have been offered, sociologists generally agree that professionals and professions act for a dual motive 'to provide service and use their knowledge for economic gain'.[40] The struggle between the 'grand old men' of commercial arbitration and the Anglo-American law firms concerning disclosure of conflicts of interest at the International Chamber of Commerce is emblematic of this mixing of principles and market competition.[41]

Assessment of the validity of these competing sociological theories for professionalism is beyond the scope of this book. However, since the book is concerned with the professionalization of the international bar, it is worth considering both of the questions that they pose. The book attempts to identify the attributes which the international bar must attain in order to become a profession and to understand the historical causes for the nascent professionalization being attempted by certain members of the international bar, for which the unique traits of the international bar are critical.

1.2.3 Fundamental Ethical Duties

One of the primary functions of the advocate is to seek to persuade the court of the righteousness of his client's cause. This may be regarded as the 'private' aspect of forensic advocacy. There is clearly a tension between the public interest in ensuring that justice is done and the private interest of the client in defending his interests. A key argument in this book is that all ethical problems of advocacy may be encapsulated within a basic dilemma, namely, conflicts between the duties owed by an advocate to justice, court, and the client. In this context, justice is mainly procedural but may also be substantive or consequential. The court refers to the institution, comprising the judiciary and registry. The client encompasses the *legal* interests that the advocate defends.

A common conception of professional ethics envisages competing duties to the court and the client. However, the court's interests may not always coincide with those of justice. Judges, arbitrators, and registrars can misbehave and the political interests of the court may pressure counsel to disregard procedural integrity. For example, the selective justice of the ICTR in not prosecuting alleged war criminals from the Rwandan Patriotic Front resulted from obstruction by the Tutsi-run Rwandan government.[42] Institutional interests require practical cooperation to function whereas justice demands the impartial exercise of the prosecutorial

[40] Krause, 'Death of the Guilds: Professions, States and the Advance of Capitalism, 1930 to the Present' (1996), ix in Evetts, 'Professionalisation and Professionalism: Issues for Interprofessional Care' 13(2) *JIC* (1999), 119–28, 120.

[41] Dezalay and Garth, *Dealing in Virtue: International Commercial Arbitration and the Construction of a Transnational Legal Order* (1996), 33–62.

[42] Reydams, 'The ICTR Ten Years On: Back to the Nuremberg Paradigm?' 3 *JICJ* (2005) 977–88.

discretion. There may also be cases in which the court is unaware of a threat to justice. For example, the ICSID arbitrators in *Foresti* were ignorant of secret meetings between the claimants and an advocate for the respondent in which a corrupt bargain was discussed.[43] The claimants eventually informed their counsel who, bound by confidentiality, advised disclosure. An overriding duty to justice requires the advocate to act even without judicial order.

1.3 Arguments for the Professionalization of Advocacy

Some of the arguments for and against the professionalization of advocacy have already been foreshadowed, which revolve around the two basic issues of the desirability and feasibility of articulating common ethical standards as a means of protecting procedural integrity. The arguments in favour of professionalization are: (1) professionalism is necessary to solve recurring problems in practice; (2) professionalism is desirable to enhance the image of the international judicial system; and (3) professionalization is achievable through progressive stages. Since professionalization is used both in a trait sense of attaining the concrete attributes of a professional bar identified above and in a functional sense of raising ethical standards to promote the legitimacy of the practice of international advocacy in wider society, these arguments address both end-goals.

1.3.1 Solving Practical Problems

The first, and most compelling, argument in favour of professionalization is that professionalism is necessary to solve real problems that have repeatedly arisen and continue to arise in practice. They point to two basic problems, both of which can seriously threaten procedural integrity: (1) conflicting national standards of conduct amongst professionals on important procedural points; and (2) the presence of non-professional advocates who are not bound by any ethical rules whatsoever. Amongst those practitioners who have participated in the nascent project of professionalization or who are otherwise in favour of it, necessity is the most frequently raised argument. Consequently, one explanation for the professionalization phenomenon is as a reaction to practical problems that are sufficiently frequent as to prompt remedial action.

However, it should not be assumed that their perception is necessarily accurate or that their personal experiences imply a wider systemic problem. It is arguable that professionalization could be said to be an overreaction to isolated or relatively infrequent problems and that, taken as a whole, the existing regulatory setup has proved itself to be adequate. Thus, the crucial test for determining whether professionalization is necessary is whether practice shows that ethical problems

[43] See Chapter 7.

threatening procedural integrity occur sufficiently frequently to justify the change. Since the necessity argument is predicated upon facts, those facts must be clearly proved.

This is one of the most important forensic tasks of this book and entails three stages of research. The first stage is to examine whether national standards of conduct, in principle, diverge from one another. This is the purpose of the inquiry into national traditions of advocacy in Chapter 2. The second stage is to determine how and why international advocacy is currently practised as it is. This is done through a historical analysis of international advocacy in Chapter 3. The third stage is to assess the practice and procedures of international courts to determine whether divergent standards of conduct actually exist and, if so, whether they have caused significant problems. This is done in scrutinizing the jurisprudence of the ICJ, ECJ, investment arbitral tribunals, and ICC in Chapters 4 to 8. An additional strand to this argument is that, even if certain problems have not yet occurred in practice or have arisen only infrequently, professionalization is nevertheless necessary to prevent rather than cure by clarifying ambiguities and deterring misconduct.

1.3.2 Enhancing the Image of International Courts

A second argument in favour of professionalization is that a professional image would be beneficial to international courts in promoting their legitimacy amongst the public and thereby boost the confidence of their constituents. For example, the respect of national judges for their international counterparts (and, by extension, for the latter's decisions) would arguably increase along with a more meritocratic, transparent, and formal system of judicial recruitment and regulation.[44] Analogically, national respect for the quality of international adjudication would presumably increase as a result of a more meritocratic, transparent, and formal system of advocacy. It may be surmised that that confidence would, in turn, be useful in attracting future business from potential litigants. Thus, this argument is essentially about using a reputation for procedural integrity and sophistication to attract business for international courts.

Whilst this argument clearly applies most readily to those international courts with consent-based jurisdictions like the ICJ and ITLOS, it may also be applied to those courts with compulsory jurisdictions such as the ECJ, ICC, and ECtHR. For the ICC and ECtHR, there is continual pressure to sustain and enhance their external legitimacy. In the case of the ICC, this is in order to attract more States to accede to the Rome Statute. In the case of the ECtHR (and, to a lesser extent, the ECJ in the EU context) this is in order to keep the existing parties within the Council of Europe and, crucially, to persuade certain States to fully implement adverse judgments.

[44] Eg Hoffman, 'The Universality of Human Rights', *Judicial Studies Board Annual Lecture* (19 March 2009), online: <http://www.judiciary.gov.uk/Resources/JCO/Documents/Speeches/Hoffmann_2009_JSB_Annual_Lecture_Universality_of_Human_Rights.pdf> (Accessed: 6 November 2011), para 38.

Consequently, the image of those courts is an important factor for their overall agenda for which professionalization could be a helpful tool. It can also be about enhancing the prestige of the court amongst professional practitioners. In the words of one judge at the Strasbourg Court:

> For me, having a code of conduct is as much a question of appearances to the outside world as it is a question of practice. It is difficult to explain to the outside world why we have ethics for judges, doctors, politicians and even for companies but we do not need them for counsel. Also, can we as a Court honestly say that we are so much better that we are not ourselves subject to temptations or to difficulties? For example, when we were considering the Resolution on Judicial Ethics, several drafts had to be prepared and put to the Plenary before an acceptable version was found. This process took between one and two years and I now think that it was a good thing that it took so much time because it really made us stop and think about these issues, particularly those judges who were sceptical at first about the whole idea. For example, on the propriety of accepting gifts or honours, can we say that accepting a small plate from a bar association leaves a judge open to accusations of bias? Clearly not. But then, can we say that accepting an all-expenses-paid holiday trip offered by a bar association or a government, for example a judge's home country, would leave that judge free from such suspicions of improper influence? Maybe not. It can often be difficult for judges, who realise that these people wish to be kind and honour them, to refuse such gifts as improper without telling a white lie to get out of it. With a Resolution that they can cite, that problem disappears completely. When you get into the details, you realise that things are more complex than they may at first appear.[45]

The counter-argument to this assertion is that it cannot be proved that professionalization would necessarily enhance the images of international courts. Furthermore, if the project is being done solely or principally for that purpose, it is arguably a weak rationale for investing effort into changing a working system if it cannot be proved that there is a real need in practice. Whilst it is impossible to predict the impact of professionalization on the image of the international judicial system, in principle it is certainly arguable that it would have a certain positive effect.

1.3.3 Stages of Professionalization

Moving from desirability to feasibility, an argument for professionalization is that it is achievable through clearly identifiable stages. In this respect, a programme for the project can be constructed that would progressively lead to the normalization of professionalism in the international judicial system. The following outline may be considered:

(1) articulation of common ethical standards based upon the consensus of practitioners from a range of professional and national backgrounds;

[45] Interview with Judge Elisabet Fura (15 October 2010), cited with permission.

(2) application of those articulated principles by individual international courts to solve problems arising in their proceedings;
(3) prescription of codes of conduct inspired by those principles into the procedural rules of individual courts;
(4) construction of a disciplinary jurisdiction harmonized across courts;
(5) harmonization of international regulatory jurisdictions with national bars; and
(6) imposition of admission requirements in international courts.

Although Chapter 10 examines the possibility of centralization into a unified international bar, self-regulation is not a requirement for professionalism. As will be seen in Chapter 9, a decentralized model reflecting the fragmented nature of the international judicial system not only achieves professionalism but is also more practicable than the centralization of regulatory authority. Whilst there would clearly an element of cross-fertilization amongst international courts in taking these steps, a centrifugal international judicial system necessarily precludes complete uniformity of professionalism. Rather, it is likelier that international courts will develop their own standards according to their particular needs and cultures whilst informally referring to each other's activity in doing so.

Of course, it cannot be predicted exactly how professionalization will take shape. In this very early stage of the process, the first stage has already begun with the articulation of the ILA Hague Principles. As will be considered in Chapter 7, those Principles are a response to the argument against professionalization set out below that the articulation of universal standards is impossible. However, even if the Principles can be accepted as an achievement of its goal, there are other practical difficulties that will need to be solved in order to complete professionalization. Those obstacles include double deontology, procedural safeguards for professional discipline, and the potential opposition of some States to the deprivation of traditional prerogatives. Thus, the crucial test for the feasibility of professionalization is the ability to craft inventive solutions for these complex problems and to persuade practitioners and States that, far from a threat to their interests, professionalization would in fact serve them.

An important question is the potential consequences of professionalization upon the international judicial system. The current system of largely unregulated advocacy creates three principal problems: (1) an imbalanced playing field, whereby some advocates are bound by standards to which others are not; (2) conflicting national standards demanding harmonization and uniformity; and (3) unaddressed misconduct for want of a clear regulatory framework. Since the rationale of professionalization is to protect procedural integrity and these problems adversely affect that integrity, the test for its success is whether it solves those problems. The scale of the impact of the project upon the practice of advocacy depends upon the incisiveness of senior practitioners and the judiciary. Although it is unlikely that professionalization would have no effect at all, moderate steps would produce only a moderate result.

1.4 Arguments against the Professionalization of Advocacy

In the emerging debate amongst practitioners concerning professionalization, cogent arguments have been made against it. Those arguments principally point towards the considerable difficulties of implementation but also, less persuasively, suggest that the end-goal of professionalism is in principle undesirable. Although the debate has hitherto focused upon the merits of the project itself, an important undercurrent is the potential impact of professionalization upon the legal services market. Thus, in addition to the need to demonstrate that professionalization is both feasible and desirable, a subtle but crucial political dimension must be accounted for to enlist the support of international law practitioners by persuading sceptics that the project accords with their interests.

The arguments put forward concerning the feasibility of the project are broadly threefold: (1) common ethical principles are impossible to articulate; (2) enforcement of those principles is impracticable; and (3) professionalization would infringe sovereignty of those parties that are States, by limiting the pool of available advocates and increasing the independence of their counsel from their control. Arguments advanced regarding desirability are: (1) codes of conduct would encourage abusive litigiousness amongst counsel; and (2) professionalization is a conspiracy of common law practitioners to remove Romano-Germanic academics from litigation. Whilst it is suggested that, on close examination, the arguments concerning feasibility are stronger than those on desirability the objections are in all cases helpful to illustrate the complexities of changing the ethos of the international bar.

1.4.1 Common Ethical Standards are Impossible

The first argument relating to feasibility is that it is impossible to articulate common ethical standards. This assertion runs counter to the existence of texts drafted by professional organizations during the past half-century identifying universal ethical principles—notably the UN Basic Principles on the Role of Lawyers and the CCBE Code of Conduct. However, a more subtle variation of the argument is that such instruments reflect consensus on only the most straightforward issues and consist of broad, vacuous principles that gloss over important national differences. Thus, it is arguable that the rationale of solving practical problems is defeated by the fact that lawyers from diverse jurisdictions are unable to agree on solutions.

At first sight, there is force in this argument. An examination of the texts that have hitherto been produced proposing universal ethical principles[46] reveals that in committees differences on key issues are often resolved by adopting a consensual

[46] See Chapter 7.

approach or by omitting the issue from the text.[47] Both of these methods defeat the very purpose of the exercise, namely, to produce *common* standards. There is also a case to be made that, on certain questions, national divergences are too great to achieve consensus. For example, witness proofing entailing pre-testimonial practice sessions between counsel and witness is unethical in England and Wales, a crime in France, and professionally negligent if *not* done in the United States. With such major differences amongst even these three jurisdictions, it appears impossible to forge consensus on practically important questions.

However, on closer examination the argument is flawed. First, it assumes that consensus is the only method by which common ethical principles can be articulated. However, it is possible through comparison of various national approaches alongside analysis of the underlying policy arguments to select or synthesize competing alternatives. An example of this may be seen in the ICC Trial Chamber's decision to depart from the ad hoc criminal tribunals' practice of accepting witness proofing in the *Lubanga* trial.[48] This does not imply that a selective or synthetic approach will necessarily be optimal but only that a lack of consensus on a particular issue is not necessarily an insurmountable obstacle to a coherent principle.

Secondly, it discounts the potential value of a minimalistic, anodyne text. This ignores the fact that the international bar is not a cohesive, organized body but rather a fragmented and mostly unregulated mass of individuals from a wide range of professional and national backgrounds. In particular, the lack of admission requirements at courts like the ICJ means that non-lawyers can and do represent parties who have no background in advocacy and are bound by no professional standards. Moreover, academic lawyers may be admitted who are similarly not bound by ethical standards and are unlikely to be experienced advocates. Hence, what may appear mundane to professional practitioners who are required to be conversant with professional ethics is not necessarily obvious to a great many of their counterparts.

Thirdly, the argument disregards the possibility of the gradual accretion of ethical norms through practice. It is arguably sensible for a universal set of ethical principles to be initially drafted in a relatively cautious and anodyne fashion to ensure sufficient consensus. The experience of the abortive CCBE Ethical Guidelines for Lawyers in Arbitration 2011, discussed in Chapter 9, is a case in point. On this approach, the priority at the beginning of professionalization is to create a framework within which the entire topic of professional ethics can be considered in international litigation. As controversial issues are addressed through court decisions, seemingly intractable problems would gradually become amenable to compromise, synthesis, or selection.

Fourthly, the argument is self-contradictory due to the critical importance of striking a balance between the need for consensus by avoiding risk and the

[47] For example, an inclusive approach to the issue of witness proofing is adopted in the ILA Hague Principles (Principle 6.2) whilst it does not feature in the CCBE Code of Conduct at all.

[48] See Chapter 8.

importance of answering the practical demand for normativity. The authority of a text depends upon that balance by avoiding a document that is so cautious that it will rarely be useful whilst also resisting the temptation of a too-ambitious text that lacks authority. This political factor is essential to inspire confidence.

Fifthly, the argument ignores the potential utility of even a conservative, anodyne text to practitioners. There is potential scope for professional negligence actions against counsel whose conduct is criticized by international courts. Without common ethical standards or organized regulation before the court in question, the determination of such a claim is likely to be complex. The applicable standards will depend upon the professional circumstances of the counsel in question and the forum of the claim, which may not fully appreciate the difficulty of applying its own norms to the individual concerned for conduct before an international court with an ethical vacuum. The potential consequences, particularly for individuals lacking professional liability insurance, can be ruinous.[49]

1.4.2 Enforcement is Impracticable

Another argument employed concerning the feasibility of professionalization is that, even if common ethical standards can usefully be identified, enforcement of them is impracticable. This is an important point that can be usefully divided into two sub-issues: (1) the competence of international courts as enforcers; and (2) conflicts of jurisdiction with national bars, known in professional ethics jargon as 'double deontology'. The argument is predicated upon the assumption that an unenforceable code is useless. Whilst a forensic study of the effects of an exhortative code as opposed to a binding one upon advocates' conduct in practice is beyond the scope of this book, it is suggested that this assumption appears to be correct in principle as there is scant cause for practitioners or courts to pay attention to an unenforceable code except as a source of inspiration for the development of binding rules to be applied in the resolution of ethical problems. Thus, since common ethical standards ultimately emanate from a regulatory jurisdiction empowered to pronounce upon matters of principle, the goal of professionalization is to development of ethical *rules* rather than exhortative *principles*.

The first sub-issue concerning the competence of international courts may itself be sub-divided into the question of jurisdiction to exercise regulatory powers over advocates ('competence' as a matter of law) and the question of the expertise of the judges and registrars who would presumably be called upon to adjudicate ethical matters ('competence' as a matter of fact). This issue is a key theme of Chapter 9, which explores not only the potential legal bases for international

[49] A recent example is *RSM* where, after having successfully represented the respondent, Freshfield Buckhaus Deringer has been sued in the US Federal District Court for the District of Columbia by the applicant for knowingly accepting a retainer paid through a corrupt relationship—Weismann, 'Freshfields Sued in International Racketeering Case', *The National Law Journal* (29 March 2010), online: <http://www.law.com/jsp/nlj/PubArticleNLJ.jsp?id=1202446897911&slreturn=1&hbxlogin=1> (Accessed: 3 July 2011). See also Sarvarian, 'Problems of Ethical Standards for Representatives before ICSID Tribunals' 10(1) *LPICT* (2011), 67–134, 99–100.

courts as regulators in detail but also the difficulties that arise from the regulation of the international bar by the international bench. However, the principal themes may be listed briefly here.

Concerning jurisdiction, the basic question is whether international courts are empowered to regulate counsel at all. The answer to this question clearly varies on a case-by-case basis and international courts have reached different conclusions for their own purposes. A critical question is whether the doctrine of inherent jurisdiction (also, perhaps erroneously, known as the doctrine of inherent powers) may be invoked by international courts in the absence of an express or implied statutory power as a legal source for such regulatory jurisdiction. The importance of this particular question is that, if the doctrine can be shown to apply, it would almost certainly apply universally to all international courts by its very nature unless it can be proved that the inherent jurisdiction is displaced by an express or implied statutory provision.

Regarding expertise, there are multiple layers to the question of whether international judges are practically capable of regulating the ethical conduct of counsel. One layer is that the qualification requirements for international judges do not require them to have practised themselves as counsel or to be conversant with the professional ethics of counsel, which is surely a basic requirement. Consequently, there are many judges and arbitrators with professional backgrounds in academia, diplomacy, or government without any expertise in counsel ethics. This is not only important in principle but also carries the grave danger of a miscarriage of justice towards a counsel who may suffer serious professional consequences from an adverse finding by an incompetent judge—in many courts (eg investment arbitral tribunals) without recourse of appeal. A second layer is the nascent professionalization of the international judiciary, a process that has begun in parallel with that of counsel. A third layer is the importance of procedural safeguards during the disciplinary process that protects basic standards of fairness for the accused counsel. Without a carefully constructed disciplinary mechanism, the authority of the court can be damaged.

The second sub-issue of enforcement is the question of double deontology. Within regulatory jurisdiction, this has both a prescriptive and a disciplinary element. The prescriptive element entails a clash between national and international codes of conduct whereby an advocate bound by both is forced to choose between them. Alternatively, an advocate who is stridently opposed to a particular ethical rule in the international code may seek to invoke his national code in order to circumvent it. The disciplinary element involves an advocate being tried twice for the same conduct. This can be envisaged if, for instance, the advocate chooses (or is ordered by the court) to follow the rule of the international code and subsequently faces disciplinary proceedings at his national bar for a violation of the national code. This has the potential to provoke a practically disruptive standoff between the international court and the national bar. This is not a far-fetched scenario in the case of, for example, a complaint by a disgruntled client or opposing party or counsel. Additionally, the national bar may be seized *ex proprio motu*. Several of these problems have already arisen in the practice of the international criminal tribunals, as explored in Chapter 6. However, despite the considerable obstacles in the enforcement problem, it is suggested that they are tricky but far from insurmountable.

1.4.3 Professionalization would Infringe Sovereignty

One of the principal objections to professionalization is that it would infringe sovereignty. This argument is classified as pertaining to the desirability of professionalization rather than feasibility because, as a matter of law, there is no basis for distinguishing between parties that are States and parties that are not in connection to the regulation of representation. This is subject to an important exception, namely, the imposition of admission requirements for agents. There, States have a statutory right to select whomever they wish as agents at courts like the ICJ and ECJ.

The argument that international courts lack the power to regulate States' representation, which is the latter's exclusive prerogative, engages the wider relationship between parties and the courts. One flaw is that it distinguishes between parties despite the fundamental principle of party equality. A second flaw is that it ignores the existence of many powers of international courts to control the presentation by parties of their case, such as the admissibility of claims or evidence. Such powers are grounded in the need for courts to control proceedings before them in order to ensure that adjudication proceeds in accordance with fundamental principles of procedural integrity. A third flaw is that it confuses the right of States to provide or withhold their consent to the jurisdiction of international courts with their procedural rights as parties once that consent has been provided.[50] A fourth flaw is that the argument explains neither the origin nor the purpose of the State prerogative to control representation.

Sovereignty etymologically derives from the Vulgar Latin term *superanus* ('chief') and the Old French term *souveraineté* ('majesty').[51] Although it is often misunderstood as denoting the *absolute* self-accountability characteristic of pre-medieval despotism, this was not its original meaning when coined by Jean Bodin in 1606.[52] Rather, Bodin asserted the divine independence of kingship from Pope, Emperor, Estates, or suzerain subject to natural law.[53] Subjects, by consequence, were generally required to obey the commands of the sovereign (*leges*) unless they contravened the laws of God (*jura*) from which the supreme legislative authority (*potestas legibus soluta*) derived.[54] Subsequently, the term was detached from its original meaning[55] to denote

[50] Higgins, 'Respecting Sovereign States and Running a Tight Courtroom' 50 *ICLQ* (2001), 121–32, 132.

[51] 'Sovereignty', *Encyclopaedia Britannica*, online: <http://www.britannica.com/EBchecked/topic/557065/sovereignty> (Accessed: 10 May 2011).

[52] Bodin, *The Six Bookes of a Commonweale* (1962).

[53] Bodin, *The Six Bookes of a Commonweale*, A15–A16, 84–113.

[54] Bodin, *The Six Bookes of a Commonweale*, A15–A16, 92.

[55] Eg Hobbes, *Leviathan* (1947), 113–20; Austin, *The Province of Jurisprudence Determined* (1968), 191–3. See also Bentham, *An Introduction to the Principles of Morals and Legislation* (1982), 11, 35.

'untrammelled authority and power and it is in such discourse that the term can be problematic'.[56] Such absolutism is diametrically opposed to the rule of law which, as the late Lord Bingham suggests, 'is the nearest we are likely to approach to a universal secular religion'.[57] The rule of law as a *grundnorm*[58] of political society was asserted as long ago as Aristotle.[59]

In the modern era, the incompatibility of sovereignty with the rule of law is illustrated by the oft-cited *Lotus* case for the proposition that States are free to do anything that international law does not specifically forbid (the so-called '*Lotus* presumption'):

> International law governs relations between independent States. The rules of law binding upon States therefore emanate from their own free will as expressed in conventions or by usages generally accepted as expressing principles of law and established in order to regulate the relations between these co-existing independent communities or with a view to the achievement of common aims. Restrictions upon the independence of States cannot therefore be presumed.[60]

Leaving aside the question of whether this statement was part of the Court's conclusive reasoning, the proposition is self-contradictory because it begins from the premise that 'international law *governs*' relations between States. The subsequent assertion that 'the rules of law... *therefore* emanate from their own free will' is illogical. Law cannot *govern* (*régit*) from *consent* (*la volonté*); rather, law can *grant* the *right* of consent. The only true 'sovereign' in the absolute sense is outside of international law (ie not a State).

Absolute sovereignty is historically inaccurate and fundamentally incompatible with the rule of law, which should be recognized as a basic or 'constitutional' norm of international law instead of the 'anachronistic idea of the total independence and autonomy of the state'.[61] Therefore, it is suggested that the argument that professionalization would infringe sovereignty is a political, not legal question. It is about potentially alienating States that cling to anachronistic privileges, often to their own detriment by retaining incompetent counsel or instructing counsel to act improperly with potentially prejudicial consequences for their own cases.

[56] Crawford, *The Creation of States in International Law* (2006), 33.

[57] Bingham, *The Rule of Law*, 8, 174.

[58] Kelsen, *General Theory of Law and State* (1946), 123–4, 406–7.

[59] Aristotle, *Politics* (2005), III.vi.1–3 (219,221), 13 (229,231).

[60] *Lotus*, 18. The paradox continues (19): 'In these circumstances, all that can be required of a State is that it should not overstep the limits which international law places upon its jurisdiction; within these limits, its title to exercise jurisdiction rests in its sovereignty.' See also the Dissents of Judges Weiss (44) and Altamira (101–2).

[61] Charney, 'Book Review: International Law Decisions in National Courts' *AJIL* (1997) 394–6, 395; Henkin, 'The Mythology of Sovereignty', *ASIL Newsletter* (Mar–May 1993), 1.

1.5 Conclusions

This book will show that the cause of the nascent professionalization of the international bar is a practical need for normativity in the area of professional ethics. The test for the success or failure of the project is whether it can be proven that that need is justified by real problems and that it is possible to meet that need by articulating coherent ethical principles that can solve those problems. The authority of a code of conduct, therefore, depends upon its ability to satisfactorily meet practical problems with practical solutions that are sustained by careful reasoning and pragmatism rather than dogmatic nationalism. This depends upon two critical criteria, namely, an overarching commitment to the pursuit of justice and the broadmindedness to jettison a priori conceptions about how advocacy is practised 'at home' in favour of reasonable, though unfamiliar, solutions.

Professionalization is neither a common law conspiracy to imperialistically colonize international courts nor a practitioners' scheme to eject the civilian professors from international litigation. Rather, it is driven by a realistic acknowledgement by practitioners of international law from a range of backgrounds that the traditional, permissive methods of glossing over divergent standards of conduct in the practice of advocacy no longer suffice. Amidst the explosion of litigation in the age of proliferation, gone are the days when teams of one or two agents would regularly appear before the PCIJ and ICJ. Nowadays, legal teams can include dozens of persons from numerous national and professional backgrounds: diplomats, academics, practising advocates, scientists, civil servants, soldiers, or even the man from the street. In these more complex times, professionalization is not a matter of narrow dogma but a response to a real and increasing demand for normativity concerning appropriate conduct by counsel in international litigation.

To be sure, there are tangible interests at stake lurking beneath the surface. Professionalization is not a wholly benign process, for change is always aimed at something or someone. It is not only aimed at resolving honest differences amongst professionals in the highest sense of the term, amongst lawyers of great stature and integrity, but it is also aimed at eliminating the pettifoggers[62] and the amateurs from the business of advocacy. It is no longer acceptable that anyone at all, without the least professional training or qualification, can represent the interests of parties before the ICJ, ITLOS, ICSID tribunals, or other courts that regularly hear cases of great gravity. Moreover, it is not enough to impose only minimal requirements: it is in the interests of the parties, the courts, and the true professionals to demand the highest standards for the practice of international law.

Neither should it be assumed that the process is fated to succeed, nor that the considerable obstacles in its path are insurmountable. The project is highly complex, littered with pitfalls and not yet universally supported. A minimal degree of consensus behind a prescribed code of conduct is an imperative to propel the

[62] See Chapter 2.

process, providing judges with the confidence to apply it. With gradual acclimatization to the new ethical dimension, bolder structural reforms such as the imposition of admission requirements cannot long await. The price for consensus, of course, is sacrificing a measure of completeness from the text to at least begin with a baseline. With growing awareness of the seriousness of the problems and the feasibility of solutions, professionalization can develop a self-sustaining momentum. Although it is likely that early doubts will delay the initiation of the process, the continuing prevalence of ethical problems in practice suggests that it will eventually succeed.

2

The Historical Development of National Ethical Traditions

In Chapter 1, one of the principal dangers identified to the integrity of international judicial proceedings within the current system of unregulated advocacy is the conflicts between ethical standards binding upon national practitioners. Within a single procedure, the absence of common rules regarding practical matters (eg the handling of evidence or appropriate contacts with judges) can result in practitioners applying their own national standards to the common problems. However, the degree to which this theoretical problem is manifested in practice depends upon the premise that national standards actually diverge and conflict on such matters. The rationale of professionalization to harmonize such conflicts also rests upon the existence of a sufficient degree of commonality amongst national cultures of advocacy.

Consequently, the purpose of this chapter is twofold: (1) to outline the historical development of professional advocacy in order to identify its rationales; and (2) to compare the architectures, ethical standards, and contemporary cultures of selected national jurisdictions. The chapter relies upon sociological studies of the historical origins of modern bars, original historical works by legal philosophers who were instrumental in the development of professional advocacy, and laws, codes of conduct, and commentaries concerning contemporary issues for the modern bars. Those bars have been selected according to three criteria: (1) their relevance to advocacy before international courts; (2) their historical impact upon the development of advocacy on a global scale; and (3) their geographical and jurisdictional diversity. By illustrating the origins, development and contemporary cultures of these bars, commonalities and divergences can be identified that shaped the practices of advocacy in the international judicial system.

The creation of an orderly narrative for a profession is somewhat artificial in tracing its historical development.[1] Nevertheless, within those realistic limitations, analysis of national ethical traditions reveals a recognizably common profession of advocacy as a classical and medieval European institution exported to other regions through imperial colonization. This, of course, was only a part of a wider historical phenomenon entailing the intensive diffusion of European laws and procedures

[1] Prest, *The Rise of the Barristers* (1986), 2.

(particularly in the commercial sphere) to Asia, Africa, and the Americas during the Age of Empire and the Industrial Age. The standardization of key architectural features of professional advocacy, such as the organization of the members of the profession into a collective bar authority, throughout the world exemplifies this legacy. Despite the standardization of most legal systems into the two broad families of legal systems (common law and civil law), considerable diversity exists not only within those two families but also between the socialist and Islamic families.

Thus, the overview provided in this chapter seeks to identify certain dynamics amongst these complex cultures—each possessing their own histories that have also been affected by a universal historical phenomenon of convergence and hybridization. Section 1.1 traces the historical genesis of professional advocacy and its ethics in classical and medieval Europe and examines the European bars of France (civil law) and England (common law). Section 1.2 addresses the North American bar of the United States (common/civil), section 1.3 the Asian bars of China (socialist/civil) and Japan (civil), and section 1.4 the Middle Eastern bars of Iran (Islamic/civil) and Saudi Arabia (Islamic). Key elements addressed are: (1) professional architecture; (2) ethical standards, especially concerning advocate's duties to client, court, and colleagues; and (3) ethical efficacy.

2.1 European Traditions

2.1.1 Historical Background

Following the Greek Dark Ages, city-states relied upon mediation and arbitration in order to strengthen social cohesion and achieve mutually acceptable settlements. Parties were self-represented and argumentation was oral and populist with emotive rhetoric and lax evidentiary rules.[2] Litigation was peculiarly Athenian: Solon's reforms transferred judicial power from magistrates to an Athenian judicial assembly of 500 plebeian citizens.[3] No judge-jury distinction existed and all participants except for the literate clerks were amateur.[4] Bribery and blackmail by paid 'sycophants' often occurred. Evidence from the torture of slaves was admissible and orators appealed to personal knowledge and private animosities. Litigiousness increased due to poorly drafted laws, court anarchy, and popular regard for litigation as entertainment.[5] This prompted the orator, who was nominally prohibited from representation without a personal interest in the case. Certain 'professional' rhetoricians would compose speeches for orators for a fee.[6] Athenian justice was an ochlocracy of rhetoric, bias, and bribery rather than proof and sobriety.

[2] Papakonstantinou, *Lawmaking and Adjudication in Archaic Greece* (2008), 20, 29, 34–7.

[3] Bonner, *Lawyers and Litigants in Ancient Athens* (1927), 35. Contrast the summary and arbitrary Lacedemonian trial—McDowell, *Spartan Law* (1986), 123–50.

[4] McDowell, *Spartan Law*, 104, 207.

[5] Forsyth, *Hortensius* (1849), 30.

[6] Forsyth, *Hortensius*, 24–6, 36–9, 44–7, 53; Bonner, *Lawyers and Litigants in Ancient Athens*, 63, 79, 206.

In the early Roman Republic, a *patronus* would sponsor his client in the forum. The illegality of fees created an aristocratic class of amateur advocates for whom forensic advocacy was a rite of passage.[7] Ignorance of the law was considered virtuous; the Roman trial judged character rather than truth.[8] *Patroni* consequently appealed to the prejudices of magistrates (and plebeian spectators) rather than to evidence.[9] Politics pervaded the forum, as when Cicero defended Ligarious for treason before Julius Caesar for aiding the vanquished Pompey.[10] Cicero was exceptional for his professionalism and articulation of the first ethical principles of advocacy. He wrote that an advocate must provide his services to all—even defending his enemy against his friend—and that he should attain mastery of law, oratory, and knowledge.[11]

In the Empire, the patricians lost their monopoly following the end of the ban upon fees by Claudius.[12] Seneca the Elder and Quintilian criticized the venality and incompetence of the infamous *advocati*.[13] Widespread corruption prompted the first historical organization, bureaucratization, and regulation of advocacy in the fourth century by the Byzantine Empire.[14] Qualification requirements, separate legal professions and a centralized bar authority were created. In the former Western Empire,[15] primitive advocacy existed during the Dark Ages with knight-advocates bound by chivalry.[16] Trials by evidence[17] and professional advocates[18] became standard by the twelfth century in ecclesiastical courts. For example, the Kingdom of Jerusalem chivalric code required advocates to advise clients for a prescribed fee, preserve confidentiality and plead honestly, fearlessly, and competently.[19] These Christian ideals laid the foundation for European professional advocacy.

2.1.2 France

2.1.2.1 Historical Development

The first professional system of advocacy in France, introduced under Charlemagne,[20] was that of the 'State bar', whose defining feature was close regulation of advocacy by the monarchy. The monarchy vested its judicial powers in the travelling *parlement*,

[7] Forsyth, *Hortensius*, 100. [8] Forsyth, *Hortensius*, 112–13, 150.

[9] Forsyth, *Hortensius*, 84–8, 102–10. See also Crook, *Law and Life of Ancient Rome* (1967), 87–97.

[10] Forsyth, *Hortensius*, 94, 193.

[11] Forsyth, *Hortensius*, 161–8, 184. See also Cicero, *De Oratore* (1942), 14–23.

[12] Forsyth, *Hortensius*, 97. See also Bablitz, *Actors and Audience in the Roman Courtroom* (2007), 141–50.

[13] Forsyth, *Hortensius*, 174. See also Schulz, *History of Roman Legal Science* (1946), 508–14.

[14] Forsyth, *Hortensius*, 204–5, 209–14. See also Honoré, *Law in the Crisis of Empire 270–455 AD* (1998), 19–29, 195–211, 263–5.

[15] Harding, *Medieval Law and the Foundations of the State* (2002), 10–11.

[16] Forsyth, *Hortensius*, 215–16, 249–59.

[17] Forsyth, *Hortensius*, 227–32; Harding, *Medieval Law and the Foundations of the State*, 10–42, 50–1, 69–98.

[18] Brundage, *The Medieval Origins of the Legal Profession* (2008), 488–92. Ethical standards included client fidelity, conflicts of interest, representation of the poor, and modest fees—181–203, 308–43.

[19] Cohen, *A History of the English Bar and Attornatus to 1450* (1929), 382–98.

[20] Cohen, *A History of the English Bar and Attornatus to 1450*, 36.

which became based at Paris under Philip the Fair.[21] Regional *parlements* were also created,[22] each exercising regulatory powers over the Order of *avocats* attached to it.[23] The Orders comprised ecclesiastical and lay members with qualification requirements (university degree, internship, and examination) and sanctions for misconduct.[24] The professions split from the fifteenth century with prosecutors (*procureurs*, later *avoués*)[25] and defence advocates (*avocats*) discharging representational functions.

In 1270, Saint Louis promulgated the first code requiring advocates to 'present no cause to the court which was not just and loyal, and to practise courtesy and forbearance towards their opponents while refuting their arguments, without using words of contumely or abuse'.[26] However, Louis XII's practice of selling judgeships led to prolix written submissions, insulting rhetoric, illegal fees, and other abuses amongst advocates.[27] Although the State bar or *noblesse de la robe* became corrupt, it left a legacy of independence, professional monopoly and ethical codification.

The 'classical bar' emerged in the mid-seventeenth century when the Paris Order wrested regulatory powers from its *parlement* in a complete break with the State-regulated regime.[28] The President of the Order (*bâtonnier*) eventually established his authority. The Order articulated core principles of probity, independence, fidelity, disinterestedness and collegiality. As ethical standards rose in practice, the popularity of the professions rose with them. Amidst widespread corruption in society, the reigns of Louis XIV and Louis XV saw high standards and a robust defence of civil liberties by advocates.[29]

Public confidence decayed in the late eighteenth century amidst political splits, as at the trial of Louis XVI.[30] The Revolution destroyed the Orders and *parlements*; most of the professionals shunned the revolutionary 'peoples' tribunals'.[31] Napoleon revived the Orders and *ancien régime* principles of probity, disinterestedness, and courtesy but abolished their independence to preserve State control.[32] The classical bar was defined by political activism and disinterestedness.[33] The Orders won public

[21] Cohen, *A History of the English Bar and Attornatus to 1450*, 232–3.

[22] Berlanstein, 'Lawyers in Pre-Revolutionary France' in Prest, *Lawyers in Early Modern Europe and America* (1981), 164–80, 165.

[23] Karpik, *French Lawyers* (1999), 21–3, 238–9.

[24] Forsyth, *Hortensius*, 234, 240, 252–3.

[25] See Chapter 6. On the functional difference between *avocats* and *procureurs du roi* in criminal trials, see Leubsdorf, *Man in His Original Destiny* (2001), 84, 101–6.

[26] Forsyth, *Hortensius*, 21. Philip's ordinance further required *avocats* to swear to, inter alia, plead with diligence and fidelity, not charge greedy fees, refrain from false citation or trickery, serve the poor, and lead a sober personal life—253–4. See also Cohen, *A History of the English Bar and Attornatus to 1450*, 398–410.

[27] Forsyth, *Hortensius*, 246–7, 263, 268–71; Berlanstein, 'Lawyers in Pre-Revolutionary France', 175; Karpik, *French Lawyers*, 22–3.

[28] Karpik, *French Lawyers*, 21, 39–41, 43–8, 51–8.

[29] Berlanstein, 'Lawyers in Pre-Revolutionary France', 165–77.

[30] Karpik, *French Lawyers*, 49–56, 87–100. See also Burrage, *Revolution and the Making of the Contemporary Legal Profession* (2006), 73–9, 95.

[31] Burrage, *Revolution and the Making of the Contemporary Legal Profession*, 79–91; Berlanstein, 'Lawyers in Pre-Revolutionary France', 177.

[32] Burrage, *Revolution and the Making of the Contemporary Legal Profession*, 95–103; Forsyth, *Hortensius*, 316–18.

[33] Karpik, *French Lawyers*, 101–54.

respect; many members served in government in the nineteenth and twentieth centuries.[34] Incremental legislation between 1971 and 2011 merged the professions of *avocat*, *avoué*, *agréé*, and *conseil juridique* to simplify legal services and strengthen market forces, causing deep rifts and public protest.[35] The modern Orders have since been characterized by a tension between classical ideals and competitive capitalism.

2.1.2.2 Ethical Standards

Under modern French law, there are two principal legal professions that exercise rights of hearing before national courts: (1) *avocat*; and (2) *procureur*. The professions are recruited and organized separately with discrete rights of hearing, though their functions interface in criminal proceedings. As noted above, *avocats* discharge advisory and representational functions; they have rights of hearing before the civil courts[36] and the exclusive right to represent defendants in criminal proceedings.[37] They are professionally defined by their independence from the State. *Procureurs*, who have rights of hearing to prosecute in criminal proceedings, are civil servants who are recruited, trained, and organized within the judicial profession. These legal professions are broadly representative of the Romano-Germanic tradition, which has historically placed a greater procedural emphasis upon judges rather than counsel. Save for ICC Prosecutors, *avocats* (and *jurisconsultes*, discussed below) are the more relevant profession before international courts.

French law on *avocats* is contained in the French Law 1971, the French Decree 1991, and the French Decree 2005. The 1971 Law concerns rights of audience and the reform of the legal professions.[38] Article 11 stipulates, inter alia, the following qualification requirements: (1) examination; (2) no criminal conviction impugning honour, probity, or good morals; and (3) no administrative sanction such as disbarment, bankruptcy, or liquidation. Article 17 empowers the Orders to promulgate internal regulations[39] and Article 22 vests each Order's disciplinary council with disciplinary jurisdiction, subject to the courts of appeal. Articles 26 to 27 provide for the civil professional liability of advocates. The 1991 Decree prescribes more detailed provisions for the organization and administration of the activities of the Orders, regional training centres, and National Council.[40] Chapter III restricts advocacy to named persons in the roll of an Order[41] and regulates professional residence, administrative matters, and fee recovery.[42] Part IV addresses the sanctions, procedure, and jurisdiction of the disciplinary councils.[43]

[34] Halpérin, 'Text and Subtext: French Lawyers' Fees in the Nineteenth Century' in Pue and Sugarman, *Lawyers and Vampires* (2003), 211–24.

[35] Halpérin, 'Text and Subtext', 157–90, 257–319.

[36] French CPC 2010, Art 411. There is a distinction between *avocats* with rights of hearing before courts of first instance and appeal (*avocats au barreau*) and the *Conseil d'État* and *Cour de cassation* (*avocats aux Conseils*).

[37] French CPP, Arts 274, 308, 417.

[38] French Law 1971, Arts 4–7.

[39] Eg Paris Code.

[40] French Decree 1991, Arts 111–23.

[41] French Decree 1991, Art 154.

[42] French Decree 1991, Arts 165–79.

[43] French Decree 1991, Arts 180–99.

The 2005 Decree articulates the ethical principles of the profession.[44] Article 1 declares that 'fundamental principles' are to 'guide the behaviour of advocates in all circumstances'. Those principles are contained in Articles 2 to 5: (1) the freedom and independence of the profession; (2) the dignity, diligence, independence, honesty, humanity, loyalty, disinterestedness, collegiality, tactfulness, courtesy, competence, and prudence of advocates in discharging their functions; and (3) strict duties of confidentiality to client and court, which may only be lifted in cases authorized by law. Article 6 commits the profession to promoting access to justice. Article 7 generally prohibits acceptance of instructions where exists risk of: (1) conflict of interest between multiple clients; (2) breach of confidentiality; or (3) impaired independence. Articles 8 to 9 require advocates to act pursuant to client instructions and to abstain from illegalities or frauds in drafting legal instruments. Article 10 stipulates that fees, subject to contract, are determined by client means, case difficulty, and advocate's prestige, efforts, and costs. Article 15 permits self-promotion within fundamental professional principles. Article 16 prescribes respect for the demands of fair trial and the rights of the opposing party.

2.1.2.3 Ethical Efficacy

The historical overview of the French professions and the professional regulation of *avocats* identify certain themes. First, the traditional ethos of disinterestedness, probity, and independence has been challenged by the radical structural change introduced since 1971 aimed at enhancing commercial competition.[45] Consequently, a greater competitiveness amongst *avocats* in practice may lead to the lowering of professional standards to attract clients. Secondly, the qualification requirements and ethical standards prescribed for the profession are relatively broad.[46] These reflect the more extensive role of the judge relative to that of counsel in the inquisitorial tradition and provide a greater freedom of action before international courts.

An additional consequence of the broadness of the ethical standards is that *avocats* have less detailed textual guidance concerning their professional duties in practising before international courts. For example, there is no equivalent of the 'international practice rules' of the English Code (see below) concerning extraterritorial applicability of home bar rules to advocacy before international courts. Whilst it is unlikely that the Orders would refrain from exercising disciplinary jurisdiction concerning alleged professional misconduct by members before international courts, the standards that they would apply in doing so would be vague. Furthermore, it is questionable whether the Orders would necessarily exercise disciplinary jurisdiction

[44] The Paris Code largely replicates these provisions and incorporates the CCBE Code (see Chapter 7). Neither statutory law nor the Regulations expressly prescribe for advocates' conduct before international courts.

[45] Leubsdorf, *Man in His Original Destiny*, 123–32.

[46] Also applicable to German *rechstanwälte*, for whom disciplinary proceedings are extremely rare and prescribed standards vague and terse. This derives in part from the historical domination of judges and civil servants. See German Code; Abel and Lewis, *Lawyers in Society: An Overview* (1995), 92–127, 92–3, 107.

concerning advocacy before international courts before which counsel perform a greater role than in France (eg in the handling of evidence). From the perspective of international courts, the reliance to be placed upon the title of *avocat* to ensure the observance of strict ethical standards may be limited.

Another important category of legal practitioner to the international judicial system is that of *jurisconsulte* ('legal adviser'). In France, as in other Romano-Germanic systems, the *jurisconsulte* is not a profession as such with its own governing body and distinctive function. It denotes a person holding a *licence en droit* who may work with the law in any number of capacities such as an employed adviser at a company, a civil servant or an academic. In the context of this book, the *jurisconsulte* refers to those civil servants employed to provide in-house legal advice and represent governments (principally as agents) before international courts. The current title of the principal legal adviser to the Foreign Ministry of the French Republic is *directeur des services juridiques du Ministère des affaires étrangères.*

Whereas in Germany 'the legal adviser's office consists largely if not entirely of regular diplomats with a legal background or even professional legal training', in France 'some members of the Quai's Direction des Affaires Juridiques are regular diplomats, for whom a period in the legal office is more or less like any other posting in Paris, and some are recruited specifically as legal advisers, for example, on secondment from the judiciary'.[47] Historically, *jurisconsultes* at the *Quai d'Orsay* who have appeared before the PCIJ and ICJ (eg Jules Basdevant, André Gros, Ronny Abraham, Alain Pellet) have also been professors of international law at the University of Paris. Whereas professors are civil servants in France, upon becoming a *jurisconsulte* the professor loses his 'professional independence' by coming under the direct authority of the Foreign Minister and is also suspended from his university post. Thus, a *jurisconsulte* (essentially a diplomat, and perhaps also academic, by vocation) is not subject to ethical standards at the national level concerning advocacy before international courts.

2.1.3 England and Wales

2.1.3.1 Historical Development

Before the Conqueror, ad hoc representation by lords for vassals existed within the feudal system.[48] Subsequently, literate cleric-advocates in ecclesiastical courts were pre-eminent as the lay-advocates of the royal courts and became notorious for prolixity, dishonesty, and venality. In 1275, statutory duties were introduced banning false causes, corruption, deceit, false delays, and excessive fees.[49] By the fifteenth century, the Inns of Court evolved from lodgings into learned societies.[50] In 1590,

[47] Wood, 'Legal Adviser', *MPEPIL*, para 5. See also Abraham, 'Le rôle du jurisconsulte au Ministère des affaires étrangères' in SFDI, *La Pratique et le droit international* (2004), 247–52.

[48] Cohen, *A History of the English Bar and Attornatus to 1450*, 4–19, 24, 30–7, 114–21, 371–82.

[49] Forsyth, *Hortensius*, 350–1.

[50] Thorne, *Essays in English Legal History* (1985), 138–9. The functions of 'counsellors' and 'attorneys' remained vague—Baker, 'Counsellors and Barristers: an Historical Study', 27 *CLJ* (1969), 205–29.

the term 'utter-barrister' was first used for student-counsellors who were outside of the (meta)-physical 'bar'. By the sixteenth century, the Inns became known as the 'third university of England' for counsellors' training[51] and in the seventeenth century excluded attorneys and solicitors.[52] By the nineteenth century, the professions of barrister and solicitor emerged split by function, recruitment and regulation.[53]

Counsellors were infamous during the Tudor and Stuart dynasties for venality and incompetence[54] and popularly stereotyped as amoral, manipulative 'intellectual prostitutes'.[55] The traditional rule of honorarium whereby barristers served without right to fee was a direct response to popular indignation.[56] They were prominent in the English Civil War, as when John Cook was hanged for high treason for prosecuting Charles I. His defence of acting pursuant to his profession was rejected in law.[57]

In the Georgian era, the apparent illogicality of defence counsel being prohibited from treason and felony trials but not misdemeanours was supported by the Bar on the grounds of dishonour for barristers to defend those accused of heinous crimes and that 'professional duels' would distort the truth. This changed with the Prisoner's Counsel Act 1836, which produced two infamous trials[58] illustrating the moral-ethical conflict of duty to court versus client, truth versus victory. The lay press attacked barristers as deceitful men saving the guilty, whereas the professional press advocated an absolute right to counsel. In 1820, Henry Brougham had articulated a so-called 'doctrine of all expedient means' whereby counsel owes an *absolute* duty to his client whereas others argued for a duty to undertake 'just causes'.[59]

The Victorian era was a formative period amidst widespread corruption.[60] Criticism focused upon inefficiency, aggressiveness, and disgraced barristers appointed as judges.[61] Discipline was primarily handled by judges and circuit messes rather than the Inns and a lax 'aristocratic ideology' replaced medieval scholarship. In 1851, the Inns created the 'Council of Legal Education'[62] and the first Consolidated Regulations for all four Inns in 1863.[63] In 1895, the General Council of the Bar ('Bar

[51] Thorne, *Essays in English Legal History*, 144.

[52] Lewis, *The Victorian Bar* (1982), 4–5, 8–9.

[53] The orders of 'civilians' and 'serjeants-at-law' became extinct—Prest, *The Rise of the Barristers*, 5, 72–82, 209–82.

[54] Prest, *The Rise of the Barristers*, 283–326.

[55] May, *The Bar and the Old Bailey* (2003), 125–32.

[56] Forsyth, *Hortensius*, 120–32, 182–94.

[57] Forsyth, *Hortensius*, 356–67, 372, 399–402.

[58] In the *Courvoisier* trial of 1840, the accused confessed his guilt to his counsel but refused to change his plea. On instruction from the bench to conduct a 'negative defence', the barrister was publicly lambasted over allegations that he had asserted a personal belief of his client's innocence in his closing speech to the jury. In the *Reid* trial of 1847, a defendant was seemingly unjustly convicted amidst rumours that his acquitted co-defendant had confessed to his counsel before trial. See May, *The Bar and the Old Bailey*.

[59] Forsyth, *Hortensius*, 368–80, 427–67.

[60] Lewis, *The Victorian Bar*, 88–164.

[61] Cocks, *Foundations of the Modern Bar* (1983), 15–33, 106–57.

[62] Roxburgh, *The Black Books: Vol V A.D. 1845-A.D. 1914* (1968), para 33.

[63] Roxburgh, *The Black Books*, 16–9.

Council') was created which promulgated the first English Code in 1979.[64] Since 2006, the Bar Council represents the profession whilst the Bar Standards Board (BSB) oversees education and discipline.[65]

2.1.3.2 Ethical Standards

As noted above, the two principal, modern legal professionals in England and Wales are barristers and solicitors. Whilst the progressive erosion of barristers' traditional monopoly over rights of audience has resulted in a degree of convergence in the late twentieth century,[66] the professions remain split. Broadly, barristers perform specialist advisory and advocacy functions connected to litigation and have virtually exclusive rights of hearing before most courts whereas solicitors conduct drafting, advisory, and other general client services. Whilst solicitors are not excluded and in fact appear as counsel before international courts, this book focuses upon barristers as the specialist profession for advocacy.[67] Barristers are regulated by the BSB, applying the English Code, legal rules and the etiquette of the profession.[68]

Whilst not intended to be totally comprehensive, the English Code is the principal textual source for the ethical standards of the Bar.[69] Its general purpose is to inculcate common standards of conduct, independence in practice, and a public duty to act for any client within a barrister's field of practice.[70] A practising barrister has an 'overriding duty to the Court to act with independence; he must assist the Court in the administration of justice and must not deceive or knowingly or recklessly mislead the Court'.[71] He must defend a lay client's interests 'fearlessly' without regard to his own or to another's interests.[72] He must not compromise his independence or integrity by lowering his professional standards to please another.[73]

A hallmark English principle is the 'cab rank rule', which prohibits barristers from withholding advocacy services on the ground that the nature of the case, the

[64] Roxburgh, *The Black Books*, 6. [65] Roxburgh, *The Black Books*, 98.

[66] Abel and Lewis, *Lawyers in Society: An Overview*, 55–7. Mayson, 'After Clementi: The Impending Legal Landscape', *LSPI* (Dec. 2006), online: <http://www.legalservicesinstitute.org.uk> (Accessed: 10 December 2011).

[67] Unlike *avocats*, barristers' rights of hearing before the English courts derive not from their admission to the Bar (requiring a qualifying law degree, completion of vocational training, and good character) but rather from 'practising certificates' that further require completion of a one-year 'pupillage' at a set of chambers and continuous training—English Code, para 202. Barristers without a practising certificate are termed 'non-practising barristers'. Unlike *avocats* in civil law jurisdictions, barristers may conditionally be employed—see Chapter 5. See also Boon and Levin, *The Ethics and Conduct of Lawyers in England and Wales* (2008), 29.

[68] In the absence of rules, barristers must rely upon conscience—Boon and Levin, *The Ethics and Conduct of Lawyers in England and Wales*, 7–8.

[69] Prior to the English Code 1979, the principal textual sources were the Bar Council's rulings published in *Annual Practices* as well as *Halsbury's Laws of England*—see Chapter 4. The most useful source in practice (particularly for junior counsel), then as now, remains the advice of senior members of the Bar.

[70] English Code, paras 104–105.

[71] English Code, para 302; Wood, 'Bar Standards Board Review of the Bar Vocational Course Report of the Working Group', online: <https://www.barstandardsboard.org.uk/media/1353435/bvc_report_final_with_annexes_as_on_website.pdf> (Accessed: 10 December 2011), para 102; Ipp, 'Lawyers' Duties to the Court' 114 LQR (1998), 63–107, 83.

[72] English Code, para 303. [73] English Code, paras 306–307.

client or the source of client's financial support is objectionable.[74] A self-employed barrister must accept instructions commensurate to his expertise and seniority regardless of the case or personal belief concerning the 'character, reputation, cause, conduct, guilt or innocence' of the client.[75] However, the degree to which this principle is enforced in practice is questionable: whereas some are noted proponents,[76] others are not.

A barrister must refuse instructions if he were to be 'professionally embarrassed' by: (1) insufficient experience or expertise; (2) inadequate preparation time; (3) fettering, unlawful, or unethical instructions; (4) prejudice to justice or to an unrepresented party; (5) conflict of interest; or (6) breach of confidentiality.[77] He may refuse instructions which: (1) require him to work outside of his ordinary working year; (2) offer an 'improper' fee; (3) require a conditional fee agreement; (4) are directly from a lay client; or (5) come from a unified professional and lay client.[78] Like other European jurisdictions, contingency fee agreements are generally illegal.[79]

A barrister must continuously assess whether the interests of justice and of the client permit him to represent.[80] For example, he must withdraw where he is professionally embarrassed, there is risk of conflict of interest or the client refuses to authorize a court-ordered disclosure.[81] He may withdraw where his professional conduct is being impugned, his advice has been ignored, or there is 'some other substantial reason' for doing so.[82] However, he must not withdraw while failing to explain his reasons to his client beforehand, for a non-professional reason or where the client cannot obtain a replacement without sustaining prejudice.[83] The Code also requires courtesy, diligence, efficiency, competence, confidentiality, and loyalty.[84] It proscribes improper arguments, unsustainable allegations of fraud, coaching witnesses, inarguable submissions, failure to inform the court of law or procedural irregularity, factual invention, personal opinion concerning a case in which he is instructed and witness vilification.[85]

A key section is the 'International Practice Rules', which provides that for 'matters or proceedings essentially arising...outside England and Wales and to be substantially performed outside England and Wales', barristers must comply with local law save where conflicting with the fundamental principles of the English Code.[86] Whilst this applies to international courts, it entails a conflict-of-law approach that assumes the existence of 'local law' that those courts generally lack. Moreover, the reservation of ultimate supremacy concerning fundamental principles creates the potential for conflict between English standards and putative international standards ('double deontology').

[74] English Code, para 601. [75] English Code, para 602. [76] See Chapter 4.

[77] English Code, para 603(a)–(f), (h). [78] English Code, para 604(a)–(f).

[79] Hardinge and Mackay, *Halsbury's Laws of England* (Vol 65) (2008), para 955; CCBE Code, Art 3.3.

[80] English Code, paras 606–7. [81] English Code, para 608.

[82] English Code, para 609. [83] English Code, para 610.

[84] English Code, paras 701–3. [85] English Code, paras 706–10.

[86] English Code, Annexe A, paras 1(a), 2.

2.1.3.3 Ethical Efficacy

This survey of the history and professional ethics of the English Bar indicates that they had relatively detailed standards and yet went through peaks and declines in terms of its reputation and integrity. This may be explained by the greater role that parties play in adversarial procedure and the historical continuity of the Bar's traditions and etiquette. The applicability of the fundamental principles of the Bar to international litigation means that barristers are bound by stricter standards, creating a distorted playing field. Without equally rigorous international standards, it is unlikely that the English Bar would fully relinquish its jurisdiction to international courts.

Despite barristers' historical independence, the twentieth and twenty-first centuries have seen increasing interference from the State.[87] The Courts and Legal Services Act 1990 increased external regulation whilst stopping an attempt to end barristers' exclusive rights of audience.[88] Contemporary issues include: reduced self-regulation, oversupply of barristers, conditional fees, and reduced adversarialism.[89] Critics suggest that the Code requires cautious interpretation,[90] anecdotal evidence indicates widespread circumvention of the cab rank rule,[91] and the BSB has published warnings concerning payments for briefs and client confidentiality.[92] As in France, the Bar is challenged by structural changes aimed at promoting commercialism that threaten its traditional professionalism.

An important category of legal professional to be considered for the practice of the United Kingdom before international courts is that of the legal adviser to the Foreign and Commonwealth Office (FCO). British legal advisers to the FCO are invariably members of one of the two legal professions.[93] Although theoretically there is a distinction between a *jurisconsulte* at the *Quai d'Orsay* who is a civil servant and not regulated by an Order and a legal adviser at the FCO who is a member of the Bar or the Law Society, in practice there are real questions concerning 'how effective [their national rules] are to control conduct before international courts'[94]—in particular due to the Bar's reluctance to investigate matters of government.[95]

[87] Abel, 'The Politics of Professionalism', 2 *Legal Ethics* (1999), 131–47.

[88] Thornton, 'Professional Responsibility and Ethics of the English Bar' in Cranston, *Legal Ethics and Professional Responsibility* (1995), 53–97, 59–64.

[89] Boon and Levin, *The Ethics and Conduct of Lawyers in England and Wales*, 25–67, 431–9; Neuberger, 'Working Party on Entry to the Bar: Final Report' (2007), online: <http://www.barcouncil.org.uk/media/164103/finalreportneuberger.pdf> (Accessed: 11 December 2011), paras 35–42; Yarrow and Abrams, 'Conditional Fees: The Challenge to Ethics', 2 *Legal Ethics* (1999), 193–213; Nicolson and Webb, 'Lawyers' Duties, Adversarialism and Partnership in UK Legal Ethics', 7 *Legal Ethics* (2004), 133–40.

[90] Cranston, *Legal Ethics and Professional Responsibility*, 4–6.

[91] Thornton, 'Professional Responsibility and Ethics of the English Bar', 69–70.

[92] 'Guidance', online: <https://www.barstandardsboard.org.uk/complaints-and-professional-conduct/professional-conduct-resources> (Accessed: 11 November 2011).

[93] Wood, 'Legal Adviser', para 4.

[94] CAHDI, 'Item 7: Organisation and Functions of the Office of the Legal Adviser of the Ministry for Foreign Affairs: Document submitted by the Delegation of the UK' (11 September 2006), online: <http://www.coe.int/t/dlapil/cahdi> (Accessed: 11 December 2011), 2 (note 1).

[95] The Attorney General (*ex officio* head of the Bar) was said to be 'in no way distinguishable from his professional brethren in being accountable to the Benchers of his Inn of Court regarding his own professional behaviour'—Edwards, *The Law Officers of the Crown* (1964), 90–118, 277–8,

FCO legal advisers operate as civil servants within a structure of formal subservience to their political masters. Whilst Sir Gerald Fitzmaurice postulated a duty of the government international lawyer to the law and Sir Franklin Berman asserted that it was for him to persuade his government to comply with the law,[96] these ideals lack a practical enforcement mechanism. Since the scrutiny of the bars is unlikely, it is arguable that as a government legal adviser the barrister's duty of independence is curtailed by the civil servant's duty to carry out policy decisions.

2.2 The American Tradition

2.2.1 Historical Development

The aboriginal nations had diverse legal systems[97] but professional advocates did not exist amongst those of New England. Aboriginal justice sought not discovery of truth but rather the preservation of social harmony. The village *sachem* administered justice by example and persuasion and the village council of clans mediated disputes.[98] Apart from the support of a friend or elder, self-representation was the norm. The seventeenth-century New England colonies consciously rejected the English common law and its legal professions as immoral.[99] The Puritan settlers opted for religious texts and self-representation in closed trials judged by the literate clergy.[100] Advocates were litigants' friends and kinsmen with laws severely restricting fees and pleadings.

The lay legal profession's genesis was in Massachusetts,[101] where burgeoning commerce with England and the consequent need for litigation to regulate commercial transactions caused the gradual adoption of professional advocacy and the common law by the eighteenth century.[102] The lack of English-trained professionals required adaptation; Massachusetts attorneys modelled their bar associations after the English attorneys' 'Society of Gentleman Practitioners' founded in 1739.[103] The professionals, seeking a monopoly to exclude the amateur 'pettifoggers', overcame resistance from the clerical bench to introduce admission requirements into

299. See also *Halsbury's Laws of England* (1954) (3rd edn) (Vol VII), 382 (notes (q), (t)). In 1963, Sir John Hobson became the first Attorney to be tried by his Inn for allegedly misleading the court. However, in 2003 the BSB found it lacked jurisdiction to hear a complaint that Lord Goldsmith had compromised his professional standards concerning his advice about the legality of invading Iraq because he was acting as a minister and parliamentarian and 'the investigation would have to consider decision-making processes of government in matters of foreign affairs'—Sands, *Lawless World* (2005), 189, 194–201, 282, 376 (note 36). See also the subsequent revelations in the evidence of former FCO legal advisers—Norton-Taylor, 'Chilcot inquiry: Lawyers expose pressure to give green light for war', *The Guardian* (26 January 2010).

96 CAHDI, 'Item 7', 2–3.

97 Kawashima, *Puritan Justice and the Indian* (1986), 5 (note 10).

98 Kawashima, *Puritan Justice and the Indian*, 3–7.

99 Gawalt, *The Promise of Power* (1979), 8–11; Burrage, *Revolution and the Making of the Contemporary Legal Profession*, 207.

100 Gawalt, *The Promise of Power*, 19.

101 Gawalt, *The Promise of Power*, 219–20.

102 Burrage, *Revolution and the Making of the Contemporary Legal Profession*, 209.

103 Gawalt, *The Promise of Power*, 11–18, 24.

the superior courts and the rank of barrister was created (though without functional specialization).

By imposing educational requirements the professionals provoked the ire of the clergy, which argued that lawyers were an evil class feeding upon the sins of wayward people.[104] The professionals retorted that the necessity for both moral and positive law to govern society demanded courts with competent professionals. However, country litigants generally preferred amateur family members due to the cost and scarcity of professionals. By 1774, a mixed picture of amateur and professional advocacy existed. As the War of Independence loomed, the courts became political arenas as in John Adams' successful defence of British soldiers for the 'Boston Massacre',[105] Patrick Henry's attack upon the Privy Council's powers,[106] and Theodore Sedgwick's defence of loyalists.[107]

After the war, the new State courts excluded loyalists but retained pre-war laws and customs except in Pennsylvania, where in 1776 a radical government created an elected judiciary—despite a bar boycott—to prosecute loyalists.[108] Massachusetts attorneys were loathed for representing wealthy creditors against poor debtors.[109] Popular antagonism (including attacks upon courthouses and attorneys) against an 'exploitative elite' became rife in the post-war period.[110] Legislation destroyed the bar associations by removing admission requirements and introducing elected judgeships. De-professionalization was caused by mistrust of professional advocacy, anti-British sentiment and class warfare. Law schools filled the gap created by the associations' demise, with universities operating them from the nineteenth century.[111]

The creation of the American Bar Association (ABA) in 1878 and contemporaneous rejuvenation of bar associations were prompted by low self-esteem amongst attorneys from rampant corruption due to virtually no regulation until after the Civil War.[112] Ethics, lacking centralized authority, were likewise highly relative. Law schools introduced ethics into curricula in the twentieth century, becoming universally taught by 1980.[113] The ABA, in its campaign to harmonize ethics, adopted the 'Canons of Professional Ethics' in 1908 and created a 'Standing Committee on Professional Ethics' in 1913 to monitor bar associations. By 1971, the Standing Committee was renamed the 'Committee on Ethics and Professional Responsibility'. In 1969, the 'Model Code of Professional Responsibility' replaced the Canons and, in 1983, the

[104] Burrage, *Revolution and the Making of the Contemporary Legal Profession*, 1–6, 24–5.
[105] Glendon, *A Nation Under Lawyers* (1994), 40.
[106] Burrage, *Revolution and the Making of the Contemporary Legal Profession*, 226–7.
[107] Gawalt, *The Promise of Power*, 48–9.
[108] Burrage, *Revolution and the Making of the Contemporary Legal Profession*, 231–2.
[109] Gawalt, *The Promise of Power*, 95–102; Witt, *Patriots and Cosmopolitans* (2007), 38–44.
[110] Burrage, *Revolution and the Making of the Contemporary Legal Profession*, 242–83.
[111] Burrage, *Revolution and the Making of the Contemporary Legal Profession*, 267–77, 281–9; Abel, *American Lawyers* (1989), 40–2.
[112] Burrage, *Revolution and the Making of the Contemporary Legal Profession*, 289–300.
[113] Rhode, *In the Interests of Justice* (2000), 200–6.

'Model Rules of Professional Conduct' ('Model Rules') replaced the Model Code. To date, California is the only state jurisdiction that has not adopted the Model Rules.[114]

Consequently, the American legal professions are separated not by function but rather by the federal system. Although the ABA has sought to represent the professions at the national level and to promote national standards, the principal regulatory functions are discharged by the state bar associations. In addition, specialist bars exist for the federal courts as well as the US Supreme Court that generally require payment of a fee and the taking of oath for admission. Thus, the 'fused profession' is something of a misnomer from the perspective of international litigation in that the Model Rules are enforceable by dozens of bar associations to regulate the conduct of attorneys before international courts.

2.2.2 Ethical Standards

The Preamble of the Model Rules identifies a lawyer's three fundamental roles: (1) representative of clients; (2) officer of the legal system; and (3) public citizen having special responsibility for the quality of justice.[115] Whilst the Preamble stipulates that the Model Rules address conflicts amongst these duties, there is no 'overriding duty' provision.[116] However, the Model Rules prioritize the client through: (1) textual prioritization; (2) structural focus; and (3) textual language. A cultural preference for partisanship has been noted in commentary by American attorneys.[117]

Concerning the 'client-lawyer relationship',[118] competence and due diligence are prescribed. Fees are subject to a broad 'reasonableness' requirement and personal financial interest in cases is permitted. A duty of confidentiality is imposed, whereby an attorney 'may' disclose privileged information only to prevent a crime believed to be 'likely to result in death or substantial bodily harm' or to provide him with a legal defence and a strict conflict of interest rule restricts multiple client representation in the same case. Contingency fees are permitted and a detailed conflict of interest provision generally prohibits, inter alia, misuse of client information, instruments providing client gifts to the attorney and financial assistance towards litigation.[119]

Refusal or termination of representation is compulsory, inter alia, upon ethical or legal violation and (unless ordered to continue) he may withdraw if without

[114] Online: <http://www.americanbar.org/groups/professional_responsibility/publications/model_rules_of_professional_conduct.html> (Accessed: 26 November 2011).

[115] ABA Model Rules, 1.

[116] The commentary states: '[A] lawyer acting as an advocate...has an obligation to present the client's case with persuasive force. Performance of that duty while maintaining the confidence of the client, however, is qualified by the advocate's duty of candor to the tribunal'—ABA Annotated Rules, 2, 305–6.

[117] See Glendon, *A Nation Under Lawyers*, 6–14, 40–59, 84–108; Rhode, *In the Interests of Justice*, 1–22, 23–80, 207–13; Rhode, *Access to Justice* (2004), 79–178; Hazard and Dondi, *Legal Ethics* (2004), 284.

[118] ABA Model Rules, r 1.1, 1.3–1.7.

[119] ABA Model Rules, r 1.8(a)–(h), (j). Direct gifts may be accepted if 'the transaction meets general standards of fairness' which would appear to equate to those of nominal value.

material adverse effect upon the client or if, inter alia, he reasonably believes that the client is perpetuating a crime or fraud involving his services, the client pursues an objective that he considers 'repugnant or imprudent' or other good cause exists.[120] An attorney must not pursue 'frivolous' arguments or knowingly mislead the court and may withhold evidence reasonably believed to be false.[121] He must refrain from falsification, sabotage, obstruction, procedural abuse, improper influence and ex parte communication with the court.[122] False or reckless public expression of doubt concerning the competence or integrity of a judge is prohibited.[123] However, the dilemma of a client's perjury, investigating the veracity of evidence and media comments remain controversial.[124]

A key provision is Model Rule 8.5, providing that an attorney admitted to practice 'is subject to the disciplinary authority of [the] jurisdiction, regardless of where the [conduct] occurs'. He may be 'subject to the disciplinary authority of both this jurisdiction and another jurisdiction for the same conduct'. A complicated 'choice of law' provision provides for the applicability of the standards of the jurisdiction in which the 'predominant effect of the conduct' occurs. Although applicable to international practice,[125] they were designed for transnational practice on a conflict-of-law approach and have been criticized by US academics for producing 'some highly problematic and ultimately unsatisfactory results when applied to international arbitration'.[126] For example, they can lead to the absurd conclusion that US attorneys are bound by Dutch standards before international courts situated in the Hague. Thus, Model Rule 8.5 is very broad and was not designed to regulate conduct before international courts.

2.2.3 Ethical Efficacy

Despite the advent of university degree requirements for law school admission in the twentieth century, the bar associations' failure to obtain admission control allowed the competition-minded law schools to form the professional culture. In 1952, an ABA investigation reported obsolete, deficient, and unenforced standards.[127] Judicial politicization hampers its ability to discipline attorneys and divergent standards from State to State constrain ABA harmonization efforts. Self-assessment has deprecated ethical efficacy, with the bars' efforts viewed as inadequate.[128] Thus, the historical background of US attorneys has been characterized

[120] ABA Model Rules, r 1.16. 'Moral conscience' is narrowly construed—ABA Annotated Rules, 244–5.

[121] ABA Model Rules, r 3.1, 3.3.

[122] ABA Model Rules, r 3.4–3.5; ABA Annotated Rules, 321–33, 344–7.

[123] ABA Model Rules, r 8.2–8.3; ABA Annotated Rules, 573.

[124] ABA Model Rules, r 3.6; ABA Annotated Rules, 316–18, 362.

[125] ABA Model Rules, r 8.5 (Comment 7).

[126] Rogers, 'The Ethics of Advocacy in International Arbitration' in Bishop and Kehoe, *The Art of Advocacy in International Arbitration* (2010), 63. Rogers, 'Lawyers without Borders', 30 *UPILR* (2009), 1035–86, 1039–40.

[127] Phillips and McCoy, *Conduct of Judges and Lawyers* (1952), 18–20, 57–8, 81–4, 150–3, 177–87, 197–200, 201–14, 319–57.

[128] Glendon, *A Nation Under Lawyers*, 6–14, 40–59, 84–108; Rhode, *In the Interests of Justice*, 1–22, 23–80, 207–13; Rhode, *Access to Justice* (2004), 79–178; Hazard and Dondi, *Legal Ethics* (2004), 284.

by de-professionalization and a market ideology that prioritizes client control over attorneys as 'hired guns'.

Consequently, the standards that apply to an American attorney diverge from those applicable in many European jurisdictions. Many of the standards that apply in the US (eg media statements, witness proofing, or contingency fees) are more permissive and the philosophy of the judicial system is considerably more party-centred and adversarial. Legal advisers in the State Department, as in the UK, are invariably qualified professionals.[129] However, the independence of US government counsel from policy direction and ideological bias (eg John Yoo[130]) is questionable.[131] Internal disciplinary procedures may exacerbate this danger by displacing the external disciplinary scrutiny of state bars when acting as agents in international litigation.

2.3 Asian Traditions

Relative to Europe, Africa, and the Americas, the participation of the Asian continent in the international judicial system through counsel has been minor. For example, China has participated in no contentious cases before the ICJ and Japan has only participated in one (pending) case. Only seven Asian States (Cambodia, India, Indonesia, Malaysia, Pakistan, Singapore, Thailand) have ever participated in contentious cases, excluding Oceania and the Middle East. China is not party to the Court's optional clause jurisdiction or the Rome Statute, though Japan is. Asian jurisdictions are not generally noted for producing lawyers who serve as counsel for States or other parties not of their own nationality before international courts.[132] There exists no regional Asian court.

Why, then, examine Asian traditions (instead of, say, African)? First, the participation of Asia in the international judicial system should be regarded as a potential growth area (eg maritime and territorial disputes). Secondly, despite its lack of modern regional integration, there is arguably a stronger basis for generalization of Asian standards than in the even more diverse and centrifugal African continent. Thirdly, examination of China and Japan as two major Asian jurisdictions that

[129] Wood, 'Legal Adviser', para 4.

[130] Office of Professional Responsibility, 'Report: Investigation into the Office of Legal Counsel's Memoranda' (29 July 2009), online: <http://www.judiciary.house.gov> (Accessed: 10 December 2011). See also Isikoff, 'Report: Bush Lawyer said President could order civilians to be "massacred" ', *Newsweek* (19 February 2010).

[131] Eg 'The Role of the Legal Adviser of the Department of State' 85 *AJIL* (1991), 358–71, 360. See also Bilder, 'The Office of the Legal Adviser', 56 *AJIL* (1962), 633–85; Koh and Zelinsky, 'Practising International Law in the Obama Administration', 35(4) *YJIL* (2009), 1–13.

[132] As of 22 September 2011 there is only one Japanese member and no Chinese members of the ICC list of defence counsel. This under-representation is even more striking in light of the fact that Japan contributed approximately 20 per cent of the ICC 2008 budget (more than Latin America, CANZ, and other Asian States combined). The linguistic bias is a factor, though counsel from non-francophone and non-anglophone jurisdictions in Europe and South America are members of the de facto bar.

share a considerable degree of common historical background (though with different modern systems) suggests the existence of distinctly Asian features of professional advocacy: restricted professional independence, small bars and a peripheral role for advocates relative to judges. It is suggested that these characteristics derive from a historical legacy of deference to the State and scepticism towards litigation with a cultural emphasis upon mediation and other non-confrontational dispute resolution techniques.

2.3.1 China

2.3.1.1 Historical Development

The Confucian foundation for imperial China emphasized a harmonious, hierarchical society promoting good morals and compromise (*li*). The competing school of legalism conceived of law as a tool for social order through deterrence and fear.[133] Mixing these two philosophies, imperial justice discouraged litigation through systematic bribery and confession by torture to compel litigants to compromise.[134] The 'officers of the court' were Confucian-trained magistrates who were consciously ignorant of laws and local customs.[135] A shadow system of private justice promoted mediation by the educated elite.

During the nineteenth century, hapless governments failed to reform the corrupt bureaucracy. As external powers sapped the economy and imperial expansion stalled, economic power was concentrated in a gentry exploiting a growing peasantry. Following the 1911 Revolution that brought the Kuomintang to power, the Republic of China unsuccessfully attempted to reform the judiciary by importing European methods, imposing new admission requirements and discarding the Confucian examination system.[136] The new bureaucracy and judiciary continued unchecked the courts' bribery and extortion and judicial reform stalled.[137] Professional advocates (introduced in 1912) were of poor standard and insufficient numbers.[138]

In the People's Republic of China (PRC), the Maoist system of 'mass line' revolutionary justice used revolutionary courts as instruments of class struggle.[139] Whilst corporeal punishment and judicial confession by torture were abolished, mediation was co-opted to compel the peasantry. As the Maoists absorbed Soviet

[133] Goh, *Law without Lawyers, Justice without Courts* (2002), 65–91; Bodde and Morris, *Law in Imperial China* (1967), 497–8.

[134] Van der Sprenkel, *Legal Institutions in Manchu China* (1962), 34–5. *Confer* Ch'en, *Chinese Legal Tradition under the Mongols* (1979), 69–98.

[135] Brady, *Justice and Politics in People's China* (1982), 36–41; Leng, *Justice in Communist China* (1967), 127; Goh, *Law without Lawyers, Justice without Courts*, 65–135.

[136] Brady, *Justice and Politics in People's China*, 49–50; Gellhorn, 'China's Quest for Legal Modernity', 1 *JCL* (1987), 1–22.

[137] Bodde and Morris, *Law in Imperial China*, 466–7.

[138] Peerenboom, *Lawyers in China* (1998) 12–3; Leng, *Justice in Communist China*, 127–8.

[139] Gellhorn, 'China's Quest for Legal Modernity', 5–8; Leng, *Justice in Communist China*, 1–14, 25–6.

ideas, the courts gradually became more bureaucratic. The Communists abolished professional advocacy in the Judicial Reforms of 1952 to 1953.[140]

The 'constitutionalist movement' campaigned for a 'socialist rule of law' espousing the slogan: 'rule by law, not by men'. The Constitution and the 'Organic Law of the People's Courts of the PRC' 1954 provided the right to defence counsel.[141] In 1956, advocates were revived as 'legal advisers'. Although originally bureaucratic 'state workers' alongside the traditional procuracy, they later created bar associations. This stab for professional independence was reversed by Mao's return to populist justice during the Great Leap Forward and Cultural Revolution.[142] The Ministry of Justice and professional advocacy were abolished from 1966 until 1976.[143]

After Mao, professional counsel and the Ministry of Justice were revived in 1979. Law schools, law offices, and local bar associations followed in 1980. An explosion in advocates' numbers created quality control problems, prompting admission requirements and the creation of the All China Lawyers Association (ACLA) in 1986. Popular discontent at widespread violation of lax standards prompted the Ministry of Justice to enact the Chinese Lawyers Law in 1996 (amended in 2007). Whilst the ACLA promulgated its 'Lawyers Code of Practice' 2004, this is not recognized by the Law and is presumably exhortatory in light of the ACLA's lack of disciplinary jurisdiction.

2.3.1.2 *Ethical Standards*

Article 1 of the Law defines its purpose: 'to improve the system of lawyers, regulate practice by lawyers, ensure that lawyers conduct their practice in accordance with the law and enable lawyers to fulfil their roles in the building of the socialist legal system.' Article 2 defines a 'lawyer' as a practitioner providing legal services to a concerned party. This definition is a compromise between 'state workers' and 'free and independent professionals'.[144] A lawyer's basic duty is ambiguous: to 'safeguard the lawful rights and interests of the concerned party, secure the correct implementation of the law and ensure social fairness and justice'. Article 3 further provides: 'In his/her practice, a lawyer must abide by the Constitution and the law, and adhere to the ethics of the legal profession and practise discipline... take facts as the bases and the law as his/her standard... subject himself/herself to monitoring by the state, the public and the concerned party.'[145]

Competence and educational attainment are problems for the legal profession. Article 5 lays down the following requirements for a practising licence: (1) upholding the PRC Constitution; (2) passage of a unified state judicial examination for judges, procurators, and lawyers; (3) completion of a one-year apprenticeship in

[140] Gellhorn, 'China's Quest for Legal Modernity', 9–10.
[141] Peerenboom, *Lawyers in China*, 14.
[142] Li, 'The Role of Law in Communist China', 44 *CQ* (1970), 66–111, 72–3, 104–11.
[143] Peerenboom, *Lawyers in China*, 15–18, 39–42.
[144] Peerenboom, *Lawyers in China*, 49–50.
[145] Lawyers' Law, Art 3.

a law firm; and (4) being of good conduct.[146] Articles 7 and 11 automatically disqualify criminals, those dismissed from State employment or disbarred and public servants. Article 42 prescribes a two-year cooling-off period for judges or procurators to serve as lawyers.

Law firms and lawyers must pay taxes pursuant and not compete for briefs through 'improper means such as denigrating other lawyers or law firms, or paying introduction fees'.[147] Article 28 of the Law provides that a lawyer has discretion whether to accept authorization to act for a client. Under Article 32, once a lawyer has accepted an appointment he may only withdraw from it with 'legitimate reason' or 'if the entrusted matter violates the law, the client uses the services provided by the lawyer to engage in illegal activities or the client deliberately conceals important facts relating to the case'.

In response to longstanding concerns about the ability of lawyers to meet with their clients in criminal proceedings, Article 33 provides for an appointed lawyer's 'right to meet the suspect or defendant and be informed of matters pertaining to the case' without being subjected to monitoring. Article 38 requires a lawyer to keep State, trade, and client secrets confidential unless pertaining to a specified ongoing or future criminal enterprise. Article 39 proscribes representation in a matter in which he or a close relative has a conflict of interest. Article 40 prohibits illicit acceptance of authorization or fees, extortion, illegal meetings with judges or prosecutors or arbitrators, bribery, forgery, suppression of concealed evidence, and obstruction.

Article 46 vests the ACLA and bar associations with powers to represent collegial interests, conduct professional training, and monitor compliance.[148] However, the Ministry of Justice retains disciplinary and admission powers. Under Articles 47 to 56, penalties for malpractice include warnings, fines, suspension, and disbarment. There is no provision addressing the applicability of the Law to conduct before international courts, though applicability may be reasonably presumed in light of the generally tight control exerted by the State over the profession.

2.3.1.3 Ethical Efficacy

The constitutionalist vision of professional advocacy based upon a socialist rule of law has in some areas been realized.[149] The Chinese Lawyers Law was a step towards professional standards of independence, integrity, and quality.[150] However,

[146] A university degree is also said to be required (though not necessarily in law)—Clark, 'An Introduction to the Legal Profession in China in the Year 2008', 51 *SULR* (2008), 833–50, 840. Originally, there was no university degree requirement so that those participating in self-study, part-time, or other *dazhuan* programmes could sit the national examination. In 1996, 25 per cent of Chinese advocates were university-educated with 46 per cent completing *dazhuan* programmes, and 29 per cent only having secondary education—Peerenboom, *Lawyers in China*, 61–2, 65. Article 8 retains a limited discretion for State approval of qualified candidates who do not meet the requirements of Art 5.

[147] Lawyers' Law, Art 26. [148] Lawyers' Law, Art 40.

[149] Dicks, 'The Chinese Legal System', 119 *CQ* (1989), 540–76, 560–8; Keith, *China's Struggle for the Rule of Law* (1994), 13–21; Feldbrugge, *The Emancipation of Soviet Law* (1992), 52; Lubman, 'Introduction: The Future of Chinese Law', 141 *CQ* (1995), 1–21, 1.

[150] Hu, *The Development of the Chinese Legal Profession Since 1978* (2000), 90–111.

the average quality of lawyers remains low, corruption rampant, and collective self-regulation weak.[151] The maladies of the legal profession are emblematic of wider problems in the judicial system: weak judicial independence, low educational standards, inadequate legislation, and the power of the Party to compromise the independence of lawyers (particularly in criminal and administrative cases).[152] The 2007 amendments to the Law have sought to address these issues, though compliance is haphazard and disciplinary proceedings rare.

In these circumstances, the development of the Chinese legal profession remains nascent. In a culture with a deep-seated prejudice against litigation and professional advocacy and an authoritarian political system with a historical suspicion of professionals seeking to limit its powers by the rule of law, this is predictable and understandable. Despite the architectural similarities to inquisitorial systems, the reality of professional advocacy in the Chinese judicial system is representative of authoritarian jurisdictions in which the State severely curtails professional independence. Whilst there is no published information on the recruitment of Chinese legal advisers, as civil servants they are precluded from practice as lawyers and appear to be primarily diplomats by training.[153]

2.3.2 Japan

2.3.2.1 Historical Development

The judicial system of medieval Japan was inspired by tenets of Shintoism and Confucianism emphasizing harmony through adherence to the hierarchical social order. As in Imperial China, judicial functions were vested in the executive, litigation discouraged, legal codes unpublished, confession by torture used, procedure judge-centred, and professional advocacy outlawed.[154] During the Tokugawa Shogunate of 1603 to 1867, only amateur advocates could represent an incompetent litigant through kinship.[155] Its feudal society delegated the administration of justice to the warrior class, which largely performed with sophisticated forensic scrutiny and without class bias. However, innkeepers near the courts (*kujishi*) who sold knowledge of legal procedures to litigants and bribed judges were despised but intermittently tolerated and suppressed.[156]

The first formative period for the modern Japanese judicial system was the Meiji Era of 1868 to 1912. European legal systems (especially Prussia) were emulated in a radical departure from Tokugawa practices, including the publication of legal

[151] Peerenboom, 'Law Enforcement and the Legal Profession in China' in Chen et al, *Implementation of Law in the People's Republic of China* (2002), 125–48.

[152] Clark, 'An Introduction to the Legal Profession in China in the Year 2008'.

[153] Eg 'Curriculum vitae of Consul-General Duan Jielong', online: <http://sydney.chineseconsulate.org/eng/zlszl/t518871.htm> (Accessed: 28 November 2011).

[154] Haley, *Authority without Power* (1991); Ch'en, *The Formation of the Early Meiji Legal Order* (1981), 30–49, 57–80, 83.

[155] Rabinowitz, 'The Historical Development of the Japanese Bar', 70 *HLR* (1956–1957), 61–81.

[156] Abel and Lewis, *Lawyers in Society: An Overview*, 128–9.

codes and abolition of judicial torture.[157] However, judicial power remained firmly embedded in the executive. Legal reforms between 1872 and 1898 sought to raise the standards of judges and procurators (who were mostly Confucian-style bureaucrats) and created the first Japanese bar for civil advocacy.[158] In 1976, the Ministry of Justice issued an 'Ordinance Concerning Attorneys' in 1876 prescribing a bar examination and rules of honour.

However, a reputation for incompetence until educational and admission reforms enacted in the early twentieth century and traditional bias against private practice meant that the Japanese bar was considered incapable of self-regulation.[159] An oversupply of attorneys and widespread corruption in the 1920s convinced bar leaders to reduce numbers in order to raise standards. However, against the bar's wishes the Lawyer's Law 1933 preserved State regulation and did not exclude non-attorneys from practice.[160] After the Second World War, constitutional reforms charged professional advocacy with the defence of human rights.[161] Self-regulation followed with the Japanese Practising Attorney Law 1949, which created the Japan Federation of Bar Associations (*Nichibenren*) and the Legal Training and Research Institute for combined training of judges, prosecutors, and attorneys under the overall supervision of the Supreme Court.[162]

A professional crisis ensued in the 1960s concerning the conduct of advocates in criminal cases involving protests against the renewal of the Japan-US Mutual Security Treaty. Attorneys obstructed, defied court instructions, and withdrew from cases to demonstrate contempt for a judicial process they considered biased towards the prosecution. The Ministry of Justice and popular media painted attorneys as immature, insubordinate, and dishonourable.[163] A proposal to abolish attorneys in criminal proceedings was narrowly averted when the head of the *Nichibenren* publicly apologized and promised to work to prevent recurrence. The Code of Ethics 1990 introduced reforms, including a narrower right of withdrawal from representation.[164]

2.3.2.2 Ethical Standards

There are three sources for the professional ethics of Japanese attorneys: (1) the Practising Attorney Law; (2) the *Nichibenren*'s articles of association and those of local bar associations; and (3) the Japanese Code of Conduct.[165] Article 1 of the Law defines attorneys' mission as the protection of fundamental human rights, realization of social justice, sincere performance of their duties whilst endeavouring

[157] Ch'en, *The Formation of the Early Meiji Legal Order*, 70–1.
[158] Hattori, 'The Legal Profession in Japan' in von Mehren, *Law in Japan* (1963), 117–29.
[159] Hattori, 'The Legal Profession in Japan', 127–8, 137.
[160] Fujikura, *Japanese Law and Legal Theory* (1996), 503.
[161] Hattori, 'The Legal Profession in Japan', 129–31, 136.
[162] Bar associations have disciplinary jurisdiction under the supervision of the *Nichibenren*, while the Justice Ministry regulates admission—Japanese Practising Attorney Law 1949, Arts 5, 45(2), 49, 56.
[163] Leonard, 'Attorney Ethics and the Size of the Japanese Bar' in Fujikura, *Japanese Law and Legal Theory* (1996), 504.
[164] Leonard, 'Attorney Ethics and the Size of the Japanese Bar', 504.
[165] Practising Attorney Law, Art 22.

to maintain social order and improve the legal system.[166] Article 2 requires them to 'strive to remain highly cultured, to build his fine character and be well acquainted with laws'.

Article 4 requires attorneys to complete vocational training at the Legal Training and Research Institute for admission. A former Supreme Court judge is *ipso facto* qualified and certain convicts, the impeached, the disbarred, the incompetent, and bankrupts are disqualified.[167] The rights and obligations of a practising attorney include: secrecy, refusal of instructions amidst conflict of interest, abstention from corruption, exclusion of non-attorneys for legal representational matters, refraining from any interest in a dispute, giving notice of refusal of instructions, and informing the bar association of any undertaking of profit-making business.[168]

Article 11 of the Articles of Association of the *Nichibenren* on the 'ethics of the practising attorney' obliges attorneys to apply law justly and to strive to rectify any discovered illegality or injustice. By Article 12, they must continuously strive to build legal knowledge and character. Article 13 stipulates duties of politeness to judges, public prosecutors, and colleagues. Article 15 declares that 'a practising attorney shall be essentially free, and shall not be influenced by power or economic interests'.

The Code of Conduct 2004 enacted by the *Nichibenren* lays down duties of professional independence, protection and development of the judicial system, fairness and integrity, personal honour, continuous professional training, and participation in public interest activities.[169] Additional standards on business matters include: dignified self-advertisement, no client solicitation or undignified litigation purpose or manner, restrictions upon fee sharing, no compensation for client referral, no promotion of unlawful conduct, no participation in immoral or degrading business, and no undignified business 'from a preoccupation with the pursuit of profit'.[170]

General standards articulated in relation to the client include: independence, not undertaking 'clearly illegitimate' cases, avoiding conflicts of interest, confidentiality where there is no 'due reason' for disclosure, and charging appropriate and reasonable fees.[171] Direct communication with a represented opposing party and the provision or acceptance of any benefit to an opposing party is forbidden.[172] Mutual respect and honour, no entrapment, no intervention, and amicable dispute settlement are required between attorneys.[173] Attorneys must strive to respect fair trial, refrain from enticing perjury or submitting false evidence, desist from negligent or 'illegitimate' delay, and avoid using personal relations with any judge or public figure towards proceedings.[174] Article 82 provides a wide discretion for individual attorneys: '[I]n consideration of diversity and individuality of the duties of attorneys, these rules shall be interpreted

[166] Practising Attorney Law, Art 1.
[167] Practising Attorney Law, Arts 6–7.
[168] Practising Attorney Law, Arts 23, 25–30.
[169] Japanese Code, Arts 2–8.
[170] Japanese Code, Arts 9–10, 12–16.
[171] Japanese Code, Arts 20–45.
[172] Japanese Code, Arts 52–54.
[173] Japanese Code, Arts 70–73.
[174] Japanese Code, Arts 74–77.

and applied so as not to impair the freedom and independence of attorneys.' There is no jurisdictional provision concerning conduct before an international court.

2.3.2.3 Ethical Efficacy

Japanese advocates enjoy a mixed reputation for high competence but questionable ethical standards.[175] The key debate in the professional media concerns the merits of increasing attorney numbers.[176] From the 1920s, this remarkably small bar has pinned its faith on its smallness rather than in ethical prescription and enforcement to ensure quality. Despite the rarity of disciplinary proceedings,[177] ethical scandals involving bribery, excessive fees, and other problems have dogged the profession.[178] In the early 1990s, the *Nichibenren* reversed longstanding policy by publishing miscreants' misconduct in a bid to win public trust. Despite internal pressure to reform the Code of Conduct and strengthen the disciplinary process, reliance upon the size rationale continues. The Code is relatively ethereal and would benefit from more specificity and practicality.

Whilst there is no published research on the backgrounds of Japanese *jurisconsultes,* both of its agents in the pending ICJ proceedings appear to be career diplomats.[179] However, Judge Oda was an academic recruited as a part-time *jurisconsulte* and Judge Owada both a diplomat and academic.[180] Thus, Japan appears to be closer to the French model rather than the English. On the rare occasions in which it participates in international litigation, it appears to rely upon diplomats as agents and eminent foreign international lawyers as counsel.

2.4 Islamic Traditions of the Near East

To an extent, as with every other category in this chapter, the adjective 'Islamic' is somewhat misleading. As within the other geographical regions and jurisdictional families, there is diversity within the group of jurisdictions that have adopted Islamic law (شريعة—*shariā*). No modern jurisdiction relies totally upon *shariā* but rather combines it, to varying degrees, with either the civil law or common law traditions. There is a lack of scholarship on the practical application of Islamic law and the ethics of the Islamic legal professions. Moreover, the degree of Islamic

175 Goodman, *The Rule of Law in Japan* (2008), 200–9.

176 Research published by the *Nichibenren* shows that from 2003 to 2010 the disparity in the *per capita* ratio of judges, attorneys, and prosecutors between Japan and the US, UK, Germany, and France has fallen from roughly tenfold to fourfold—*Nichibenren*, 'White Paper on Attorneys' (2010), online: <http://www.nichibenren.or.jp/library/en/about/data/WhitePaper2010.pdf> (Accessed: 30 November 2011), 5.

177 *Nichibenren*, 'White Paper on Attorneys', 61–2.

178 Leonard, *supra* note 160, 504–15.

179 Koji Tsuruoka, Deputy Vice-Minister for Foreign Policy and Minoru Shibuya, Ambassador to the Netherlands—*Whaling in the Antarctic*, 2. Similarly, the agent in an UNCLOS Annex VII ad hoc arbitration was another career diplomat (Shotaro Yachi)—*Southern Bluefin Tuna*, para 17.

180 McWhinney, 'The Many Capacities of Shigeru Oda as International Law-Maker: Publicist, Jurisconsult and Judge' in Ando et al, *Liber Amicorum Judge Shigeru Oda* (2002)(Vol I), 41–56, 43; 'President Hisahi Owada', online: <http://www.icj-cij.org/court> (Accessed: 30 November 2011).

influence varies considerably from one jurisdiction to the next so that generalizations become difficult to sustain.[181] Theological divisions within *shariā* further complicate the task.

However, within the narrow scope of the legal professions, it remains possible to identify Islamic traditions. As explained below, historically the principal profession is that of the judge (قاضي —*qadi*)—almost invariably a member of the clergy (علماء—*ulama*). Professional advocates were not indigenous to the Islamic traditions but rather a European importation. The relevance of these traditions to international courts is that there are some States (eg Saudi Arabia and Iran[182]) that employ them to varying degrees. Whilst Saudi Arabia is not active in international litigation, Iran has been party to four ICJ contentious cases as well as the Iran-US Claims Tribunal. As the principal Islamic quasi-theocracies, the salient features of their Islamic and non-Islamic legal professions within authoritarian political systems provide a useful comparative template with the European ideal of professional independence.

2.4.1 Saudi Arabia[183]

2.4.1.1 Historical Development

The modern Kingdom of Saudi Arabia, created in the early twentieth century from Ottoman territory, is based upon the Wahabbi movement of Sunni Islam through an alliance between the House of Saud and the Wahabbi clergy. Founded in the eighteenth century by the theologian Muhammad ibn Abd al-Wahhab, it aims to revive a classical Islam as a living reality purified of cultural innovations.[184] This goal is aided by the historical isolation in the nineteenth century of the Wahabbists in the Arabian hinterland from European legal influences.[185] Initially, the judicial system created by royal decree (نظام—*nizām*) was separated into *shariā* courts applying Islamic jurisprudence (فقه—*fiqh*) whilst the interior and commercial courts used French-derived Ottoman legal codes (قانونين—*qanunin*) for the cosmopolitan Hijaz region. Only in 1992 was the judicial system unified under reformed *shariā* courts.

Classical judicial procedure under *shariā* relied exclusively upon the Islamic judge to adjudicate in accordance with *shariā*. The appointment of judges in Saudi Arabia is a royal prerogative that is in practice made upon the advice of a senior

[181] Vogel, *Islamic Law and Legal System* (2000), xi–xvii.

[182] Possibly including parallel or hybrid jurisdictions. For example, the legal professions in Yemen are recognizably civilian apart from '*shariā* attorneys' exempted from the usual admission requirements and a *shariā* knowledge requirement—al-Hubayshi, *Legal System and Basic Law in Yemen* (1988), 165–75. Similarly, professional advocacy in Bahrain is a secular British importation apart from a *shariā* requirement—Radhi, *Judiciary and Arbitration in Bahrain* (2003), 146–62. The quality of Middle Eastern bars such Egypt is said to be 'depressing'– Mallat, *Introduction to Middle Eastern Law* (2007), 415.

[183] There is a dearth of scholarship on the Kingdom's judicial system—Vogel, *Islamic Law and Legal System*, xi.

[184] Vogel, *Islamic Law and Legal System*, xvi.

[185] Vogel, *Islamic Law and Legal System*, 87–97, 279–308.

cleric (مرجع—*marjah*) to nominate, supervise, and discipline judges.[186] Since judicial procedure was highly informal (largely oral) and expeditious, professionalism was an alien concept. The Judiciary Act 1975 now prescribes standards of independence, qualification (*shariā* knowledge), and training (three years as judicial assistants) under the disciplinary jurisdiction of the Supreme Judicial Council (the apex court).[187]

Against this historical background, Saudi *shariā* courts 'oppose the use of advocates because they feel that they would tend to expand, instead of simplify, the dispute and drive the parties apart instead of together'.[188] Indeed, there is a latent cultural scepticism of professional advocacy:

> Islamic society did not know legal practice as an organized social practice... unlike other societies, Islamic societies did not value those who represented litigants; the occupation was rather seen as a degrading career, and many of those with piety had avoided playing this role. In a society that holds this view... falling standards in this occupation are to be expected. No surprise then... if the history of the Islamic judiciary is one of great caution towards representation.[189]

The only representative recognized under classical procedure is the agent (وكيل—*vakil*) who is a proxy (typically a senior male relative) rather than a defender to assist an incompetent litigant but without an autonomous status as an 'officer of the court'.

Consequently, despite the existence of a statutory right of litigants to counsel in principle, in practice the right was not recognized in the Kingdom until 2001 when royal decrees enacted laws of civil and criminal procedure before *shariā* courts.[190] However, litigants have the right to self-representation or to be assisted by lay counsel—there is no exclusivity over rights of hearing for professionals. Although two professional bars now exist in the Kingdom (one for the *shariā* courts and another for regulatory agencies and tribunals), neither is a member of the International Bar Association. Whereas in practice professionals regularly appear in commercial cases, they are rare in criminal trials.[191] There is a separate legal profession of crown prosecutors, though their regulatory infrastructure has yet to be researched.

2.4.1.2 Ethical Standards

Unsurprisingly, there is scant information in the public domain concerning the admission requirements, ethical standards, and disciplinary procedures governing

[186] Vogel, *Islamic Law and Legal System*, 88. Royal discretion over appointments is said to be limited—al-Eshaikh, 'Human Rights and the Trial of the Accused' (Unpublished PhD book), online at: <https://theses.ncl.ac.uk/dspace/handle/10443/754> (Accessed: 30 November 2011), 270–1. For a sceptical view, see al-Jarbou, 'Judicial Independence: Case Study of Saudi Arabia', 19(1) *ALQ* (2004), 5–54.

[187] Al-Ghadyan, 'The Judiciary in Saudi Arabia', 13(3) *ALQ* (1998), 235–51, 236–8, 241.

[188] Vogel, *Islamic Law and Legal System*, 160–1.

[189] Al-Kelanee in al-Eshaikh, 'Human Rights and the Trial of the Accused', 192.

[190] Al-Kelanee in al-Eshaikh, 'Human Rights and the Trial of the Accused', 195–201.

[191] Vogel, *Islamic Law and Legal System*, 161.

professional lawyers. The Code of Law Practice (Rights and Duties of Lawyers) 2001 is the governing legislation, applicable to professional lawyers appearing before *shariā* courts, the Board of Grievances, or any other tribunals. In line with the traditional scepticism towards professional advocacy, the Code recognizes broad powers for the client in matters like termination of representation and case strategy.

However, a lawyer must refrain from offensive language or referring to personal matters concerning the opposing party or his representative. A lawyer cannot without legitimate cause decline to represent his client before the conclusion of the case, though he must not represent multiple clients in cases of conflicts of interest. A lawyer is bound by client confidentiality 'unless such non-disclosure constitutes a violation of a *shariā* requirement'.

Although breaches of professional standards are subject to disciplinary sanction under the Code, since the law does not require evidence obtained through breach of confidentiality there is the residual possibility that criminal defendants could be convicted in this way. In a legal culture to which professional representation and confidentiality are alien, the likelihood of professional sanction for such breaches may be doubtful. Moreover, the Code makes no mention of effectiveness or competence standards and the judiciary has been unwilling to lay down any such requirements. It is also unknown what qualification requirements are laid down to be called to the Saudi bar.

2.4.1.3 Ethical Efficacy

Professionalism is an alien and novel concept to Saudi Arabia. In a political system based upon authoritarianism and neo-classical Islam, the monarchy and clergy have historically been sceptical of professional advocacy. Notwithstanding the Judiciary Act, the symbiotic political relationship between the two may curtail judicial independence—though it is also likely that the monarchy exercises self-restraint in its regulation of the judiciary to preserve its Islamic legitimacy. Consequently, the European ideal of professional independence through ethical standards to preserve the integrity of judicial procedure appears to be contrary to classical Islamic tradition.

In a political system consciously striving to emulate classical Islam with its reliance upon informal procedure and judicial inquisition, the introduction of professional advocacy in 2001 was likely to be difficult. In such a short time and on such stony ground, it is likely that local standards are relatively weak. In particular, the Saudi Code prescribes very few and vague standards for professional counsel that are not accompanied by legal and architectural safeguards. The traditional scepticism towards the concept of professional counsel likely accounts for the highly client-oriented nature of the Code and the lack of exclusive rights of hearing for professionals. Saudi attorneys are unlikely to enjoy social prestige when their very existence is regarded as at least questionable according to *shariā*, which creates a vicious circle of low professional standards.[192] Moreover, the Saudi Foreign

[192] A United Arab Emirates court ruled in 1984 that legal practice is prohibited in *shariā*—al-Eshaikh, 'Human Rights and the Trial of the Accused', 193 (note 19).

Ministry does not appear to employ legal advisers on international law. On those rare occasions when it has participated in international litigation, its agents have been diplomats and it has not employed foreign counsel.[193]

2.4.2 Iran

2.4.2.1 Historical Development

The ancient history of the judicial system of the Iranian civilization has also been defined by two key institutions: the autocratic monarchy and the clergy. Pre-Islamic ancient Persia[194] was a despotic political system in which all power was vested in the monarchy as a living deity. In practice, judicial power was delegated to judges and public prosecutors (learned Zoroastrian clerics or *mubadan*) who developed sophisticated procedural rules of evidence, precedent and jurisdiction.[195] Unlike contemporary practices in ancient Greece and Rome, rigorous standards of legal scholarship, procedural fairness, and evidentiary inquiry were placed upon the judiciary. It appears that ancient Persia developed an indigenous professional advocacy well before medieval Europe. Paid advocates who were subject to strict ethical standards were regularly employed in the courts.[196]

This judicial system appears to have been largely destroyed under the Muslim Caliphates and replaced by modified versions of the classical Islamic system described above.[197] Judicial authority was generally delegated to *shariā* courts, though there was right of appeal to the court of last resort of the ruler (المظالم—*al-māzālem*). Whilst this system somewhat increased the independence of the judiciary from the ruler relative to ancient Persia, its procedure was arguably more primitive and in any case excluded professional advocacy.[198] The adoption of Shia Twelver Islam as the official religion of the Safavid dynasty in the sixteenth century resulted in the organization of the Shia clergy into a bureaucracy overseen by a royal appointee (صدر—*sadr*).

Amidst the civil strife from the decline of the late Safavid to the fall of the Qajar dynasty in 1925, the relationship between monarchy and clergy was competitive rather than cooperative with legitimacy flowing to the latter at the expense of the former.[199] During this time, the traditional cooperation of the two institutions was frayed and parallel judicial systems (State and *shariā*) competed with one another. Attempts by rulers to impose educational requirements upon the clergy, centralize the judicial system under the Ministry of Justice and ban judicial torture and harsh punishments (eg blinding, firing at people by cannon, burying people alive,

[193] In this respect, see in particular *Buraimi*—Chapter 4. See also *Kosovo*.

[194] Loosely used to signify the successive Achamaenid, Selucid, Parthian, and Sassanid Empires from 648 BC until the Arab conquest of Persia and the death of Yazdegerd III in 651 AD.

[195] Mohammadi, *Judicial Reform and Reorganization in 20th Century Iran* (2008), 34–6.

[196] Lawyers had to take an oath and could not act contrary to their clients' cases, speak irrelevantly, disobey court orders or charge excessive fees—Bulsara, *The Laws of the Ancient Persians* (1937), 46.

[197] Mohammadi, *Judicial Reform and Reorganization in 20th Century Iran*, 36–43.

[198] Mohammadi, *Judicial Reform and Reorganization in 20th Century Iran*, 51.

[199] Mohammadi, *Judicial Reform and Reorganization in 20th Century Iran*, 42–54.

or placing them alive in a wall) were rare and largely unsuccessful. The judicial systems during these eras were defined by their inaccessibility to the people, lack of judicial independence and competence, and corrupt, arbitrary and an ineffective State that sought legitimacy from the *shariā* courts.

The European (principally French) legal traditions were introduced into Iran on a significant scale during the Pahlavi dynasty that followed the Constitutional Revolution of 1906. Under Reza Shah Pahlavi, there was a conscious effort to subordinate the judicial system to a State overtly emulating European legal tradition whilst preserving its authoritarian nature.[200] The professional lawyer (called *vakil*, despite the originally non-professional status in classical Islamic procedure) was first recognized in 1912 as the equivalent of the *avocat*, though licensed by the judiciary rather than bar associations.[201]

Following the subordination of the judiciary to the State, the judiciary was mostly purged of the clergy in 1936 by a new requirement that judges (still called *qadi*, though no longer required to be clergy) and prosecutors (*mostanteq*) hold a university law degree. The Iranian Bar Association was founded in 1935 under the supervision of the Ministry of Justice. By the Codes of Law Practice of 1935 and 1936, the Bar Association board was composed of Ministry appointees and the profession was subject to Ministry regulations and disciplinary jurisdiction. During the reign of Mohammad Reza Shah from 1941 until 1979, the only period in which judicial and professional independence was pursued was during the premiership of Mohammad Mosaddeq of 1951 to 1953 during which major disciplinary efforts were made to stamp out judicial corruption and the Bar Association was recognized as a financially and legally independent institution in the Bar Independence Act 1952. This Act vested licensing, regulatory, and disciplinary powers in the Bar Association.

The Revolution of 1979 that subsequently resulted in the creation of the Islamic Republic of Iran severely damaged the independence and integrity of the legal professions.[202] Based upon the controversial theological doctrine of 'guardianship by jurist' (ولايت فقيه—*velayat-e faqih*), the judiciary was purged of non-clerics and constitutionally subordinated to the Supreme Leader (رهبر انقلاب—*rahbare enghelab*) with Revolutionary Courts.[203] Severe shortages resulted for lack of qualified judicial candidates from religious seminaries. Particularly notorious amongst the new judiciary was Ayatollah Sadegh Khalkhali, who as Chief Justice of the Revolutionary Courts summarily and arbitrarily executed thousands of individuals and thereby earned a reputation as Iran's chief 'hanging judge'.[204] From 1979 until 1991, there was no right to counsel in the Revolutionary Courts until a constitutional amendment passed over the resistance of the judiciary who were threatened

[200] Mohammadi, *Judicial Reform and Reorganization in 20th Century Iran*, 80–108.

[201] Mohammadi, *Judicial Reform and Reorganization in 20th Century Iran*, 69.

[202] Mohammadi, *Judicial Reform and Reorganization in 20th Century Iran*, 126–32.

[203] For an overview of the current constitutional position with respect to judicial power, see Abghari, *Introduction to the Iranian Legal System and the Protection of Human Rights in Iran* (2008), 21–4, 69–92.

[204] Abghari, *Introduction to the Iranian Legal System*, 136–47.

with disciplinary proceedings if they refused to hear counsel. Only in 1997 were professional advocacy and the Bar Association revived.

2.4.2.2 Ethical Standards

Despite the upheavals of the immediate post-revolutionary period described above, the full revival of professional advocacy in 1997 appears to have included a reversion to the Bar Independence Act 1952 as the governing legislation for the profession.[205] Standard admission requirements for advocates are to be at least 25 years of age, have an LLB degree, complete a prescribed training regimen over 18 months, and pass the written and oral examinations of the Iranian Bar Association.[206] In addition, Article 2 of the Manner of Acquiring an Advocacy Licence Act 1997 requires that candidates, inter alia: (1) believe and undertake to practise *shariā*; (2) believe in the Islamic Republic of Iran with its principles of 'guardianship by jurist' and Constitution; (3) have no record of membership or activism in groups opposed to Islam or based on negation of theistic religion; (4) not be dependent on the Pahlavi regime; and (5) not be a member of or be giving support to illegal groups opposed to the Islamic Republic of Iran.

Since 2002, an ongoing problem has been the legal right of the judiciary to issue advocacy licences so that there are two licensing regimes in force. Moreover, there is right of appeal to the judiciary from the Advocates' Disciplinary Courts (which is presumably under the aegis of the Bar Association) and the judiciary vets candidates for the Board of Directors of the Bar Association. At present, the ethical standards applied by the Advocates' Disciplinary Courts and their disciplinary decisions are not published in English or French and appear also to not be published in Persian.[207]

2.4.2.3 Ethical Efficacy

The long history of the Iranian legal culture reveals that, after the sixth century, professional advocacy disappeared in line with judge-centred Islamic tradition. Thereafter, the judicial system was characterized by a power struggle between the successive monarchies and the Islamic clergy. When it was created anew more than a thousand years later in 1906, it was part of a political programme of conscious Europeanization. However, this professionalization was limited by an authoritarian political system that subordinated the profession to the State.

In the aftermath of the 1979 Revolution that effectively destroyed the civilian legal professions, the clergy has replaced the monarchy as the dominant force in the judicial system. Given the history of the professionals and the traditional scepticism of classical Islamic procedure towards them, the initial destruction of the legal professions in favour of summary justice in revolutionary courts is explicable. With the judiciary under the authority of the Supreme Leader and the advocacy

[205] Abghari, *Introduction to the Iranian Legal System*, 95–9.

[206] There are exceptions for clerics as well as former judges, parliamentarians, and army officers who satisfy prescribed conditions of length of service and education.

[207] Online: <http://www.iranbar.org> (Accessed: 1 December 2011).

profession subordinated to the judiciary, professional independence does not exist. This dependence upon the State, coupled with the lack of ethical standards and with the hostility of the judiciary towards professional advocacy, is unlikely to create a reputation for competence and integrity.[208] The Foreign Ministry Department for International Legal Affairs appears to be comprised of career diplomats, not necessarily with legal training, who act as agents before the Iran-US Claims Tribunal and ICJ assisted by foreign counsel.[209]

2.5 Conclusions

This overview of the national ethical traditions of national jurisdictions has illustrated a number of themes. First, it shows that professional advocacy as understood today is a peculiarly European institution that was subsequently spread throughout the world during the Age of Empire and afterwards. Consequently, there are certain architectural and functional commonalities that derive from this history. This provides a tenuous foundation for the articulation of common ethical standards for advocacy before international courts in that the concepts (eg confidentiality or conflicts of interest) are shared.

Secondly, it demonstrates the significant differences in the histories and professional standards of the respective bars. A crucial factor to consider is the legal system and cultural context in which the bar is situated. For example, for the bars operating within liberal democracies professional independence through self-regulation is considered to be an imperative virtue as a bastion against State power. By contrast, for the bars operating in authoritarian systems and/or in legal cultures that are traditionally sceptical of professional advocacy the self-conception will be more likely to be service to the State or to God. However, it is noteworthy that professional advocates in authoritarian systems worldwide almost invariably come to agitate for professional independence and the rule of law. Thus, despite cultural differences concerning the role of professional advocacy it is arguable that justice and the rule of law are universal principles.

Thirdly, although historical and cultural context are important factors in determining the success of a bar the history also shows that bars have a degree of power to professionalize themselves by raising their own standards. The age and social status of the profession is a critical factor for the standards that it adheres to in its practice, through which virtuous and vicious cycles of integrity and corruption

[208] Allegations of grave misconduct by Iranian agents before the Iran-US Claims Tribunal have been made. For example, they have reportedly burglarized the Registry and spied on internal deliberations—Mosk, 'Attorney Ethics in International Arbitration', 5 *BJILP* (2010), 32–7, 35. Another case featured the suppression of evidence— JI *Case v Iran*. See also Khan, *The Iran-United States Claims Tribunal: Controversies, Cases and Contribution* (1990), 41–7, 61–77.

[209] Eg *Oil Platforms*, 4. An example is Mr Mohammad Akhundzadeh Basti, Director-General from 2003–2005 who is a career diplomat with a background in engineering—online: <http://www.mfa.gov.ir/NewsShow.aspx?NID=749&menu=167&lang=en> (Accessed: 1 December 2011).

emerge. At various points, bar leaders seized the initiative to stamp out corruption, exclude amateurs and impose higher standards on the profession. A successful outcome appears to create a virtuous circle of high standards and social prestige. These historical examples can guide the professionalization of the international bar.

Fourthly, it shows that there are significant differences in the professional backgrounds of *jurisconsultes* in foreign ministries. These are more often career diplomats and academics rather than members of national bars. Consequently, when they appear as agents for their governments before international courts they are unlikely to be bound by professional codes of conduct. However, despite the theoretical distinction of British or American legal advisers belonging to self-regulating national bars, the lack of history of national bars disciplining members serving as government lawyers calls into question its practical effect. Whilst this lack of independence is likely to endanger the integrity of international judicial proceedings where a State pressures counsel to engage in corrupt practices, it is even more likely to occur where the legal culture of the State is authoritarian and sceptical of professional independence.

These are real challenges facing the professionalization of international advocacy, which necessarily entails the creation of a professional autonomy for counsel bound by standards that require them to resist such pressures under threat of disciplinary sanction. Common ethical standards articulated in the absence of common ideology necessitate value judgements and a conscious, *a priori* articulation of the fundamental role of the advocate. Whilst it is right that justice and the international rule of law form the core values of a new profession, the realities of diverse legal cultures must be reckoned with.

3

The Historical Development of International Advocacy

Having examined select national traditions, this chapter considers the historical development of international advocacy preceding the Second World War. From classical ad hoc arbitral tradition through to the Permanent Court of International Justice (PCIJ), the ethics of advocacy was an almost completely ignored topic. Scholars and statesmen who were engaged in the creation of the first international judicial institutions at the turn of the century, culminating with the PCIJ, were far more concerned with the impartiality of the international judiciary. In line with the diplomatic tradition from which international arbitration derived, procedural rules concerning the representation of parties were minimal. A laissez-faire culture prevailed in this era, by which arbitral tribunals and the PCIJ declined to regulate advocacy in deference to 'State sovereignty'.

However, this did not preclude ethical issues connected to counsel from arising before those early institutions. Such problems included the forgery of documents, conflicts of interest arising from arbitrators seeking to serve as counsel and the propriety of scientific experts appearing as counsel rather than witnesses. Such issues persist before modern international courts and tribunals. This not only indicates that they are long-term procedural problems but also that the laissez-faire policy adopted by the early courts and tribunals was unsuccessful. Whilst a degree of homogeneity was present before the PCIJ due to the emergence of a tiny de facto bar, with small legal teams of typically one or two counsel representing each party, this could not wholly preclude the regulation of counsel from international judicial procedure. Moreover, certain PCIJ judges supported the creation of an 'international bar' attached to the Court in order to break the link between advocacy and nationality and ensure the quality of advocates.

Thus, this chapter serves two main purposes. First, by describing the historical development of advocacy before the early international courts, it explains the original reasons why modern advocacy has been hitherto unregulated. Secondly, it identifies early (and largely unknown) problems arising in this unregulated and quasi-diplomatic culture that recur before modern courts. Through analysis of these two themes, the longevity and recurrence of ethical issues for counsel becomes evident. Despite (or because of) the laissez-faire culture before the early international tribunals, problems such as forgery, experts and qualification requirements for counsel repeatedly arose. Strikingly, these and others remain live issues before the ICJ and other modern tribunals that also lack common ethical standards for counsel.

An important theme that this chapter engages is the role of counsel as an autonomous intermediary between the parties and the court. It does so by examining the early models of representation before arbitral tribunals and the PCIJ, which eventually became standardized with the distinction between 'agents' and 'counsel and advocates' within Article 42 of the ICJ Statute. The attempts to delineate the respective functions of the two were connected to the control of parties over case presentation. Since agents were diplomatic representatives considered to be beyond the regulatory jurisdiction of the judiciary, abortive proposals to professionalize counsel and advocates were especially significant. After briefly examining classical and early modern arbitration, the narrative principally addresses the practices of the Permanent Court of Arbitration (PCA) and the Permanent Court of International Justice (PCIJ). Section 3.1 concerns ancient and classical arbitration, section 3.2 relates the early institutionalization of the international legal system, and section 3.3 examines the creation and practice of the PCIJ and other courts and tribunals between the two World Wars.

3.1 Ancient and Classical Arbitration

3.1.1 Antiquity

The degree to which arbitration was employed by the independent polities of antiquity is debatable.[1] However, scholars agree that the Greek city-states most frequently utilized 'public' arbitration[2]—defined as the submission by independent and legally equal polities of a dispute to an impartial arbiter.[3] In the ancient world, the modern 'fiction'[4] of juridical equality within a co-existential legal system did not generally exist. Whilst domination by conquest was the order of the day, expediency and morality prompted resort to some 81 recorded instances of inter-municipal arbitration in the Hellenes.[5] In these arbitrations, natural justice principles of equal hearing and impartiality were observed.[6] Arbitration was not conducted with non-Greeks, probably due to hostility and arrogance.[7]

The majority of known Greek arbitrations arose within alliance systems, either by *clause compromissoire* or by ad hoc agreement.[8] Disputes were most often

[1] Ralston, *International Arbitration from Athens to Locarno* (1929), 155; Phillipson, *The International Law and Custom of Ancient Greece and Rome* (1911) (Vol II), 127, 130–1; Raeder, *L'Arbitrage international chez les Hellenes* (1912), 237–40.

[2] Ralston, *International Arbitration from Athens to Locarno*, 128–9.

[3] Phillipson, *The International Law and Custom of Ancient Greece and Rome*, 127–9.

[4] Phillipson, *The International Law and Custom of Ancient Greece and Rome*, 8.

[5] Raeder, *L'Arbitrage international chez les Hellenes*, 237.

[6] Ralston, *International Arbitration from Athens to Locarno*, 155, 161; Phillipson, *The International Law and Custom of Ancient Greece and Rome*, 135–6.

[7] Phillipson, *The International Law and Custom of Ancient Greece and Rome*, 127.

[8] Ralston, *International Arbitration from Athens to Locarno*, 156–8.

territorial but would also concern religious, proprietary, or other matters.[9] No unified code of procedural law governed arbitrations, which varied immensely in form and content; for example, whilst the usual number of arbitrators was three or five, the range was between one and six hundred.[10] Arbitral procedure depended upon parties; often, it was agreed that a neutral third city or institutions like the Amphictyonic Council and the Delphic Oracle be designated to constitute a tribunal.[11] There were no qualification requirements for arbitrators (in one arbitration, they were chosen by lot[12]) but they were often required to swear an oath to the gods that they had not received a bribe and that they would judge impartially according to the truth.[13]

Advocates were routinely employed to present arguments,[14] yet no oath appears to have been required of them. Advocates and 'trustworthy men' would be entrusted with the conduct of the case but had no right to amend the procedural rules of the *compromis* without instructions.[15] Parties were entitled to equal numbers of advocates by arbitration agreements, which also often limited the number of advocates to two or four each.[16] Advocates' speech time—as in Athenian law—was limited and procedures governed the production of documents.[17] However, no personal duties appear to have been placed upon advocates who were also invariably citizens of their instructing city.

Early Rome largely rejected participation as litigant in arbitration and when acting as arbiter frequently did so for self-benefit; its eventual domination over most of the known world precluded the utilization of arbitration between independent polities but rarely.[18] Advocates' ethics being unknown in archaic Greece and only really developed from the time of Cicero onwards, the exclusion of such ethics from international arbitration is readily understandable. The principal legacy of ancient arbitration was the principle of equality before and impartial decision by international arbitral tribunals and a precedent of unregulated advocacy.

3.1.2 Middle Ages

The two most powerful authorities in Catholic Christendom during the Middle Ages were the Papacy and the Holy Roman Empire. The Papacy claimed to and often actually did dispense title and judgement amongst the princes of Europe. It did so, literally and figuratively, *ex cathedra* as God's vice-regent—his judgements

[9] Ralston, *International Arbitration from Athens to Locarno*, 247–9.
[10] Ralston, *International Arbitration from Athens to Locarno*, 158–60.
[11] Ralston, *International Arbitration from Athens to Locarno*.
[12] Ralston, *International Arbitration from Athens to Locarno*, 159.
[13] Ralston, *International Arbitration from Athens to Locarno*, 161.
[14] The existence of an 'international law' of the Hellenes is debatable—Ralston, *International Arbitration from Athens to Locarno*, 154–5.
[15] Ralston, *International Arbitration from Athens to Locarno*, 274, 292.
[16] Ralston, *International Arbitration from Athens to Locarno*, 291.
[17] Ralston, *International Arbitration from Athens to Locarno*, 298–9.
[18] Ralston, *International Arbitration from Athens to Locarno*, 168–73; Phillipson, *The International Law and Custom of Ancient Greece and Rome*, 152–65.

were nigh-absolute rather than 'judicial' in any restricted sense.[19] Whilst this largely excluded law, the princes' methods of pleading before the Pope remain unexplained. The incremental surrender of papal authority as the summit of feudal Christendom to absolute monarchy[20] produced several arbitrations involving the Pontiff as arbitrator as well as an arbitration submitted to the Paris *parlement* as party against the Emperor.[21] Besides the Papacy, arbitrators included the Emperor, princes, cardinals and bishops, municipalities, and even occasionally individuals of lesser rank.[22]

Little is described concerning the procedure of these arbitrations.[23] Cases have been cited of the use of advocates and delegates in arbitrations.[24] Whether they were employed to advocate the pleadings of princes who appeared before the Pope or arbitrator and whether the ethical duties of the ecclesiastical courts bound such advocates in doing so remains unknown. The principal legacy of feudal adjudication and medieval arbitration was twofold: an overtly pacifistic ideal to achieve *pax inter christianos* and, pursuant to that aim as well as expediency, the establishment of a fragile principle of co-existentialism within initially a feudal hierarchy beneath the Supreme Pontiff and later an anarchical Europe of sovereigns—each with an equal right to rule bestowed directly by God, not by Pope.

3.1.3 Early Modern Age

Scholars generally date the beginning of the early modern age of international arbitration from the signing of the Jay Treaty between Great Britain and the USA in 1794.[25] Early modern arbitration can be said to span the nineteenth century until the creation of the Permanent Court of Arbitration (PCA) by the first Hague Convention 1899 as the first permanent arbitral institution. One reckoning of the number of arbitration treaties agreed between 1796 and 1900 shows 177 in total, with 134 of them occurring after 1860.[26] The great majority of these arbitrations involved European and American parties in which arbitrators were vested with remarkably broad procedural powers, as *compromis* were often silent or terse on procedure.[27] Whilst it has been observed that the incremental increase of arbitrations brought greater procedural homogenization, their general flexibility has also

[19] Ralston, *International Arbitration from Athens to Locarno*, 175; Revon, *L'Arbitrage international* (1892), 122.

[20] Higgins, 'The Papacy and International Law' 9 *JSCL* (1908), 252–64, 254; Nys, *Droit international* (1912), 349–76.

[21] Ralston, *International Arbitration from Athens to Locarno*, 176; 181–4. Revon, *L'Arbitrage international*, 125–9.

[22] Ralston, *International Arbitration from Athens to Locarno*, 176–85.

[23] Ralston, *International Arbitration from Athens to Locarno*, 185.

[24] Ralston, *International Arbitration from Athens to Locarno*, 185–6.

[25] Bishop, *International Arbitral Procedure* (1931), 1–2, 191–3.

[26] Bishop, *International Arbitral Procedure*, 1.

[27] Bishop, *International Arbitral Procedure*, 3–4. See also Mérignhac, *Théorique et pratique de l'arbitrage international* (1895), 245.

been noted.[28] Arbitrators were stated to have been permitted to draw upon general rules for the administration of justice to safeguard their decisions.[29] Agents and advocates appear to have invariably been expressly or impliedly permitted in the arbitrations to which the United States was party during this period, mostly claims commissions.[30]

Periodically, arbitrators would have to address procedural issues concerning advocacy in an ad hoc fashion. Whilst diplomats were more likely to appear for parties than professional advocates, there was considerable diversity. In the *Behring Fur Seal* arbitration of 1892, the arbitrators directed that they would recognize the agent's standing to present a motion but not to argue it because argumentation was held to be the function of counsel.[31] The Chilean Claims Commission directed that certain offensive briefs submitted by private counsel be withdrawn and that in future no briefs be submitted without prior authorization by agents. The Spanish-American Commission and Venezuelan Protocols directed that it would only receive petitions and arguments from individual claimants through State-appointed advocates and agents, arbitrators in a US-Russian whaling arbitration directed that Russia must communicate with the USA through its appointed agent, and the Spanish Commission held that a former secretary in its offices—having had access to its documents—would not be permitted to act as counsel before it.[32] An oath to faithfully perform their duties was administered by an arbitrator to the agents appearing for the USA and Great Britain (the US agent was a Massachusetts attorney) in the *St Croix River Arbitration* of 1814.[33]

Whilst these cases are exceptional, the matters upon which arbitrators ruled—conflicts of interest, oaths, offensive pleadings and the functions of agents—would today be covered by professional ethics. This not only demonstrates that such issues were arising within historical arbitrations but also that arbitral tribunals were ready in certain instances to assert an authority to regulate advocacy when necessary. Consequently, though the prevailing diplomatic culture resulted in minimalistic procedural rules, this did not preclude arbitral tribunals from issuing ad hoc directions and otherwise controlling advocacy in the interest of the proceedings. This indicates that, in even the most unregulated era of modern international litigation, international tribunals could and did exercise regulatory authority over counsel.

[28] Bishop, *International Arbitral Procedure*; Mérighnac, *Théorique et pratique de l'arbitrage international*, 246–8.

[29] Mérighnac, *Théorique et pratique de l'arbitrage international*, 246.

[30] Moore, *History and Digest* (1898) (Vol III), 2133–276. A functional distinction between 'representation' and 'defence' has been drawn between the two—Monaco, 'Représentation et défense des parties devant les instances internationales' in Diez et al, *Festschrift für Rudolf Bindschedler* (1980), 373–5.

[31] However, this direction was exceptional in that agents generally had standing to discharge all of the functions of counsel—Ralston, *International Arbitral Law and Procedure* (1910), 130–1.

[32] Ralston, *International Arbitral Law and Procedure*, 131–3.

[33] Moore, *International Adjudications, Ancient and Modern* (1933) (Vol VI), 19, 22.

3.2 The Permanent Court of Arbitration

The *Institut de Droit International* was founded in 1873 with the aim of contributing to the development of international law independent of governmental influence. Its third resolution was the Code of Arbitral Procedure 1875,[34] which was the first attempt to codify arbitral rules of procedure. In 1927, the Institute considered that certain Code provisions had attained the status of positive law.[35] The Code, with only 27 articles, left many matters to individual tribunals. Article 12 of the Code provided that a tribunal must conform to its statutory procedure but was free to create rules conforming to governing principles. Article 13 (adopted without debate) ambiguously stipulated that each party may appoint 'a' representative.[36] Article 15 prescribed that tribunals should have the power to, inter alia, create procedural rules and control evidence.[37] The Code's provisions have been stated to represent contemporary 'best practice' and were a model for ad hoc arbitration and the PCA.[38]

The PCA is the oldest currently operating international arbitral institution. Its statute is contained within the Conventions for the Pacific Settlement of International Disputes 1899 and 1907. Its provisions were intended to be 'fundamental' rules rather than comprehensive with broad discretion for individual arbitral tribunals.[39] The *travaux préparatoires* reveal that the two issues causing most debate were the compulsion of arbitral dispute settlement and the composition of tribunals.[40] Representation was barely discussed.[41]

Article 37 of the 1899 Convention couched the right of parties to appoint agents and 'counsel and advocates' in absolute terms. There was no limitation upon the number of counsel; in the *Pious Fund* arbitration, as many counsel as desired were permitted to plead on behalf of each party.[42] However, adverse criticism was provoked when members of the PCA appeared as counsel in the *Pious Fund* and *Venezuelan Preferential Question* arbitrations.[43] A proposal was made at the 1907 Conference to exclude 'Members of the Court' from representing parties whilst in office on grounds of judicial impartiality but was opposed because the pool of high-quality arbitrators and counsel would be reduced.[44] Article 62 of the

[34] Online: <http://www.idi-iil.org/idiF/navig_chron1873.html> (Accessed: 10 December 2011).

[35] Bishop, *International Arbitral Procedure*, 8–9.

[36] Goldschmidt, 'Projet de Règlement pour Tribunaux Arbitraux Internationaux' 6 *RdDI* (1874) 421, 439–40; Goldschmidt, 'Procédure arbitrale internationale' 7 *RdDI* (1875), 418–26, 421.

[37] Goldschmidt, 'Projet de Règlement pour Tribunaux Arbitraux Internationaux', 441; Goldschmidt, 'Procédure arbitrale internationale', 421.

[38] Bishop, *International Arbitral Procedure*, 8, 11.

[39] Bishop, *International Arbitral Procedure*, 12.

[40] Scott, *The Proceedings of the Hague Peace Conferences* (1920) (Vol I), 746; (Vol II), 143–62.

[41] Scott, *The Proceedings of the Hague Peace Conferences (Vol I)*, 737–8, 747; Hull, 'Obligatory Arbitration and the Hague Conferences' 2 *AJIL* (1908), 431–742; Hicks, 'The Equality of States and the Hague Conferences' 2 *AJIL* (1908), 530–61.

[42] Ralston, *International Arbitral Law and Procedure*, 135.

[43] Ralston, *International Arbitral Law and Procedure*, 130.

[44] Scott, *The Proceedings of the Hague Peace Conferences (Vol II)*, 720–1.

1907 Convention adopted a compromise proposal whereby 'the Members of the Permanent Court may not act as agents, counsel, or advocates except on behalf of the Power which appointed them Members of the Court'. An attempt to remove the exception[45] was defeated due to the 'freedom of the parties to be represented by those of their nationals whom they desire'.[46]

Article 45 of the 1899 Convention (Article 70 of the 1907 Convention) provides absolute discretion for agents and advocates submitting oral arguments 'which they may think expedient to the defence of their case'. However, the original draft was narrower in authorizing them to present 'all the explanations or proofs which will aid the defense of the cause'.[47] No explanation for this change is revealed by the drafting committee minutes.[48] Article 46 (Article 72 of 1907) prescribes a right for agents and counsel to 'raise objections and points' to the tribunal, whose decisions concerning those points are 'final'. Article 47 (Article 71 of 1907) creates a converse right for the tribunal to 'put questions to the agents and counsel of the parties, and to demand explanations from them on doubtful points'. Article 44 (Article 69 of 1907) provides that the tribunal may 'take note of refusal'.

Despite the prescription of a detailed procedure for the hearing of witnesses and expert for international commissions of inquiry, the PCA's provisions for arbitration were virtually silent concerning them. Article 50 (Article 77 of the 1907 Convention) provides that 'when the agents and counsel of the parties have submitted all the explanations and evidence in support of their case the President shall declare the discussion closed' and Article 90 of the 1907 Convention (concerning summary arbitral procedure) provided for a right for the parties and the Tribunal to call witnesses and experts. Article 90 originated from a French proposal of amendments to arbitral procedure, yet the Committee incorporated it into summary procedure (Article 90) only.[49]

A treaty signed at the 1907 Hague Conference, but subsequently not ratified, was the International Prize Court Convention 1907 to hear appeals from national jurisdictions.[50] The Court was to have been given power to compose its own procedural rules, to have been undertaken within a year of ratification.[51] Article 17 forbade members of the Court from hearing cases who had participated in the judgments of the national courts involved or had appeared as counsel for one of the parties and also prohibited them from appearing as agent or advocate before the Court or 'act[ing] in any capacity whatever'.[52] Article 27 provided for calling

[45] Scott, *The Proceedings of the Hague Peace Conferences (Vol II)*, 720–1: '[T]he mentality of a lawyer is or must readily become different from that of a judge and can but be harmful to the court'.

[46] Scott, *The Proceedings of the Hague Peace Conferences (Vol II)*, 751–2.

[47] Scott, *The Proceedings of the Hague Peace Conferences (Vol I)*, 803.

[48] Scott, *The Proceedings of the Hague Peace Conferences (Vol I)*.

[49] Scott, *The Proceedings of the Hague Peace Conferences (Vol II)*, 735–6.

[50] Bishop, *International Arbitral Procedure*, 19.

[51] Bishop, *International Arbitral Procedure*, 21.

[52] 'Convention Relative to the Establishment of an International Prize Court', 2 (Suppl) *AJIL* (1908), 174–202, 183.

witnesses and experts and Article 25 for the right to be represented by agents and counsel.[53]

Article 26, by contrast, made representation by advocate compulsory for private persons appearing before the Court; moreover, qualification requirements were imposed that the 'attorney... must be either an advocate qualified to plead before a court of appeal or a high court of one of the signatory States, or a lawyer practicing before a similar court, or lastly, a professor of law at one of the higher teaching centers of those countries'.[54] This provision appears to have been the first attempt in the history of the modern international legal system to impose a formal 'bar' upon rights of hearing for advocacy. The *travaux préparatoires* reveal that these provisions—drafted by representatives from Germany, USA, France, and Great Britain—were adopted without debate.[55] The contrast between Articles 25 and 26 is also unexplained by the materials, though it plausibly stems from the traditional deference to State control over arbitral proceedings as opposed to the weaker power of the individual. Whether it was assumed that national ethics would apply to advocates appearing for States remains likewise unknown.

The International Prize Court, however, never came into being due to the failure of the signatories to agree to an applicable law for the Court as well as a procedure for the appointment of judges. The failure of the Convention to come into effect, or else the adoption of a generally more conservative view of international litigation, may have been why Article 26 did not catalyse later initiatives to create qualification requirements for advocates.[56] The Court was an early example of the bifurcation between qualification requirements for State and non-State Parties, whereby the former were not subject to such requirements whereas the latter were. This distinction continues to be made before modern courts. Moreover, it is likely that the character of the Prize Court as a 'court' rather than an arbitral tribunal was a factor in the reduced State control over advocacy.

An early regional court was the Central American Court of Justice (CACJ), which was created by a 1907 treaty inspired by the Hague Conferences and ideas for a Central American federation.[57] Article 26 empowered the Court to formulate its procedural rules, contained within its 1911 Regulations and 1912 Procedural Ordinance.[58] Article 25(2) provided a ground of challenge to a judge's competence 'to have been counsel or attorney for any party in the pending suit or to have been such before a national court or a court of arbitration or international commission of inquiry in the controversy which gave rise to the suit'. Representation was implied by Article 53 of the Ordinance requiring that all pleas be filed by the party

[53] 'Convention Relative to the Establishment of an International Prize Court', 186.

[54] 'Convention Relative to the Establishment of an International Prize Court', 186–7.

[55] Scott, *The Proceedings of the Hague Peace Conferences (Vol II)*, 820, 838, 1062–3.

[56] However, a draft provision for the Rules of the PCIJ contained very similar requirements—Series D, No 2 (1922), 263.

[57] 'Convention for the Establishment of a Central American Court of Justice', 2 (Suppl) *AJIL* (1908), 231–43. Hudson, 'The Central American Court of Justice', 26 *AJIL* (1932), 759–86, 759–61.

[58] 'Regulations of the Central American Court of Justice' 8 (Suppl) *AJIL* (1914), 179–94; 'Ordinance of Procedure of the Central American Court of Justice' 8 (Suppl) *AJIL* (1914), 194–213.

or 'his attorney or legal representative'.[59] Articles 35 and 37 of the Regulations prohibited judges from practising as lawyers and from intervening 'as counsel or advisers for any of the parties in the cases before the court for its decision'.[60]

The CACJ heard ten cases over the course of its ten years of existence, of which three were initiated *ex proprio motu* and only two came for judgment on the merits.[61] The closure of the CACJ following ten years of existence has been attributed to its lack of practical independence, extraordinarily broad jurisdiction, and unsatisfactory procedure.[62] Whilst advocates pleaded before the Court,[63] its incomplete procedural rules, light docket, and short existence precluded its operation from impacting on the development of agents and counsel in international courts.

3.3 The Permanent Court of International Justice

3.3.1 The Creation of the PCIJ

The late nineteenth-century movement advocating international institutionalization and the creation of a permanent international court largely derived from pacifism.[64] Progressive jurists regarded ad hoc arbitration and other mechanisms as valuable but insufficient to prevent war. Proposals at the Second Hague Peace Conference for a 'Court of Arbitral Justice' were never realized.[65] When the PCIJ was being created, the drafting of its Statute was entrusted to an 'Advisory Committee of Jurists' comprising ten members from the judicial, diplomatic, academic, and political fields (five nationals of the 'Great Powers' and five of 'smaller Powers') which met between 16 June and 24 July 1920.[66] Following the conclusion of the Committee's work, its draft was amended by the League Council as well as the Third Committee of the First Assembly of the League and again in 1929.[67]

The Rapporteur in his initial Report to the League outlined the recent history of the creation of arbitral and judicial institutions and noted that the most sensitive points concerned the appointment of judges and compulsory jurisdiction.[68] The official language of the Court was the only procedural matter discussed. Except as affecting the judiciary, the provisions of the Statute pertaining to the representation were drafted with little scrutiny at each stage. Preoccupied with the two

[59] See also Art 43.

[60] Although strictly concerning judicial ethics, they remain relevant for conflicts of interest in modern international arbitration for simultaneously held 'judicial' and advocacy roles.

[61] Hudson, 'The Central American Court of Justice', 768.

[62] Hudson, 'The Central American Court of Justice', 785.

[63] Hudson, 'The Central American Court of Justice', 776.

[64] Bustamente, *The World Court* (1925), 8–39.

[65] Scott, 'The Proposed Court of Arbitral Justice' 2 *AJIL* (1908), 772–810; Oppenheim, *International Law* (1912), 524–5.

[66] Hudson, *The Permanent Court of International Justice 1920-1942* (1943), 114–5; Spiermann, 'Who Attempts to Do Too Much Does Nothing Well', 73 *BYIL* (2003), 187–260.

[67] Hudson, *The Permanent Court of International Justice 1920-1942*, 142, 144.

[68] League of Nations Advisory Committee of Jurists, *Draft Scheme of the Committee* (1920), 70–2, 83–92.

major diplomatic issues, the Committee considered representation a minor matter that was addressed by resorting to arbitral practice which left it almost entirely to parties.

3.3.2 Statute

In the Committee of Jurists, arguments similar to those at the Hague Conferences were made for and against the restriction of judges' extra-judicial activities.[69] The Committee opted for stronger controls than those at the PCA. Article 17 of the PCIJ Statute forbade them from acting as agent or counsel in any case of an international nature or from sitting on any case in which he had previously acted as such.[70] The Committee declared that 'once the judge has taken up his duties, he may no longer act as representative, counsel or advocate in any case of an international nature, even on behalf of his own country. This incompatibility, though not recognised by the Court of Arbitration, must be taken into account by a Court of Justice'.[71]

Articles 42, 51, and 54 of the PCIJ Statute concerned representation. Article 42 provided: 'The parties shall be represented by agents. They may have the assistance of counsel or advocates before the Court.' Although Article 42 was barely discussed, the Committee reported that only agents could represent parties but that agents might also act as counsel.[72] Whilst consistent with the PCA functional distinction, Article 42 differs from the *Behring Fur Seals* precedent. In addition, it is illogical that agents might also act as counsel if the latter have no defined role. Article 51 provided for the Court's power to question agents and advocates[73] and Article 54 for case presentation by representatives 'under the control of the Court'.[74]

3.3.3 Rules of Procedure

The terseness of the Statute's provisions concerning advocacy is explicable by the Advisory Committee's intention that the PCIJ should have wide discretion to create rules of procedure governing its proceedings.[75] The Court proceeded to adopt the first Rules in 1922 with amendments in 1926 and 1931. In 1936, the Court enacted the PCIJ Rules 1936 in response to the amendments to the Statute instituted by the Revision Protocol of 1929.[76] The PCIJ Rules 1922 mentioned representatives only secondarily within Part III ('Oral Procedure')

[69] League of Nations Advisory Committee of Jurists, *Draft Scheme of the Committee*, 164–7.
[70] League of Nations Advisory Committee of Jurists, *Procès-verbaux* (1920), 574, 599, 613, 717.
[71] League of Nations Advisory Committee of Jurists, *Procès-verbaux*, 716.
[72] Hudson, *The Permanent Court of International Justice 1920-1942*, 199.
[73] Hudson, *The Permanent Court of International Justice 1920-1942*, 202–3.
[74] Hudson, *The Permanent Court of International Justice 1920-1942*, 204; League of Nations Advisory Committee of Jurists, *Procès-verbaux*, 590, 740–1.
[75] Hudson, *The Permanent Court of International Justice 1920-1942*, 270.
[76] Hudson, *The Permanent Court of International Justice 1920-1942*, 271.

concerning matters such as order of speaking. The 1936 Rules, although substantially based upon the previous versions, differed in structure and content.[77] The 1926 and 1931 amendments did not contain changes concerning the conduct of representatives.[78]

3.3.3.1 Qualifications

In creating the 1925 Rules, the Court relied upon drafts submitted by Judges Loder and Altamira as well as the Secretariat.[79] Article 38 of the Secretariat's draft[80] required that 'advocates' be: (1) 'persons admitted to practise as advocates before the highest Court of their own country'; (2) 'University professors of International Law'; or (3) 'members of the great international academies of International Law'. It further stipulated:

> In each particular case the Court shall fix the number of counsel which each party may employ in the conduct of the case. The counsel of the different parties shall be called upon to speak in the order laid down for the presentation by the parties of the written proceedings. Agents shall always speak after counsel.

Article 40 of the draft provided that 'the representatives of the parties may be heard as witnesses' and that the Court may grant a request by a party to administer an oath to the other party of the truth of its assertions.[81] Judge Altamira's draft was to have excluded an agent from addressing the Court in oral proceedings where an advocate conducted a case as in *Behring Fur Seals*.[82]

All of these proposals were ultimately not adopted. The judges rejected any limitation of rights of pleading before the Court.[83] Lord Finlay articulated the rationale for restricted pleading in national courts as preventing abuse of procedure but asserted that that rationale did not apply 'when the persons pleading represented States; moreover, the difficulty in laying down rules in such a matter was almost insurmountable'. The Court decided that 'no rule limiting the right of pleading before the Court should be introduced into the Rules of Procedure. Any person appointed by the Court to represent it should be admitted by the Court'. In practice, advocates were commonly university professors or national practitioners fluent in the Court's official languages.[84] Judge Hudson speculated that a qualification requirement would be ill-received by States in light of the 'quasi-political functions of agents' and, if imposed, may have resulted in the non-appointment of advocates in favour of agents.[85]

In practice, agents were far more significant than advocates. Whilst agents were almost invariably appointed in contentious proceedings, advocates were not. Advocates were introduced into advisory proceedings after agents were.[86] Agents

[77] Hudson, *The Permanent Court of International Justice 1920-1942*, 732–55.
[78] Series D, Second Addendum to No 2 (1931).
[79] Hudson, *The Permanent Court of International Justice 1920-1942*, 272.
[80] Series D, No 2 (1922), 263.
[81] Series D, No 2, 264. [82] Series D, No 2, 277. [83] Series D, No 2, 78–9.
[84] Hudson, *The Permanent Court of International Justice 1920-1942*, 537–8.
[85] Hudson, *The Permanent Court of International Justice 1920-1942*, 537.
[86] Hudson, *The Permanent Court of International Justice 1920-1942*, 532–3.

could entirely conduct proceedings without advocates whilst advocates lacked agents' power to commit their parties, did not engage in case correspondence and were not usually questioned by the Court in oral proceedings.[87] Whilst the language of Article 42 of the Statute required the appointment of agents, Judge Hudson described it as exhortatory due to the Court's inability to enforce.[88] Regardless of the legal issue of compulsoriness, it would seem that the utilization of agents in contentious proceedings was invariable in practice.[89] Agents were likewise utilized in advisory proceedings by States and organizations, though initially termed 'representatives'.[90] As with advocates, the Court did not regulate the quality of agents.[91]

The Court similarly permitted parties to employ however many advocates and agents they wished. Proposals to restrict numbers in the 1922 and 1936 Rules failed.[92] However, on 15 June 1923 the Court 'held that, in order to avoid useless repetition, the maximum number of speeches or oral statements made in the same interest should not as a general rule exceed two. It was however understood that, if necessary, several persons might share the task of stating a case.'[93] In *Legal Status of Eastern Greenland* 'the President pointed out that, according to the practice of the Court, there was no objection to several persons dividing between them the main speech on behalf of each Party, providing however that the various speakers dealt with different points or with different aspects of the subject, which was moreover strictly limited'.[94] Despite the absence of a prescribed rule, the Court controlled the number of representatives. This suggests that its general laissez-faire approach towards representation was tempered in practice.

3.3.3.2 Experts

The impact of the Court's decision to allow States' absolute discretion concerning the quality of its representatives was profound. The overlap with the role of witness (despite the relative rarity of witnesses) was a very important one whereby in practice expert witnesses (and, theoretically, lay witnesses) could give evidence as advocates, thus avoiding the 'solemn declaration' and cross-examination without right of reply. Under the 1922 Rules, no discrete category of 'expert witness' existed; only a 'witness' category was prescribed under Articles 48, 50, and 51.

[87] Hudson, *The Permanent Court of International Justice 1920-1942*, 531–2.

[88] Hudson, *The Permanent Court of International Justice 1920-1942*, 527. In *Belgium v China*, China did not appoint an agent and eventually Belgium withdrew its action; those proceedings terminated early. In the *Castellorizo* case, the proceedings were soon terminated by common agreement so that Italy's failure to appoint an agent was irrelevant.

[89] *Confer* Hudson, *The Permanent Court of International Justice 1920-1942*, 528–9.

[90] Hudson, *The Permanent Court of International Justice 1920-1942*, 530–1.

[91] Hudson, *The Permanent Court of International Justice 1920-1942*, 529.

[92] Hudson, *The Permanent Court of International Justice 1920-1942*, 532; Series D, Second Addendum to No 2.

[93] 'Annual Report from 1926-1927', Series E, No 3, 204.

[94] *Eastern Greenland*, 17–18.

Nevertheless, 'experts' were considered in the *Personal Work of Employers Case* (1926) (Advisory Opinion No 13):

> ...the Court decided...[that] the International Federation of Trades Unions should be allowed to produce experts. It was further decided that: (1) the experts should not to be treated as witnesses and (2) they should be invited to reply to questions put by the representatives of international organisations and, if necessary, by the Court. It was also agreed that the representatives of organisations might reply orally to the arguments advanced at the first hearings (Cf. *Rules*, Article 46). Ultimately, these experts were not heard, as the organisation concerned considered that their evidence was not required and the right of reply was not used.[95]

Although these 'experts' were apparently to have been treated as representatives rather than witnesses, it was crucially the Court which decided the matter rather than the party. Thus, there was no absolute right to call experts under the PCIJ regime.

There was only one case where 'expert witnesses' ('témoin-expert') so called were employed.[96] In *Upper Silesia*, Germany called four expert witnesses and Poland one—the Court had made an order inviting the parties to furnish 'by any means they think fit, further information regarding the points reserved by the Court for this purpose'.[97] The witnesses gave evidence and were cross-examined by the opposing party's agent and then by the judges. All of the witnesses were treated according to the procedure then prescribed by Article 50 of the Rules, whereby they made a 'solemn declaration' to 'speak the truth, the whole truth and nothing but the truth'.[98] Here, by contrast, it was not the Court but the parties which decided how the 'experts' were to appear according to the wide discretion given by the Court in its order.

The PCIJ Rules 1936 introduced an 'expert' category into Article 53 with a separate procedure.[99] This was prompted by a desire to harmonize the positions of experts called by parties with those called by the Court under Article 57.[100] However, in only one post-1936 case was an 'expert' ever utilized. In *Diversion of Water from the Meuse*, the Belgian agent requested that M le professeur Delmer—'secrétaire général du ministère des Travaux publics de Belgique, est la père du projet du canal Albert'—be permitted to present a statement to the Court, which the President approved.[101] Designated 'conseil technique du gouvernement belge', M Delmer proceeded to address the Court on two scientific issues. He neither made a 'solemn declaration' nor was he examined by the opposing agent. Notwithstanding the Court's right to question advocates under Article 52(1) of the Rules, he was not questioned.

[95] 'Annual Report from 1926-1927', 213.

[96] Hudson, *The Permanent Court of International Justice 1920-1942*, 569 (note 71).

[97] *Upper Silesia*, 25–34.

[98] *Upper Silesia*, 27–8.

[99] Hudson, *The Permanent Court of International Justice 1920-1942*, 289; Series D, Third Addendum to No 2, 237, 439–40, 618–9.

[100] Series D, Third Addendum to No 2, 624–5.

[101] *Diversion of Water from the River Meuse*, 218–20, 331–69.

Belgium did not assert a procedural right to designate M Delmer as 'technical counsel' rather than as 'expert witness' but applied to the Court. Thus, it was the Court which permitted him to appear as advocate rather than the party. This implies that it was the Court which governed the admission of advocates and evidence rather than litigants, an approach consistent with the fact that it was the Court which decided not to impose qualification requirements in the 1922 Rules. The amendments to the Rules and their redrafting in 1936 further show that the Court retained the power to change its position concerning advocates' qualifications—as when it invented the 'expert witness' in 1936.

3.3.3.3 Functions

Article 51 of the 1922 Rules came closest to defining representational functions: 'witnesses shall be examined by the representatives of the parties under the control of the President'. The Rules seemingly envisaged representatives' functions to be oratorical since they are only mentioned for oral proceedings. However, in practice the agent acted for his party in all matters including diplomatic and political functions alongside legal ones.[102] In the drafting of Article 35 of the 1936 Rules, it was decided that only agents could represent parties on procedural matters and the agent's superior role was emphasized.[103] An amendment to Article 32[104] governing the Court's general procedural power was proposed but not discussed.[105]

Whilst the Court declared in the *Prince von Pless Administration* case that 'according to the doctrine of the Court, statements by Agents of the governments…engaged the responsibility of those governments, whereas observations offered by Counsel or Advocates only engaged the responsibility of the latter', the following day it narrowly adopted a contravening amendment to Article 51 of the Rules changing 'representatives' (which had been applied as 'agents') to 'agents, counsel or advocates' all having the right to question witnesses.[106] In any event, the Court's former position did not explain an advocate's 'responsibility' in practical terms; given the Court's general laissez-faire approach, it is unlikely that it envisaged an ethical dimension.

3.3.3.4 Documentary Evidence

A crucial link exists between counsel, witnesses, and evidence. Article 68 of Judge Nyholm's redraft of the 1922 Rules[107] had empowered the Court to 'on [its] own initiative, or at the request of one of the parties, order the production of any evidence which [it] consider[s] necessary…for instance, order the appearance or the interrogation of the representatives'. Despite the use of 'representatives', the following

[102] Hudson, *The Permanent Court of International Justice 1920-1942*, 533–6.

[103] Series D, Third Addendum to No 2, 260, 817.

[104] 'Should a case arise that is not provided for in the present Rules, it shall be decided by the Court, which shall be guided by the general principles of procedure recognized by civilized nations.'

[105] Series D, Third Addendum to No 2, 260, 845.

[106] Series D, Third Addendum to No 2, 233–7.

[107] Series D, No 2 (1922), 370.

Articles 69 to 71 referred exclusively to 'agents' in the administration of an oath ('serment décisoire ou supplétoire') and interrogatory examination. Article 77 had stipulated that 'the agents of the parties and persons whose individual responsibility might be involved by their replies shall not be heard as witnesses'.[108] However, these provisions were ultimately not adopted.

The 1926 Revision of the 1922 Rules amended Article 35 ('institution of proceedings') to require 'whenever possible' agents to be resident at the Hague.[109] The Court debated[110] the following amendment proposed by President Huber:

> *Article 33 bis:* States...which are Parties to a dispute or which furnish information to the Court in the course of advisory procedure, shall be held solely responsible for the production of any particular document and for any statement made on their behalf during the proceedings...The Court, when deciding upon [a] request that the proceedings shall be secret, shall at the same time decide whether the evidence in question is admissible.

President Huber explained the reasoning for his proposal:

> Again it might happen that a representative of a Party made statements or proposals which, in the opinion of the other Party, were of an invidious nature. Cases of this kind had actually occurred. Now, it was a very regrettable matter when one of the representatives made a protest to the Court. Of course, the President could always break off the hearing in order that the Court might withdraw to decide the point, but nevertheless it would be well for the Court to establish once and for all the principle of the exclusive responsibility of Parties. Parties appearing before the Court were invariably sovereign States, but the corollary of such sovereignty was the absolute responsibility of the representatives of such States. That principle having been established, the President should simply say: 'under the Rules of the Court all responsibility rests on States appearing before it and on their representatives'...The President also observed that the principle of responsibility also covered that of secrecy.

The ensuing debate focused exclusively upon the principal aim of President Huber's proposal, namely, to establish *exclusive* responsibility of Parties 'in order to relieve the Court of responsibility'.[111] Judge Weiss proposed to amend the provision to refute the Court's responsibility on the ground that the Court lacked the power to enforce any sanction which it may prescribe for party responsibility.[112] The President ultimately withdrew his proposal.[113]

Whilst the principal focus of the debate concerned the role of the Court in regulating evidence, President Huber's proposal placed responsibility not only upon parties but also upon their representatives. Whilst this aspect was not debated, the proposal engaged an important theme pervading the procedure of international dispute settlement, namely, the tension between the power of international courts and tribunals to regulate their own procedures on the one hand and the State control over case presentation on the other. Concerning the practical question of approval

108 Series D, No 2 (1922), 372.
109 Series D, Addendum to No 2 (1926), 75.
110 Series D, Addendum to No 2 (1926), 126–32.
111 Series D, Addendum to No 2 (1926), 127.
112 Series D, Addendum to No 2 (1926), 128.
113 Series D, Addendum to No 2 (1926), 131–2.

by agents, advocates, or witnesses of court records of their statements, a distinction was drawn between 'the position of agents, advocates and counsel, on the one hand, and witnesses on the other; there could be no question as to the integrity of persons representing a government, and the Court could not dictate to them what the record of their speeches was to be'.[114] President Huber's proposal could potentially have created personal responsibility for agents and counsel who, for example, colluded to suppress documentary evidence on false grounds of secrecy.[115]

An interesting historical example of forged documents occurred in the *Behring Fur Seals* arbitration. An American counsel, studying Russian documents in his leisure hours, discovered obvious discrepancies in the translations from Russian to English which, on investigation, were found to have been forgeries by the translator employed by the American legal team.[116] This raises two ethical questions, namely, whether counsel should be obliged to take reasonable steps to scrutinize documentary evidence that they intend to adduce and whether they should be required to notify the tribunal and the opposing party of reasonable suspicions concerning the veracity of evidence. There is some evidence to suggest that the British legal team had previously discovered the discrepancies and, seemingly to prejudice the American case by ambushing them at oral hearings, deliberately decided to keep silent.[117]

During the *Lighthouses* case, one of the agents referred to a document which he intended to file but whose authenticity he could not verify. The agent, upon being questioned by the President, stated that since he attached little importance to the document it would not be worthwhile to authenticate so that he 'consented' to withdraw it.[118] This control by the Court concerning the veracity of evidence would appear to have gone further than the laissez-faire admissibility approach in the Rules. The debates concerning President Huber's proposal in the framing of the rules of procedure, coupled with *Behring Fur Seals* and *Lighthouses*, illustrates two important dynamics concerning responsibility for the veracity of documents. The first is the link between parties' control over counsel and case presentation and the danger of false evidence. Since parties' principal motivation is to win cases, there is a considerable risk that absolute control over case presentation entices some parties to attempt to mislead the court. The second is the personal responsibility of counsel as an intermediary between court and client to ensure the veracity of documentary evidence as an important safeguard for the integrity of the judicial process.

3.3.4 Calls for an International Bar

In a lecture and debate of the Grotius Society in 1931 concerning the future of the PCIJ, Judges Caloyanni and Hurst expressed qualified support for the

[114] Series D, Addendum to No 2 (1926), 144–5.

[115] See *Corfu Channel*, Chapter 5.

[116] Marston, 'Falsification of Documentary Evidence before International Tribunals' 71 *BYIL* (2000), 357–73, 373.

[117] It has even been suggested that the translator was bribed or assisted in his fraud—Marston, 'Falsification of Documentary Evidence before International Tribunals', 362, 373.

[118] 'Sixteenth Report of the PCIJ', Series E, No 16, 194–5.

concept of an 'international bar' as part of the Court.[119] For Judge Caloyanni, the crucial motivation was ensuring that men of the highest standard appear before the Court:

> At this moment anybody, without restriction... with regard to qualifications, may plead before the Permanent Court... [t]he States responsible for sending representatives have sent men who were up to their task, but with the number of cases increasing, I should say in the interests of the Court a Bar should be formed... a great deal... of the Judges' education is owed to... the high standard of the men who compose the Bar—I do not mean morally, I mean scientifically... The men who plead before the Permanent Court are either practitioners or men who have never had the slightest practice at the Bar—professors—and, in countries where professors are not allowed to practise at the Bar, sometimes men who have only known the Bar because they are eminent political men. If there were formed a body with strict rules not only with regard to the conduct of cases but also to the organisation of the Bar, we should have there a great opportunity with regard to the choice of Judges when the day comes, if it ever comes, when it will not be left entirely in the hands of the National Group to submit the names of the Judges to the League of Nations.[120]

Thus, for Judge Caloyanni the rationale for the professionalization of advocacy before the Court was twofold: (1) to raise the standards of its practitioners (particularly professors and politicians) by requiring them to be experienced advocates; and (2) to raise the standards of the judiciary by providing recruits from the bar.

For Judge Hurst, there were two reasons for the existence of a Bar, namely, 'to ensure that those who are responsible for the preparation of the case shall see to it that the individuals they are representing—whether it is a State or a private person—shall have their case put before the Court in a proper way, and, above all, to ensure that all the material essential to a proper decision by the Court is laid before the Court for its consideration'.[121] He also dwelt upon the official languages excluding more able advocates in favour of less able 'professors'.[122]

Dr Bisschop advocated the creation of a 'School of International Law' alongside a professional bar attached to the Court in order to increase independence of advocates from States.[123] Dr Idelson expressed scepticism, in that he favoured a 'law of natural selection' that would solve such practical problems due to the difficulty of creating such a bar.[124] Mr Bewes supported the idea of replacing the national group system as it produced 'too many professors':

> It seems to me that the first thing... is to get the very best men. If you have a wide rule... the little fish will no doubt come through because the net is so wide, and you cannot keep them out. It may be that all these Courts suffer from 'professors', sometimes on the Bench and sometimes at the Bar... after all a Court must protect itself, if and when troublesome or

[119] Caloyanni, 'The Judicial Policy for the Settlement of International Disputes' 17 *TGS* (1931), 85–111, 90–1, 97–9, 108–11; Caloyanni, 'L'organisation de la Cour permanente de justice' 38 *RdC* (1931), 651–786, 768–76.

[120] Caloyanni, 'The Judicial Policy for the Settlement of International Disputes', 90–1.

[121] Caloyanni, 'The Judicial Policy for the Settlement of International Disputes', 97.

[122] Caloyanni, 'The Judicial Policy for the Settlement of International Disputes', 98.

[123] Caloyanni, 'The Judicial Policy for the Settlement of International Disputes', 99.

[124] Caloyanni, 'The Judicial Policy for the Settlement of International Disputes', 100–2.

wearisome advocates come before it. It must have the courage, even if the advocate is an advocate for a Government, to shut him up if he ought to be shut up. The difficulty…is very much greater if the Government is going to go off the deep end and say: 'how can anyone representing us be otherwise than perfect?' But in the end it can be done…It may be, as [Judge Hurst] pointed out, that for disciplinary reasons the creation of a Bar may be necessary which the man who wishes to plead can join as of right and by joining would submit himself to the discipline of the Court.

Judge Caloyanni replied that 'a Court is responsible for its Bar because the Bar is responsible to the Court'. He declared:

…when a Government appoints a member of the bar, the first is that the Government will take care he is a man of their own political views. That is a danger. The Government, knowing that there are two languages there, will choose from amongst the most eminent men…It might mean that, in that way we should have a very good selection of barristers. That number should be fixed, but not by the Permanent Court…When you have had those men chosen, they will form a Bar. The Bar, directly it is appointed, will be denationalised…and that body will grow and in time create an atmosphere in which they will even stand up against their own Governments…they will also be in a panel of barristers put up by the Bar Council itself, who will say: 'These men are qualified to go and plead.' Then the Governments must [support them]…His qualifications would have to be studied by…a private Committee appointed by the League of Nations itself, and he would have to submit something to the League of Nations by way of qualifications.[125]

These Grotius Society proceedings, unknown to us today, paint a remarkable picture of the practice of advocacy before the PCIJ. Despite the modern tendency to regard the PCIJ as, in some respects, more successful than the ICJ there was general criticism offered in the debate concerning the quality of its judges and practitioners.

First, there was a general dissatisfaction with the academics who regularly appeared before the Court. Although no specific cases or individuals were cited, there was a collective perception that 'the professors' were verbose, tiresome, or otherwise incompetent advocates and that qualification requirements were needed to weed the 'little fish' out. Judge Caloyanni's statement that there was a need to attract advocates and judges of higher quality suggests that, contrary to the modern perception of the Court, it did not generally meet that standard. In particular, he criticized the political motivations for States' recruitment of counsel and the restrictions imposed by the official languages. Secondly, contrary to Lord Finlay's assertion in 1922 that the rationale of qualification requirements before national courts to prevent procedural abuses did not apply to States, there was a clear recognition that States' representatives could misbehave.

The debate reveals the great tension between Court and States with a clear desire to increasing the independence of advocates in order to improve the quality of argumentation and restrict the ability of States to control evidence. Interestingly, despite the general laissez-faire culture of the Court, at no time during the debate were

[125] Caloyanni, 'The Judicial Policy for the Settlement of International Disputes', 110–11.

concerns raised about the power of the Court to exercise such regulation. Judge Caloyanni, in a paper presented later that year, amplified his views by proposing a constitution for an international bar with a senior-junior division and 'denationalization' scheme which would break the tradition of national election which he ascribed to the principle of State equality.[126] That these issues were being discussed in 1931 reveals that, despite the tradition of State control over international litigation, those arrangements were considered problematic by some insiders.

3.4 Conclusions

This narrative of the historical development of international advocacy has identified several important themes. The first is the tension between party control (especially States) and tribunal control over the case presentation, which stems from the origin of the international legal system in inter-State arbitration where State control is imperative. The second, related theme is the role of professional counsel as autonomous intermediaries between parties and tribunals. The history of international arbitration leading to the PCIJ illustrates that desire of States to retain control over their representatives and the belief of some judges, like Lord Finlay, that the integrity of States could not be questioned created an unregulated space within which States at times misbehaved. The propensity of such procedural abuses and the criticisms made by insiders like Judges Hurst and Caloyanni suggest that the standards being observed by agents and counsel in practice were problematic.

A third theme is the readiness of international tribunals to regulate counsel. The research indicates that two opposing dynamics were occurring. On the one hand, the historical era was strongly characterized by a laissez-faire mentality by which the judiciary formally allowed parties a virtually absolute discretion concerning the appointment and control of their representation. For example, the PCIJ considered but rejected proposals to impose qualification requirements for counsel in its rules of procedure. However, when procedural problems arose within this unregulated space international tribunals demonstrated a remarkable willingness to regulate in an ad hoc fashion. Orders made by the *Behring Fur Seal* arbitration concerning the function of agents and by the PCIJ regarding the use of experts as counsel fall within this category. At no time were the powers of the arbitral tribunals and the PCIJ to make such orders questioned. Regulating counsel was as a matter of policy rather than law.

Consequently, modern concerns about the powers of international courts (particularly for inter-State courts like the ICJ and ITLOS) to regulate counsel on the ground that they lack the power to do so are historically unfounded. First, representation was not considered in any detail by State delegates at the Hague Peace Conferences or by the Advisory Committee and other organs involved in the drafting of the PCIJ Statute. Those delegates, being preoccupied by the great

[126] Caloyanni, 'L'organisation de la Cour permanente de justice', 770–5.

issues of compulsory jurisdiction and the judiciary, left procedural matters (including representation) entirely to the courts. The broad statutory power of the PCIJ (identical to that of the ICJ) to frame rules of procedure was intentional. The subsequent consideration by the PCIJ in drafting its first rules to impose qualification requirements for counsel was rejected not because the Court considered that it lacked the power to do so but on policy grounds. This suggests that the ICJ has the implied power to regulate counsel under its statutory power to frame rules of procedure.[127]

The final theme illustrated by this chapter is the link between professional advocacy and procedural integrity. This is demonstrated not only by specific cases such as *Behring Fur Seals* and *Pious Fund* but also by more general considerations such as the competence and efficiency of counsel. The criticisms voiced of the quality of counsel in the Grotius Society debates of 1931 are revealing and have circumstantial support in attempts in the 1920s to impose time limits and make agents personally responsible for the production of documents. These early problems concerning the integrity and efficiency of proceedings appear to have been more serious than is understood today and to have foreshadowed virtually identical problems that would arise before the ICJ. They are longstanding issues dating from the beginnings of international adjudication that are today beginning to be addressed.

[127] See Chapter 7.

4

The International Court of Justice

Having set out the historical background of international advocacy, this chapter begins examination of the ethical standards for counsel before three modern courts that differ considerably from one another. As explained in Chapter 1, a key question is whether the professionalization of advocacy through the articulation of common ethical standards for counsel would be desirable. Following historically from the PCIJ analysis in Chapter 3, this chapter analyses the procedural rules and practice concerning advocacy before the ICJ with supplementary reference to other inter-state courts and tribunals.[1] Parties are allowed absolute discretion concerning whom they appoint as their agents and counsel so that anyone regardless of training, vocation or character can represent a party before the Court.

Despite (or because of) this laissez-faire diplomatic tradition of nineteenth-century advocacy explored in Chapter 3, the role of representatives before the Court has been attracting greater attention from prominent judges[2] and practitioners[3] in recent years. These commentators have expressed two broadly opposed views. The progressive view is that that there ought to be a professional bar at the Court because this would be theoretically desirable or practically necessary. The conservative view argues for the *status quo* because there is no practical need, the project would be prohibitively onerous or States would resist professionalization in order to defend their 'sovereignty' with detrimental consequences for the Court's docket.[4]

In examining the practice of the Court, two questions are posed. The first is whether problems concerning the conduct of party representatives have arisen and, if so, to what causes are such problems attributable. This may be termed the corrective aspect of professionalization in that it seeks to rectify existing problems by providing a regulatory framework within which they can be better handled by the Court. The second is whether, in the absence of common ethical standards, there are potential problems that would threaten the integrity of the Court's proceedings

[1] Namely, the International Tribunal for the Law of the Sea (ITLOS) and ad hoc arbitration.

[2] Cot, 'Appearing "for" or "on behalf of" a State: The Role of Private Counsel before International Tribunals' in Ando et al, *Liber Amicorum Judge Shigeru Oda* (2002), 835–47, 837, 839; Higgins, 'Ethics and International Law' (2010) 23(2) *LJIL* 277–89, 288–9; Crawford, 'Advocacy Before the International Court of Justice and Other International Tribunals in State-to-State Cases' in Bishop and Kehoe, *The Art of Advocacy in International Arbitration* (2010), 303–30, 304.

[3] Zimmerman et al, *The Statute of the International Court of Justice: A Commentary* (2006), 967–76, 975–6.

[4] Zimmerman et al, *The Statute of the International Court of Justice*, 977–1038; Peck and Lee, *Increasing the Effectiveness of the International Court of Justice* (1997), 118–21.

in the wrong circumstances. This may be called the preventative aspect of professionalization whereby it serves to preclude potential problems through prescription. Through analysis of the cases in which ethical questions have arisen, it is suggested that common ethical standards for counsel are desirable for both corrective and preventative purposes.

This chapter also serves a second purpose, namely, to identify the main issues concerning professionalization within the specific cultural context of the Court. As explained in Chapter 1, each international court has its own historical, procedural and jurisdictional identity that delineates its ability to undertake professionalization. The historical legacy of the Court, for example, makes clear that the laissez-faire culture of the PCIJ towards representation deriving from the nineteenth-century diplomatic tradition explored in Chapter 3 derived not from statute but rather from a decision of the judiciary when it was framing its 1922 Rules of Procedure. This decision indicates an implied power for the Court under Article 30(1) of the Statute to regulate representation within its rules of procedure. However, it is clear that professionalization would encounter a degree of resistance from a culture that remains considerably deferential toward governmental officials. Thus, the debate is likely to largely focus upon the attitude of those officials towards professional representation.

4.1 Historical Background

Procedural matters received scant attention from the various organs that drafted the ICJ Statute.[5] The PCIJ Statute provisions concerning representation, judicial disqualification and case presentation under Articles 17, 30, 42–3, 51 and 54 were retained virtually intact and caused little discussion in the ICJ Statute at the San Francisco Conference.[6] In adopting the ICJ Rules 1946, the Court retained the laissez-faire provisions in the PCIJ Rules 1936 concerning representation.[7] However, amidst a 'crisis of unemployment' following the unpopular *South West Africa* and *Barcelona Traction* judgments, several States complained that the Court's procedure was costly and cumbersome.[8] The Court responded to these complaints by enacting the ICJ Rules 1972 to improve its efficiency by exercising greater control over proceedings and compelling parties to plead more succinctly.[9]

[5] Hilderbrand, *Dumbarton Oaks* (1990); Rosenne, *The Law and Practice of the International Court 1920-2005* (2006) (Vol I), 55–7.

[6] Hudson, 'The Twenty-Fourth Year of the World Court' 40 *AJIL* (1946), 1–52, 21, 28, 37–40; *UNCIO Documents* (1945) (Vol XIII), 57–9, 136–7, 155, 163, 170, 386; (Vol XIV), 50, 57–65, 85–6, 172, 202, 283, 798–853; (Vol XVIII), 589–601.

[7] Rosenne, *The Law and Practice of the International Court 1920-2005*, Vol III, 1032 (note 25).

[8] 25 *UNGAOR* (1970), 201 (para 19), 220 (para 26); (1971), UN Doc A/8382, 102–9 (paras 306–356), 114 (para 342), Add No 1, 8 (para 19); UNGA Res 2723 (XXV), 15 December 1970; 25 *UNGAOR* (1970), Annexes, UN Doc 8042 and Add No 1 and 2, 11. In *Barcelona Traction*, documentary evidence amounted to some 18,000 pages—25 *UNGAOR* (1970), Supplement No 5, UN Doc A/8005, 2 (para 20).

[9] 4 *ICJ Acts and Documents* (1978), 92–161; Jiménez de Aréchaga, 'The Amendments to the Rules of Procedure of the International Court of Justice' 67 *AJIL* (1973), 1–22, 1, 6. See also Guyomar,

This greater judicial oversight over parties' pleadings was welcomed by States,[10] indicating that government officials were willing to exchange a measure of their control over case presentation for improved procedural efficiency. These amendments on case presentation remain in force to this day.[11] Similarly, the ICJ Practice Directions[12] introduced in 2001 to augment the Rules and improve courtroom discipline have been generally welcomed by States. As explored below, though Practice Directions are not legally binding they are in practice treated as such by parties. Not only have greater judicial oversight into party representation in Practice Directions VII and VIII do not appear to have had any negative impact upon the Court's docket but, on the contrary, have arguably improved the attractiveness of the Court to potential litigants as an efficient and rigorous judicial institution.

This background suggests two points concerning the regulation of party representation: (1) that procedural inefficacy arising from a party-controlled litigious process can undermine the Court's legitimacy and docket; and (2) that at least some States welcome tighter judicial control in the interest of procedural efficiency and rigour. Whilst this book has not undertaken research into the attitudes of States towards the professionalization of advocacy and the corresponding reduction of their control over their representatives, this historical background concerning increases in the Court's regulation of advocacy suggests that the tighter procedural integrity that would accompany the advent of professionalism would be welcomed by States as another progressive step in the continuous improvement of the Court's procedure. Since States regularly conform to compulsory professional representation before their own national courts, it is illogical to suppose that the conformity of the ICJ to that national standard would be met with hostility by those same government officials. On the contrary, it is arguable that professionalization would enhance the Court's attractiveness to States by providing even stronger assurances of procedural integrity, fairness and efficiency in settling their disputes by judicial means.

4.2 Admission Requirements

Article 42 of the Statute[13] is identical to the PCIJ Statute. From the *Corfu Channel* case onwards, the ICJ has followed PCIJ in imposing no admission requirements

Commentaire du règlement de la Cour internationale de justice: interprétation et pratique (1973); Lachs, 'The Revised Procedure of the International Court of Justice' in Kalshoven et al, *Essays on the Development of the International Legal Order* (1980), 21–52, 34–8.

[10] 27 *UNGAOR* (1972); 29 *UNGAOR* (1974); UNGA Res 3232 (XXIX), 12 November 1974, OP3.

[11] 32 *ICJ Yearbook* (1977–1978), 112; Rosenne, *The Law and Practice of the International Court 1920-2005*, Vol III, 1033–4; Guyomar, *Commentaire du règlement de la Cour internationale de justice*. For a table of concordance, see Rosenne, *The Law and Practice of the International Court* (1985), 760–7.

[12] Watts, 'New Practice Directions of the International Court of Justice' 1 *LPICT* (2002), 247–56; Rosenne, 'International Court of Justice: Practice Directions' 1 *LPICT* (2002), 223–45.

[13] '(1) The parties shall be represented by agents; (2) They may have the assistance of counsel or advocates before the Court.'

for representatives. Whilst Professor Rosenne opines that representation 'is a matter for each litigating State to settle for itself with due regard for the status of the Court, on a level with its own Supreme Court',[14] litigants' powers to appoint representatives under the current Rules are limited only by the Court's power under Article 58(2) to restrict the number of advocates (a 1972 amendment).

Concerning the question of whether the Court has the power to regulate the appointment of parties' representation, judges are broadly divided into two camps:

> Subject to the Statute, the Court does have the authority [to prescribe admission requirements]. Concerning the Court's consent-based jurisdiction, there is one camp within the Court that gives priority to 'State sovereignty' and there is another camp that says 'this is a courtroom!' This is not a regional dividing line. I have always taken the view that sovereignty stops at jurisdiction and that litigants are subject to courtroom discipline.[15]

An interesting innovation in *Bosnia Genocide* was a 'code of conduct' for journalists backed by exclusion from proceedings for the good administration of justice. Other judges believe that since only 'sovereign States' can appear before the Court, sovereignty 'does not stop at the jurisdictional door'.[16] Another view is that 'it is at the risk and peril of the party concerned to [appoint] non-lawyers as counsel and they are the ones who stand to lose by it.'[17] Four admission issues arise from practice: (1) the appointment and functions of agents; (2) expertise in international law; (3) expertise in advocacy skills; and (4) the appointment of experts as counsel rather than witnesses.

4.2.1 Agents[18]

As explored in Chapter 3, the agent is the most procedurally powerful representative of the party and (for logistical, political, and other reasons) is usually a diplomat or other government official in practice. Objection has been made to Practice Direction VIII on the ground that the Court lacks the power to regulate the appointment of diplomats.[19] However, Judge Oda was critical in *DRC v Uganda* of a private lawyer as agent because of a recent history of 'abusive' unilateral applications brought without the prior exhaustion of diplomatic channels for the private interest of the lawyers rather than the interest of the party.[20] A similar

[14] Rosenne, *The Law and Practice of the International Court 1920-2005*, 1133.

[15] Interview with Dame Rosalyn Higgins (30 September 2010), cited with permission. See also Higgins, 'Respecting Sovereign States and Running a Tight Courtroom' 50 *ICLQ* (2001), 121–32, 131–2.

[16] Interview with Judge Abdul Koroma (4 August 2011), cited with permission.

[17] Interview with former Registrar Eduardo Valencia-Ospina (19 August 2010), cited with permission.

[18] Valencia-Ospina, 'International Courts and Tribunals, Agents, Counsel and Advocates' *MPEPIL* (2010); Rosenne, 'The Agent in Litigation in the International Court of Justice' in Kaplan and McRae, *Law, Policy, and International Justice* (1993), 41–70; Matheson, 'Practical Aspects of the Agent's Role in Cases before the International Court', 1 *LPICT* (2002) 467–79; Monaco, 'Représentation et Défense des Parties Devant les Instances Internationales' in Diez et al, *Festschrift für Rudolf Bindschedler* (1980), 373–84.

[19] Rosenne, *The Law and Practice of the International Court 1920-2005*, 225–7.

[20] *DRC v Uganda*, Declaration of Judge Oda, 132–3.

problem arose before the ITLOS in the *Grand Prince* case, where a Spanish *abogado* appeared as agent for Belize.[21] In that case, there were not only practical difficulties for the agent in obtaining instructions from his principal but 'one of the difficulties the Tribunal had to face was that of an eventual conflict of interest between the lawyer acting as an agent for Belize and as counsel for the ship-owner.'[22] The comments of Judges Oda and Cot suggest an unhealthy degree of control being exerted by private counsel over vulnerable States in certain cases.[23]

This problem of conflicts of interest also begs the question of defining the fundamental role of the agent before the Court. Historically, the agent derives from the 'diplomatic tradition' of nineteenth-century arbitration. In the context of diplomatic functions, the ICJ has defined an 'agent' in permissive terms:

> The Court understands the word "agent" in the most liberal sense, that is to say, any person who, whether a paid official or not, and whether permanently employed or not, has been charged by an organ of the organization with carrying out, or helping to carry out, one of its functions—in short, any person through whom it acts.[24]

The agent also has exclusive authority under the Rules to perform procedural acts.[25] The agent also fulfils an important, practical role as the legal team's chief administrator and intermediary with the instructing government.[26] Thus, it is sensible for practical and political reasons that the party have a diplomat within its legal team.

However, the ability of agents to perform representational functions is problematic because such persons (unless members of national bars) are not bound by ethical standards of conduct or required to have expertise in international law or advocacy. There are two ways to address this: (1) to exclude agents from advocacy by restricting their rights of hearing to diplomatic statements and performing procedural acts required of them under the Statute;[27] or (2) to require agents to meet admission requirements and standards of professional conduct. The former would require parties to appoint professional 'counsel and advocates', which is inconsistent with the permissive text of Article 42. However, the latter would comply with Article 42 because it would still permit a party to choose to be represented by an agent alone. Since the character of an agent is not defined by Article 42, the Court is free to require agents to satisfy its requirements. Whilst this in itself would not solve the conflict of interest problems arising in cases such as *DRC v Uganda* and *Grand Prince*, those conflicts could be dealt with by conjunctly prescribing ethical

21 Cot, 'Appearing "for" or "on behalf of" a State', 842–3.

22 Cot, 'Appearing "for" or "on behalf of" a State', 842.

23 Sarvarian, 'Problems of Professional Ethics for Representatives before ICSID Tribunals', 10(1) *LPICT* (2011), 67–134.

24 *Reparation for Injuries Suffered in the Service of the United Nations (Advisory Opinion)*, [1949] ICJ Rep 174, 177.

25 Rules, Art 40(1).

26 Bowett, 'The Conduct of International Litigation' in Wickremasinghe and Gardner, *The International Court of Justice: Process, Practice and Procedure* (1997), 1–20, 12, 14, 17–18.

27 See *Behring Fur Seals*, Chapter 3.

standards forbidding agents and counsel from serving interests other than those of the client.[28]

4.2.2 Membership of a National Bar

The only admission requirement common to the ECJ, ECtHR and ICC is membership of a national bar.[29] There are three advantages to this requirement. First, advocates would be subject to the admission requirements of national bars—theoretically ensuring that they have received some advocacy training. Secondly, national bars have disciplinary sanctions (eg suspension and disbarment) that international courts lack.[30] Thirdly, national bars can provide practical assistance to international courts' disciplinary systems.[31]

It is arguable that a top practitioner with no specialist background in international law is nevertheless capable of advocating effectively before the Court.[32] However, not all non-specialist practitioners would be competent. For example, Maître Jacques Vergès[33] was reportedly discharged by the DRC for poor performance in *Arrest Warrant*.[34] According to one judge:

> 'I would favour robust standards of admission—eg 'great expertise in international law'. For example, in two African cases a French counsel representing the Applicants clearly did not know what he was doing and knew nothing of the Court's procedures. It was a vexing experience and people were surprised to see this individual appear again before the Court as counsel.'[35]

Since membership of a national bar does not necessarily ensure competence before the ICJ, a requirement of 'expertise in international law' would be appropriate.

[28] Hague Principles, Principles 2.2, 3.1.

[29] ECJ Statute, Art 20; ECtHR Rules, Art 36(4); ICC Rules, Art 22(1); Court Regulations, Reg 69(2)(b).

[30] ICC Code, Arts 22(5), 41(4).

[31] ICC Code, Arts 36(5), 38(2).

[32] For example, Sir Frank Soskice QC had no academic background in international law yet successfully represented the UK in *Corfu Channel*, Cambodia in *Preah Vihear*, India in *Right of Passage*, and Greece in *Ambatelios*—Pearce, 'Soskice, Frank, Baron Stow Hill (1902-1979)', *Oxford Dictionary of National Biography* (2004), online: <http://www.oxforddnb.com/view/article/31703> (Accessed: 10 March 2011).

[33] 'Jacques Verges: "The Devil's Advocate"', online: <http://news.bbc.co.uk/1/hi/world/europe/3578421.stm> (Accessed: 10 March 2011).

[34] *Arrest Warrant*, Verbatim Record (20 November 2000). He is not listed in the judgment—*Arrest Warrant*, 5. He later appeared for the Republic of the Congo in *Certain Criminal Proceedings*, Verbatim Record (28 April 2003), 4.

[35] Interview with Dame Rosalyn Higgins. This is corroborated by Judge Jean-Pierre Cot, Interview (13 September 2010), cited with permission. Other judges had a more positive impression of his performance—Interview with Judge Koroma.

4.2.3 Academic Lawyers

Advocacy work before the Court is dominated by an elite 'mafia'[36] of professors. The professionalization of advocacy before the Court is a sensitive proposal in part because of academics' fear that it would result in the end of their domination. However, precedent exists for the admission of academics before international courts. Exceptions for academic lawyers from the general admission requirement of membership of a national bar are prescribed by both the ECJ[37] and ICC.[38] Thus, it does not necessarily follow that a generic admission requirement of membership of a national bar results in the exclusion of academics.

There are cogent arguments for the admission of specialist academics. First, by definition they have the international law expertise that practitioners from other specialities lack. Whilst the very best practitioners may be able to plead effectively before the Court without an academic background in the discipline, it is a strong argument that the majority of practitioners without such a background would struggle to do so. Secondly, the prescription of common ethical standards would arguably deal with academics' lack of advocacy expertise by obliging them to abide by those standards.[39] Thirdly, it may be suggested that academics have greater practical independence from their clients than diplomats or government lawyers.

There are also powerful arguments for the restriction of academics' admission. First, in the absence of common ethical standards, academics have an unfair competitive advantage vis-à-vis practitioners who are bound by their own national standards. Secondly, there is an argument for requiring academics to complete advocacy training because university lecturing requires different rhetorical skills:

> ... the written pleadings should not be excessively argumentative, nor should they be academic or pedantic in their presentation. It is not the function of advocates (including those also known as professors) to give lectures to tribunals; it is not the function of written pleadings to substitute for textbooks. Cases can usually be presented clearly and eloquently without over-elaborate disquisition on legal issues.[40]

Thirdly, academics arguably lack the forensic skills required to be a complete advocate.[41] For example, an oft-repeated criticism is that professors have poor witness examination technique:

> This common law art of questioning in examination and cross-examination of a witness is one of those skills which can only be learned by doing it. It is, one may say with conviction, not one that the academics and professors of international law who so often plead in the ICJ would be well advised to attempt. The few times it has been attempted have not shown

[36] Pellet, 'The Role of the International Lawyer in International Litigation' in Wickremasinghe, *The International Lawyer as Practitioner* (2000), 147–62, 147–61, 147.

[37] ECJ Statute, Art 20.

[38] Persons with 'specific competence in international or criminal law and procedure' may 'assist' counsel—ICC RoPE, Rule 22; ICC RoC, Reg 68; ICC Regs, Reg 124.

[39] Mackenzie et al, *Selecting International Judges: Principle, Process, and Politics* (2010), 52–3.

[40] Crawford, 'Advocacy Before the International Court of Justice and Other International Tribunals in State-to-State Cases', 301–30, 322.

[41] Mackenzie et al, *Selecting International Judges: Principle, Process, and Politics*, 53–7.

the professors at their best. Good cross-examination has indeed happened in the ICJ but that has only been when a party has been wise enough to include in its team some experienced and proven practising counsel, often not an international lawyer at all, but who is used to dealing with witnesses and with the art of examination and of cross-examination.[42]

It may be suggested that the cause of this particular weakness is not professional but procedural in that academics typically come from inquisitorial jurisdictions. However, there may also be a difference between *avocats* and academics insofar as the former have greater experience in interrogating witnesses after the judge.

A nuanced approach would reflect the dual need both for international law expertise and competent advocacy. One way to reflect these priorities would be to exempt sufficiently qualified academic international lawyers from a putative admission requirement of membership of a national bar. However, academics should be required to adhere to common ethical standards to provide parity with practitioners who are already subjected to national ethical standards. Such standards would also oblige academics to refrain from performing those advocacy functions for which they lack due expertise; for example, a due diligence rule would be infringed by an academic who attempts witness examination to his client's detriment.[43]

4.2.4 Experts

Despite the experts witness procedure in the Rules, litigants are able to designate their experts as 'counsel' instead of witnesses. The tactical advantages to be gained from this method of adducing 'evidence' is that counsel are, unlike witnesses, not subject to cross-examination and the substance of that material can be presented in a more controlled and favourable manner to the Court. The central issue concerns the independence of these experts from their clients and, from that, the integrity of their statements. Examination of the Court's practice reveals that the anomalous privilege of parties to present expert evidence in the form of pleadings by counsel not only impinges upon the Court's ability to accurately weigh the evidence but also provides a loophole through which it can be corrupted.

In *Corfu Channel*, Albania sought permission for its 'experts' to interrogate witnesses. The President directed Albania to clarify whether they were appearing as 'expert counsel' or 'expert witnesses'.[44] Upon being reminded that, if appearing as the latter, they would not have the right to interrogate witnesses Albania ultimately decided to designate the experts as witnesses rather than counsel.[45] In the *South West Africa* cases, the President declared that the evidence of a governmental official called as an 'expert' was admissible but his status as a governmental official 'may bear upon the weight to be given to his evidence'.[46] Following statements

[42] Jennings, 'The Work of the International Bar' in Vohrah et al, *Man's Inhumanity to Man* (2003), 443–66, 450. This observation is supported by former President Higgins, Interview.

[43] Hague Principles, Principle 3.3.

[44] *Corfu Channel (Merits)*, Vol III, 429–30.

[45] *Corfu Channel (Merits)*, Vol III, 429–30. Albania argued that the experts in question 'were strangers to the facts of the case'—*Corfu Channel (Merits)*, Vol III, 690–1.

[46] *South West Africa Cases (Merits)*, Vol X, 122–3.

of personal opinion by an 'expert' in *Burkina Fasoe v Mali*, the presiding judge declared that his statements would be treated as those of a representative.[47]

This permissive policy proved to be problematic in the *Pulp Mills* case,[48] in which scientific evidence was pivotal. Argentina and Uruguay appointed 'scientific experts' as part of their legal teams. In its pleadings, Argentina characterized some of these persons as 'independent experts'. Uruguay argued that Argentina, by 'cloaking them in the garb of advocates' and thereby insulating them from cross-examination, had forfeited their independence. Argentina argued that independence depends upon the experts' relationships to the instructing party and case issues. The Court held:

> Regarding those experts who appeared before it as counsel at the hearings, the Court would have found it more useful had they been presented by the Parties as expert witnesses... instead of being included as counsel in their respective delegations. The Court indeed considers that those persons who provide evidence before the Court based on their scientific or technical knowledge and on their personal experience should testify before the Court as experts, witnesses or in some cases in both capacities, rather than counsel, so that they may be submitted to questioning by the other party as well as by the Court.[49]

Pulp Mills illustrates the danger of permitting litigants to conflate the roles of witness and advocate; as Sir Arthur Watts put it, it becomes a matter of 'forensic tactics'.[50] A potential benefit is that the inclusion of experts in legal teams improves their arguments.[51] However, the exposure of the experts to the parties' strategies—compounded by lack of cross-examination[52]—can compromise their credibility upon which their value to the Court depends.[53]

[47] *Frontier Dispute*, Verbatim Record (26 June 1986), 59. In another case, the parties agreed in advance and the President confirmed that a scientist's statements would be treated as those of an advocate rather than an expert witness—*Gabčikovo-Nagymaros Case*, Verbatim Record (25 March 1997), 39.

[48] *Pulp Mills*, Verbatim Record (24 September 2009), 4–10, 33 (para 2), 34 (para 9); Verbatim Record (22 September 2009), 59 (para 35); Verbatim Record (29 September 2009), 22–7 (paras 20–6)

[49] *Pulp Mills*, Judgment, para 168; Separate Opinion of Judge Greenwood, paras 27–28. For criticism of the Court's 'passive approach', see the Joint Dissenting Opinion of Judges al-Khasawneh and Simma, paras 6–17; Dissenting Opinion of Judge ad hoc Vinuesa, paras 92–94; Declaration of Judge Yusuf, paras 1–14. *Confer* Separate Opinion of Judge Keith, paras 9–11; Separate Opinion of Judge Cançado Trindade, paras 148–51.

[50] Watts, 'Burden of Proof, and Evidence before the ICJ' in Weiss, *Improving WTO Dispute Settlement Procedures* (2001), 289, 299; Watts, 'Enhancing the Effectiveness of Procedures of International Dispute Settlement' in Wolfrum, 5 *MPYUNL* (2001), 29–30.

[51] Zimmermann et al, *The Statute of the International Court of Justice*, 1013 (note 293).

[52] See *Islamic Republic of Iran v United States of America*, 169–70, paras 3–5. The Claimant objected to the appointment of five Ernst & Young and LBC International employees as expert witnesses after they had already addressed the Iran-US Claims Tribunal as counsel. The Respondent argued that 'it has met all of the requirements provided for in the Tribunal Rules... if it is not allowed to present its evidence [in this way]... it will be fundamentally deprived of the ability to present its case because evidence presented under oath subject to cross-examination carries greater weight'. The Tribunal ruled: '[they] may appear at the Hearing to make their statements, but they will not make the declaration [of witnesses]. They will, however, be subject to cross-examination by the Claimant.'

[53] Rosenne, *The Law and Practice of the International Court 1920-2005*, 1137.

4.2.5 Legal Aid

An important facet of equality of arms entails parties' ability to retain competent counsel. In forming a legal team, 'the real objective...would seem to be that a State, presenting its case, should use the best counsel and advocates available, no matter what their nationality'.[54] Judge Owada wrote in 1971:

> [T]here is a vast difference between...a country which can employ her own legal experts in the service of the government and...a country which has to hire illustrious names from abroad. A possible solution to this might be found in the establishment of a panel of lawyers from whose list the parties may choose their own counsel before the Court and the establishment of a system under which the cost incurred will be borne, *in toto* or in part, by the United Nations.[55]

The creation by the Court of a list system comprising expert counsel would be a useful and feasible project. A legal aid mechanism would help to ensure that all parties can retain good counsel. Currently, the UN Secretary-General's Trust Fund provides only financial assistance and is somewhat cumbersome.[56]

An apposite case is *Corfu Channel*, which was litigated in the tense atmosphere of the nascent Cold War between a relatively wealthy and experienced Applicant (the United Kingdom) and a poor and novice Respondent (Albania) then ruled by a Communist government. Judge Jean-Pierre Cot's sketch of the two parties' legal teams reveals a significant imbalance,[57] though he notes that the degree of inequality was 'a situation quite unimaginable today in the Hague Court'.[58] However, according to a confidential source there have been cases in which the Registrar has had to bend his strict neutrality by informally helping parties to retain competent counsel. A legal aid mechanism would bring structure to this de facto practice.

4.3 Ethical Standards

In the absence of common ethical rules for counsel, it might be asked whether the standards of counsel who regularly appear before the Court are nevertheless harmonious. However, the question is not entirely to the point because, although it is true that the group of regular counsel is relatively homogenous,[59] there are also counsel who appear before the Court in only one or two cases.[60] Whilst the standards of the counsel who regularly appear before the Court (the so-called

[54] Peck and Lee, *Increasing the Effectiveness of the International Court of Justice*, 144.

[55] Owada, 'What Future for the International Court of Justice?' 65(4) *AJIL* (1971) 268–74, 274.

[56] Zimmerman et al, *The Statute of the International Court of Justice*, 1396–8. By contrast, the Advisory Centre on WTO Law established by the WTO Agreement 2001 provides counsel to indigent States for both advisory and representational services.

[57] Cot, 'The Bar' in Bannelier et al, *The ICJ and the Evolution of International Law: The Enduring Impact of the Corfu Channel Case* (2012), 21–38.

[58] Interview.

[59] Pellet, 'The Role of the International Lawyer in International Litigation' in Wickremasinghe, *The International Lawyer as Practitioner* (2000), 147–62, 147.

[60] For two recent examples, see the legal teams in *Georgia v Russia*, 4–6 and *Pulp Mills*, 5–9.

de facto bar) clearly have the most scope to shape its culture of advocacy, the lack of admission requirements for counsel common ethical standards are necessary not only to harmonize divergent standards amongst senior ICJ counsel (eg Professors James Crawford SC or Alain Pellet) but also amongst junior counsel.

The ICJ Practice Directions provide a precedent for compromise between the progressive and conservative schools of thought concerning the jurisdiction of the Court to regulate counsel. Were the Court unwilling to prescribe a binding code as part of its Rules, it could partially base such a code upon the consent of counsel by issuing a Practice Direction containing a voluntary code of conduct and inviting counsel to sign and deposit a copy of the code with the Registrar at the commencement of new proceedings. Non-mandatory provisions of the code could potentially be amended by the common consent of the counsel in a particular case:

> Although I for one believe that the Court ought to adopt its own Code of Conduct for counsel, I believe that the Court might find such an idea interesting. I do not personally see a problem with it, if that is part of the agreement of the States Parties.[61]

A quasi-compulsory set of ethical standards would not only be useful in addressing practical issues but also circumvent the debate concerning the Court's powers.

4.3.1 Duties to the Client

In considering counsel's duties to his client, the role of counsel as intermediary between Court and client is crucial. Counsel not only articulates his client's cause to the Court but also explains the Court's procedure and its wishes to his client. The paradox that emerges is that clients that consider the pursuit of a course of action that they perceive to be in their best interests—defined narrowly as 'winning the case'—can sometimes act contrary to their best *legal* interests. The perceived dichotomy between, on the one hand, the client's interests and, on the other hand, the interests of justice is fallacious. Counsel must be persuasive in dissuading his client from pursuing a course of conduct that, in endangering the integrity of proceedings, concordantly carries the grave risk that his client's cause will be prejudiced. Thus, by serving the supreme interests of justice and those of the Court counsel is also serving his client's legal interests.

An important factor to consider in examining this counsel-client dynamic is that not only do client profiles and attitudes differ but so too do those of counsel. Although the pool of senior counsel at the Court is relatively concentrated, there is a wider range of junior counsel. They, too, will encounter ethical problems in advising and representing their clients. It is conceivable that, in doing so, they may be compelled to act without the benefit of advice and supervision from senior counsel. The dynamics of the counsel-client relationship clearly change, in that the authority accrued by senior advocates will necessarily be nascent for juniors. Even eminent counsel may not always be successful in persuading (or dissuading) their

[61] Interview with Dame Rosalyn Higgins.

clients. A code of conduct serves not only as a shield to empower counsel to resist client pressure but also as a sword to pressure clients to 'do the right thing'.

4.3.1.1 Acceptance of Instructions

There exists a variety of national practices concerning the circumstances in which advocates may enter into a representation agreement.[62] The problem that arises from these differences is that, without a uniform rule based upon a clear philosophical approach, parties may well face difficulties in retaining objective and disinterested representation. Two issues in practice have been incompetent counsel representing inexperienced parties and counsel being pressured to not represent 'pariah States'.

A relatively trite and universal principle is that counsel should only accept briefs for which they are 'competent' in expertise and resources.[63] The problem of counsel subjectively selecting clients or being pressured to reject clients by third parties is more difficult.[64] The *Corfu Channel* experience of a 'pariah State' unable to retain counsel from the de facto bar is arguably unlikely to recur:

> This is not such a problem because the international marketplace is very open. States will always be able to find someone to defend them, which is a case where ethical flexibility is actually good because someone will always be available.[65]

By contrast, the late Sir Ian Brownlie was a famous proponent of the English 'cab rank rule' in his representation of States hostile to the UK as a manifestation of the rule of law.[66] Whilst his ideal that counsel should be independent and apolitically loyal to the rule of law has much to offer in politically sensitive litigation, agreement amongst counsel may be difficult to achieve due to divergences in national standards.

4.3.1.2 Conflicts of Interest

Conflicts of interest are a particularly sensitive area,[67] including where counsel: (1) is a former judge or registrar of the Court; (2) has professional or personal links with the Bench or the opposing party; and (3) is likely to be called as a witness. Opinions diverge on whether appropriate remedies are disclosure,

[62] Eg English Code, paras 601–607, Annexe A (para 3); New York Code, Rules 1.1, 1.7; German Code, para 3; Paris Code, Arts 1.1, 4; CCBE Code of Conduct, Arts 3.1.1, 3.1.3.

[63] Hague Principles, Principle 3.3; CCBE Code of Conduct, Art 3.1.3.

[64] Hague Principles, Principle 2.2. Professor John Dugard criticized the omission of the 'cab rank rule' from the Principles—Chinkin et al, *Report of the Seventy-Fourth Conference* (2010), 957.

[65] Interview with Judge Cot. *Confer*, eg *Oil Platforms*, 7; *NATO Cases*, 7; *Lockerbie*, 116–17.

[66] Eg *Nicaragua*; *Lockerbie*; *NATO Cases*; *Bosnia Genocide*. See also Brownlie, 'The Perspective of International Law from the Bar' in Evans, *International Law* (2003), 11–14, 14; Owada, 'Sir Ian Brownlie, KT, CBE, QC (1932-2010): The Professor as Counsel', *BYIL*, online: <http://www.bybil.oxfordjournals.org> (Accessed: 28 October 2011), 6–7; Brownlie, 'International Law at the Fiftieth Anniversary of the United Nations', *Recueil des Cours*, 255(1995), 9–228, 22; Crawford, 'Ian Brownlie: 1932-2010', online: <http://www.lcil.cam.ac.uk/Media/lectures/Brownlie_British_Academy.pdf> (Accessed: 12 November 2012), 16–18.

[67] Hague Principles, Principle 4.

withdrawal, or waiver. In examining these conflicts, it is suggested that client waiver would be unsatisfactory because parties may not be well-placed to judge their own legal interests and such conflicts also affect the Court. Thus, a stricter standard of disclosure or withdrawal would better protect the integrity of proceedings.

(a) Former Judges and Court Officials

The Court has sought to sharpen the boundary between judges and representatives.[68] In February 2002, the Court issued Practice Direction VII directing parties not to appoint as ad hoc judge one who has acted as agent or advocate within the previous three years.[69] Practice Direction VIII directs parties not to appoint as agent or advocate one who has been a judge, ad hoc judge or official within the previous three years. Whilst there was no single incident that prompted these Directions, there was disquiet at a growing trend of ad hoc judges contemporaneously acting as counsel. As the President at the time relates:

> Speaking generally, I would say that I believe the pre-PD practice of an *ad hoc* judge addressing the Court as counsel in another case was professionally not right and needed changing. On a more personal level, it can make one feel quite uncomfortable when counsel in an ongoing case is sitting with you in Judges' quarters as a judge *ad hoc* in another case. It had to change.[70]

Whilst the Directions have been welcomed as 'a demonstration of the Court's growing judicial self-confidence and maturity',[71] doubts have also been raised concerning their propriety, compulsoriness, and enforceability.

The interaction between the Statute and Rules on the one hand and the ICJ Practice Directions on the other has been described as 'unclear'.[72] Although it may be suggested that the requirement in Practice Direction VII has a defensible rationale on the ground that the neutrality of ad hoc judges who have recently acted as counsel for the appointing party may be challenged, the Directions are clearly exhortatory. As former President Higgins explains:

> *All* Practice Directions have the same legal character. The Bench was fully aware that Directions are not binding and their language reflects that. That said, sensible counsel are well aware that there is no point in antagonising or irritating the Bench and so the Directions have been treated in practice as if they were obligatory.[73]

[68] Rosenne, *The Law and Practice of the International Court*, 238; Watts, 'New Practice Directions of the International Court of Justice', 254. Article 17 of the Statute for judges has been applied several times—Rosenne, *The Law and Practice of the International Court 1920-2005* (Vol III), 1063–4.

[69] Subsequently, two ad hoc judges in pending cases resigned—Rosenne, *The Law and Practice of the International Court 1920-2005* (Vol III), 1090–1. See also Pellet, 'Remarks on Proceedings before the International Court of Justice' 5 *LPICT* (2006), 163–82, 177–9; Watts, 'New Practice Directions of the International Court of Justice', 252–5; Rosenne, *The Law and Practice of the International Court*, 223–38.

[70] Interview with Dame Rosalyn Higgins.

[71] Watts, 'New Practice Directions of the International Court of Justice', 247.

[72] Watts, 'New Practice Directions of the International Court of Justice', 255.

[73] Interview.

Whilst Practice Directions VII and VIII have largely been respected by parties and counsel, there has been at least one case of non-compliance. In *Bosnia Genocide*, Judge ad hoc Sir Elihu Lauterpacht QC resigned on 22 February 2002.[74] On 21 January 2003, Sir Elihu addressed the Court as counsel for the Respondent in *Avena*.[75] According to a confidential source, the Applicant in that case was aware of the issue but, to avoid antagonising the Court or embarrassing an eminent advocate, it made no formal objection but informed the Registrar. Whilst it is arguable that the Court should have nevertheless examined *ex proprio motu* whether to exclude him due to appearance of bias, it is conceivable that the Court decided that the 'damage' had already been done by the speech.

The question remains whether, where a party appoints an ad hoc judge or advocate contrary to these directions, an ethical duty ought to exist for that person. Acceptance of both appointments risks a 'conflict of interest' between judicial impartiality and client fidelity. A judgment appearing to have been influenced by the presence of a former judge or registrar on a legal team endangers 'not just the reputation and interests of the personalities in this field... but [also] the fair administration of international justice'.[76] International justice serving elite interests risks undermining confidence in the Court, which is detrimental for the 'invisible bar' because history has shown confidence to be necessary for the Court's docket.

(b) Professional and Personal Links

In the small world of the Court in which counsel and judges are often close colleagues and personal friends, caution is necessary to prevent the appearance of bias or corruption.[77] The merest suggestion[78] that an advocate or judge could have been biased would damage the Court's reputation. This applies emphatically to contacts between judges, ad hoc judges and representatives of the same nationality.[79] This does not mean, however, that withdrawal is necessarily the appropriate remedy in all cases. Disclosure would in most cases satisfy integrity through transparency. However, withdrawal may be more appropriate in cases of exceptional proximity such as spouses serving on opposite legal teams. Nuanced cases include barristers from the same set of chambers or solicitors from the same firm appearing on opposite sides or joining proceedings after a judge who is a former member of the same chambers or firm.[80]

[74] *Bosnia Genocide*, para 29.

[75] *Avena*, Verbatim Record (21 January 2003), 4, 34.

[76] Malintoppi, 'Remarks on Arbitrators' Independence, Impartiality and Duty to Disclose in Investment Arbitration', 7 *LPICT* (2008), 351–6, 356.

[77] Hague Principles, Principle 5.5.

[78] Eg Malleson, 'Judicial Bias and Disqualification after Pinochet (No 2)', 63(1) *MoLR* (2000), 119–27.

[79] Sarvarian, 'Problems of Professional Ethics for Representatives before ICSID Tribunals', 108 (note 146).

[80] Sarvarian, 'Problems of Professional Ethics for Representatives before ICSID Tribunals', 96–9.

(c) Witnesses of Fact

There have been several cases in which representatives have made reference to personal knowledge concerning the facts of the case in the course of pleadings, including *ELSI*, *DRC v Uganda* and *Costa Rica v Nicaragua*. In *ELSI*, Mr Guiseppe Bisconti (an Italian *avvocato*) was instructed as an 'adviser' to the United States. However, in addressing the Court as counsel:

> [H]e had occasion to refer to matters of fact within his knowledge as a lawyer acting for Raython Company, the President of the Chamber acceded to a request by the Agent of Italy that Mr. Bisconti be treated *pro tanto* as a witness. Mr. Bisconti, who informed the Chamber that both Raytheon Company and Mr. Bisconti himself waived any relevant privilege, was cross-examined by [counsel for Italy].[81]

In *DRC v Uganda*, the President interrupted the speech of the Defence Minister for Uganda acting as counsel when he referred to personal knowledge to remind him that he was speaking for Uganda rather than as a witness.[82] A similar statement occurred in *Costa Rica v Nicaragua*, in which Mr Paul Reichler referred to his personal familiarity with a river in contradistinction to opposing counsel.[83]

Whilst these were ultimately not major slips, they were nevertheless inappropriate[84] because they conflated the role of counsel as an *interpreter* of the facts with the role of a witness as a *narrator* of those facts. The effect is to impinge upon counsel's professional objectivity and create the appearance of distortion of the facts. This conflict unnecessarily complicates the Court's task to test evidence with the objective assistance of counsel. Ethical standards requiring counsel to segregate the roles of advocate and witness would preclude this.[85]

4.3.1.3 Withdrawal

As already discussed, withdrawal may well be the appropriate remedy for ethical problems that emerge during the course of representation (as opposed to those that appear prior to acceptance, for which the technical equivalent is refusal of instructions). These may include conflicts of interest, such as an unforeseen factual issue upon which counsel has personal knowledge such as renders him 'reasonably likely' to be called as a witness. This test of reasonable likelihood is suggested as appropriate, in that it does not impose an excessively strict standard of automatic withdrawal where it is merely *possible* that the counsel will be called as a witness. Counsel would be required to take steps to ascertain whether his knowledge would be required by the Court and, if so, to disclose its existence.

[81] *ELSI*, 19; Vol III, 300–4.

[82] Verbatim Record (18 April 2005), 42, 53.

[83] *Costa Rica v Nicaragua*, Verbatim Record (6 March 2009), 23 (para 39). See also *Gabčikovo-Nagymaros*, Verbatim Record (11 April 1997), 24; (15 April 1997), 17; *Nicaragua*, Vol V, 8; *Bosnia Genocide*, Verbatim Record (24 March 2006), 13.

[84] Watts, 'New Practice Directions of the International Court of Justice', 256.

[85] Hague Principles, Principle 4.3.3.

There are, however, situations in which withdrawal is the only reasonable course. For example, a client may insist upon giving an instruction to make manifestly abusive arguments lack a legal and/or factual basis. As one senior counsel explains

> But it is not the function of a written pleading to present purely argumentative or rhetorical material. Unfortunately it is not uncommon for written pleadings to be presented in an overwritten—indeed at times even hysterical—style. No doubt there can be legitimate differences in forensic taste, but in my opinion the written pleadings are better and more effective if they are relatively understated. They need to express the party's case, and to do so clearly, convincingly and without equivocation. But they do not need to pour abuse on the other side or to use language which is overblown or unsustainable.[86]

Such pleadings are likely to be made by parties that enjoy a generally hostile relationship or are engaged in a particularly charged dispute. Whilst senior counsel may have the personal authority to dissuade clients from such pleadings, junior counsel will likely struggle to do this. They are not only bad advocacy but can cross an ethical threshold of professional embarrassment if they are vexatious, insulting or manifestly unsustainable in fact or law.[87]

4.3.1.4 Diligence

Criticism has been made in debates on the Court's procedural efficiency of advocates' volubility in their pleadings[88] alongside common law practitioners' and civil law academics' tendency to respectively indulge in 'procedural chicaneries' and unnecessary 'intellectual jousting'.[89] Here, there is a fine line between indifferent advocacy and professional misconduct due to inefficiency or lack of diligence.[90] Like a 'game of ping-pong',[91] bench and bar have blamed one another for inefficient advocacy. Counsel are said to indulge in irrelevant debate and insufficiently focus their pleadings whilst judges are said to insufficiently direct the parties to enable advocates to sharpen their pleadings.[92] Clients sometimes insist upon legally weak but politically important arguments[93] and pressure counsel to 'keep all issues open' and resist any concessions, however sensible.[94] As Professor Crawford has written:

> Evidently it is the function of the advocate to comply with the instructions of the government or other party, and to present the case in as forceful and vigorous a way as possible.

[86] Crawford, 'Advocacy Before the International Court of Justice and Other International Tribunals in State-to-State Cases', 321–2.

[87] Hague Principles, Principles 6.1, 7.1.

[88] Pellet, 'The Anatomy of Courts and Tribunals' 7 *LPICT* (2008), 275–87, 280–4.

[89] Pellet, 'Remarks on Proceedings before the International Court of Justice', 167. See also Practice Directions II and III.

[90] Hague Principles, Principles 2.3, 3.3.

[91] Peck and Lee, *Increasing the Effectiveness of the International Court of Justice*, 117.

[92] Peck and Lee, *Increasing the Effectiveness of the International Court of Justice*, 112–13, 115–16, 123–4, 141–3; Teitelbaum, 'Recent Fact-Finding Developments at the International Court of Justice' 6 *LPICT* (2007), 119–58, 123; Higgins, 'Respecting Sovereign States and Running a Tight Courtroom', 127–8.

[93] Zimmermann et al, *The Statute of the International Court of Justice: A Commentary*, 1038.

[94] Crawford, 'Advocacy Before the International Court of Justice and Other International Tribunals in State-to-State Cases', 320.

At the same time it is not the function of the advocate simply to say things for money; nor unquestioningly to present the client's case in the way the client would have it, without regard to any of the actual difficulties. Rather it is the function of the advocate to seek to persuade the tribunal in such a way as to preserve the essentials of the client's case. This is a delicate matter, requiring trust between the client (through the Agent) and the advocate. In the search for a proper outcome, the advocate is not merely a mouthpiece but rather an active intermediary.[95]

Ethical standards of efficiency and diligence can oblige and empower counsel to resist such pressures in the interest of justice and of the client by retaining 'the independence of approach which is characteristic of the professional lawyer. Confidential advice to the client must involve frankness and objectivity, otherwise it is worthless, and probably harmful.'[96]

A related problem is the bringing of manifestly unfounded unilateral applications to the Court.[97] According to one former Registrar:

There were a few times when, as Registrar, I would receive applications that were so clearly improper that I would on my own authority have to indicate to the applicant the defects in their application so that, if possible, they could re-submit it properly. There is a distinction between the roles of counsel and Registrar. The Registrar cannot address the merits of a case. Perhaps admission requirements for counsel are inevitable in this respect.[98]

In 1999, the Democratic Republic of the Congo ('DRC') brought two applications against Burundi and Rwanda. Both of them were subsequently withdrawn whilst 'reserv[ing] the right to invoke subsequently new grounds of jurisdiction of the Court', implying that the DRC belatedly understood that its applications were ill-founded.[99] Judge Jean-Pierre Cot, an ITLOS judge and ICJ ad hoc judge in four pending cases, explains:

Burundi did not waste much of the Court's time but rather the parties' time as it was withdrawn fairly quickly. Inter-state tribunals are constrained by sovereignty of States. Consequently, they are very cautious with them in their procedures. For example, in *Nicaragua v. Colombia* there will be a full week of pleadings from Costa Rica and Honduras which could be done in two days. There will be a great deal of repetition and waste for which the Court will pay. The same happened in *Black Sea* with matters unnecessarily protracted. The Court basically lacks the authority to control this. The Strasbourg and Luxembourg Courts have much stronger mandates.[100]

Thus, although frivolous applications may not have a great deal of adverse effect upon the Court's docket there is a more fundamental problem concerning the seeming inability or unwillingness of certain counsel to plead succinctly. However,

[95] Crawford, 'Advocacy Before the International Court of Justice and Other International Tribunals in State-to-State Cases', 330.

[96] Brownlie, 'The Perspective of International Law from the Bar', 14.

[97] See discussion on the agents in *DRC v Uganda* and *Grand Prince*.

[98] Interview with Mr Valencia-Ospina.

[99] *DRC v Burundi*, 4; *DRC v Rwanda*.

[100] Interview with Judge Cot.

there arguably have been manifestly ill-founded applications[101] that the Court should have dismissed *in limine litis*.

4.3.1.5 *Confidentiality*

The principle of professional secrecy or confidentiality is sensitive. For obvious reasons, it is central to the counsel-client relationship because trust with one's client is considered to be impossible without discretion.[102] Exceptions to the principle may be commonly found in national codes for evidence of future crimes or frauds or in the advocate's own defence.[103] However, there have been cases where its strictness may arguably be detrimental to the interests of justice by preventing advocates who know of abusive misconduct by parties from informing the Court.

For example, in *Qatar v Bahrain* (discussed in greater detail below) Qatar adduced 82 false documents as 'evidence' at the written stage of pleadings for which its official explanation concerning their provenance is weak. In particular, there is no record of these documents' existence prior to their sudden appearance at those archives during the case.[104] In the absence of a convincing alternative explanation, *lex parsimoniae*[105] suggests that those documents were forged by someone within Qatar's archives. In such circumstances, if counsel 'knows' that a client is endangering the integrity of proceedings by intentionally submitting documents of dubious veracity and that client disregards counsel's professional advice to confirm their authenticity, then counsel should withdraw from representation and inform the Court. A disclosure exception to the confidentiality principle[106] would empower counsel to dissuade clients from misconduct.

4.3.1.6 *Fees*

The Court, by Article 64 of the Statute, has the power to make costs orders. However, like the PCIJ, it has never elected to depart from the general rule that each side should bear its own costs.[107] Apart from general statements that costs orders are exceptional and require express reasoning, the Court has yet to elaborate the principles upon which it would base a putative decision to impose costs

[101] Eg *DRC v Rwanda (New Application)*, 16–21. Although the Court rejected Rwanda's request to dismiss the application for 'manifest lack of jurisdiction', it ultimately found overwhelmingly that it lacked jurisdiction. All of the DRC's representatives were Congolese and most were government officials—*DRC v Rwanda(New Application)*, 6–7.See also the abrupt switch in the jurisdictional position of Serbia and Montenegro in the *NATO Cases*, which should arguably have prompted the Court to remove them *in limine litis*—Müller, 'Procedural Developments at the International Court of Justice' 4 *LPICT* (2005), 141–63, 159–63.

[102] Eg CCBE Code of Conduct, para 2.3.

[103] New York Code, Rule 1.6(b); German Code, para 2(3); English Code, para 702; Paris Code, Art 2.1.

[104] Al-Arayed, *A Line in the Sea*, 356.

[105] Blackburn, 'Ockham's razor', *The Oxford Dictionary of Philosophy* (2008), online: <http://www.oxfordreference.com/views/ENTRY.html?subview=Main&entry=t98.e2230> (Accessed: 28 October 2011).

[106] *Confer* Hague Principles, Principle 3.4.

[107] Zimmerman, *The Statute of the International Court of Justice: A Commentary*, 1393–400; Rosenne, *The Law and Practice of the International Court 1920-2005*, 1280 (note 191); Hudson, *The Permanent Court of International Justice 1920-1942* (1943), 530.

orders.[108] Commentators have surmised that costs orders may be made for 'manifest abuse of legal process or in cases of *prima facie* unfounded claims' or 'vexatious or abusive tactics...employed or the proceedings conducted in an improper manner'.[109]

Two ethical issues arise for advocates: personal liability and proportionality of fees. If a party were to blame its advocate for procedural impropriety, the question arises whether the Court could make a 'personal costs order' directed at that advocate—a potentially useful tool for enforcement purposes. Further, the scale of an advocate's fees would eventually become relevant should the Court ever utilize its dormant power. Professor Pellet has provided estimates of $250,000 to $8 million to conduct litigation before the Court,[110] sums which may be burdensome for poor States.[111] This may require that advocates' fees be subject to a 'proportionality test' in order to ensure that all litigants can obtain access to good counsel at affordable cost.[112] Additionally, as considered above in the context of a putative legal aid system, a requirement that 'list counsel' undertake to a certain percentage of cases *pro bono* would be a useful and feasible requirement in promoting access to top counsel for poor States.

4.3.2 Duties to the Court

General principles of ethics that one may identify in an advocate's interaction with an international court or tribunal include loyalty, candour, and courtesy.[113] Counsel should not disobey, disrespect, or lie to the bench. Whilst these principles may appear at first sight to be relatively straightforward, practice has shown them to be more complex owing to diverging national standards of appropriate professional conduct. In particular, the exact standard of honesty expected in counsel's pleadings is a tricky and delicate problem. The resolution of such problems depends upon the hierarchical supremacy of duties to court over counsel's duty of loyalty to the client, which entails a conceptualization of the role of the advocate as an independent intermediary between Court and client and a servant of justice. This notion runs counter to the current laissez-faire culture of the Court, in which counsel are not empowered by ethical standards and procedural rules in their relations with their clients.

Additional problems have arisen in the Court's practice concerning ex parte contacts between counsel and judges as well as the handling of documentary and testimonial evidence. Witnesses, in particular, have historically been a difficult procedural area in which normativity is greatly lacking. Since these are areas in

[108] Zimmerman, *The Statute of the International Court of Justice: A Commentary*, 1395–6.

[109] Zimmerman, *The Statute of the International Court of Justice: A Commentary*, 1396 (note 18); Rosenne, *The Law and Practice of the International Court 1920-2005*, 1279 (note 189); UNCLOS, Art 294.

[110] Peck and Lee, *Increasing the Effectiveness of the International Court of Justice*, 118.

[111] Peck and Lee, *Increasing the Effectiveness of the International Court of Justice*, 112.

[112] Peck and Lee, *Increasing the Effectiveness of the International Court of Justice*, 156.

[113] Hague Principles, Principles 5.1, 5.3, 6.1.

which the integrity of proceedings has the potential to be seriously undermined—and with it the legitimacy of the Court's judgments to the public—the lack of appropriate safeguards is a major procedural lacuna. Here, ethical standards can be particularly useful in providing counsel and judges with practical guidance in difficult and awkward situations. Moreover, an ethical rubric would enable the Court to handle such problems as may arise without recourse to *ex post facto* law. Finally, ethical standards would provide an even stronger appearance of institutional maturity.

4.3.2.1 Loyalty and Courtesy

A duty of loyalty to the court is an uncomfortable term for many counsel.[114] Loyalty entails a general duty to diligently implement the rules and orders of the Court. In *Corfu Channel*, the President took the very unusual step of publicly admonishing counsel for both sides for lack of discipline in breaching an order of the Court.[115] Obedience of the procedural rules and orders of the Court is vital to preserve its control over proceedings. However, it is suggested that there may be rare occasions in which the Court itself seriously breaches procedural integrity or fair trial standards. Judges, however eminent, are only human and can therefore be corrupted. Thus, counsel's duty of loyalty to the Court as an institution should take precedence over whether a judge whom counsel reasonably suspects of having breached judicial standards is expected to vote favourably to his party's case. Moreover, the desire to spare the Court, or the judge himself, embarrassment should not outweigh the overriding need that justice be clearly seen by the outside world to have been done.

A duty of courtesy is largely self-explanatory in that counsel should always address a court or tribunal, including registrars and officials, with respect and decorum. Insulting or abusive language or behaviour should be strictly forbidden. Vitriolic, intemperate, or otherwise disrespectful language should be avoided at all times. Whilst seriously disruptive incidents are relatively rare in oral proceedings before the Court,[116] disrespectful language has been known to be employed in written pleadings.[117] Not only do these not serve the best interests of the client but disrespectful language towards either the Court or one's colleagues in oral proceedings may disrupt the smooth functioning of the Court.

4.3.2.2 Ex Parte Communication

In practice, the danger of apparent or actual bias[118] from ex parte communications between counsel and judges has been illustrated in two cases: 1) allegations

[114] Eg Hague Principles, Principle 5.1: '[C]ounsel shall *abide by* the rules of conduct, orders and directions of the international court or tribunal' (emphasis added).

[115] *Corfu Channel (Merits)*, Vol III, 188; Vol IV, 305–16.

[116] *Corfu Channel (Merits)*, Vol III, 188; Vol IV, 305–16.

[117] Crawford, 'Advocacy Before the International Court of Justice and Other International Tribunals in State-to-State Cases', 321.

[118] Mahoney, 'The International Judiciary—Independence and Accountability' 7 *LPICT* (2008), 313–49.

of judicial leaks;[119] and 2) informal meetings between a judge and a member of the de facto bar. In *Nuclear Tests*, a statement by the Australian Prime Minister was published speculating that the Court would rule in favour of Australia by eight votes to six. The Registrar (Mr Stanislas Aquarone) was an Australian national. Australia's agent denied that the statement was based upon a leak[120] and the Court unsuccessfully investigated. The case demonstrates the danger of the appearance of bias:

> I think that in general counsel and judges are sensible about their social arrangements. For example, if I were to invite my friend to a social function who happens to be counsel in a pending case I would also invite opposing counsel to ensure that there is no appearance of bias. Certainly *ex parte* communications are a real issue, we have had leaks in the past. Of that there is no doubt. Some judges are too familiar with their national embassies and certainly there is an issue with ad hoc judges' links with appointing States.[121]

Professor Pellet also relates an informal encounter with a judge in a pending case:

> In [*Nauru*] I was acting for Australia and the written pleadings had been drafted in cooperation with Counsel, but by the Australians themselves... sometime before the oral hearings I met one of the "civil law" Judges, who said to me, "Well Alain, I have read all of this material, but to be honest, I am not sure I have understood all of the reasoning". I answered "Well Judge, I am not sure I have understood it myself". There was a pause before he asked "Who is going to plead that part at the hearings?" When I answered "I think I should do it", I had the feeling he was somewhat relieved. Then, after the oral hearings we met again and he told me "I think I have understood now". However he voted against Australia and I am not sure it would not have been better from our point of view if he had not understood that part of the argument.[122]

Although there is no indication that Professor Pellet was 'pleading', it is arguably improper for pleadings to be discussed one-on-one with a judge in a pending case. The exchange illustrates the proximity of the bench and bar created by a small and tight-knit legal community.

4.3.2.3 Candour

The principle of candour in an advocate's pleadings to the Court is misleading in its seeming simplicity in that the precise *standard* of honesty is difficult to determine. Should counsel be obliged to disclose information adverse to their own case, even if the Court does not directly solicit it? What steps should counsel take to 'reasonably'[123] confirm evidentiary veracity? Closing one's eyes to suspicions of falsehood has implications for client confidentiality. Counsel may be obliged to not disclose that a grave breach of procedural integrity had occurred in the absence

[119] Statute, Art 54. See, eg *Buraimi* in Wetter, *The International Arbitral Process: Public and Private (Vol III)* (1979), 355–400.

[120] *ICJ Yearbook* (Vol 28) (1973–1974), 128.

[121] Interview with Dame Rosalyn Higgins. See also Crawford, 'Advocacy Before the International Court of Justice and Other International Tribunals in State-to-State Cases', 313.

[122] Pellet, 'The Role of the International Lawyer in International Litigation', 152.

[123] Hague Principles, Principle 6.1.

of client consent. Thus, counsel may be required, even where they have real suspicions, to silently witness the Court being misled by false evidence.

The counter-argument is that, since counsel may be ignorant of potentially misleading information until informed by their clients, they will necessarily not be in a position to persuade their clients to inform the Court because the latter would be unwilling to share such sensitive information with their counsel knowing that the latter would be obliged to independently disclose it. The relationship of trust empowers counsel to persuade the clients to ultimately 'do the right thing' and removing confidentiality from the equation would threaten that trust.

An example of this dilemma is the *Nicaragua* case, in which the agent for Nicaragua allegedly misled the Court by affirming that his Government was not supplying Salvadorean rebels with military munitions. The Court found that Nicaragua had not in fact provided such support during the relevant period.[124] Judge Stephen Schwebel, who dissented from the Court's judgment, opined that this conclusion was wrong.[125] Concerning the 25th anniversary of the case, Judge Schwebel wrote an editorial in which he alleged that a 'fraud' had been perpetrated upon the Court by Nicaragua.[126] He debated the matter with Mr Paul Reichler, counsel to Nicaragua, in a series of replies and rejoinders.[127]

A distinction should be drawn between the Nicaraguan agent (who, by his very nature, could not be described as independent of his principal) and the 'external counsel' (Paul Reichler, Ian Brownlie, Abram Chayes, and Alain Pellet), which incidentally supports the argument made earlier in this chapter for regulation of agents as well as counsel. As Paul Reichler has written *à propos* the *Nicaragua* case:

> Judge Schwebel's editorial raises concerns not only for Nicaragua, but also for its counsel. As officers of the Court, we have an ethical obligation not to submit, or to allow a client to submit, false evidence. Judge Schwebel's editorial is susceptible of being read as implying that Nicaragua's counsel failed properly to exercise this obligation...
>
> As I have previously written, prior to going to the ICJ, Nicaragua was advised by its counsel not to bring the case if it were then engaged in, or intended to engage in, the trafficking of arms to El Salvador (or anywhere else)... Our clients assured us... that they would take no actions that might undermine Nicaragua's prospects for success, including providing arms or other material support to Salvadoran or other rebel forces. We believed them, and the evidence proves we were right to do so. The Court's judgment was firmly grounded in that evidence.

Putting to one side the question of the veracity of the evidence concerned (a disputed point between Judge Schwebel and Mr Reichler), the central question concerning counsel conduct is whether counsel 'knew' of *potential* falsehood and nevertheless made submissions *potentially* misleading to the Court. Taking Mr Reichler's

[124] *Nicaragua* (Merits), para 160.

[125] *Nicaragua* (Merits), Dissenting Opinion of Judge Schwebel, paras 28–32.

[126] Schwebel, 'Celebrating a Fraud on the Court' 106(1) *AJIL* (2012), 102–5.

[127] Reichler, 'Nicaragua Case: A Response to Judge Schwebel' 106(2) *AJIL* (2012), 316–21; Schwebel, 'Nicaragua Case: A Response to Paul Reichler' 106(3) *AJIL* (2012), 582–3; Reichler, 'Paul Reichler's Rejoinder' 106(3) *AJIL* (2012), 583–4.

assertion of his client's 'assurances' as an example, should such assurances (assuming that they were not supported by tangible evidence) be enough to absolve counsel of responsibility for the veracity of potentially misleading arguments?

On balance, there is a real need for an autonomous actor to disclose grave and potential threats to procedural integrity that outweighs the potential erosion of trust between counsel and client. Whilst it is evidently not the primary function of counsel to 'turn in' his own client, nor is it counsel's role simply to say whatever his client instructs him to say without regard to the truth-seeking function of the judicial process. International justice being compromised by false evidence as counsel watches in silence is surely not the solution. It may be orthodox to say that, in the ideal scenario, counsel will act as a 'filter' by digging deeper in his own preparation of his brief and persuade his client to redact arguments based upon unsubstantiated or potentially false evidence. In the real world, this will not always happen. In such a case, the professional course should be withdrawal from representation and (more controversially) independently informing the Court of the circumstances.

In the ITLOS case of *Louisa*,[128] St Vincent and the Grenadines argued that the purpose of the Louisa company entailed hydrocarbon exploration to the exclusion of archeological excavation – a point contested by Spain. Following the conclusion of hearings and in response to questioning by the Tribunal, St Vincent and the Grenadines submitted the relevant document concerning the mission of the vessel, which made repeated reference to the recovery of historical artefacts. In paragraph 47 of its judgment, the Tribunal noted 'with regret that a copy of this agreement was not provided by the Applicant until after the request was made by the Tribunal'. In his Separate Opinion, Judge Jean-Pierre Cot concluded, inter alia, that a fraud had apparently been attempted to be perpetrated upon the Tribunal by counsel for St Vincent and the Grenadines. Noting the resemblance to the *Qatar v Bahrain* case and regretting the absence of a professional bar, Judge Cot concluded that the late production of the document had 'polluted the case'.

Besides the question of the appropriate standard of candour, another issue is the relevance of the ultimate factual veracity of the evidence. Should counsel be required to disclose suspicions of falsehood to the Court even where those suspicions ultimately prove to be unfounded? To invert the proposition, is it a good defence for counsel to assert that the evidence was substantively truthful to a charge of failure to disclose suspicions of falsehood? If the essence of the duty is procedural justice, then the conclusion must be that counsel must disclose where he has reasonable (that is, sustainable or substantial) suspicions of falsehood but that the ultimate veracity of the evidence is immaterial to the propriety of counsel's professional conduct. Furthermore, counsel is not a tribunal of fact: it is not for counsel to definitively determine the veracity of evidence but rather to assist the Court to do so. In performing that duty, it is not for counsel to suppress real doubts about the veracity of evidence and submit arguments that he reasonably believes may be false. In making those submissions, counsel assumes professional responsibility for them with potential consequences to his reputation for professional integrity and competence.

[128] *The M/V 'Louisa' Case*, Opinion individuelle de M. le juge Cot.

4.3.2.4 Documentary Evidence

Written pleadings are a crucial facet of the Court's procedure,[129] which correspondingly increases the importance of the veracity of documentary evidence. Following naturally from the general duty of candour, the role of counsel in undertaking a professional assessment of documentary evidence before the Court is critical. For example, an American counsel in *Behring Fur Seals* discovered forged translations with only a rudimentary knowledge of the Russian alphabet.[130] Thus, as intermediary between Court and client, counsel is well-placed to protect evidentiary integrity. Two problems in practice have been the suppression of adverse documents on false grounds and the submission of false documents.

Governments may attempt to abusively invoke 'executive privilege' to conceal documents adverse to their case.[131] In *Corfu Channel*, the 'XCU' Admiralty orders that arguably disproved the British argument of innocent passage were suppressed by the British legal team to the point of refusing to produce them on the ground of naval secrecy.[132] Professor Carty's study suggests that the documents had no information justifying secrecy and that the British advocates were principally motivated not from any genuine belief in the documents' military sensitivity but rather to suppress adverse documents in order to win the case.[133] A memorandum dated just days before the oral hearings from the Attorney General and leader of the British legal team (Sir Hartley Shawcross QC) to the Prime Minister (Clement Attlee, also a barrister) is telling:

> It is a fundamental principle of the practice of the Courts of our country and of the conduct of our legal profession that parties to litigation are not entitled to use merely those documents which they think will assist their case and to suppress others which are inimical to it. I must make it clear that neither the Solicitor General, nor myself, nor, I am sure, any of the other members of the Bar who are assisting us in this matter, would for a moment contemplate being parties to the course of conduct now forced upon us by the Admiralty's failure to procure and produce these documents earlier had our country's international position not been so gravely involved. As it is, we retain great misgiving about the propriety of what is being done, which we can only justify on the principle 'my country [...] right or wrong, my country'. We all feel that we must insist that circumstances such as these are not allowed to recur [...].[134]

It is difficult to resist the conclusion that the eminent counsel were knowing parties to misleading the Court, both concerning the reason for the refusal to disclose and

[129] Crawford, 'Advocacy Before the International Court of Justice and Other International Tribunals in State-to-State Cases', 304–5.

[130] Marston, 'Falsification of Documentary Evidence before International Tribunals: An Aspect of the *Behring Sea* Arbitration, 1892-3', 71 *BYIL* (2000), 357–73, 373.

[131] Teitelbaum, 'Recent Fact-Finding Developments at the International Court of Justice', 129–31.

[132] Carty, 'The Corfu Channel Case—and the Missing Admiralty Orders' (2004) 3 *LPICT* 1–35, 30–4. See further Keith, '"Naval Secrets", Public Interest Immunity and Open Justice' in Bannelier et al, *Due Diligence, Self-Help and the Rise of International Law*, 124–46.

[133] Carty, 'The Corfu Channel Case', 4, 12–13, 28–9.

[134] Carty, 'The Corfu Channel Case', 11.

the suppression of evidence. National ethics and discipline appear to have been completely ineffective.[135]

As discussed above, issues concerning the authenticity of documents arose in *Qatar v Bahrain* where Qatar adduced eighty-one 'historical documents' to its written pleadings in support of its claim to the Hawar Islands.[136] Expert analysis commissioned by Bahrain indicated that documents adduced by Qatar from its own archives were forged.[137] Qatar declined to elaborate upon the provenance of the documents, asserting only that they had been obtained through 'academic and private channels' and submitted in good faith.[138] Qatar's subsequent analysis also cast doubt on the documents' authenticity, following which it withdrew them.[139] Although the Court only referred to the issue in passing, Judge Fortier (seemingly adopting the words of Sir Elihu Lauterpacht QC, counsel for Bahrain[140]) in a separate opinion characterized Qatar's case as 'polluted' and 'infected' by the documents.[141]

Counsel for Qatar, numerous and from diverse national jurisdictions, have been described as 'seasoned, experienced, respectable... and very embarrassed'.[142] From the ethical perspective, the incident is troubling in two respects. The first is that documents of doubtful authenticity were adduced to the Court. The government of Qatar's unsubstantiated and vague explanation that it had acquired the documents from 'a number of sources... through official, academic and private channels... all over the world'[143] is circumstantially weak.[144] That these documents, which contained several obvious anomalies,[145] were submitted without detecting by Qatar's external counsel[146] appears not to be collusion but rather a

[135] Although the first English Code was not enacted until 1979, the Bar Council's published rulings clearly prohibited misleading the court—*Halsbury's Laws of England* (1953) (Vol III), 59 (paras 81, 88); *Halsbury's Laws of England* (1931) (Vol II), 510–33 (paras 692–725); *Annual Practice* (1941), 2761–71. However, no Attorney General had yet been subjected to the disciplinary jurisdiction of the Bar at that time—see Chapter 3.

[136] *Qatar v Bahrain*, Memorial of the Government of the State of Qatar (30 September 1996), 'Chapter V: The Territorial Integrity of Qatar and Qatar's Sovereignty over the Hawar Islands'; Counter-Memorial of the Government of the State of Qatar (31 December 1997), 1–3 (paras 1.2–1.8). See also the oral arguments of Sir Elihu Lauterpacht, counsel for Bahrain, Verbatim Record (8 June 2000), 11–15. See also the false documents incident in the Ir-USCT *Gabay* arbitration—Sarvarian, 'Problems of Professional Ethics for Representatives before ICSID Tribunals', 111–12.

[137] An account of the matter from the standpoint of Bahrain is given by Bahrain's Agent in the case. See al-Arayed, *A Line in the Sea* (2003), 355–93.

[138] Al-Arayed, *A Line in the Sea*, 388.

[139] Al-Arayed, *A Line in the Sea*, 389.

[140] Sir Elihu Lauterpacht, counsel for Bahrain, Verbatim Record (8 June 2000), 12 (para 8), 14 (para 14).

[141] Sir Elihu Lauterpacht, counsel for Bahrain, Verbatim Record (8 June 2000), 452 (para 4).

[142] Cot, 'Appearing "for" or "on behalf of" a State, 837.

[143] *Qatar v Bahrain*, 'Interim Report Submitted by the State of Qatar' (30 September 1998), para 14.

[144] Al-Arayed, *A Line in the Sea*, 356.

[145] Eg references to 'Her Majesty's Government' at a time when the British monarch was King George VI and a letter purportedly written by a ten-year-old official—Al-Arayed, *A Line in the Sea*, 358.

[146] For a list of counsel, see *Qatar v Bahrain*, 41–2.

failure to verify.[147] In ethical question is the standard of 'reasonable knowledge'[148] expected of counsel in a duty not to mislead the court. This would accord with the standard of diligence owed to clients to require counsel to take reasonable steps to confirm the authenticity of documents. Whilst counsel for Qatar may not have had access to the documents prior to submission,[149] had ethical standards existed the resulting prejudice sustained by the client would likely have raised questions about negligence.

4.3.2.5 Testimonial Evidence

Testimonial evidence has been relatively rare[150] but a difficult area for several reasons. First, the Court's procedural rules[151] concerning testimonial evidence are silent on important issues on the role of counsel like witness preparation, examination technique and extra-testimonial contact. Secondly, national standards diverge on these matters.[152] Thirdly, parties can appoint counsel inexpert in handling witnesses. Memory[153] is especially vulnerable to contamination so that robust procedural safeguards are necessary to protect evidentiary integrity. Problems arising from conflicting national standards on witness statements, contacts with witnesses and examination procedure were particularly acute in *Corfu Channel* but have also arisen in subsequent cases.[154] In recent cases (particularly *Bosnia Genocide*) the earlier problems have been somewhat ameliorated by the Court's adoption of common law procedures and parties' use of common lawyers to interrogate witnesses. Nevertheless, the lack of common ethical standards leaves scope for contamination of evidence through inappropriate procedures.

In *Corfu Channel*, the UK legal team were all members of the English Bar.[155] The first English Code of Conduct was not enacted until 1979, which expressly permitted barristers to accept 'foreign work' subject to local law and the Code.[156] In 1946, the Bar Council had not made a general ruling on barristers being extraterritorially bound by home ethics. However, the ruling of the Bar Council in 1946 prohibiting a barrister from representing an accused before the Nuremberg Tribunal implies the general applicability of the 'cab rank rule' and other ethical standards. Albania was represented by two diplomats, a French professor and three *avocats* of the Paris Order.[157] In 1948, the French Orders were in disarray following

[147] Mendelson, 'The Curious Case of *Qatar v. Bahrain* in the International Court of Justice', 72 *BYIL* (2001) 183–212, 211 (para 4). See, however, the author's disclaimers at 183 (note **) and 211 (note 70).

[148] Hague Principles, Principle 6.1.

[149] Pleadings are signed not by counsel but by agents—Bowett, 'The Conduct of International Litigation', 1–20, 12, 14, 17–18.

[150] Witnesses have been heard in ten contentious cases: *Corfu Channel (Merits)*; *Preah Vihear*, 8–9; *South West Africa*, 9–10; *Tunisia v Libya*, 25; *Gulf of Maine*, 256; *Libya v Malta*, 17–18; *Nicaragua*, 18; *ELSI*, 19; *El Salvador v Honduras*, 361; *Bosnia Genocide*, paras 58–59.

[151] Statute, Arts 43(5), 51; Rules, Arts 57, 58(2), 62–5.

[152] See Chapter 2.

[153] Eg Kirby, 'Witness Preparation: Memory and Storytelling', 28(4) *JIntA* (2011) 401–6.

[154] Rosenne, *The Law and Practice of the International Court 1920-2005*, 1305–21.

[155] *Corfu Channel (Merits)*, 5.

[156] English Code 1979, Annex 14.

[157] *Corfu Channel (Merits)*, 5.

the political splits of the 1930s and the Vichy era.[158] Although in Vichy France the Orders' personal jurisdiction over advocates was essentially retained,[159] the Orders' oversight may have been practically curtailed.

During the case, there was a clear conflict between French and English civil procedure and counsel ethics. In France, the interrogation of witnesses is principally a matter for the judge at a hearing (*enquête*).[160] Pre-testimonial contact with witnesses by advocates is forbidden and can even be a crime.[161] However, advocates may ask supplementary questions in the *enquête* to witnesses with relatively few technicalities.[162] This is attributable to the dominant role of the judge in the process of gathering evidence. By contrast, evidence-gathering within common law systems is formally[163] weighted towards the parties.[164] There are detailed legal and ethical rules concerning preparation of testimony[165] and myriad technicalities regarding interrogation technique.[166] Using *Corfu Channel* as the principal case study, six problems have arisen in practice from diverging national standards: (1) witness statements; (2) showing documents to witnesses; (3) impugning a witness' credibility; (4) limits to questioning; (5) communication with a witness; and (6) leading questions.

(a) Witness Statements

In *Corfu Channel*, Sir Hartley Shawcross objected to a witness on the ground that Albania had failed to provide a 'proof of evidence' and the witness might modify his testimony after hearing the opposing party's opening statement.[167] President José Gustavo Guerrero of El Salvador inquired whether Albania was able to supply 'un résumé de la deposition ... ainsi que le prévoit le Règlement.'[168] However, Professor Pierre Cot for Albania argued that Article 48 of the Rules required 'l'indication en termes généraux du ou des points sur lesquels doit porter la déposition' and that, '[c]onformément à nos habitudes françaises, nous sommes incapables de dire en quell sens ils déposeront.'[169] Following argument, the President ruled that Article 49 required only an enumeration of topics rather than a summary of testimony.[170]

[158] Ozanam, 'Histoire des avocats' in Beignier, Blanchard and Villacèque, *Droit et déontologie de la profession d'avocat* (2002), 19–26.

[159] Ozanam, 'Histoire des avocats', 17, 22, 27.

[160] Bishop and Kehoe, *The Art of Advocacy in International Arbitration*, 24–5, 511–12; Sandifer, *Evidence before International Tribunals* (1975), 288, 303–5. See also the French CPC, Arts 204–31.

[161] French CPC, Arts 132–142.

[162] French CPC, Art 214.

[163] *Confer* English CPR, r 32.1.

[164] *Halsbury's Laws of England* (2009) (Vol 11), paras 1037, 1046.

[165] English CPR, r 33.2 *et seq*; *Halsbury's Laws* (2009) (Vol 66), paras 1207 (notes 1 and 4), 1208, 1209 (note 4).

[166] *Halsbury's Laws* (Vol 11), paras 1037–49; (2006) (Vol 11(3)), paras 1433–43.

[167] *Corfu Channel (Merits)*, Vol III, 245–7.

[168] *Corfu Channel (Merits)*, Vol III, 246.

[169] *Corfu Channel (Merits)*, Vol III, 246.

[170] *Corfu Channel (Merits)*, Vol III, 247–8.

There was clearly a conflict between diverging national standards. English civil procedure demands early disclosure of the *substance* of testimony to preclude witnesses from manipulating their evidence to suit a party's case. French civil procedure requires advocates to refrain from preparing testimony to preclude manipulation by counsel.[171] The procedure under Article 48 (now Article 57) of the Rules was too vague to resolve this conflict. Witness statements were in general use in *Bosnia Genocide*,[172] which is logical in light of the Court's general dependence upon parties to adduce evidence due to remoteness and lack of coercive powers.[173] However, the danger that counsel may influence testimony is a real one and should be addressed by ethical standards governing the preparation of witness statements.

(b) Showing Documents to Witnesses

In *Corfu Channel*, the President's initial direction explained the order of questioning with a 'very liberal' procedure and no limit to questioning.[174] This direction was consistent with the laissez-faire PCIJ procedure and the President's background as a career diplomat and academic from a civil law jurisdiction who was the last PCIJ President.[175] However, it soon proved inadequate to deal with a variety of procedural issues. The use of documents was an especially protracted and difficult problem. As noted above, compounding this was the disparity between the legal teams.

In Professor Cot's cross-examination of Commander Kovavic, he presented a photostatic copy to the witness. Sir Frank Soskice objected on the ground that, under English procedure, 'one cannot produce a copy of a document unless one can account for the fact that the original is not being produced.'[176] Following debate, the Court directed the parties to adduce only original documents.[177] However, the documents issue was revisited several times with British objections[178] and Professor Cot apologizing for his unfamiliarity with the procedure.[179] The need for rigour to ensure the veracity of testimony was underlined by a challenged copy used by Albania in cross-examination.[180] Counsel argued the issues from their own national perspectives.[181] The President had to reprimand counsel for 'breach of discipline'.[182]

[171] French CPC, Art 214. The author has regrettably been unable to consult the French CPC in force in 1946 but it is presumed that an equivalent provision existed.

[172] *Bosnia Genocide*, Verbatim Record (17 March 2006), 10.

[173] Eg subpoena or perjury powers—Rosenne, *The Law and Practice of the International Court 1920-2004* (Vol III), 1308–9.

[174] *Corfu Channel (Merits)*, Vol III, 428–9.

[175] 'Biografiá del Dr. José Gustavo Guerrero', online: <http://ieesford.rree.gob.sv/index.php?option=com_content&view=article&id=26&Itemid=82&limitstart=1> (Accessed: 10 March 2011).

[176] *Corfu Channel (Merits)*, Vol III, 539.

[177] *Corfu Channel (Merits)*, Vol III, 541–2, 545.

[178] *Corfu Channel (Merits)*, Vol III, 553–5, 560–4, 568–70; *Corfu Channel (Merits)*, Vol IV, 303–14.

[179] *Corfu Channel (Merits)*, Vol III, 560, 563. Professor Cot had not practised as an *avocat* for many years, was not an international law specialist and did not have the benefit of an extensive support team—see Cot, note 57.

[180] *Corfu Channel (Merits)*, Vol III, 568–70.

[181] Eg *Corfu Channel (Merits)*, Vol IV, 314, 578.

[182] *Corfu Channel (Merits)*, Vol IV, 316. Counsel apologized the next day—*Corfu Channel (Merits)*, Vol III, 188.

(c) Impugning the Credibility of a Witness

During cross-examination, Professor Cot commented that 'I thought I heard the witness state on a former occasion that he understood French and English, but I see that he understand both languages only for the examination and not for the cross-examination.'[183] Sir Frank objected:

> Mr. President, while that document is being fetched—of course I will not attempt to copy M. Pierre Cot in making that kind of observation about the witness, which we, at any rate, in our Courts, and I hope that you in this Court would regard as offensive and unnecessary, but that is entirely of course a matter for his judgment and for his taste.[184]

This exchange[185] illustrates another conflict between diverging standards whereby English barristers must refrain from gratuitously insulting a witness or from impugning his credibility without reasonable grounds[186] whereas French *avocats* are not so bound. In this instance, the former standard[187] would appear to be more appropriate for decorum and the burden of proof.

(d) Communication with a Witness under Solemn Declaration

Sir Frank, in applying to recall a witness, made the following declaration:

> Now I want to be perfectly frank with the Court and say that after Commander Kovavic finished his evidence yesterday I personally spoke to him. *Ordinarily, of course, one does not speak to a witness under examination.* The Court may say that in those circumstances they will not allow him to be recalled any further, but I should like the Court to know that I spoke to him about that... [n]eedless to say, I have not told him what I want him to say; that goes without saying. Ordinarily, of course, I would not have spoken to him when under examination, *but yesterday his evidence was concluded.* However, on speaking to him I find there is a little further evidence on that point which I would be very grateful to be allowed to place before the Court.[188]

Although neither Professor Cot nor the Court made objection to the application to recall the witness,[189] the statement is noteworthy for two reasons. First, Sir Frank impliedly felt himself to be obliged by English standards which generally prohibit a barrister from communicating with a witness until his evidence has been concluded.[190] Secondly, it illustrates the danger that may arise in an ethical vacuum wherein a non-professional advocate may influence or appear to influence a witness' evidence. For example, during a lunch break an advocate may ask a witness one-on-one whether he enjoyed his meal which, from afar, could appear to be a conversation about the testimony. This danger accordingly demands ethical

[183] *Corfu Channel (Merits)*, Vol IV, 578–9.
[184] *Corfu Channel (Merits)*, Vol IV, 578–9.
[185] See also *Corfu Channel (Merits)*, Vol IV, 573, 600–1, 672–6.
[186] Boulton, *A Guide to Conduct and Etiquette at the Bar of England and Wales* (1953), 59.
[187] *Confer* Hague Principles, Principle 7.1.
[188] *Corfu Channel (Merits)*, Vol IV, 665 (emphasis added).
[189] *Corfu Channel (Merits)*, Vol IV, 666.
[190] *Annual Practice* (1941), 2771.

rules prohibiting such contacts unless authorized by the Court or in the presence of opposing counsel.

(e) Leading Questions

Sir Frank objected to certain questions put by Professor Cot as 'leading':[191]

> ... it is of little assistance to the Court if the advocate examining him tells him in the form of his question almost exactly that which he wants him to say. I quite accept that it is not always practicable to avoid doing so. One has, to a certain extent, to indicate the type of answer which one is endeavouring to elicit, and I have not raised any complaint against Professor Cot doing so. I do, however, respectfully submit that there is a limit beyond which Professor Cot should not go ... I simply make the comment because I do respectfully submit that either he should not do it, or, if he does, it should be recognized that the answer he elicits, it being such a very leading question, really can be of very little value as evidence, because in effect it is Professor Cot giving the evidence and not the witness.[192]

After Professor Cot apologized and rephrased,[193] the President declared: 'The Court, in assessing the evidence given by witnesses, will bear in mind the method employed, and therefore the Agents need have no fear that any method employed will prejudice the Court one way or the other in reaching its decision.'[194] This disregarded the prejudice of leading questions whereby counsel can influence testimony.

In *Preah Vihear*, the President was Judge Winiarski of Poland and the legal teams had a mixture of French academics and Belgian, Thai, American, and English practitioners. During examination-in-chief of the former governor of Kompong Thom[195] (a Cambodian province) Professor Roger Pinto of the University of Paris asked the witness: '[l]e temple de Préah Vihéar est-il situé dans la province de Kompong Thom?'[196] Sir Frank objected for leading. Professor Pinto re-phrased: 'S[s]avez vous, M. le gourverneur, dans quelle circonscription administrative du Cambodge est situé le temple de Préah Vihéar?' The ensuing exchange is revealing:

> [T]he whole issue in the case ... is whether or not Preah Vihear is in Cambodia. The question was whether the witness knew in what district of Cambodia Preah Vihear was. He therefore puts to the witness the whole issue in the case. I say it was not in Cambodia at all. I respectfully submit that there is a plain case of a leading question and ask that it should be withdrawn.
>
> LE PRÉSIDENT: Je crois que la règle que sir Frank Soskice vient de formuler comme une règle anglo-saxonne ou anglaise n'est pas particulière au Royaume-Uni, aux pays anglo-saxons, c'est une règle générale, mais d'autre part, il est difficile de voir ici une question qui suggère qoi que ce soit au témoin ...

[191] Being those which 'suggests the answer which the questioner wishes to receive or which suggests the existence of disputed facts to which the witness has not already testified'—Stephen, *Digest of the Law of Evidence* (1936) in *Halsbury's Laws* (2006), para 1434.

[192] *Corfu Channel (Merits)*, Vol IV, 256.

[193] *Corfu Channel (Merits)*, Vol IV, 256–7.

[194] *Corfu Channel (Merits)*, Vol IV, 258.

[195] *Preah Vihear*, Vol II, 331.

[196] *Preah Vihear*, Vol II, 332.

SIR FRANK SOSKICE: Mr. President… to ask the witness in what province of Cambodia Preah Vihear is, in my submission, clearly offends against the rule. If Professor Pinto cannot put his question in a different form which does not offend against the rule, I would respectfully ask that the Court should say he must not ask the question at all.

M. ROGER PINTO: Monsieur le Président, je vais essayer, malgré le manqué d'habitude des jurisdictions anglo-saxonnes, mais avec l'aide de la delegation thailandaise, de formuler la question d'une façon qui puisse paraître satisfaisante à mon eminent confrere. Et, Monsieur le Gouverneur, je vous demanderai simplement ceci: dans quelle province du Cambodge croyez-vous que se trouve situé le temple de Préah Vihear?

LE PRÉSIDENT: Voulez-vous répondre à cette question?

M. SUON BONN: Je ne crois pas, mais il est incontestable que Préah Vihéar se trouve dans le district de Cheom Ksan qui est du resort de la province de Kompong Thom.[197]

The witness' answer demonstrates the wisdom of the rule against leading because the witness, having heard two leading questions by counsel for Cambodia, knew the answer that counsel wished to elicit and gave a highly biased answer to a third formulation that was *still* leading.

Leading was also problematic in *South West Africa* with frequent objections by counsel.[198] One exchange is revealing:

MR. GROSS: May I be permitted to be heard? Mr. President, it will be apparent that in this Court rules of procedure and of evidence are not as easy to come by as in municipal courts; the line that is sought to be drawn between cross-examination, objection and comment will therefore present serious difficulties which may be prejudicial to the Applicants…

THE PRESIDENT: Mr. Gross, the procedure before this Court is not greatly different from any other court. The counsel will direct questions to the witness; either their question is a leading question, in which event objection can be taken to the question, or the answer of the witness is not responsive to the question which is put, in which event again objection can be taken to it.[199]

Although the President was Australian and both parties' legal teams were South African and American practitioners,[200] the terseness and opaqueness of the Rules on nuanced procedural matters caused confusion. National standards on issues like combativeness towards witnesses diverged. Despite the President's activism, he was ultimately unwilling to forbid questions.[201]

The need for common ethical standards to protect the integrity of testimonial evidence and clarify procedure is evident. Although the Court was unwilling to prescribe uniform rules for counsel from mixed cultures it was unable to avoid the resulting delay, confusion and even acrimony. Perhaps due to those experiences, testimonial evidence has remained rare even though common law

[197] *Preah Vihear*, Vol II, 332–3 (emphases added).

[198] *South West Africa*, Vol X, 26, 44, 107–8, 172, 175, 340–2, 345, 348–9, 455, 511–13, 515–16; Vol XI, 660–1, 693.

[199] *South West Africa*, Vol X, 122–3.

[200] *South West Africa*, Judgment, 7–8.

[201] *South West* Africa, Vol XII, 13.

procedures have been used from *Preah Vihear* onwards.[202] In *Bosnia Genocide*, the Court heard nine witnesses over six days under a more rigorous regime than in *Corfu Channel* (where one of the witnesses needed three days). President Higgins adopted common law procedures[203] with rules on timing, referencing, witness statements, and leading.[204]

4.4 Disciplinary Jurisdiction

There exist no prescribed disciplinary powers for the Court. As discussed in Chapter 9, the two potential bases are an implied power under Article 30(1) of the Statute or an inherent jurisdiction. Since exclusion from proceedings is a severe form of sanction, it may be posited that more moderate sanctions such as public admonishment, fines, suspension from proceedings and reporting to national bar authorities would also be available to the Court. Clearly, the authority of common ethical standards depends upon their being backed by a disciplinary jurisdiction. However, a fair and carefully constructed framework incorporating natural justice principles is required to ensure that such powers are exercised wisely. Counsel should have a right to a fair hearing before the Court with, *inter alia*, a right to be heard, to be represented by counsel, and to appeal. Sanctions should be proportionate and the disciplinary judge(s) should have expertise in professional ethics.[205]

There is no reason why such a framework cannot be created with a disciplinary chamber to investigate complaints against counsel. Although *ex post facto* application of ethical rules can be safely done with flagrant examples of dishonesty or incompetence, this would be controversial regarding nuanced issues. As previously suggested, a way for the Court to achieve compromise between conservative and progressive schools of thought would be to require counsel to sign and deposit a copy of a code of conduct at the commencement of proceedings. By putting counsel on notice of the standards of conduct expected of them, this would not only act as a deterrent upon flagrant misconduct and a clarification of the nicer issues but would also provide tribunals with a textual basis for the imposition of sanctions. Counsel would not be in a position to complain of lack of notice.

[202] Eg *Tunisia v Libya*, Vol V, 182–98; *Libya v Malta*, Vol IV, 199–282; *El Salvador v Honduras*, Verbatim Record (29 May 1991), 10–49. However, in *Nicaragua* the agent for the Applicant (a diplomat) conducted an examination-in-chief and asked several leading questions without objection—Vol V, 93–8.

[203] *Bosnia Genocide*, Verbatim Record (17 March 2006), 10–11.

[204] *Bosnia Genocide*, Verbatim Record (17 March 2006), 30, 61–2; (20 March 2006), 25, 32–3, 43; (23 March 2006), 22–3; (24 March 2006), 12–3, 48–9; (27 March 2006, CR 2006/7), 24, 26.

[205] See Chapter 7.

4.5 Conclusions

This chapter has shown that problems caused by divergent ethical standards have occurred on several occasions in practice. The laissez-faire PCIJ culture has proved increasingly inadequate to meet these challenges. The history of the ICJ Rules 1972 and the ICJ Practice Directions suggests that States, far from opposing greater regulation of their case presentation, have welcomed it in the interests of efficiency and rigour. Under President Higgins, the Court had a greater confidence in issuing directions to counsel (eg *Bosnia Genocide*). There exists momentum for the prescription of admission requirements, common ethical standards, and disciplinary jurisdiction as another step to promote that efficiency and rigour.

Complaints regarding the succinctness of pleadings continue due to parties' control over pleadings, the Court's unwillingness to direct them with greater firmness and certain advocates' loquacity. Parties' ability to manipulate the use of experts by appointing them as 'technical counsel' detracts from the Court's ability to assess evidence. The absence of admission requirements—allowing agents, government officials, experts or anyone else to conduct forensic advocacy—restricts counsel's independence and creates unnecessary and dangerous conflicts of interest. Certain cases seemingly saw abuses such as manifestly inarguable applications or claims, the suppression of evidence, the submission of false evidence and ex parte communications with judges. More commonly, cases have seen questionable practices like leading, inappropriate contacts with witnesses and references to counsel's personal knowledge that did not result in serious incidents but could have done so in different circumstances. In any event, such practices are both detrimental to the Court's procedural integrity and image as well as avoidable through the professionalization of advocacy.

The beginnings of a movement towards a professional bar at the Court in order to address such issues can be seen. Although warnings about the resistance of States towards encroachment upon their traditional prerogatives in ICJ litigation are still made, the progressive view that the Court is politically and institutionally prepared to advance to a higher level of procedural maturity appears to be increasingly persuasive. If government officials were prepared during the Court's post-*South West Africa* nadir to sacrifice traditional prerogatives to redress inefficient practices which those privileges had caused, it would seem unlikely that they would resist reforms during the busiest period in the Court's history. The case for the professionalization of advocacy is persuasive from the practical and the political perspectives.

If one accepts that reforms for advocates and case presentation are desirable, how then should they be implemented? One possibility is for the Court to do so, as it is well-placed to regulate advocates due to its broad power to prescribe procedural rules compatible with its Statute.[206] As explained above, the Court cannot exclude

[206] Zimmerman et al, *The Statute of the International Court of Justice: A Commentary*, 481–93.

agents from forensic advocacy without amendment of Article 42 of the Statute. In opposition, it is argued that the Court ought not to potentially antagonize litigants by constraining their ability to control their advocates. Treating States who have submitted their dispute to the Court for resolution as 'litigants' rather than as 'sovereigns' is compelling. Practically, the Court would appear to be best-placed to create a professional bar through admission and ethical requirements. However, should the Court decline to do so, advocates could themselves seek through the aura of professionalism to establish its authority over advocacy.[207]

[207] This was how the English and Massachusetts bars came into existence—see Chapter 2.

5

The European Court of Justice[1]

If the ethical framework of the ICJ concerning advocates exemplifies a 'diplomatic tradition' of laissez-faire regulation, that of European Court of Justice (ECJ) appears at first sight to be considerably more stringent. Unlike the ICJ, it has prescribed admission requirements for representatives of individual litigants as well as disciplinary powers for professional misconduct. The requirement that advocates be members of national bars seemingly ensures that they be subject to professional ethics and discipline for their conduct before the European Courts. These requirements and powers are rare amongst 'civil' international courts and tribunals.

However, on closer inspection, the Courts' regulation of advocates is superficial. The lack of admission requirements, common ethical standards, and disciplinary powers in ICJ proceedings is replicated before the European Courts. The requirement that advocates be 'members of national bars' applies only to *individual* litigants' representatives; States and EU organs, by contrast, continue to be privileged in their right to be represented by agents who are insulated from the Courts' oversight. Thus, two sets of representation requirements result. The EU Courts have yet to exercise their disciplinary powers, at least in part due to the lack of common ethical standards against which to judge advocates' professional conduct.

Nevertheless, such ethical problems as have arisen in practice have been rare and largely isolated. This lack of practice is attributable to the narrow, review-based jurisdiction of the ECJ in which matters of fact and evidence are largely absent so that the role of counsel and scope for professional misconduct is accordingly diminished. For historical reasons, there is also a greater degree of procedural homogeneity before the Court due to the influence of the 'original Six' founding members of the European Coal and Steel Community (ECSC). The smallness of the de facto bar of regular practitioners also ensures a degree of uniformity of standards. Although expansion to 27 Member States may challenge this homogeneity, hitherto there have been no serious cases reported in which professional misconduct has featured heavily.

However, this is not to suggest that ethics have no practical relevance before the Court. This relaxed regulation of counsel creates certain dangers, several of which have emerged (albeit rarely) in practice. First, the lack of common ethical

[1] This chapter includes previously published material in the following article: Sarvarian, 'Common Ethical Standards for Counsel before the European Court of Justice and European Court of Human Rights', 23(4) EJIL (2012), 991–1014.

standards creates the potential for conflicting national and personal standards concerning fundamental principles of professional conduct. Secondly, a weak regulatory regime creates gaps into which unscrupulous advocates may indulge in abusive conduct and thereby threaten the integrity of judicial proceedings with potentially serious implications for fair trial and equality of arms. Indeed, it is possible that such misconduct has gone undetected in the past 50 years of practice. Thirdly, the bifurcation of regulation of States as opposed to that of individuals creates the potential for agents to behave abusively without the threat of sanction by the Courts. Fourthly, although the Courts both have prescribed disciplinary powers to sanction misconduct the lack of prescribed codes of conduct containing clear and stringent ethical rules deprives all concerned of prior notice of the precise *standards* of conduct expected of counsel. If and when ethical problems do arise in proceedings, the EU Courts would be able to address them within a prescribed framework. For these reasons, it is recommended that the ECJ prescribe a code of conduct for counsel in order to fill a procedural lacuna.

5.1 Historical Background[2]

The ECJ was created in 1952 by the ECSC Protocol as the judicial institution of the ECSC annexed to the Treaty of Paris 1951.[3] In 1958, the current ECJ Statute was annexed to the Treaty of Rome 1957 and is the Court's current statute. The ECSC Rules[4] were 'inspired by' the ICJ Rules and national administrative and civil codes.[5] Unfortunately, the *travaux préparatoires* to both the Statute and Rules remain unavailable for research.[6]

The admission requirements imposed by Article 20 of the ECSC Protocol were historic, in that they marked the first time that litigants' discretion to appoint counsel was fettered before an international court. Contemporary works by treaty protagonists,[7] judges, advocates-general, and registrars[8] as well as other

[2] Mackenzie et al, *The Manual on International Courts and Tribunals* (2010), 278–333.

[3] Paris Treaty, Arts 7, 31.

[4] Delvaux, *La Cour de Justice de la Communauté Européenne du Charbon et de l'Acier* (1956), 251–313.

[5] Delvaux, *La Cour de Justice de la Communauté Européenne du Charbon et de l'Acier*, 45–6. See also Riese 'Die Verfahrensordnung des Gerichtshofes der Europäischen Gemeinschaft für Kohle und Stahl', 6 *NJW* (1953), 521–5, 521.

[6] A limited source is Schulze and Hoeren, *Dokumente zum Europaischen Recht Bandz Justiz (bis 1957)* (2000). Neither the ECJ Library, *Fondation Jean Monnet Pour l'Europe*, nor the EU University Institute in Florence hold the *travaux* to the ECSC Protocol.

[7] Reuter, 'Le Plan Schuman', 81 *RdC* (1952-II) 523–628, 559–71; Reuter, *La Communauté Européenne du Charbon et de l'Acier* (1953), 66; Schuman, *Pour l'Europe* (1963), 151–76; Monnet, *Mémoires* (1976), 318–35.

[8] Delvaux, *La Cour de Justice de la Communauté Européenne du Charbon et de l'Acier*; van Houtte, 'La Cour de Justice de la Communauté Européenne du Charbon et de l'Acier', II *Annuaire Européen* (1956), 183–222; Lagrange, 'La Cour de Justice de la Communauté Européenne du Charbon et de l'Acier', 70 *RDP* (1954), 417–35, 433; Lagrange, 'La Cour de Justice des Communautés Européennes: du Plan Schuman à l'union Européenne' *RTDE* (1978), 2–17.

commentators[9] do not explain why the drafters opted to depart from the settled policy of the ICJ permitting litigants absolute control over their representation. However, since Professor André Gros, *jurisconsult* of the French delegation,[10] almost certainly was involved in drafting the Protocol and was also a delegate to the London Conference that created the Nuremberg Charter—the first 'international' tribunal to impose admission requirements for counsel—it may be speculated that an indirect link existed.[11]

Moreover, Article 6 of the ECSC 'Supplementary Rules of Procedure Concerning the Rights and Obligations of Agents and Advocates, etc.' prescribed the first-ever disciplinary power of an international court to exclude agents and advocates from proceedings for 'behaviour incompatible with the dignity of the Court'.[12] Publications by the Court protagonists of the day merely describe the existence of the powers without explaining the reasons for their creation.[13] Without the *travaux* to the Supplementary Rules or other explanatory material, one might tentatively speculate that they were prescribed to generally strengthen the Court's control over its procedural integrity and thereby promote its image as a sophisticated judicial institution. Article 6 of the Supplementary Rules is retained as Article 35(1) of the current ECJ Rules of Procedure.

In 1957, when the Court became the shared judicial institution of the three Communities, its Statute was substantively renegotiated. Whilst the ECSC Court of Justice was vested with the power to frame its own rules of procedure,[14] the EEC Treaty required the ECJ to obtain the approval of the EU Council.[15] Uniquely amongst the courts and tribunals examined by this work, the Court still lacks exclusive control over its own Rules.[16] This arrangement is understandably unpopular with the Court.[17] Although the Court has the right to request amendment of its Statute or be consulted, its consent is not required.[18] The Court's control over its own procedure is consequently limited due to the oversight of the Council.

[9] Antoine, 'La Cour de Justice de la C.E.C.A. et la Cour internationale de Justice', 57(3) *RGDIP* (1953) 210–61, 221, 252–3; Jeantet, 'Les intérêts privés devant la Cour de Justice de la Communauté Européenne du Charbon et de l'Acier', 70 *RDP* (1954), 684–713, 709; Valentine, *The Court of Justice of the European Coal and Steel Community* (1955), 149–51; Robertson, 'Legal Problems of European Integration', 91(I) *RdC* (1957) 105–211, 149–53; Van Reepinghen and Orianne, *La procedure devant la Cour de justice des communautés européennes* (1961), 26–7.

[10] 'List of the delegations to the Paris Conference on the Schuman Plan (20 June 1950)', online: <http://www.ena.lu> (Accessed: 9 February 2011).

[11] Circumstantial support for this hypothesis may be found in a textual comparison between the French versions of Art 23 of the Nuremberg Charter ('Les fonctions de défenseur peuvent être remplies... par tout *avocat régulièrement qualifié pour plaider dans son propre pays...*') and Art 20 ECSC Protocol ('assistées par un avocat *inscrit à un barreau* de l'un des États membres').

[12] ECSC Protocol, Art 20; Delvaux, *La Cour de Justice de la Communauté Européenne du Charbon et de l'Acier*, 310.

[13] Delvaux, *La Cour de Justice de la Communauté Européenne du Charbon et de l'Acier*, 50–1; Riese, 'Die Verfahrensordnung des Gerichtshofes der Europäischen Gemeinschaft für Kohle und Stahl'.

[14] Paris Treaty, Art 44. [15] Rome Treaty, Art 188. [16] Lisbon Treaty, Art 253.

[17] Rodríguez Iglesias, 'Réformer la Cour de justice européenne', *Le Monde* (28 April 2000).

[18] Lisbon Treaty, Art 281.

Several works in French and English discussing the Court's procedure or advocacy before the Court only briefly describe the admission requirements, privileges, immunities and disciplinary powers concerning advocates and do not discuss the subject of professional ethics.[19] Brown and Kennedy observe:

> Rules governing lawyers' professional ethics ... vary widely between Member States. Moreover, apart from the notes for the guidance of counsel for the parties at the hearing, which are intended to ensure the efficient management of court business, there are no common rules governing the conduct of lawyers before the Court of Justice and the Court of First Instance and it would be invidious for the Court of Justice to attempt such a labour of Sisyphus.[20]

Similarly, Anderson writes:

> ... there is no code of conduct for lawyers practising before the European Court, whether in preliminary reference cases or direct actions. The construction of such a code might have advantages but it would be a formidable task, bearing in mind the very different traditions from which European advocates, procurators and legal advisers have evolved.[21]

Whilst it seems surprising that the subject should not have been comprehensively discussed in more than half a century of practice, this may be partially explained by the fact that the Court has never formally invoked its disciplinary powers for professional misconduct.[22] The absence of practice is also attributable to the rarity of serious misbehaviour.[23]

In considering the ECJ, it is important to bear a number of considerations in mind. The first is language. Uniquely amongst the courts that this work examines, the ECJ is not confined to one or two official languages. The only authentic language of the ECSC Protocol and Rules of Procedure was French,[24] though the four languages of 'the original Six' founding members (French, German, Dutch, and Italian) were adopted as the official languages of the Court.[25] However, these were adopted as the authentic languages of the ECJ Statute in 1957.[26] The English

[19] Valentine, *The Court of Justice of the European Communities* (Vol I: Jurisdiction and Procedure) (1965), 47–50; Toth, *Legal Protection of Individuals in the European Communities* (Vol II: Remedies and Procedures) (1978), 11–12; Usher, *European Court Practice* (1983), 113–17, 220–3; Philip, *La Cour de Justice des Communautés Européennes* (1983), 12; Lasok, *European Court of Justice: Practice and Procedure* (1984), 66–88; Darmon, 'L'avocat devant la Cour de Justice des Communautres Européennes' in Schaffer, *L'avocat et l'Europe des 12 et des 21* (1988), 177–84; Yaqub, 'Lawyers in the European Transnational Courts' in Tyrrell and Yaqub, *The Legal Professions in the New Europe* (1996), 33–62; Chavrier, 'L'avocat devant les jurisdictions européennes', 52 *L'observateur de Bruxelles* (2003), 21–31; Mouton and Soulard, *La Cour de justice des Communautés Européennes* (2004), 63–4; Boudant, *La Cour de justice des Communautés Européennes* (2005), 48. Others do not mention representational requirements at all, eg Wall, *The Court of Justice of the European Communities: Jurisdiction and Procedure* (1966), 209–70; Vaughan and Grey, 'Litigating in Luxembourg and the Role of the Advocate at the Court of Justice' in Arnull et al, *Continuity and Change in EU Law: Essays in Honour of Sir Francis Jacobs* (2008), 48–69, 51–4.

[20] Brown and Kennedy, *The Court of Justice of the European Communities* (2000), 302–3.

[21] Anderson and Demetriou, *References to the European Court* (2002), 252–3 (9-051).

[22] Letter from the Registrar (22 October 2009), on file with the author.

[23] Telephone interview with Mr David Vaughan QC (22 July 2010) cited with permission.

[24] Paris Treaty, Art 100.

[25] ECSC Rules, Art 27(1).

[26] Rome Treaty, Art 248.

versions of the Statute and Rules are translations done upon the accessions of the UK and Ireland in 1973.

In examining the evolution of the Court's Statute and Rules, it is consequently necessary to do so in French—as the sole continuously authentic tongue—and to recall that the English version, as a translation, necessarily cannot always provide a perfect reflection of the originally intended meaning. The same precaution should be extended to the jurisprudence of the Court, as the official language of a given case may in principle be any one of the (currently 23) official EU languages.[27] In interpreting the Court's jurisprudence concerning the relevant provisions, it is important to compare the official language of the *case* with the translation into one of the original languages.

The second factor is the functional and structural differences of the various legal professions of the national systems. For example, the functional purpose of an *avocat* within Article 19 of the Statute takes concrete form once the original, national role of *avocats* is considered to contextualize the meaning of the term. Thus, the purely linguistic differences should be overlaid with the architectural distinctions between legal systems—particularly those between the common law and civil law jurisdictions. In this way, potential causes of confusion arising from the evolution of the texts may be dispelled.

The third factor is the Court's intricate jurisdiction, which has great ramifications for its procedure—in particular, it is directly responsible for the comparative rarity of factual issues—and, thus, evidence—in its proceedings. There are two main categories of proceedings: (1) direct actions; and (2) preliminary references concerning points of EU law from national jurisdictions.[28] Direct actions are subdivided into two categories: (1) actions brought between 'privileged parties'; and (2) actions brought by individuals against institutions. A particular point to note is that the Statute only prescribes procedure for the former category; the Rules, supplementing the Statute, address the latter.[29] Since 'staff cases' are now delegated to the EU Civil Service Tribunal[30] factual issues are now rare in judicial review actions brought by individuals against institutions because the Court relies upon national courts in preliminary reference cases for factual assessment.[31] This restricts the role of counsel before the Court and thus the scope for professional misconduct.

5.2 Admission Requirements

Representation of litigants before the Court is governed by Article 19 of the Statute, supplemented by Article 104(2) of the Rules. In order to fully explain the

[27] ECJ Rules, Art 29(1). [28] Lisbon Treaty, Arts 263, 267–8, 270.

[29] ECJ Statute, Art 63; ECJ Rules, Art 104.

[30] Lisbon Treaty, Art 257; 2004 Decision.

[31] However, reassessment of factual matters is possible—Interview with President Eric Jaeger, Judge Nicholas Forwood, and Registrar Emmanuel Coulon (14 October 2010), cited with permission.

admission requirements, it is necessary to compare the various linguistic versions. Article 20 of the ECSC Statute originally provided:

Les États ainsi que les institutions de la Communauté sont représentés devant la Cour par des agents nommés pour chaque affaire; l'agent peut être assisté d'un avocat inscrit à un barreau de l'un des États membres.

Les entreprises et toutes autres personnes physiques ou morales doivent être assistées par un avocat inscrit à un barreau de l'un des États membres.

[. . .]

La Cour jouit à l'égard des avocats qui se présentent devant elle des pouvoirs normalement reconnus en la matière aux cours et tribunaux, dans des conditions qui seront déterminées par le même règlement.

Les professeurs ressortissants des Etats membres dont la législation leur reconnaît un droit de plaider jouissent devant la Cour des droits reconnus aux avocats par le présent article.

Article 17 of the ECJ Statute 1957 was formulated in almost identical terms. Although mostly the same, Article 19 of the current Statute differs in two parts:

Les États membres ainsi que les institutions de l'Union sont représentés devant la Cour de justice par un agent nommé pour chaque affaire; l'agent peut être assisté d'un conseil ou d'un avocat. [. . .]

Les autres parties doivent être représentées par un avocat.

Seul un avocat habilité à exercer devant une jurisdiction d'un État membre ou d'un autre État partie à l'accord sur l'Espace économique européen peut représenter ou assister une partie devant la Cour.

The English version states:

'The Member States and the institutions of the Union shall be represented before the Court of justice by an agent appointed for each case; the agent may be assisted by an adviser or by a lawyer.

[. . .]

Other parties must be represented by a lawyer.

Only a lawyer authorised to practise before a court of a Member State . . . may represent or assist a party before the Court.

[. . .]

As regards such advisers and lawyers who appear before it, the Court shall have the powers normally accorded to courts of law, under conditions laid down in the Rules of Procedure.

University teachers being nationals of a Member State whose law accords them a right of audience shall have the same rights before the Court as are accorded by this Article to lawyers.

Article 17 applies in essentially identical terms at the General Court, the specialised courts and Court of Justice of the European Free Trade Association States (EFTA).[32]

[32] Statute of the EFTA Court, Art 36.

5.2.1 Agents

The first observation is that there exists a bifurcation of representational requirements for States and EU organs ('privileged litigants') on the one hand and for individuals and companies ('unprivileged litigants') on the other hand. Although all litigants' *advocates* are subject to the same admission requirements, States and institutions are permitted to appoint agents who are not subject to such requirements. The language of the provision, coupled with the fact that the ECSC Court's procedure was largely 'inspired' by the ICJ,[33] renders it likely that the rule on State representation derives from the ICJ Statute.[34]

The reason for this dichotomy stems from the functional role of the *avocat* in civil law systems as an *agent* empowered to perform acts of procedure in civil proceedings. Privileged litigants are required to be 'represented' (*répresenté*) by agents whereas 'counsel or advocates' merely 'assist' (*assisté*). As before the ICJ, counsel consequently do not bear personal responsibility for the procedural actions of the privileged litigants whom they 'assist'.[35] The requirement that unprivileged litigants be 'represented' by an *avocat* derives from the ban upon self-represented litigants within certain civil law jurisdictions. An *avocat*, by virtue of that title, is empowered under French law (to take one example) to perform administrative acts of procedure for his client.[36] Thus, the requirement that unprivileged litigants be represented by an *avocat* was occasioned by the need to create a counterpart to the procedural role of the agent as well as the prohibition upon self-representation within certain national jurisdictions.

Although agents are in principle not required to have any legal expertise, in practice they are usually employed government lawyers.[37] As before the ICJ, sometimes 'experts' are appointed.[38] Whilst there does not appear to generally be any great harm in practice from the use of agency,[39] it is suggested that the ideal procedure would require all parties to the litigation to be represented by professional counsel who are subject to common admission requirements, ethical standards, and disciplinary rules. However, this would be unlikely to be approved by the Parliament and especially the Council which, as privileged litigants, benefit from the status quo.

In this respect, the author is aware on a confidential basis that when the new Civil Service Tribunal wrote its Rules of Procedure, it wished to include agents within the scope of its disciplinary powers.[40] It was required as part of the process

[33] Antoine, 'La Cour de Justice de la C.E.C.A. et la Cour internationale de Justice', 252; de Richemont, *Communauté européenne du charbon et de l'acier: La cour de justice, code annoté guide pratique*, (1954), 103; an alternative hypothesis is that it mirrors French civil procedure—Lasok, *European Court of Justice: Practice and Procedure*, 66.

[34] Schulze and Hoeren, *Dokumente zum Europaischen Recht Bandz Justiz (bis 1957)* (Vol II), 464.

[35] *FTA*, Order (24 February 2000), para 25.

[36] French CPC, Art 411. The German text of Art 17 was even more explicit on this point, under which the term *bevollmächtigte* or 'duly authorised agent to perform certain administrative or procedural acts' is used for *both* privileged and unprivileged litigants.

[37] Lasok, *European Court of Justice: Practice and Procedure*, 70.

[38] Eg *Azienda*; *FTA*.

[39] Interview with Judge Sir David Edward (27 August 2010), cited with permission.

[40] EU Civil Service Tribunal Rules, Arts 31–2.

to send its proposed Rules to the ECJ for positive advice before submitting them for approval to the Council.[41] However, the proposal was ultimately not included in the Rules and the ECJ has not proposed to amend Article 19 in its draft amendments.[42] Thus, it appears that there has been greater concern on the part of some members of the EU judiciary concerning agents than meets the eye.

5.2.2 Lawyers

The second issue is the meaning of the term 'lawyer' within the English text.[43] As seen in the three French versions, there has been consistent use of *avocat* to describe the representative of unprivileged litigants. This naturally accords with the requirements of civil law jurisdictions, in which the title of *avocat* provides the right to perform procedural acts on behalf of a party in civil litigation. However, upon the accession of the anglophone, common law jurisdictions of the UK[44] and Ireland in 1973 this provision needed to be translated into English legal language. The drafters of the English version of the Statute were attempting to find the *equivalent* in English legal terminology for the representational function of an *avocat*. Instead of inserting the terms 'advocate, barrister, or solicitor' into the provision, they opted for 'lawyer' as the 'least cumbersome' term.[45] However, since 'lawyer' is not a legal term of art in either jurisdiction its use may cause confusion. Nevertheless, it is evident that the drafters of the English version of Article 19 intended to designate barristers, advocates, and solicitors as 'lawyers'.[46] Concerning the requirement that a 'lawyer' be 'authorised to practise before the court of a Member State', this was an attempt to distinguish between practising and non-practising lawyers.[47]

Thus, upon the accession of the UK and Ireland there was a discrepancy between the requirements of Article 19 in the English version and those of the other versions. This led to a third problem, namely, the change in the admission requirements for an *avocat*. Under Article 20 of the ECSC Statute, retained in the original Article 17 of the ECJ Statute, an *avocat* was defined as *inscrit à un barreau* or 'admitted to a bar' of a Member State. In the original French, this is a clear requirement because the title of *avocat* derives from membership of one of the regional Orders. The EEA Treaty provided for amendment of the Statute to ensure that EFTA lawyers could appear before the Court. Accordingly, all of the linguistic versions of the Statute were amended by the EU Council to provide literal

[41] EU Civil Service Tribunal Rules, Preamble.

[42] Draft ECJ Amendments to the Statute, online: <http://curia.europa.eu/jcms/jcms/Jo2_7031> (Accessed: 2 February 2013). *Confer* Art 46, Draft ECJ Rules.

[43] Although Art 19 suggests that parties are restricted to a single lawyer, in practice there is no limit—Lasok, *European Court of Justice: Practice and Procedure*, 70.

[44] With the partial exception of Scotland—Edward, 'Different Assumptions—Different Methods', *S.S.C. Biennial Lecture 1990*, 13.

[45] Interview with Judge Edward. See also Usher, *European Court Practice*, 114–15.

[46] Articles 1(2) of the 1977 and 1998 Directives on transnational legal services define 'lawyers' as 'advocates, barristers and solicitors'.

[47] At the time, 'practice certificates' distinguishing between practising and non-practising legal professionals had not yet been introduced.

linguistic harmony with the English version.[48] Thus, although the various versions of Article 19 are now linguistically consistent with one another, the redaction of *inscrit à un barreau* has left no textual definition of an *avocat* and its equivalents. The use of the English version of Article 19 as the template rather than the French version has introduced ambiguity.

Despite this omission, it appears that the old definition has been implicitly retained in the Courts' application of Article 19. In *Comunidad Autónoma de Valencia*, the CFI refused admission to an employed lawyer of a Spanish local governmental authority (who had rights of audience before Spanish courts) because he was not a member of the Spanish Bar. The CFI, citing a key passage from the competition case of *AM & S Europe*,[49] seemingly applied Article 19 in its original meaning in French[50] whereby only a person inscribed to the College of Advocates would be considered to be an *abogado*.[51] However, the Court did not cite the original text but rather confusingly relied upon the principle of 'independence' from *AM & S Europe*.

Since the harmonization of the various linguistic versions of Article 19, the Courts have interpreted it to stipulate two separate requirements: (1) that a person be a 'lawyer'; and (2) that he be 'authorised to practise before the Court of a Member State'. As the *Comunidad Autónoma* case demonstrates, the original French definition of 'lawyer' is implicitly retained. This has become a contentious area for 'patent agents' or 'patent litigators' who have unsuccessfully sought admission in their own right to representation before the Courts for intellectual property cases.

In *Alto de Casablanca*, the claimant wished to be represented by a 'patent attorney' who was entitled to 'represent clients before the courts and tribunals of the United Kingdom in litigation concerning intellectual property'.[52] However, the CFI (again citing *AM & S Europe*[53]) rejected this argument because the person in question was 'neither a solicitor nor a barrister... [so] it remains the case that he is not a lawyer'.[54] The Court cited the specific exception within Article 19 for university teachers as illustrating the strictness of the general rule.[55] Thus, the original intention of 'lawyer' as meaning 'solicitor, barrister, or advocate' was applied to exclude a patent agent.

In the *Wilfer* case, a *patentanwalt* or 'patent attorney' applied for right of hearing before the Court. In Germany, *patentanwälte* are entitled to represent parties only before patent courts.[56] The CFI, citing *Alto de Casablanca*, held that the *patentanwalt* could only address the Court in the presence and under the supervision of a *rechstanwalt*.[57] This pragmatic compromise to an immediate problem reinforces the rule that only *rechstanwälte* may represent or assist parties.

[48] The clearest version is in the 1994 Decision (in French).

[49] See note 65.

[50] The first Spanish version of Art 19 mirrored the English one.

[51] *Comunidad Autónoma de Valencia* (French translation), para 12 (sub-paras 10–11).

[52] *Alto de Casablanca*, para 7.

[53] *Alto de Casablanca*, para 10.

[54] *Alto de Casablanca*, paras 7, 11.

[55] *Alto de Casablanca*, para 12.

[56] Bayer, 'Litigators at Community Patent Proceedings—Whose Representation Is It?' 34 *IRIPCL* (2003), 351–73, 361–2 (note 4).

[57] *Wilfer*, para 11.

Finally, in the *Imperial Chemicals* case the applicant sought to distinguish *Alto de Casablanca* on the ground that 'patent attorney litigators' differ from 'patent attorneys' in that they are 'governed by special rules of professional discipline and special rules of conduct' and are defined as 'lawyers' under UK law.[58] The CFI rejected these arguments and defined the term 'lawyer' narrowly because the Chartered Institute of Patent Attorneys 'cannot be assimilated to an authorised institution for the purposes of the case-law' and (citing *Comunidad Autónoma*) the need for an 'independent and uniform interpretation [of 'lawyer'] throughout the Community' overrode the position of patent attorney litigators under UK law.[59] However, the CFI also cited EU transnational legal services directives.[60] Although it acknowledged that their purpose is not 'representation of a party by a lawyer before the Community judicature', it concluded that 'the concept of lawyer must be given a uniform interpretation' in order to 'avoid the paradox of permitting a person to represent a party before the Community judicature when he would not be authorised to represent that party before the national courts and tribunals of the Member States other than his State of origin'.[61]

Although the issue of patent attorneys recently arose again in the *Enercon* case, there is no reference to it in the judgment and it appears that the matter was disposed of summarily.[62] Whilst the Courts' consistent rejection of patent attorneys has been explained as motivated by judicial scepticism of their professional competence,[63] the more convincing explanation is that patent attorneys were not designated as 'lawyers' within Article 19. Whilst there may be an argument for amendment of Article 19 to allow one or more versions of patent attorneys to be admitted in their own right as 'lawyers' before the Courts for trademark cases, the jurisprudence is consistent with Article 19 restricting representation to solicitors, barristers, advocates and *anwälte.*

Hitherto, the discussion has focused upon the admission rules for direct actions. There is a somewhat looser rule for preliminary reference cases, for which Article 104(2) of the ECJ Rules of Procedure provides:

> As regards the representation and attendance of the parties to the main proceedings in the preliminary ruling procedure the Court shall take account of the rules of procedure of the national court or tribunal which made the reference.

It is somewhat ambiguous whether this provision obliges the Court merely to *consider* national procedures or to *apply* them.[64] Nevertheless, in practice the Court has been flexible in preliminary reference cases where parties were self-represented

[58] *Imperial Chemicals*, paras 11–12. [59] *Imperial Chemicals*, paras 19-21.

[60] *Imperial Chemicals*, paras 23–8. The relevant provisions are Arts 1(2) of the 1977 and 1998 Directives.

[61] *Imperial Chemicals*, paras 27–8.

[62] Morcom, 'Representation of parties before the European Court of Justice—Is There a Need for Reform?' 31 *EIPR* (2009), 223–6, 223.

[63] Bayer, 'Litigators at Community Patent Proceedings—Whose Representation Is It?', 364–5.

[64] The French text does not clarify the matter.

in the national courts.[65] Although the Court has never given a reasoned decision, it is suggested that the phrase 'take account of' is not obligatory in scope.

Throughout the jurisprudence concerning patent litigators, there is frequent reference in the decisions of the General Court to the need for representatives of unprivileged parties to be subject to professional ethics and discipline. In that context, the Court has cited a key passage from *AM & S Europe*:

> ...the requirement as to the position and status as an independent lawyer...is based on a conception of the lawyer's role as collaborating in the administration of justice by the courts and as being required to provide, in full independence, and in the overriding interests of that cause, such legal assistance as the client needs. The counterpart of that protection lies in the rules of professional ethics and discipline which are laid down and enforced in the general interest by institutions endowed with the requisite powers for that purpose. Such a conception reflects the legal traditions common to the member states and is also to be found in the legal order of the Community, as demonstrated by article 17 of the Protocols on the Statutes of the Court of the E.E.C. and the E.A.E.C., and also by article 20 of the Protocol on the Statute of the Court of Justice of the E.C.S.C...[s]uch protection may not be extended beyond those limits, which are determined by the scope of the common rules on the exercise of the legal profession as laid down in Council Directive of March 22, 1977 ...which is based in its turn on the mutual recognition by all the member states of the national legal concepts of each of them on this subject.[66]

As discussed below,[67] *AM & S Europe* concerned a specific issue, namely, the existence and scope of the legal principle of professional secrecy in EU law. Specifically, this passage concerned the ruling that the principle does not extend to employed or 'in-house' lawyers. Thus, notwithstanding the Court's citation of the Statute, *AM & S Europe* did not concern the issue of admission requirements for counsel before the Court.

Nevertheless, the consistent citation by the General Court of this passage in the admission cases suggests that 'professional ethics and discipline' guaranteeing 'independence' is an underlying rationale for the restriction of admission to the traditional legal professions. The greater European reliance upon a more 'paternalistic'[68] relationship between counsel and client than is usual in the United States is predicated upon the assurance that, in exchange for such authority, counsel will be bound by professional ethics to ensure client confidence.[69] The authority to perform procedural acts (often, if not almost always, irrevocable) on behalf of clients is, in many ways, one of the greatest manifestations of this trust. Although the ECJ is bound to apply its Statute according to its original meaning, should amendment of Article 19 be considered to extend rights of hearing to non-traditional 'lawyers' the value of independent counsel bound by professional ethics and discipline should be central.

[65] Anderson and Demetriou, *References to the European Court*, 9-046. See, eg *Haegeman*; *Coenen*; *Gullung*.

[66] *AM & S Europe*, 950, paras 24, 26.

[67] Section 5.3.2.2.

[68] Terry, 'An Introduction to the European Community's Legal Ethics Code Part I: An Analysis of the CCBE Code of Conduct' 7 *GJLE* (1993-1994), 1–87, 32.

[69] Terry, 'An Introduction to the European Community's Legal Ethics Code Part I', 46–51.

5.2.3 Employed Lawyers

Although questions concerning confidentiality have not yet arisen in proceedings before the Court, the *AM & S Europe* case established that the principle exists in Union law. The Court's citation of its Statute in its key holding arguably excludes employed counsel by implication from representing or assisting parties before the Court.[70] However, although the Court decided that the confidentiality does not yet extend to employed lawyers, its judgment did not directly engage with the underlying issue of the practical independence required of counsel. Although the case principally addresses the *legal* dimension of the confidentiality principle, its converse *ethical* dimension was pivotal because professional ethics (backed by professional discipline) provide a vital safeguard against lawyers concealing client misconduct behind the veil of confidentiality.

The underlying question is: who is to be trusted not to be subverted in this way? One of the two Advocates-General in *AM & S Europe*, Sir Gordon Slynn (as he then was), opined that employed lawyers should be treated in the same way as lawyers in private practice because the latter is no more 'independent' than the former but the Court based its decision to exclude employed lawyers from the confidentiality principle on the 'common legal principles' of EU national systems.[71] Since those legal systems diverge on employed lawyers, the Court's prioritization of consensus resulted in the extension of the confidentiality privilege to communications with self-employed lawyers only—requiring that the definition of a lawyer be unanimous amongst the (now 27) EU Members' legal systems rather than based upon the underlying question of principle.[72]

The arguments for the inclusion of employed lawyers, as advanced by Advocate-General Slynn, are that professional ethics and discipline constitute sufficient safeguards in themselves against subversion of an employed lawyer's independence and that there is little practical difference between a self-employed lawyer dependent upon a single client for his practice and a lawyer employed by his client. There is also the suspicion that the exclusion of employed lawyers is motivated not so much by ethical considerations as by protectionism. The arguments for the exclusion of employed lawyers are that there is a difference between a lawyer whose entire living is dependent upon his employer and one who, by virtue of his self-employment, is *capable* of financial independence by acting for multiple clients.

The *AM & S Europe* decision was subsequently applied by the General Court in *Akzo Nobel*, in which the Court found, inter alia, that *AM & S Europe* defined the role of 'lawyer' in negative terms to exclude employed counsel and that a re-examination of the laws of the EU Member States revealed that 'even though it is the case... that specific recognition of the role of in-house lawyers and the protection of communications with such lawyers under LPP is relatively more common

[70] Usher, *European Court Practice*, 216; Brown and Kennedy, *The Court of Justice of the European Communities*, 304–5.

[71] *AM & S Europe*, 914, 949 (para 21) and 951 (paras 26–7).

[72] *AM & S Europe*, 909; Calhoun, 'Globalization's Erosion of the Attorney-Client Privilege and What U.S. Courts Can Do to Prevent It' 87 *TxLR* (2008), 235–65, 242 (notes 54–55).

today than when the judgment in *AM & S* was handed down, it is not possible, nevertheless, to identify tendencies which are uniform or have clear majority support in that regard in the laws of the Member States'.[73] Before the ECJ, the appellants' grounds of appeal were rejected by the Grand Chamber, which held that the General Court had correctly interpreted *AM & S Europe* and that there was no 'predominant trend' amongst the Member States to justify an extension of legal confidentiality to communications with employed lawyers under EU law.[74]

On the first point, the Grand Chamber was more explicit than in *AM & S Europe* in setting out the rationale for the exclusion of employed lawyers from confidentiality:

Notwithstanding the professional regime applicable in the present case in accordance with the specific provisions of Dutch law, an in-house lawyer cannot, whatever guarantees he has in the exercise of his profession, be treated in the same way as an external lawyer, because he occupies the position of an employee which, by its very nature, does not allow him to ignore the commercial strategies pursued by his employer, and thereby affects his ability to exercise professional independence.

It must be added that, under the terms of his contract of employment, an in-house lawyer may be required to carry out other tasks... which may have an effect on the commercial policy of the undertaking. Such functions cannot but reinforce the close ties between the lawyer and his employer.

It follows, both from the in-house lawyer's economic dependence and the close ties with his employer, that he does not enjoy a level of professional independence comparable to that of an external lawyer.[75]

Despite the overlap in the analysis with the debate concerning the attitudes of national jurisdictions concerning employed counsel, the *Akzo Nobel* judgment is clearer in articulating a principled basis for the exclusion of employed lawyers.

Despite the express reference by the ECJ to Article 19 of its Statute in *Akzo Nobel*,[76] it is nebulous whether the Courts would exclude employed counsel from their proceedings. According to the Registrar of the General Court:

It would be interesting to examine whether the *Akzo Nobel Chemicals* decision has consequences for employed counsel appointed by parties before the Court. It is interesting and an open matter. Of course, although the confidentiality cases have analogies they do not necessarily raise identical issues concerning Article 19. It is to be noted that is not always possible to detect in-house lawyers by knowing that a member of a national bar is also employed. For example, the practising certificates of barristers and solicitors do not indicate whether they are self-employed or employed. Nor does a certificate of admission to the English Bar or Law Society state whether the individual is a practising or non-practising member, which is why the General Court requires that counsel produce their practising certificates.[77]

73 *Akzo Nobel* (General Court), paras 168–170.
74 *Akzo Nobel* (ECJ), paras 40–51, 69–76.
75 *Akzo Nobel* (ECJ), paras 49–51.
76 *Akzo Nobel* (ECJ), para 42.
77 Registrar Coulon, Interview.

It is 'almost certain' that employed counsel has appeared before the EU Courts without their knowledge since the Courts have no means of detection.[78] However, the judiciary's discomfort with employment suggests that they would be excluded.

5.2.4 Experts

As before the ICJ, the possibility exists for parties to present expert evidence through the medium of representation. One commentator suggests that 'there are certain practical advantages for a member state or Community institution to be assisted by an adviser who, while having no legal training, is an expert in any technical matters relevant to the case'.[79] Insofar as those advantages encompass effective argumentation through embellishment with expert knowledge, there seems to be no reason why that knowledge should not be tested by cross-examination. This apparent procedural inequality between privileged and unprivileged litigants does not appear to be regarded as a major problem.[80]

From the perspective of the judiciary, the current practice is to permit experts and other non-lawyers to address the Court under the supervision of a lawyer:

Judge Forwood: This must also be seen in the context of the practice of allowing unqualified persons to address the Court under the supervision of qualified counsel. For example, case handlers on the Respondent's side and also in-house counsel on the Applicant's side. See also big, complex cases such as *Microsoft* in which non-lawyers were giving submissions under supervision. This facility is very generally used to cover even non-lawyers addressing the Court.

President Jaeger: There is a practical element to this practice, in that it saves time for counsel having to continuously ask the Court for time to consult the non-lawyer experts on technical matters and then repeating exactly what they were told, possibly mishearing as well. It is simpler to have them address the Court directly. Case-law and practice are well-established, covering especially economists but other technical experts as well. This practice of supervision is intended to ensure both that the Court's procedure complies with the Statute and Rules and the presence of an ethical element concerning counsel. We expect the lawyer to interrupt the non-lawyer if there have been misstatements and that control exerted by the lawyer is linked to the deontological responsibility of an *avocat*. It is important, in this respect, to have a bar association as interlocutor to assimilate these matters. Lawyers have tried sometimes to explain that their national rules are all the same, when they are not.[81]

Thus, notwithstanding the absence of major problems in practice concerning the limited facility for non-lawyers to directly address the Court, it is clear that the supervision of a lawyer is regarded as necessary to ensure the presence of professional responsibility.

[78] Judge Forwood interview. Whilst an employed lawyer was 'directed to withdraw for being unqualified' in *Endesa*, there is no record of this in the judgment. See also *DB Schenker II*, paras 24–38, in which the European Free Trade Area Court purported to apply ECJ jurisprudence in rejecting an objection to representation by an 'external law firm'.

[79] See note.

[80] Interview with Mr Vaughan QC.

[81] Interview.

5.3 Ethical Standards

As previously indicated, there is little practice to draw upon concerning ethical problems before the ECJ. The Court's Statute, Rules of Procedure, and 'Notes for the Guidance of Counsel' (originally created for oral hearings only[82]) address legal and practical matters, not professional ethics. Whilst some authors cite the Council of Bars and Law Societies of Europe (CCBE) Code of Conduct 1988 as a source,[83] the Code is inapplicable to ECJ proceedings because it was expressly designed for transnational practice[84] rather than for proceedings before international courts.

The Court has never invoked its disciplinary powers towards advocates and generally ignores such problems as arise on rare occasions. The lack of practice must also in part be attributable to the comparative rarity of evidence before the Court which, as explained above, derives from its largely review-based jurisdiction. However, one judge has noted unevenness in quality of counsel:

A judge of the European Court of Justice comments that there are some excellent lawyers who regularly appear before his court. 'Then on the other end, you have some poor lawyer who's coming from a small town and who has no experience of European Community law. And then, maybe even against his own preference, the judge of that national court decides to ask us for a preliminary ruling, and then the poor guy has to come here. And then for some reason he doesn't even bother to find out exactly what customarily happens, so he comes here with a long speech, which repeats what he already said in writing. That's the other extreme. And we have everything in between.'[85]

Other problems have been dealt with summarily and consequently are not in the public domain. According to two members of the General Court:

Judge Forwood: The General Court tends to deal with such matters on an ad hoc basis. Only if real problems arise, would a real incentive be provided to justify the intellectual effort and energy required to draft a comprehensive code of conduct. That said, [there are] some particular issues which are problems that, if they have not already arisen, may do so in the future. Confidentiality issues particularly come to mind in the context of counsel passing on to their client confidential material made available to him by the Court on a restrictive basis. This could be particularly relevant for business secret material in competition cases, for example. One future area where this potentially could be important is in terrorist asset cases, though it has not yet arisen. For example, cases could arise concerning the 'special advocate' procedures or the equivalent, in which lawyers are required to keeping information secret from their client; even where it is central to the substance of the case.

President Jaeger: Although I can anticipate that many national bars would not be in favour of a 'European bar', I can see intellectual arguments in favour of such an idea. We have some 700,000 lawyers who now may plead before the Court, from 27 Member States all with their own deontological rules, so there are strong arguments for the Court to only deal with one bar and one set of rules.

[82] Usher, *European Court Practice*, 233.
[83] Brown and Kennedy, *The Court of Justice of the European Communities*, 302 (note 14).
[84] CCBE Code, Art 1.3.1. [85] Terris et al, *The International Judge* (2007), 85.

Judge Forwood: There are trends now towards the liberalisation of rights of hearing in national jurisdictions, e.g.—the expansion of solicitors' rights in England and Wales. There is an argument for a list of counsel to be maintained by the Court with a specialist EU Bar like the US Supreme Court. However, because of the requirement before the ECJ to take account of national rules in preliminary reference cases, this idea would only work for the General Court. We could have a common code of conduct without having to refer to 27 sets of codes.[86]

Thus, irrespective of the rarity of real problems before the EU Courts, there is interest in the prescription of common ethical standards for counsel for its potential utility.

The question may be posed: why have ethical issues not arisen more often before the Court? It may be hypothesized that there are multiple causes: (1) the generally narrow, law-based jurisdiction of the Court excluding evidentiary matters; (2) the concentrated number of specialist practitioners who regularly appear before the Court, helping to instil collegiality and similar etiquette; and (3) the relative procedural homogeneity of the 'original Six' jurisdictions, narrowing certain differences in national standards. At first sight, since there are few problems in practice, ethical conduct is not problematic because the existing admission requirements and disciplinary powers have proved adequate.

However, it is suggested that this is not the case. First, although the Court's homogenous procedure would appear to be enduring despite membership expansions, the diversity of counsel qualifying for admission has considerably expanded. Ethical standards are consequently far more diversified and jurisdictions with formerly authoritarian political systems and limited experience of independent, self-regulating bars may not be able to adequately regulate their memberships. Moreover, national regulation is inadequate to ensure observance *common* standards because national standards diverge. The dormancy of the Court's disciplinary powers may also be attributable to the absence of prior notice for counsel through prescribed standards.

It is arguable, however, that the best-placed organization to undertake the task of drafting such a code would be the CCBE. In the words of one judge:

If the CCBE were to adopt a code of conduct for cases before international courts, such as the CJEU, the judges of both the EU Courts would necessarily be consulted as part of that process for our views. That would likely be the way in which such a project could be achieved. Having previously served as the CCBE Representative to the ECJ as part of its Permanent Delegation, I can imagine that there would be interest within the CCBE to undertake such a project.[87]

The participation of national bars through the CCBE would ensure that the resulting text would be integrated at the national level. This would not only ameliorate the double deontology problem but also strengthen the legitimacy of the code amongst counsel by constituting a shared text. However, the principal danger of this approach is to prescribe a low standard as the price for consensus amongst

[86] Interview. [87] Judge Forwood, Interview.

dozens of jurisdictions by avoiding the difficult issues. This would defeat its very purpose by perpetuating conflicts between national rules rather than setting a common standard.

In the absence of agreement by the EU Council to such a code, it is arguable that the Court could nevertheless prescribe one by invoking an inherent jurisdiction:

> If there were a serious enough case, for my part I would be willing to do so by relying upon the Court's mission to judge cases justly. In this respect, it is important to take into account the position of agents, who are not covered by Article 41. I can see a distinction in this sense between States and institutions, in that States would presumably be more jealous over their control over agents than would institutions.[88]

Thus, it seems plausible that States would seek to block a code applicable to agents through their representation on the EU Council. However, it is suggested that a sufficiently serious case of dishonesty or other misconduct by an agent[89] would justify the unilateral prescription of ethical rules to protect the integrity of its proceedings.

5.3.1 Duties to the Client

There are neither procedural rules nor precedents prescribing the circumstances in which an advocate may (or must) accept a brief or withdraw from one such as competence, conflict of interest, or professional embarrassment. Whilst this suggests that such issues have not yet come to the Court's attention, this does not necessarily mean that they have not surreptitiously occurred in practice. Moreover, the controversial *AM & S Europe* and *Akzo Nobel* confidentiality issues demonstrate that divergence of national standards and cultures results in deeply opposed views concerning shared problems. Within the common proceedings before the Courts, this divergence could lead to differences in advocates' handling of such sensitive issues.

5.3.1.1 Conflicts of Interest

Before other international courts, conflicts of interest are an increasingly important issue. The ECJ has also addressed the issue within Article 6(2) of the ECJ Code of Conduct 2007 for judges, which prohibits them after holding office from, inter alia, acting as representatives of parties for a three-year period. This is a practical problem:

> [The three-year freezing period] is the Court of Justice's considered response to a potential problem. Several former Advocates-General, judges and even a President of the General Court have subsequently returned to practice and appeared as counsel. This is, moreover, a practical issue because EU judges are appointed for only six years or even shorter, rather than as a lifetime career, and (particularly if they have been appointed early) it would be severe to require them to sacrifice rights of audience permanently in the future, upon becoming judges.[90]

[88] Judge Forwood, Interview. [89] Section 5.3.2.1. [90] Judge Forwood, Interview.

Moreover, it is also interesting that the freezing period is the same as that of the ICJ—suggesting cross-fertilization between international courts. This indicates that the adoption of a code of conduct for counsel by one court would provide an example for others to do likewise.

In the pending case of *DB Schenker II*, the President of the EFTA Court rejected an application to exclude counsel on the ground of conflict of interest. There, an application for leave to intervene was made by Norway Post in an application for annulment of an EFTA Surveillance Authority decision denying public access to documents.[91] One of the arguments deployed by the applicant, DB Schenker, to resist the third-party application was that 'the application is inadmissible because Norway Post is not independently represented before the Court [pursuant to Article 17 of the EFTA Statute]'. The applicant argued that 'reliance placed by Norway Post on allegedly erroneous expert advice provided by its law firm in 2002 means that the law firm in question, which presently represents the applicant intervener, cannot be objectively perceived as being without its own interests tied to the subject matter before the Court in this case following the judgment in *Norway Post* v *ESA*'.

Applying the *AM & S Europe* test, the President rejected the application on factual grounds:

> In the present proceedings, the applicant intervener has chosen to be represented by a particular law firm as external counsel. Such external counsel must be perceived as a genuine intermediary between Norway Post and the Court unless the conduct of counsel towards the Court is, pursuant to Article 31 RoP, incompatible with the dignity of the Court or with the requirements of justice, or if such adviser or lawyer is using his rights for purposes other than those for which they were granted. No such concerns exist in the present proceedings.[92]

In this case, the question was not the standing of the external counsel to appear before the Court in general but rather whether a conflict of interest could disqualify counsel in this particular case. The conflict of interest could be said to have arisen from the potential exposure of the law firm in question to professional negligence proceedings, which the documents comprising the target of the application could affect. Whilst the President's Order comprises a reasonable outcome to a tricky problem, it also underscores the need for prescribed standards to more effectively address such issues.

5.3.1.2 Confidentiality

The principle of confidentiality of communications between lawyer and client, documents belonging to a litigant, and communications between litigants intended to be treated as confidential has both legal and ethical dimensions. The legal protection of the principle ensures that third parties may not generally view

[91] *DB Schenker II*, para 12. [92] *DB Schenker II*, para 38.

such confidential or privileged communications without client consent. The ethical principle of confidentiality exists in order to encourage trust between lawyer and client.

However, the legal protection of such communications from the eyes of others creates a danger that it may be abused. Legal and ethical safeguards are accordingly needed, wherein the former allows for limited circumstances for a court to view confidential communications and the latter requires counsel to disclose such material in abusive circumstances. Although the procedural rules of the Court provide for the former, its powers have never been invoked. Article 32(2)(a) of the Rules[93] provides:

> P[p]apers and documents relating to the proceedings shall be exempt from both search and seizure; in the event of a dispute the customs officials or police may seal those papers and documents, they shall then be immediately forwarded to the Court for inspection in the presence of the Registrar and of the person concerned…

De Richemont, commenting upon the rule, wrote:

> *Le principe du secret professionel* auquel tout défenseur est astreint s'impose aux tiers, autorités publiques ou privées. Le cabinet d'avocat est inviolable… [c]e privilege s'étend aux dossiers de l'avocat, soit à son cabinet, soit au cours de leur transport…
>
> Par papiers et documents, il faut entendre non seulement les actes de procedure… mais encore la correspondence échangée entre le défenseur et son client… sous la reserve suivante:
>
> Il est nécessaire que la correspondence et les documents aient trait à l'affaire soumise à la Cour et que les seconds ne constituent pas le corps d'un délit qui aurait été commis dans l'affaire en cause ou dans un connexe.
>
> La justice peut s'emparer, partout où elle la trouve, d'une pièce constituent le corps meme du délit—une pièce arguée de faux par exemple—sous condition qu'elle soit representée en original; une copie ou un photostat ne pourraient être saisis.[94]

Thus, the robust protection afforded to the confidentiality principle under French legal ethics is here invoked to interpret the Court's procedural rules. An advocate's duty to preserve secrecy extends even to confessions or admissions of wrongdoing, so that a client admitting, for example, that his case or a particular argument is a sham[95] would be able to disclose to his advocate without fear that the latter would disclose that fact to the Court. Although de Richemont was commenting upon the Court's powers as a legal principle, it cannot be defined without also addressing its ethical counterpart.

The legal protection of confidential or privileged material is qualified. In writing that *justice* may demand material comprising a legal wrong, such as forgery, de Richemont probably intended that it would be for the Court alone to order disclosure. Article 24 of the Statute is expressed in very wide language: '[t]he Court of Justice may require the parties to produce *all* documents and to supply

[93] Originally Art 1(2)(a) of the ECSC Supplementary Rules—de Richemont, *Communauté européenne du charbon et de l'acier*, 105–2.

[94] De Richemont, *Communauté européenne du charbon et de l'acier*, 105–2.

[95] Namely, a case or argument unfounded in fact or law or otherwise made for abusive, vexatious, or frivolous purposes.

all information which the Court considers *desirable*' (emphases added).[96] This is reinforced by Article 34 of the ECJ Rules (originally Article 3(1)(2) of the ECSC Supplementary Rules):

> The privileges . . . specified in Article 32 of these Rules are granted exclusively in the interests of the proper conduct of proceedings. The Court may waive the immunity where it considers that the proper conduct of proceedings will not be hindered thereby.

Commenting upon the provision, de Richemont wrote:

> La défense doit être libre; les défenseurs doivent jouir d'une *independance totale et absolue* tant au point de vue moral que materiel . . . *Assurer ces conditions, c'est également garantir le fonctionnement harmonieux de la procedure et par suite preserver et garantir l'intérêt de l'instance* . . . Le cas pourrait se presenter, *si le défenseur s'était rendu coupable à l'égard des parties* ou des tiers d'imputations diffamatoires ou injurieuses, graves ou renouvelées.
>
> *La Cour decide souverainement* (emphases added).[97]

Thus, protection of confidential material is a privilege, not a right. The Court may order disclosure of such material if it considers it to be in the interest of justice.

The question may be posed: why would an international court ever order disclosure of confidential material? The answer is that serious alleged misconduct threatens the integrity of the judicial process. This is not only hypothetical, but practical in light of certain questionable cases before international courts and tribunals concerning bribery, forgery, and other forms of serious misconduct.[98] Since the advocate is the only person besides the client (who has a vested interest to keep secret his own wrongdoing) privy to the information that would prove that the judicial process is endangered, it follows that a safeguard is required in order to alert the Court. An advocate ought not to be suborned into protecting a client who bribes, deceives, coerces, spies, or otherwise seeks to corrupt proceedings. Thus, it is suggested that an ethical duty of confidentiality would prescribe a duty to disclose confidential material where there is reasonable suspicion of such serious misconduct.

As previously discussed, *AM & S Europe* and *Akzo Nobel* exclude employed counsel from the scope of legal confidentiality. The 'independence' of the lawyer from the client, particularly in the context of client misconduct, was crucial to that determination. Whilst this author respectfully agrees with the justification offered in *Akzo Nobel* for that finding, the cases illustrate by analogy the problem of divergent ethical standards within the context of potential client misconduct being shielded by the confidentiality principle. The need for a general, rather than absolute, ethical duty of confidentiality would accordingly be appropriate in striking the correct balance between lawyer-client trust and protecting the integrity of judicial proceedings.

[96] See also ECJ Rules, Art 57; ECSC Rules, Art 48(1).

[97] De Richemont, *Communauté européenne du charbon et de l'acier*, 105–8.

[98] Sarvarian, 'Problems of Ethical Standards for Representatives before ICSID Tribunals', 10(1) *LPICT* (2011) 67–134.

5.3.2 Duties to the Court

Within the procedural rules of the Court, there are no general principles articulated concerning the ethical duties of advocates towards it. The umbrella terms 'dignity of the Court' and 'proper administration of justice' underpinning the Court's disciplinary powers within Article 35(1) of the Rules are the only such duties in the rules. 'Dignity of the Court' may be interpreted, *sensu stricto*, as a requirement to address the Court with civility and decorum. However, the phrase 'proper administration of justice' is too broadly drafted to extrapolate much concrete meaning. Particularly important but unaddressed matters include ex parte communications with the Court and the handling of evidence so as to preclude its contamination or fabrication by counsel or the parties.

5.3.2.1 Candour

A basic principle to be considered upon which there are differing standards in practice is that of honesty to the Court. At least two cases have occurred, discussed within 'documentary evidence' below, in which this has been an issue. It was commented above that there ought to be an ethical duty upon counsel to disclose otherwise confidential information to the Court, as when a client is insisting upon bringing a 'sham case'—that is, a case or argument unfounded in fact or law or otherwise brought for vexatious or frivolous purposes. It should be noted that the risk of such 'sham' cases being brought before the Court is generally slight. As a former judge has commented:

> I suppose this could arise in a cartel case where a client says 'of course we were part of an illegal cartel but the Commission's evidence is insufficient to prove it'. However, in thirty years of practice before going to the Court I never experienced this kind of outright confession. One should distinguish between an out-and-out admission of a false case (which, if happening at all, will be very rare) and the more common situation of: 'We've been fined EUR 50 million...what can you do for us?' Decent counsel will say: 'We can certainly argue that the Commission's evidence is insufficient but this may not hold water in court.' I remember as a judge, and I have said it in lectures then and afterwards, that 'you can tell an illegal cartel when you smell it.' Some counsel more than others will attempt to run every conceivable argument, which is not really a question of ethics but simply bad advocacy.[99]

Apart from the issue of misleading the Court by putting forward argumentation that counsel 'knows' to be false, it may be suggested that 'bad advocacy' of sufficient seriousness could infringe an ethical standard of due diligence or competence. If counsel is running every conceivable argument without regard to merit in the forlorn hope that one of them sticks, this would be not only a waste of the time and money of his client but also that of the Court.

[99] Interview with Judge Edward.

The importance of candour appears in the *List D* case:

> The Hellenic Republic admits that the provisions of Community law referred to by the Commission prohibit the introduction by Member States of quantitative restrictions with regard to matches from Bulgaria and Sweden. It claims, however, that 'List D' was abolished in 1980 by Decision E6/8196/2600 in order to adapt Greek rules with a view to the accession of Greece to the Communities...
>
> It is therefore common ground that the Hellenic Republic, before accession, applied a system of import authorization referred to as 'List D' or 'Procedure D', the purpose and effect of which was to restrict imports of certain products. The Hellenic Republic has not produced any instrument providing for the abolition of that system. Contrary to the Hellenic Republic' s claim, Decision E6/8196/2600 does not expressly abolish 'Procedure D'; paragraph 2 of that decision merely rescinds the distinction between Procedures 'Delta' and 'Epsilon' for the granting of an authorization to import.
>
> ...the Commission has produced to the Court photocopies of the two import application forms...[o]n each form the refusal of the application is hand-written, accompanied by the Greek letter 'D', also hand-written. The refusal of an import application bears no relation to a purely statistical procedure. On the contrary, the fact that the refusal of the application was accompanied by the letter 'D' proves the continued existence of a so-called 'List D' or 'Procedure D' system designed to restrict imports, which did in fact have the precise effect of preventing the imports concerned.
>
> In the absence of any other convincing explanation from the Government of the Hellenic Republic it must therefore be concluded that there was in existence in that State a 'Procedure D', the effect of which was to prevent the importation of the products appearing on a 'List D', and in particular matches from non-member countries.[100]

Here, there was certainly a failure to sufficiently scrutinize the Commission's documentary evidence. Had the agent for Greece examined that evidence thoroughly, she would have noticed the handwritten 'delta' symbols undermining her assertion that the 'List D' procedure had been abolished. This may be attributed to an attempt to mislead the Court by an assertion that the agent 'knew' to be unfounded (namely, that the 'List D' system had been abolished when the agent knew that it had not) and/or to a failure to exercise due diligence in scrutinizing the evidence of the other side.

Although one could argue that the client in such cases bears the consequences for engaging bad counsel or insisting upon bringing a bad case, it does not account for the impact upon the Court. It also does not acknowledge the injustice of a *client* bearing the consequences of bad advocacy by *counsel*. If counsel vexes the Court with prolix or mendacious argumentation, then in principle it should be for counsel to reap what he has sown. To the argument that counsel may simply be advancing a case or argument which his client is insisting upon regardless of its merits, there is the answer that 'independent' counsel must not compromise his professional standards to please his client. An example of this is the *Koelman* case,[101] concerning which the author is aware on a confidential basis that the applicant was nominally represented by a Luxembourgois counsel who, in order to

[100] *List D*, paras 6–10. [101] *Koelman*.

comply with the deadline for filing, signed pleadings that the applicant had himself drafted—presumably to assist the client in circumventing the Court's general prohibition upon self-representation. Subsequently, the advocate refused to answer questions put by the Court at the oral hearing—apparently because he was insufficiently unfamiliar with the applicant's case.[102]

5.3.2.2 Documentary Evidence

It is important to recall the preliminary *caveat* that the Court's jurisdiction generally precludes fact and evidence. However, when it does arise the Court's procedure is weighted towards written pleadings to which supporting documentary evidence is attached.[103] Where there is an issue of fact, the integrity of the judgment accordingly relies greatly upon the credibility of such evidence due to the comparative rarity of other evidence to refute it. Under the ECSC Rules, Article 33(7) provided that, in the event of the authenticity of a document being contested, the Court may *ex proprio motu* or on the application of the Advocate-General or one of the parties order verification measures to be taken.[104] This provision is omitted from the current Rules. Lacking the *travaux préparatoires* to the Rules, it is unknown why or when the rule was redacted.

Notwithstanding the procedural safeguards by which the Court may test the authenticity of written evidence, in most national ethical traditions an advocate is obliged to refrain from misleading the court. The enduring and universal nature of this problem is demonstrated by the forged documents incident in the *Qatar v Bahrain* case before the ICJ.[105] Although it clearly behoves the Court that advocates be placed under a professional duty to refrain from misleading it by false evidence, *Qatar v Bahrain* further shows the necessity for advocates to actively control evidence. Thus, it is argued that procedural justice demands that advocates not only be obliged to refrain from misleading the Court but also to shield it from false evidence.

Documentary evidence problems have arisen in at least one case. In *Società Italiana Vetro*, the General Court noted:

> It emerges from the inquiry carried out by the Court that when the Commission prepared the documentary evidence... certain relevant passages were deliberately deleted or omitted, even though they did not relate to business secrets. In particular, nine words were deleted without trace in a handwritten note from SIV of 20 January 1985 (374)...
>
> The Court considers that is self-evident and indisputable that the tenor of the note is changed completely by the omission of those nine words. With those nine words the note could be taken as clear evidence of a competitive struggle between SIV and FP on the one hand and VP on the other. At the hearing, the Commission tried in vain to supply an objectively justifiable reason for the deletion of those words.
>
> The Court must record that that is not the only example of such a proceeding, other examples of which will be commented upon below...

[102] *Koelman*, para 18. [103] ECJ Rules, Art 37(4).
[104] De Richemont, *Communauté européenne du charbon et de l'acier*, 125. [105] Chapter 4.

Accordingly, the Court considers that it is incumbent on it, in assessing the applicants' second general plea, to check meticulously the nature and import of the evidence taken into consideration by the Commission in the decision.[106]

The redaction of those nine words from a document, for which there was no 'objectively justifiable reason', can be attributed either to dishonesty or to a failure to sufficiently inspect the document and provide an explanation for the redacted words. The Commission was 'represented' by two members of its Legal Service as agents who were 'assisted' by an Italian *avvocato* and a French *avocat*. Since only agents can perform procedural acts that bind their principals before the Court, the ultimate responsibility for the documentary evidence is theirs. In this respect, it is noteworthy that although the Court was critical of this redaction in its judgment it lacks disciplinary powers concerning agents. Thus, even if the Court had been minded to discipline the agents in that case on grounds of candour or diligence it would not have had the ability to do so. A similar problem of failing to sufficiently scrutinize documentary evidence arose in the *BP Chemicals* case, in which certain documents submitted in support of the Commission's position were seemingly reconstructed from memory by the legal team or case team.[107] This, however, did not appear to have been an attempt at deceit but rather a failure on the part of the legal team to sufficiently analyse the documents prepared by the case team.

5.3.2.3 Testimonial Evidence

It has been noted that, due to the review-based jurisdiction of the Court, testimonial evidence by witnesses and experts is very rare.[108] The broadly drafted procedural rules of the Court are virtually identical to those of the ICJ, giving scant guidance to advocates.[109] Although the Court's original policy was to permit advocates to question witnesses only indirectly through the President of the Court, the Rules were amended in 1974 to allow direct interrogation.[110] There is no rule that regulates witness statements,[111] which are a requirement in England and a taboo in France. Surprisingly, witness examination before the Court is not addressed by much of the English literature.[112] However, Usher writes:

Since all witnesses are ultimately called by the Court on matters decided by the Court, distinctions known to common lawyers between witnesses called by one side or the other are

[106] *Società Italiana Vetro*, paras 90–95. [107] *BP Chemicals*, paras 27, 133–5.

[108] The Court had heard witnesses in only forty-four cases and appointed only sixteen experts in thirty-six years of existence up to 1 January 1989—Brown and Kennedy, *The Court of Justice of the European Communities*, 279. Another reason for the rarity of witnesses may be that 'civil lawyers do not generally know how to cross-examine, so they rarely bring witnesses to the Court'—Interview with Mr Vaughan.

[109] ECJ Statute, Arts 26, 32; ECJ Rules, Art 47(4); Van Reepinghen and Orianne, *La procedure devant la Cour de justice des communautés européennes*, 44.

[110] Brown and Kennedy, *The Court of Justice of the European Communities*. This does not appear to accord with Art 42 of the ECSC Rules—Delvaux, *La Cour de Justice de la Communauté Européenne du Charbon et de l'Acier*, 283.

[111] This problem has seemingly also arisen on the rare occasions when witnesses are called before the Court—Interview with Mr Vaughan.

[112] See note 19.

not recognised. In particular... there is no real distinction between examination-in-chief and cross-examination, and no prohibition upon leading witnesses.[113]

Although the distinction between witnesses called by the parties as opposed to those called by the Court may be technically accurate, it is suggested that it is an unsatisfactory one. Like all international courts and tribunals, the Court is almost always far removed from the vicinity of the disputed facts. Whilst the Court is vested with inquisitorial powers to collect evidence, in reality parties will have much greater access to potential witnesses. The conditions for the relaxed rules governing witness examination at the national level do not exist for international courts.

Brown and Kennedy also observe:

> The taking of evidence from a witness conforms, for the most part, with the normal practice of continental courts—practice which common lawyers generally regard as much inferior to their own for the establishment of facts where this depends on the credibility of a witness... [t]he witness is heard by the Court in the presence of the parties or their representatives. After the witness has given his or her evidence, questions may be put to the witness by the presiding judge, the other judges or the advocate general. Until the revision of the Rules of Procedure in 1974, the parties' lawyers could only put questions through the medium of the presiding judge, but now they may be permitted to put their questions directly, as in cross-examination—although the different context of the Luxembourg questioning makes it no more than a pale shadow of the English original.[114]

To illustrate this perceived cultural difference, they cite a case in which '[t]he parties were each represented by distinguished leading counsel from the English bar who were repeatedly admonished by the presiding judge for attempting to turn the inquisitorial hearing of witnesses into an adversarial trial'.[115] According to one of the barristers in the case, the incident was actually quite minor in that counsel for both sides had wished to cross-examine witnesses but were instructed by the President that, as those witnesses were 'the Court's witnesses', they must be examined through the Court.[116] In the event, the interrogations 'came off in a similar way to a normal cross-examination, in that the same progress was made but in a less confrontational manner'.[117] This procedure, wherein the judges' questions precede those of counsel, is more representative of a civil law jurisdiction than a common law one.[118] The role of counsel is correspondingly diminished, though of course not eliminated.

Instead of the technicality of calling witnesses, the more compelling explanation for the Court's relaxed rules of witness examination is historical in that there

[113] Usher, *European Court Practice*, 199.

[114] Brown and Kennedy, *The Court of Justice of the European Communities*, 278.

[115] Brown and Kennedy, *The Court of Justice of the European Communities*, 278 (note 11). No record appears in the judgment itself—*Adams*.

[116] Interview with Mr Vaughan.

[117] Interview with Mr Vaughan.

[118] Another similarity may be seen in the Court's rule of administering the oath to witnesses at the *end* of their testimony rather than at the beginning (Rules, Art 47(5)) reflecting German procedure, allowing the witness an opportunity to recant or rephrase their evidence.

was not a single common law jurisdiction within the 'original Six' members of the ECSC. Naturally, the protagonists drew upon their own national experiences and practices, as well as the laissez-faire regime of ICJ, in shaping the procedure of the Court. However, in light of the practical reality of the Court as a distant court of reference from national jurisdictions (apart from direct actions) there is a need for strict ethical standards binding upon advocates from common law and civil law jurisdictions alike concerning contact with witnesses and treatment of testimonial evidence—including witness examination—in order to preclude contamination of evidence. Although certain common law rules concerning evidence, such as those governing 'hearsay evidence', are unsuitable for the Court due to the absence of a jury the stricter common law rules concerning 'leading' witnesses and particularly upon appropriate communication between counsel and witnesses may be appropriate due to the relatively greater access of parties to evidence.

The Court's procedural rules concerning experts are generally similar to those for witnesses.[119] Thus, the foregoing analysis concerning testimonial evidence by witnesses of fact applies to expert witnesses with one important difference discussed above, namely, that the 'experts' utilized by privileged litigants may, as before the ICJ, be insulated from cross-examination by opposing counsel (though not from questioning by the Court[120]) by designating them as agents rather than as expert witnesses. By contrast, unprivileged litigants must adduce experts as witnesses.

5.3.3 Duties to Colleagues

Apart from the broad provision under Article 35(1) of the Rules concerning the 'dignity of the Court', there are no formal rules concerning collegiality or courtesy between advocates. Whilst counsel generally observe similar standards of decorum and courtesy,[121] there is still some scope for divergent standards of conduct in practice. According to one senior English practitioner, in one case a minor incident occurred in which a German lawyer had effectively accused him in pleadings of attempting to mislead the Court.[122] Although the judges from civil law jurisdictions did not take notice of it, the British judge (Lord Slynn of Hadley) 'gave the lawyer hell' for it. When the lawyer, upon being questioned by Lord Slynn as to whether he had any evidence to sustain the allegation, replied that he had none to offer he was told to withdraw it.

This minor incident demonstrates the scope for divergent standards of conduct between counsel. At the English Bar, an allegation against the integrity of another advocate is considered to be very serious. However, it was seemingly considered to be trivial by the accusing lawyer and the civil law judges. An incident that could result in disciplinary sanctions for a barrister could pass off without notice for a German *rechtsanwalt*. It is conceivable that differences of national ethical standards could disrupt proceedings, whether from simple misunderstanding or reckless accusations.

[119] ECJ Rules, Arts 47–53.
[120] ECJ Statute, Art 24; ECJ Rules, Art 57.
[121] Interview with Mr Vaughan.
[122] Interview with Mr Vaughan.

5.4 Disciplinary Jurisdiction

Whilst the ECJ has not yet legislated common ethical rules for advocates, it has prescribed disciplinary powers. Article 19 of the Statute provides: '[a]s regards such advisers and lawyers who appear before it, the Court shall have the powers normally accorded to courts of law, under conditions laid down in the Rules of Procedure'. Article 35(1) of the current Rules states:

> If the Court considers that the conduct of an adviser or lawyer towards the Court, a Judge, an Advocate General or the Registrar is incompatible with the dignity of the Court or with the requirements of the proper administration of justice, or that such adviser or lawyer is using his rights for purposes other than those for which they were granted, it shall inform the person concerned. If the Court informs the competent authorities to whom the person concerned is answerable, a copy of the letter sent to those authorities shall be forwarded to the person concerned.
>
> On the same grounds, the Court may at any time, having heard the person concerned and the Advocate General, exclude the person concerned from the proceedings by order. That order shall have immediate effect.[123]

The Court was vested with positive disciplinary powers grounded in the inherent powers of courts and tribunals, including national courts. Moreover, the omission of agents from the exercise of these powers continues the bifurcation of representation whereby privileged litigants' representatives are subject neither to admission requirements nor disciplinary sanctions. As seen in the *List D* and *Società Italiana Vetro* cases above, agents are not immune from questionable conduct. However, amendment of Rule 35(1) of the Rules (and, ideally, Article 19 of the Statute as well) to include agents would require the approval of the Council, an unlikely prospect.

An interesting point is whether the Court could financially sanction a lawyer *personally*, as opposed to the party he represents, for wasteful or abusive pleading. Whilst there have been cases in which the Court has sanctioned parties through costs orders for such pleading,[124] it is arguable that counsel should bear personal costs for their own inefficiency or misconduct. However, it is contestable whether the Court would have the power and need to do so:

> There is no scope for personal costs orders because it is unlikely that they would be within the Court's powers and in any event this would usually concern only respondents' costs, which in this respect are not excessive and in any event form a tiny fraction of the institution's budget.[125]

[123] See also ECSC Protocol, Art 20; ECSC Supplementary Rules, Art 6. The ECSC Court's disciplinary power was circumscribed by the approval of the Council and agents were always excluded—de Richemont, *Communauté européenne du charbon et de l'acier*, 106–1.

[124] Eg *Impala*, paras 544–554. Inordinately lengthy written pleadings by the Applicants also appears to have factored into the costs decision in *Atlantic Container*, paras 1646–7.

[125] Interview.

However, assuming the Court did have such a power, it is likely that the mere existence of personal costs orders would help to deter lawyers from such pleadings.

The Court has yet to invoke its disciplinary powers. Although this reflects a general lack of serious professional misconduct by counsel, as seen above this does not necessarily mean that no ethical problems have arisen during the Court's history:

Registrar Coulon: On the Court having 'never invoked its disciplinary powers', this is formally correct. However, in only one case (*Goldstein v. Commission*) the President explained to a lawyer that if he intended to proceed with the 25th or 26th proceeding by one litigant concerning the same subject-matter before the Court then the Court's disciplinary powers under Article 41 would be invoked.

Judge Forwood: I was the reporting judge in that case. It was also clear that the lawyer in question had not drafted the party's applications himself but had merely signed them. This clearly concerns not just the multiplicity of actions by the same party but also issues like the duty of the lawyer to present tenable arguments, the independence of the lawyers and the duty of the lawyer to assume personal responsibility for the content of pleadings. However, the isolated nature of this case demonstrates that this sort of occurrence is not a general problem.[126]

Such difficulties appear to have been handled in an informal way on the rare occasions that they have arisen through admonishment by the President or indirect criticism in the judgment.[127] According to a former judge:

In general, the tendency is to not to make an issue of such things because it will probably not make a difference to the outcome of the case... Certainly, some counsel make extravagant claims or 'over-egg the pudding' in presenting their case. I have certainly pressed counsel to face up to difficulties; once counsel replied 'I do not want to answer that question'! However, I do not remember any extreme incidents.

I suppose that with expanding EU membership there may be some new jurisdictions where the Bar take a different view of their role, particularly where the State has been seen as an enemy. It may be that as the Union enlarges, different ethical values will lead to conflicts of behaviour. Ethical problems are in practice more likely to arise in: (1) competition cases; or (2) staff cases.[128]

In the absence of practice or a prescribed code of conduct, the question remains as to what misconduct would be regarded as 'incompatible with the dignity of the Court or with the requirements of the proper administration of justice'. This applies *a fortiori* with respect to difficult issues with divergent 'good faith' views amongst national ethical traditions, such as conflicts of interest or confidentiality. In a nice case of alleged professional misconduct, the absence of prescribed ethical rules would undermine the legitimacy of the Court's *ex post facto* disciplinary sanction by depriving advocates of prior notice of the exact *standard*.

Due to the comparatively rare nature of disciplinary problems before the Court, the problem of 'double deontology' entailing regulatory conflicts of jurisdiction

[126] Interview.

[127] De Richemont observed that such admonishments do not constitute disciplinary sanctions—*Communauté européenne du charbon et de l'acier*, 106–1.

[128] Interview with Judge Edward.

between international courts and national bars has not yet arisen. In discussing double deontology, one judge has surmised:

On that problem, it is likely that the EU Courts would be in a stronger position than the international criminal tribunals towards national bars because they can invoke the Article 10 duty of cooperation of the Member States, which is broad, to compel national bars to respect the jurisdiction of the Courts.[129]

Thus, one may hypothesise that the crux of the prescription of common standards for counsel before the Court is the articulation of principles acceptable to national bars rather than compelling the bars to respect the Court's regulatory jurisdiction.

5.5 Conclusions

To recapitulate, the regulation of advocacy before the ECJ and ECtHR is currently in a state of partial development. Whilst both Courts have prescribed admission requirements and disciplinary powers concerning advocates, their policies in practice have been to delegate the regulation of advocates to national bars. This explains the otherwise surprising fact that neither Court has yet prescribed common ethical standards for advocates in over 50 years of existence.

Thus, the procedural rules of the Courts concerning advocates are, like those of the ICJ, relatively lax. Although they have prescribed admission requirements and disciplinary powers for advocates, in practice the Courts have adopted a similarly passive posture. On the rare occasions in which it has been compelled to consider ethical problems with divergent national views, such as the confidentiality principle and the status of employed lawyers in *AM & S Europe* and *Akzo Nobel*. Where cultural conflicts have occurred, they have largely been dealt with by the ECJ in an informal way. However, more serious problems have not been avoided entirely.

One might argue that there is no pressing need for common ethical standards or for active regulation by the Courts because of the lack of serious problems. However, this ignores not only that theory is merely practice waiting to happen but also the occurrence of dubious professional conduct before the ECtHR and other 'civil' international courts and tribunals. Furthermore, even if one discounts flagrant professional misconduct there nevertheless remains the important problem of good faith differences amongst divergent national and personal ethical standards. The Courts' principal admission requirement—that advocates be subject to *national* professional ethics and discipline—arguably creates problems arising from conflicts between divergent standards of professional conduct. However, this is not merely a fact of life to be accepted, but a problem to be solved.

Admission standards, ethical rules, and discipline are interlinked. The continuing diplomatic tradition of privileged litigants insulates their representatives from

[129] Interview with Judge Forwood.

the Courts' regulation. Not only is this dichotomy between litigants intrinsically prejudicial to equality of arms by creating a double standard of acceptable professional conduct, but the underlying rationale of different standards for fair trail for different litigants—by which States are not considered to need professional representation whereas individuals do—is disproved by practice. Thus, the case for the abolition of privileged representation to ensure uniform regulation for *all* litigants and thereby promote fair trial is compelling.

Although the ECJ has emphasized that professional ethics and discipline lie at the heart of its admission requirements, it has nevertheless declined to engage with underlying ethical issues in its jurisprudence. This must at least partially explain the otherwise curious fact that the Court has yet to exercise its disciplinary powers in its entire history. Prescribed ethical rules that fail to resolve the critical issue of the prioritization of conflicting, fundamental duties are of limited value. In order to provide the norm of 'independence' with practical meaning, advocates must be both *empowered* and *obliged* to behave independently according to common and robust standards. The rule of justice demands that advocates—as professionals—should be held not to the lowest common denominator but to strict standards of conduct so that the procedural efficacy of international courts may be held in the highest regard.

6

The European Court of Human Rights[1]

Having examined the European Court of Justice in Chapter 5, this chapter addresses a separate yet related institution in the European Court of Human Rights (ECtHR or 'Strasbourg Court'). Whilst the political and philosophical origins of both Courts lie in the post-War Reconstruction of Europe, they belong to discrete international organizations that were originally designed to serve very different purposes. Whereas the ECSC was an essentially 'economic' organization, the Council of Europe started as an overtly political body advocating solidarity, human rights, and the rule of law in Europe. One of its cornerstones is the European Convention on Human Rights and Fundamental Freedoms 1950 (ECHR or 'the Convention').[2]

Whilst there is no code of conduct for agents or counsel before the Strasbourg Court, the procedural rules applicable to representation are similar to those of the Luxembourg Court. Counsel are required to meet admission requirements (to be admitted to the bar of a Member State and proficient in one of the two official languages of the Court) and the Court has prescribed disciplinary powers (eg exclusion of counsel from the proceedings) in the event of counsel misconduct. As before the ECJ, there is a clear bifurcation between applicants (who must be represented by counsel) and respondents (which may be represented by agents to whom these rules do not apply).

However, there are also important differences between the ECJ and the ECtHR. Whereas the jurisdiction of the former is primarily review-based, that of the latter has greater scope for factual inquiry. This entails a greater role for parties and their representatives in the truth-seeking evidentiary process. In addition, whereas the control of the ECJ over its own procedural rules is circumscribed by the European Council, the ECtHR resembles the ICJ in having control over its procedural rules subject to the Convention. Consequently, the Strasbourg Court is in a stronger position to enact a code of conduct for counsel.

Moreover, in examining the practice of the Court, there have been considerably more frequent issues concerning the conduct of agents and counsel. From conflicts of interest to courtesy to competence, there have been a number of occasions in which agents and counsel alike have behaved in an ethically questionable manner.

[1] This chapter includes material previously published in the following article: Sarvarian, 'Common Ethical Standards for Counsel before the European Court of Justice and European Court of Human Rights', 23(4) *EJIL* (2012), 991–1014.

[2] Statute of the Council of Europe 1949, Arts 1, 3.

This greater frequency is attributable not only to the greater role for evidence before the Court but also to the even more diverse range of national jurisdictions from which counsel appear before it. The array of legal traditions with their own standards of conduct for counsel, particularly from jurisdictions with authoritarian backgrounds or systems, can be evident before the Court with clear implications for fairness, integrity, and equality of arms. Thus, there is a more pressing need for clearer regulation of counsel in practice for the Strasbourg Court than the Luxembourg Court.

As explored below, the principal institutional challenge confronting the Strasbourg Court at present is the elimination of the backlog of pending applications in its docket. At least part of this problem arises from unmeritorious claims or defences, such as 'repeat applications' concerning issues already decided by the Court in recent jurisprudence, the contestation of evidently meritorious claims by certain respondents and the failure by some respondents to implement decisions of the Court at the national level. In this sense, and in light of the historical connection between professional representation and the docket, it is suggested that greater professionalization of counsel can contribute towards the resolution of the backlog problem.

6.1 Historical Background

The statute of the Strasbourg Court is contained within Section II of the Convention. Although the *travaux préparatoires* of the Convention are published,[3] those of the Court's Rules of Procedure are not. Scholarship on the Court's procedure does not generally address ethical standards applicable to counsel.[4] Since the advent of rights of litigation for applicants in 1998, the Court's most pressing problems have included its backlog and uneven compliance by States with adverse judgments. Resource problems amid expanding membership and a low application threshold have also contributed even while efficiency reforms have doubled productivity.[5] The long-anticipated entry into force of Protocol No 14 in June 2010—designed

[3] *Collected Edition of the Travaux Préparatoires* (1975).

[4] Robertson, *The Law of International Institutions in Europe* (1961), 68–86; Mosler, 'The Protection of Human Rights by International Legal Procedure', 52 *GLJ* (1964), 800–23; Monconduit, *La Commission Européenne des Droits de l'Homme* (1965); Gormley, *The Procedural Status of the Individual before International and Supranational Tribunals* (1966), 92–115; Krüger, 'The European Commission of Human Rights', 1 *HRLJ* (1980), 66–87; Mikaelsen, *European Protection of Human Rights* (1980), 38–59; Mahoney, 'Developments in the Procedure of the European Court of Human Rights: the Revised Rules of Court', 3 *YEL* (1984) 127–68, 128–34; Eissen, 'L'avocat devant la Cour européenne des Droits de l'Homme' in Matscher and Petzold (eds), *Protecting Human Rights: The European Dimension* (1988), 159–69; O'Boyle, 'Procedure before the European Court of Human Rights' 2 *AEHRY* (1992), 93–104, 102–3; Konstantinov, 'Procedure of the New Permanent European Court of Human Rights', 3 *EEHRR* (1997) 101–16, 114; Leach, *Taking a Case to the European Court of Human Rights* (2011); Chavrier, 'L'avocat devant les jurisdictions européennes', 52 *L'observateur de Bruxelles* (2003), 21–31, 27–8; Reid, *A Practitioner's Guide to the European Convention on Human Rights* (2008), 21–3; Lambert, 'L'avocat devant la Cour européenne des droits de l'homme' in *Liber Amicorum Jean-Pierre Cot: le procès international* (2009), 171–84.

[5] Shelton, *The Regional Protection of Human Rights* (2008), 493–7, 1013–23.

to improve efficiency by empowering the Court to better filter applications—may help to reduce the docket.[6] In considering the historical development of rights of litigation and representation for applicants before the Court, it is clear that the role of professional counsel has been linked to the need to filter unmeritorious applications within the context of expanding rights of litigation for applicants.

From 11 May 1949 to 4 November 1950, the 'Committee on Legal and Administrative Questions' ('Legal Committee') drafted the Convention. Sir David Maxwell Fyfe chaired the Committee and Pierre-Henri Teitgen served as *rapporteur*.[7] Maxwell Fyfe declared that the right of individual petition was 'perhaps the most troublesome of [the Committee's] problems'.[8] Teitgen's original proposals called for the creation of a Court and a Commission,[9] in which the Commission was to be 'a kind of barrier—a practical necessity well known to all jurists—[to] weed out frivolous or mischevious applications'.[10] Amidst considerable debate, the Report of the Legal Committee endorsed the right of petition for individual applicants.[11] A recurring argument against individual petition was that it may be abused through frivolous or vexatious applications.[12] Supporters and opponents of the Court were united in their support for filtering mechanisms, such as the Commission and admissibility requirements.[13]

Whilst the early drafts of individual petition permitted individuals to directly apply, Lord Layton asserted on the issue of abusive petitions that '[i]t is clear from [the Legal Committee's] Report that some such sifting will take place, and that in due course the Commission will, in certain cases, hear the cases through the medium of legal representatives'.[14] M Pernot of France (Chair of the Drafting Sub-Committee) proposed an amended right of petition providing, inter alia, that individual petitions may be received by the Commission only when 'signed by counsel or through other similar legal channels'.[15] Whilst the amendment was unanimously adopted,[16] the Committee's Explanatory Memorandum states that '[o]n the provision that the petitions should be signed by a lawyer there was a difference of views, and the proposal was carried by 15 votes to 7'.[17]

M Pernot explained his reasons for compulsory representation as 'purely practical... not on grounds of principle... to facilitate the work of the Commission... by excluding appeals, as it were, through the obligation to make use of the services

[6] Shelton, *The Regional Protection of Human Rights*, 1014. See also Leach, 'On reform of the European Court of Human Rights', 6 *EHRLR* (2009), 725–35.

[7] *Collected Edition of the Travaux Préparatoires* (Vol I), 154.

[8] *Collected Edition of the Travaux Préparatoires* (Vol VI), 78.

[9] *Collected Edition of the Travaux Préparatoires* (Vol I), 47–8.

[10] *Collected Edition of the Travaux Préparatoires* (Vol I), 48.

[11] *Collected Edition of the Travaux Préparatoires* (Vol I), 202, 224; (Vol II), 154, 167–8, 178–80, 182, 192, 200; (Vol III), 22, 196; (Vol V), 62–4, (Vol VI), 22–4, 78, (Vol VII), 162 (para 17), 172.

[12] *Collected Edition of the Travaux Préparatoires* (Vol II), 182, 190, 198.

[13] *Collected Edition of the Travaux Préparatoires* (Vol II), 198.

[14] *Collected Edition of the Travaux Préparatoires* (Vol II), 196.

[15] *Collected Edition of the Travaux Préparatoires* (Vol VI), 34 (Doc A 2299).

[16] *Collected Edition of the Travaux Préparatoires* (Vol VI), 38–40.

[17] *Collected Edition of the Travaux Préparatoires* (Vol VI), 64 (para 6).

of a barrister or a jurisconsult'.[18] However, the provision was redacted due to the opposition of Mr Mitchinson of the United Kingdom. In proposing 'professionocide', he invoked the common law right to self-representation and argued that the Commission should itself decide the issue in its Rules of Procedure.[19] In exchange for Mitchinson withdrawing his opposition to the Convention rights to property and to education, Pernot agreed to redact the requirement of compulsory professional representation.[20] Thus, the Assembly endorsed a diplomatic bargain whereby compulsory professional representation was not legislated but merely left over for the Commission to decide.[21]

Although the principal debates were focused upon individual petition to the *Commission*, a largely but not wholly unnoticed[22] change was the elimination of direct individual petition to the *Court*. The Commission was originally intended to act as a filtering buffer, yet due to the elimination of individual access to the Court,[23] its role would necessarily expand to represent applicants. To discharge its task, the Commission relied not only upon the Convention and its Rules of Procedure but also upon 'an established practice in dealing with individual applications... [which] does not always emerge from the decision itself of the Commission but is often recorded in the minutes on the case concerned, which are not public'.[24]

In Rules 36 and 37(1) of the Commission's Rules of Procedure, as before the ECJ representation was bifurcated between individuals and States whereby the former were generally required to be represented by a 'solicitor' or 'professor of law' whereas the latter could be represented by agents.[25] The Court's first Rules of Procedure of 18 September 1959 followed the practice of the ICJ[26] and the ECSC Court of Justice[27] in requiring States (and the Commission) to be 'represented by agents who may have the assistance of advocates or advisers'.[28] Thus, an individual applicant was not originally entitled to directly litigate as a 'party' before the Court.[29]

[18] *Collected Edition of the Travaux Préparatoires* (Vol VI), 170–1. In the original French, 'barrister' and 'jurisconsult' were *avocat* and *docteur en droit*.

[19] *Collected Edition of the Travaux Préparatoires* (Vol VI), 98.

[20] *Collected Edition of the Travaux Préparatoires* (Vol VI), 166.

[21] *Collected Edition of the Travaux Préparatoires* (Vol VI), 166–72.

[22] *Collected Edition of the Travaux Préparatoires* (Vol VII), 172.

[23] Article 44: 'Only the High Contracting Parties and the Commission shall have the right to bring a case before the Court.' Article 48: 'The following may bring a case before the Court... (a) the Commission; (b) a High Contracting Party.'

[24] Council of Europe, *Bringing an Application before the European Commission of Human Rights (Procedure and Practice of the Commission)* (1972), 1. See also the works cited at note 4.

[25] In its practice, the Commission extended the right to self-representation to virtually all applicants—Council of Europe, *Bringing an Application before the European Commission of Human Rights*, 7 (notes 22–3). *Confer* the application of Rule 37, at 9.

[26] Mosler, 'La procédure de la Cour Internationale de Justice et de la Cour Européenne des Droits de l'Homme. Observations à l'occasion de la nouvelle procédure interne de la Cour Internationale de Justice' in *René Cassin Amicorum Discipulorumque Liber I: Problèmes de protection internationale des droits de l'homme* (1969), 196–212, 197.

[27] Mahoney, 'Developments in the Procedure of the European Court of Human Rights', 127–68, 167.

[28] ECtHR Rules of Procedure 1959, Rules 28–29.

[29] Mahoney, 'Developments in the Procedure of the European Court of Human Rights', 128.

The resulting lacuna forced the Commission to adopt a dual 'objective and impartial' stance whilst simultaneously representing individual applicants' interests.[30] The Commission considered itself to be principally a fact-finding body rather than a representational or judicial one.[31] However, the Court considered that, in light of its 'duty to safeguard the interests of the individual' it was 'in the interests of the proper administration of justice' that the Court hear the applicant's views directly or through the Commission.[32]

The conflict of interest created by this dual role climaxed ten years later in the *Vagrancy* case, in which the Commission designated as its assisting counsel the advocates who had represented the applicant before it. The Court rejected Belgium's objection that this would undermine the Convention's ban upon rights of litigation for applicants but declared that 'the person assisting the Delegates must restrict himself in his statements to presenting to the Court explanations on points indicated to him by the Delegates, and this always subject to the control and responsibility of the Delegates'.[33] Thereafter, the 'customary procedure' was that the Commission Delegates would 'transmit the applicant's written observations to the Court...and the applicant's lawyer...would appear at the hearing "assisting" the Delegates under Rule 29 paragraph 1'.[34]

However, the procedural imbalance between individuals and States continued to invite criticism. This included the irony that this inequality under the Court's own procedure may not have satisfied the Convention right to a fair trial.[35] Public criticism by Professor De Meyer (counsel for Belgium in the *Vagrancy* case[36]), alongside subsequent cases in which respondents welcomed the presence of applicants' lawyers, prompted the Court to grant individuals standing to directly participate in its proceedings in its revised Rules of 1983.[37] Since Articles 44 and 48 of the Convention continued to preclude applicants from initiating proceedings, the Court widened their rights of hearing whilst continuing to deny them rights of litigation.[38]

Clearly, it was the change in certain States' views concerning individual participation that encouraged the Court to adopt this measure.[39] However, the Court also declared that compulsory legal representation for the applicant would be desirable 'as a precaution to prevent abuse and to ensure a proper administration of justice'.[40] Rule 30 of the new 1983 Rules accordingly required applicants to be professionally represented except with the leave of the President. Following the abolition of the

[30] Mahoney, 'Developments in the Procedure of the European Court of Human Rights', 128–9,

[31] Mahoney, 'Developments in the Procedure of the European Court of Human Rights', 128 (note 11).

[32] *Lawless*, 11, 15–16.

[33] *Lawless*, 8.

[34] Mahoney, 'Developments in the Procedure of the European Court of Human Rights, 130.

[35] Mahoney, 'Developments in the Procedure of the European Court of Human Rights', 130–1.

[36] De Meyer, 'La situation des "personnes physiques", "organisations non gouvernmentales", et "groupes particuliers" dans la procédure devant la Cour européenne des droits de l'homme,' 34 Rtdb (1974), 65–74, 70–3.

[37] Mahoney, 'Developments in the Procedure of the European Court of Human Rights', 132.

[38] Mahoney, 'Developments in the Procedure of the European Court of Human Rights'.

[39] Mahoney, 'Developments in the Procedure of the European Court of Human Rights'.

[40] Mahoney, 'Developments in the Procedure of the European Court of Human Rights', 134.

Commission in 1998, the current system permits applicants to litigate before the Court whilst generally requiring them (unlike States) to be professionally represented. In considering the intended role of counsel as an autonomous actor or filtering mechanism between applicants and the Court, the prescription of ethical standards to regulate counsel is arguably a natural next step in this historical narrative.

6.2 Admission Requirements

Representation is bifurcated before the Court in that individuals are generally required to be represented by professionally qualified counsel whereas the States must be represented by agents.[41] After an application has been submitted, applicants must be represented by 'an advocate authorised to practise in any of the Contracting States…or any other person approved by the President of the Chamber' with 'an adequate understanding of one of the Court's official languages'.[42] By contrast, no comparable admission requirements are prescribed for agents.

In practice, agents are typically in-house government lawyers.[43] As the UK delegation to the Council of Europe Committee of Legal Advisers on Public International Law (CAHDI) has noted, whilst legal professionals from the United Kingdom who serve as legal advisers in the Foreign and Commonwealth Office are bound by domestic rules of conduct, 'how effective [their national rules] are to control conduct before international courts is another matter'.[44] Despite the assumption that agents are qualified to represent States and that States are wise enough to engage qualified professionals, in practice States do not always do so and agents are not immune from dubious conduct.

In light of certain negative experiences at the application stage involving vexatious petitions,[45] offensive language,[46] baseless accusations against the Court,[47] and deceit,[48] compulsory representation at point of application may be a useful filtering mechanism. However, vulnerable applicants may struggle to retain counsel:

> There are three filtering ideas being considered now: (1) applications to be drafted in one of the official languages; (2) an application fee; and (3) compulsory professional representation…[t]he problem with imposing the professional representation option is that a legal aid system at that stage would be required, for which there is little funding at the moment…[c]urrently the filtering costs are borne by the Court and the financial case would need to be made that requiring applicants to engage a lawyer would be more effective.[49]

[41] ECtHR Rules, Rules 35-36.

[42] ECtHR Rules, Rule 36(4)(a), 36(5)(a).

[43] ECtHR Rules, Rule 70.

[44] CAHDI, 'Item 7: Organisation and Functions of the Office of the Legal Adviser of the Ministry for Foreign Affairs' (32nd Meeting, 13–14 September 2006), online: <http://www.coe.int/t/dlapil/cahdi> (Accessed: 11 December 2011), 2 (note 1).

[45] *M v UK*.

[46] *Varbanov*, paras 36, 63–66; *Manoussos*, 20–21; *IS v Bulgaria*, No 32438/96 (6 April 2000), 6; *Akdivar*, paras 51–54; *Aslan*; *Assenov*, 68.

[47] *Duringer*, 2; *Řehák*, 4–5.

[48] *Jian*, 10–13; *FM v Spain*, 194.

[49] Interview with Ms Clare Ovey (15 October 2010), cited with permission.

One way to address the financial difficulty of legal aid may be to make exceptions for vulnerable applicants such as prisoners, residents in war zones or the indigent. Whilst the overall filtering effect may be modest, abusive and vexatious applications could at least be filtered to the benefit of all concerned (including the applicant).

6.3 Ethical Standards

Like the Luxembourg Court, the Strasbourg Court lacks prescribed standards of conduct for counsel. However, in 2008 the Court enacted the 'Resolution on Judicial Ethics'.[50] According to an architect of the Resolution:

> For me, having a code of conduct is as much a question of appearances to the outside world as it is a question of practice. It is difficult to explain to the outside world why we have ethics for judges, doctors, politicians and even for companies but we do not need them for counsel. Also, can we as a Court honestly say that we are so much better that we are not ourselves subject to temptations or to difficulties?... [w]hen you get into the details, you realise that things are more complex than they may at first appear. Another aspect is that a code of conduct, backed by disciplinary sanctions, clearly has a deterrent effect upon bad behaviour. Who knows what might happen? Everyone can fail and everyone can make mistakes. It would be naïve, or even foolish, to say 'don't do anything because nothing has happened yet'. It would be better to already have rules ready in such a situation than to have *to invent* rules on the spot to deal with it once it has already occurred.[51]

Thus, ethical standards can be useful not only to address existing problems but also to prevent potential problems, more effectively address future problems and promote institutional legitimacy. Such issues may be simple yet important: for example, counsel makes an urgent application for interim measures in a torture case but cannot be contacted or fails to notify the Court that he no longer represents the applicant.[52]

Ethical standards can be a particularly useful shield for junior counsel against client pressure:

> [T]his is something that I as a former practising lawyer can detect in observing the demeanour of counsel and client from the Bench. For example, colleagues of mine who say 'why did that counsel make such a silly point?' who have not been practising lawyers having to deal with clients in the past have not observed that it was because of the client that the lawyer had to say that. For a junior counsel, it *can* often be very difficult to deal with this and there will be all sorts of reasons why, such as age difference, client literacy, dealing with government officials as clients and so on. A senior counsel will find it easier, though problems will still arise for them too. They arise for judges. For example, during the drafting of the Resolution the point was made that 'one day, one of us will have problems and we will need to refer to the Resolution to support us'.[53]

[50] Resolution on Judicial Ethics 2008.
[51] Interview with Judge Elisabet Fura (15 October 2010), cited with permission.
[52] Interview with Judge Elisabet Fura.
[53] Interview with Judge Elisabet Fura.

The authority of counsel towards his client varies considerably and, in the event of pressure by his client or others to commit misconduct, a text can be a useful tool.

There is a substantial amount of practice entailing questionable conduct by counsel. Amidst an even greater diversity of national cultures and standards amongst the 47 current members of the Council of Europe, one judge has observed:

> Generally the standard of advocacy is not good in our court...but that's largely because we don't have professional advocates most of the time. It's only when we have the British, as we have quite a lot, that we have really good professional advocates. Then they're very well argued. Most of the time the arguments are conducted on behalf of the government by civil servants who work in their various departments. They have absolutely no experience or skill or qualification as an advocate and it shows. They're very poor at the presentation of the cases.[54]

Consequently, it would appear that some judges believe the quality and general evenness of advocacy in practice could be improved. This opinion is corroborated by a number of cases in which agents and counsel have engaged in dubious conduct. The enactment of a code of conduct for counsel would potentially promote not only procedural efficacy but also fairness by reducing disparity in quality amongst agents and counsel.

6.3.1 Duties to the Client

Due to the special features of human rights litigation, issues concerning ethical duties to the client can be manifested in ways differing to other international courts. For example, cases before the Strasbourg Court often perform a dual function: to obtain redress for the applicant and to promote legal reform in national jurisdictions. In the course of litigation, these priorities may conflict with one another and, ironically, it may even be the applicant pushing for the latter interest over the former. Conversely, respondents' priorities may not be simply to defeat a particular claim but also to resist legal changes or to generally protect national reputation by preventing adverse judgments. For counsel, these can present special challenges of advocacy.

Before the ECtHR, there is no rule prohibiting judges from serving as counsel following their term of office. However, in one case a former judge (Loukis Loucaides of Cyprus) sought to appear as counsel. While the application of the Court's power to exclude counsel was considered, the problem was ultimately resolved when Mr Loucaides voluntarily withdrew. Since the average age of Strasbourg judges (like Luxembourg judges) is relatively low compared with those of other courts such as the ICJ, there would appear to be a practical need for normativity concerning the apparent conflict of a former judge or registrar acting as counsel before his past colleagues. The inclusion of a 'freezing period' for such persons would be a useful precaution against allegations of bias or unfairness.

Another issue particularly affecting human rights organizations is a conflict between the duty of loyalty to an individual client and a campaign interest for human rights reform. For example, in Roma, Chechen, and Kurdish cases claims are

[54] Interview with Judge Elisabet Fura.

necessarily propelled more by the lawyers than by the applicants. Whilst this provides vulnerable applicants with an opportunity to seek a remedy, the question arises how far counsel should go in pushing the campaign interest. According to a confidential source, in the *Tahsin Acar* case the applicant rejected a substantial offer from the respondent in friendly settlement negotiations.[55] The Grand Chamber ruled that the 'unilateral declaration' should not be imposed upon the applicant but the Court found only minor violations. Either the applicant rejected the offer or the lawyer convinced the client to reject it. Although human rights organizations have brought cases that would otherwise never have come before the Court, they may adversely affect applicants' interests by prioritizing a campaign interest.

6.3.2 Duties to the Court

Rules 44A ('Duty to cooperate with the Court[56]) and especially 44D ('Inappropriate submissions by a party'[57]) articulate general principles of courtesy, honesty, and competence in an advocate's relations with the Court. In particular, the use of the term 'representative of a party' rather than 'advocate' suggests that Rule 44D is intended to apply not only to advocates but also to agents. In light of experiences concerning inappropriate submissions,[58] the addition of this provision on 13 December 2004 is understandable and supports the argument for common and rigorous ethical standards.

6.3.2.1 Misleading the Court

The danger of counsel misleading the Court is considerable due to the importance of factual issues, lax admission requirements and considerable diversity of counsel. Apart from asserting facts that counsel actually knows to be false, there are grey areas such as suppressing or otherwise failing to disclose adverse evidence and making unsupported factual assertions. Not only do these practices endanger judicial integrity but they can also result in a waste of judicial resources on factual matters that could be properly agreed between the parties.

In the *Foxley* case, the applicant's original representative (whose professional status is not clear from the judgment) was alleged to have prior convictions for perjury and perverting the course of justice. He was found by the Court to have attempted to deceive it (and to have succeeded in deceiving his unfortunate client) by clumsily forging letters of acknowledgment by the Commission in order to

[55] *Tahsin Acar*, paras 21–26.

[56] 'The parties have a duty to cooperate fully in the conduct of the proceedings and, in particular, to take such action within their power as the Court considers necessary for the proper administration of justice…' Although the term 'party' refers to the litigants themselves rather than to their advocates, it is difficult to conceive of any real difference for these purposes.

[57] 'If the representative of a party makes abusive, frivolous, vexatious, misleading or prolix submissions, the President of the Chamber may exclude that representative from the proceedings, refuse to accept all or part of the submissions or make any other order which he or she considers it appropriate to make, without prejudice to Article 35(3) of the Convention.'

[58] See notes 45–8.

prove that the application had been made within the deadline.[59] In another case, a Bulgarian advocate was found to have not concealed 'events of central importance' in his client's application because he had not had opportunity to confer with his client prior to hearing and had subsequent to the hearing done so *ex proprio motu*.[60] These examples illustrate not only the importance of an ethical duty for advocates to not deceive the court, but also that the duty must extend beyond deception to one of positive disclosure of facts material to justice—even without a client's consent. Although the material facts in *al-Nashif* were not subject to confidentiality, the potential for prejudice had the advocate failed to disclose the information had it been confidential nevertheless illustrates the potential conflict between an advocate's duty to the client and his duty to the court.

In cases where parties without excuse fail to produce evidence that the Court demands there is a compelling argument for the sanction of agents and counsel who actively collaborate in such concealment.[61] A particular problem concerning applicants entails attempts to deceive the Court by omitting to inform it of compensatory payments by respondents[62] or cases in which 'applicants' representatives did not bother to inform the Court that the respondent had indeed complied [with] and enforced the judgment'.[63] Collaboration by counsel in such deception or in the suppression or manipulation of evidence by intimidation, coercion or other tactics in circumstances where the representative would be in a position to reasonably 'know' of it may attract sanction.

Whilst compelling one side to prove its case is not necessarily misleading as it flows naturally from the burden of proof, it would depend upon how the arguments are presented. Each party can comment upon the other's evidence and the Court takes into account only the agreed facts. If a respondent does not comment upon an applicant's version, then the Court can accept it. Since respondents know this, one can find examples in the Chechen cases where the Court draws adverse inferences from lack of challenge. If a challenge does occur, the Court can demand substantiation and, under Article 38 of the Convention, it can find against a respondent for non-cooperation. Whilst unfounded challenges do not delay cases, as they arise early in the procedure, they can waste resources by sending weak or incomplete files.

The docket of the Court also creates a particular challenge for applicants' advocates who should be ethically obliged to protect the Court from frivolous cases whilst advancing meritorious ones. Agents, particularly those appearing for States facing many applications, may be pressured to contest every case regardless of merits and

[59] *Foxley*, 6–8.

[60] *Al-Nashif*, paras 88–9.

[61] See, eg *Tekin*, 1530.

[62] For examples of cases in which applicants represented by counsel have been found to have abused the right of application in this way, see *Keretchachvili*, 3–4; and *Lozinschi and Rujavnita*, 3–4. In *Sumila*, the application for enforcement was declared to be inadmissible for tardiness rather than abusiveness—a decision possibly attributable to the fact that the application was only for enforcement rather than for compensatory payment for late enforcement as well.

[63] Interview with Clare Ovey.

acquiesce to other tactics to compel applicants to abandon their cases by attrition. The disparity from State to State can be striking:

> For the UK, there are some 4000 cases pending and we have 4 permanent lawyers and 2 temporary lawyers as well as a large amount of high-quality interns. This is very manageable and we have good resources to stay on top of the docket. The principal problem for us is the large number of Rule 39 applications concerning asylum seekers.
>
> On the other hand, Russia has some 30000 cases pending. The Court's policy changed from chronological handling to prioritisation on the basis of urgency and importance, as we used to deal with cases indiscriminately as they came in. Now, the main problem with the docket is simply the volume of cases. It should be said that right across the Court, regardless of Respondent, around 90% of applications are filtered as inadmissible.
>
> [Concerning the question whether] there is a problem of certain agents contesting every case regardless of the merits and thus cluttering the Court's docket unnecessarily, this may vary from government to government, certainly one cannot say that about either the UK or Moldova agents. One problem is ensuring that counsel for applicants are adequately protected. Something needs to be done to ensure that counsel are able to do their work in physical safety.[64]

As seen in the history of the right of petition, compulsory professional representation is a vital safeguard for the Court against abusive or frivolous applications for which the extension of the rule to the application stage is desirable. Ethical standards are the necessary counterweight to encourage counsel to behave appropriately regardless of pressures emanating from their clients or even themselves (eg pleasing the client for fear of one's livelihood).

6.3.2.2 Documentary Evidence

Like the ICJ and ECJ, the proceedings of the ECtHR are weighted towards written pleadings. Although there is no specific provision addressing the veracity of documentary evidence, Rule 44D in referring to 'misleading submissions' presumably includes those based upon forged documents. Less clear, however, is whether an advocate who omits to disclose the existence of documents or who fails to seek to verify their veracity but who did not actually 'know' them to be false[65] would similarly be penalized.

There is no specific provision addressing the veracity of documentary evidence.[66] The Court has experienced dubious documentary evidence, as in *Foxley*. Although an advocate who knowingly adduces false documents would presumably commit misconduct, it is less clear whether a failure to disclose the existence of probative documents or to take steps to verify the authenticity of documents where he could be reasonably expected to do so would be sanctioned.

In light of the importance of written pleadings, safeguards certifying the veracity of documents are critical to procedural integrity. A duty for counsel not only to refrain from submitting documents that he actually knows to be false but also actively to

[64] Interview with Clare Ovey.

[65] Eg *Qatar v Bahrain*, Chapter 4.

[66] 'Misleading submissions' in Rule 44D is presumably broad enough to cover false documents.

take steps to certify the authenticity of documents could be a useful safeguard. While Principle 6.1 of the Hague Principles requires counsel to 'refrain from presenting or otherwise relying upon evidence that he or she knows or has reason to believe to be false or misleading', this arguably places the bar too low by catching actions but not omissions.

6.3.2.3 Testimonial Evidence

Rules 38(1)[67] and 39(1)[68] of the original Rules provided for witnesses and experts to be called by the Court or by the parties. Rule 42 ('Questions put during the hearing') provided that any judge could question the witnesses and that, 'subject to the control of the President who has the power to decide as to the relevance of the questions put' they may be examined by agents, advocates or advisers of parties or by delegates and assistants of the Commission. Testimonial evidence, however, was primarily the task of the Commission. Provision was made in Rule 54 for parties to arrange for witnesses and experts to appear, subject to the agreement of the Commission, and in Rule 56 for them to be examined by the parties with the permission of the President of the Commission with similar provision to 'decide as to the relevance of the questions put'. A witness was not heard by the Court until the *Syndicat* case in 1975 but was not permitted to be questioned by the parties under Rule 42(2).[69] Rules A1(1)[70] and A7(2)[71] now provide for examination of witnesses by parties.

Witnesses are rare[72] and the practice of the Commission and the Court concerning witness examination is vague.[73] Although one experienced advocate advises that '[f]or each witness, a summary should be provided as to the evidence that that witness is expected to give (where you already have witness statements), or at least in the areas which the witness is expected to cover (if you have no witness statements)',[74]

[67] See note 32.

[68] 'Witnesses, experts and other persons whom the Chamber decides to hear shall be summoned by the Registrar. If they are called by a Party…'

[69] Eissen, 'La présentation de la preuve dans la jurisprudence et la pratique de la Cour européenne des Droits de l'Homme' in *La presentation de la preuve et la sauvegarde des libertés individuelles* (1977), 143–214, 168.

[70] 'The Chamber may, at the request of a party or of its own motion, adopt any investigative measure which it considers capable of clarifying the facts of the case. The Chamber may…decide to hear as a witness or expert or in any other capacity any person whose evidence or statements seem likely to assist it in carrying out its tasks.'

[71] 'Witnesses, experts and other persons appearing…may, subject to the control of the head of the delegation, be examined by the Agents and advocates or advisers of the parties. In the event of an objection to a question put, the head of the delegation shall decide.'

[72] Leach, *Taking a Case to the European Court of Human Rights*, 62. See, eg *Lawless Case*, Series B (No 1), 53 (para 41) *et seq*; *France et al v Turkey*, 35 (para 20); *Ireland v UK*, 128 (para 3) *et seq*.

[73] The former Registrar Marc-André Eissen 'La présentation de la preuve dans la jurisprudence et la pratique de la Cour européenne des Droits de l'Homme', 143–214, 169 (note 73) posed the question: 'La Cour aurait-elle adopté la notion "continentale" de témoin, de préférance à la notion "anglo-saxonne"?' Ironically, in the case of *Ireland v UK*, 138–42, the argument was heard on the Respondent's (successful) application to the Commission to take evidence from certain of 'its' witnesses without affording the Applicant an opportunity to cross-examine.

[74] Leach, *Taking a Case to the European Court of Human Rights*, 69.

this common law procedure is unlikely to apply in cases with civil law advocates.[75] On witness examination, he writes:

> The President of the delegation of three judges will preside over the hearing. The President may lead in questioning witnesses, or other judges may be requested to do so. For an 'applicant's witness', the applicant's representative will then be given the opportunity to question the witness, followed by the Government (with a 'state witness' the Government precedes the applicant). However, Court delegations do vary in the procedure they follow. Some will extensively question the witnesses before the parties' representatives are given the chance to do so, others will not.[76]

Thus, the Court's procedure on witness examination varies according to the backgrounds of the judges and counsel in the case. It can broadly follow the comparatively flexible civil law model of an *enquête*[77] but can also adopt certain common law features, such as the use of witness statements. There are no rules concerning appropriate conduct in contacts with witnesses or interrogation techniques. Whilst the limited scope for cross-examination of witnesses within this procedure provides scant incentive for respondents to insulate 'experts' or other witnesses from cross-examination[78] by designating them as agents, they have the right to do so.

In practice, parties are likelier to have readier access to witnesses and, unlike in the civil procedures of civil law jurisdictions, advocates are not excluded from the evidentiary process. This justifies the inclusion of common law standards designed to protect procedural integrity from questionable practices such as coaching witnesses, communication with witnesses under oath, preparation of witness statements and interrogation technique (eg 'leading' questions and impugning the credibility of a witness). More detailed ethical standards for counsel designed to protect the integrity of testimonial evidence would be a useful addition to the European Courts' procedural rules to provide tighter safeguards for the hearing of witnesses.

[75] For example, in the *Lawless Case* (167, para 130(a); 169, para 132(b)), the advocates for applicant and respondent States were all from common law jurisdictions and 'affidavits' were used. Similarly, in *Ireland v UK* (131, 133, 135, 141–2). By contrast, in *Ringeisen* (283) in which the President, the Respondent and almost all of the advocates were from civil law jurisdictions, the President declared: 'I would draw Mr. Nettel's attention, with [*sic*] regard to the examination of the original applicant who of course is not a party before the Court, to what is expressly laid down in the Rules of Court: we would not treat him as a "witness" because *in our continental idea* it is difficult for anyone who could be challenged to be regarded as a witness; he cannot for example be sworn in a case in which he is directly concerned. But on the other hand it is possible to hear him in order to obtain information, i.e. to attempt to arrive at the truth and to discover what witnesses should be heard. The Court has made provision for this in its Rules and I don't think that we can depart from that procedure' (emphasis added, original: *notre conception continentale*).

[76] Leach, *Taking a Case to the European Court of Human Rights*, 70.

[77] Giovannini, 'The Continental European Perspective and Practice of Advocacy' in Bishop and Kehoe (eds), *The Art of Advocacy in International Arbitration* (2010), 499–517, 512; Sandifer, *Evidence before International Tribunals* (1975), 288, 303–5. See also the French CPC, Arts 204–31.

[78] See, however, the tactic of the UK on its lay witnesses in *Ireland v UK*.

6.3.2.4 *Judicial Orders*

An issue that has arisen in ECtHR proceedings is the violation of judicial orders[79] on confidentiality. Whilst there are no detailed rules concerning confidentiality owed to the client, Rule 62(2) provides for confidentiality of settlement negotiations:

> [i]n accordance with Article 39(2) of the Convention, the friendly-settlement negotiations shall be confidential and without prejudice to the parties' arguments in the contentious proceedings. No written or oral communication and no offer or concession made in the framework of the attempt to secure a friendly settlement may be referred to or relied on in the contentious proceedings.

This trite rule is intended to encourage free negotiation by ensuring that a court's deliberations cannot be affected by impressions of the parties' assessments of the merits of their cases during those negotiations. In *Popov*, the applicant (represented by one 'Mr V Jereghi of the Moldovan Helsinki Committee'[80]) disclosed the content of friendly-settlement negotiations to the Court in alleging that Moldova had attempted to coerce the applicant into a settlement. In response to that point as well as the respondent's counter-allegation that the applicant's assertion was 'offensive and defamatory' and, as such, an 'abuse of process', the Court observed:

> The Court reiterates the importance of the principle that friendly settlement negotiations are confidential and that communications made by the parties within the context of such negotiations are not to be relied upon in contentious proceedings. Moreover, it cannot be excluded that a breach of the principle could, in certain circumstances, justify the conclusion that an application is inadmissible on grounds of abuse of the right of petition. However, this principle cannot be interpreted in such a manner as to allow improper coercion by any of the parties to the proceedings. Nevertheless, this being said, since the applicant has made no complaint under Article 34 of the Convention that he has been hindered in the presentation of his complaint, the Court sees no reason to pursue the issue of its own motion and thus leaves open the question whether or not the allegation of improper coercion is well founded.
>
> As to the Government's submission concerning the alleged abuse, the Court considers that an application would not normally be rejected as abusive under Article 35 § 3 of the Convention on the basis that it was 'offensive' or 'defamatory' unless it was knowingly based on untrue facts (see the *Varbanov v. Bulgaria*, no. 31365/96, § 36, ECHR 2000-X or *Rehak v. Czech Republic*, (dec.), no 67208/01, 18 May 2004). However, on the basis of the material in its possession, the Court is unable to conclude that the applicant has based his allegations on information which he knew to be untrue. Accordingly, this submission fails.[81]

In another case, the Commission had occasion to investigate whether a Spanish *abogado* breached the confidentiality of its proceedings by speaking with Spanish media and whether effectively deceived the Commission by deliberately concealing the existence of parallel domestic proceedings:

> The Commission has first examined whether the application could be considered an abuse of the right of petition because of a breach of the confidentiality prescribed by Article 33

[79] ECtHR Rules, Rule 44(B): 'Where a party fails to comply with an order of the Court concerning the conduct of the proceedings, the President of the Chamber may take any steps which he or she considers appropriate.'

[80] *Popov*, para 2.

[81] *Popov*, paras 48–9.

of the Convention. It notes that in his letter to the Commission of 11 March 1990 the applicant's representative asserted that he had merely answered questions put to him by the press, who had secured their information from other sources. While regretting the fact that the press had access to confidential information concerning proceedings before it, the Commission considers in this case it does not have conclusive evidence that the applicant's representative was responsible for the disclosure of the information.

The Commission has next examined whether by omitting to inform it about the civil proceedings in progress in Spain the applicant has acted in bad faith. The Commission notes in this connection that the present application had already been introduced when the applicant instituted the civil proceedings referred to and that in the applicant's opinion these proceedings were not capable of affording him redress with regard to the complaint he has submitted to the Commission. Consequently the Commission does not consider that the applicant deliberately concealed information it needed in order to examine the application.[82]

These findings were not made pursuant to the advocate's professional duties but to the applicant's procedural duties as a party. The incident not only shows a need for robust ethical standards but also for *common* ones because matters like contacts with the media about ongoing proceedings and disclosure of parallel proceedings are subject to divergent national standards. It is unclear whether the conduct in *FM* would be have breached domestic standards[83] or whether they even apply before the Court.[84]

A similar problem arose in the case of *B and P*, in which two fathers 'complained that, in their residence applications concerning their sons, each was denied a public hearing and a public pronouncement of the judgment'.[85] The principal issue was whether the presumption in English law that legal proceedings concerning children would be held in private violated the fathers' right to a fair trial. In the proceedings before the ECtHR, the first applicant was represented by Mr Andrew McFarlane QC and Mr Tim Eicke (both barristers) instructed by Mr James Welch (solicitor) of the National Council for Civil Liberties (a prominent human rights charity) whereas the second applicant represented himself.[86] The Court 'noted with considerable displeasure that during the [oral] hearing, in breach of the Vice-President's order of 2 November 2000, Mr McFarlane and the second applicant referred to the full names of the applicants, their former partners and their children'.[87]

Thus, not only did the self-represented applicant and the professional advocate (to all appearances) knowingly breach the Court's order but they did so when the very subject matter of their application (namely, the confidentiality of children's

[82] *FM v Spain*, 194. See also *Drozd*, in which a self-represented applicant breached the Commission's confidentiality rules by publishing information concerning the proceedings in a newspaper of which he was an editor.

[83] *Real decreto 648/2001*, Art 24(2): 'Se considerará contraria a las normal deontológicas de la abogacía la publicidad que suponga: (a) Revelar directa o inderectamente hechos, datos o situaciones amparados por el secreto profesional.' Although there are several references to 'el secreto profesional' in the decree, there is no comprehensive definition so as to include tribunal-ordered confidentiality.

[84] *Real decreto 648/2001*, Arts 4(h), 68(y).

[85] *B and P v United Kingdom*, para 31.

[86] *B and P v United Kingdom*, para 8.

[87] *B and P v United Kingdom*, para 9.

identities in judicial proceedings) was intimately connected with that order. Although the Court noted its 'considerable displeasure', it did not take disciplinary action against either person. This case preceded the entry into force of Rule 44B (though Rule 36(4)(b) was in force) and the Court took no disciplinary measures. The case may have been one to have prompted the Court's decision to add Rules 44A and 44D. Whilst it is uncontroversial that an advocate who breaches Court confidentiality acts unethically, it is less clear whether the advocate should be required to take steps to prevent his client from breaching confidentiality. It is suggested that the appropriate standard is that of reasonable knowledge, whereby counsel must take such steps in circumstances in which he might objectively be expected to do so. These may include expressly advising his client and potentially alerting the Court.

6.3.3 Duties to Colleagues

Rudeness and insults by counsel towards opposing parties and their representation has frequently occurred before the ECtHR.[88] Harassment and intimidation towards opposing parties or their counsel has also been known to occur.[89] Apart from a reference to 'abusive submissions' in Rule 44D there are no specific procedural rules concerning standards of courtesy expected by the Court. Although overt insults by counsel would presumably constitute misconduct, matters like 'impeaching the credibility of a witness' or accusing other counsel of dishonesty are more subtle. There is also need for a professional duty of cooperation with the opposing party's representatives to promote orderly and expeditious proceedings. The lack of detailed rules concerning such matters renders it difficult to draw the line between zealous advocacy and professional misconduct.

6.4 Disciplinary Jurisdiction

The ECtHR has prescribed disciplinary powers under Rule 36(4)(b):

> In exceptional circumstances and at any stage of the procedure, the President of the Chamber may, where he or she considers that the circumstances or the conduct of the advocate or other person appointed under the preceding sub-paragraph so warrant, direct that the latter may no longer represent or assist the applicant and that the applicant should seek alternative representation.

Additionally, Rule 44D ('Inappropriate submissions by a party') provides:

> If the representative of a party makes abusive, vexatious, misleading or prolix submissions, the President of the Chamber may exclude that representative from the proceedings, refuse to accept all or part of the submissions or make any other order which he or she considers it appropriate to make...

[88] See note 46.

[89] See, eg Goldhaber, *A People's History of the European Court of Human Rights* (2009), 125–7, 138, 142–4.

Since Rule 44D was added in 2004 rather than appearing in the original 1998 version, it is reasonable to assume that it was prompted by occurrences of the very types of 'abusive' submissions at which it is aimed.[90] Moreover, the reference to 'representatives' rather than 'advocates' suggests that the power applies equally to 'agents'. This implies that these problems arose not only from individuals' representatives but also from those of States, thus supporting the argument for the abolition of the class of the privileged litigant.

Despite the lack of a prescribed power under the Convention or its Rules, the Commission excluded one lawyer from proceedings 'whose conduct was considered to be objectionable'.[91] As explored above,[92] although the Commission had occasion to investigate the professional conduct of an advocate in *FM v Spain* it did not appear to be considering exclusion of the advocate but rather procedural consequences for his client. Since the abolition of the Commission, the Court has exercised its power to exclude rarely. In the case of *Media Pro SRL v Moldova*, the President invoked Rule 36(4)(b) 'to exclude [Mr Tudor Cojocaru] as representative from all the cases lodged by him before the Court and prohibit him to lodge any new application before the Court as a representative' on the ground that Mr Cojocaru was discovered to have fraudulently filed an application on behalf of an unaware 'applicant' naming himself as its representative.[93]

An interesting manifestation of the 'double deontology' problem appeared in one case before the Commission in which, due to communications with the Solicitor's Complaints Bureau, 'the applicant alleged that his solicitor felt constrained in presenting his arguments to the Court in the knowledge that they might subsequently form the basis of disciplinary proceedings and he invoked his rights under Article 25 of the Convention [to self-representation]'.[94] Since the matter was not pursued by any of the parties, the Court did not find it appropriate to examine it. This example illustrates the need for *exclusive* disciplinary jurisdiction for international courts in order to ensure that counsel can represent their clients before the Court free from fear of parallel disciplinary proceedings by national bars and with full confidence in the transparency, consistency and integrity of the disciplinary architecture applicable to them for the purposes of their representation in such cases.

In addition to the problem of articulating common ethical standards for the divergent European professions, their enforcement is equally important. In the absence of

[90] Eg *Varbanov*.

[91] *Northern Irish Cases*, 35, 37. The advocate in question, one Mr James Heaney (an American attorney from New York), had written letters to the Secretary of the Commission making certain unspecified 'accusations' against him that the Commission considered as 'transgressing the limits for the proper conduct of such proceedings and not serving the interest of the applicants' and decided 'not to accept any further…submissions from him on behalf of the applicants'. The Commission did not invoke any statutory or other power to justify its decision. The applicants were informed and offered legal aid for a replacement advocate of their choice, Mr Ciaran McAnally (an Irish solicitor), who 'indicated that, *for professional reasons*, he was unable to accept instructions from the applicants until they had formally discharged Mr. Heaney.'

[92] See note.

[93] 'Letter in Media Pro' and 'Letter to applicants' provided by a confidential source (on file with author).

[94] *Findlay*, paras 64–5.

an international bar authority, the Court itself is the logical forum to uphold the integrity of common standards. The disciplinary framework does not at present provide for procedural rights (eg hearing, representation, and appeal) for impugned counsel enshrined in Article 6(1) of the ECHR.[95] An important point is whether there are enough judges with the requisite expertise to exercise such powers:

> Absolutely correct, and this seems to me to be self-evident. For example, I have an advantage in this area over *those of* my colleagues who have principally been academics, for example... [f]or these types of matters, it is important that judges called upon to deal with disciplinary matters concerning counsel have the background necessary to see all of the issues.[96]

A disciplinary architecture needs to ensure that counsel can be confident that the judges and registrars are familiar with the realities and ethics of forensic advocacy.[97]

6.5 Conclusions

The work of the Strasbourg Court in the specialized field of human rights has seen special problems concerning counsel ethics arise in practice. Whereas the frequency and nature of such issues is more limited and rare before the Luxembourg Court for the reasons explored in Chapter 5, the greater prominence of facts and evidence in the procedure of the Strasbourg Court coupled with its even greater diversity of national jurisdiction from which cases emanate results in considerably more frequent and varied ethical problems. Consequently, the case for greater regulation of agents and counsel before the ECtHR is not only a question of prevention and image but also of immediate practical utility.

In this respect, a key factor is the control of the Strasbourg Court over its Rules of Procedure. Whilst the Luxembourg Court lacks the power to enact a code of conduct for counsel without the approval of the European Council, the Strasbourg Court resembles the ICJ in its ability to prescribe such a code at its discretion. This is exemplified by the additions of Rules 44B and 44D in 2004 as a plain reaction to problems arising in practice concerning counsel conduct. In light of the connection described in Chapter 9 that is often made between the prescription of standards for judges on the one hand and counsel on the other, it is somewhat ironical that the Court has already enacted a code of conduct for the judiciary but has not yet legislated a counterpart for counsel.

A potentially sensitive issue is the bifurcation of agents and counsel previously observed in ICJ and ECJ procedure. In addition to the instances of questionable conduct discussed in Chapters 4 and 5, this chapter has examined additional examples. From discourtesy to dishonesty, there is nothing in the character of a representative of a State that precludes the possibility of human error and misbehaviour that

[95] Clayton and Tomlinson, *The Law of Human Rights* (2009), 860 (para 11.425).

[96] Interview with Judge Fura (emphasis in original text).

[97] Mackenzie et al, *Selecting International Judges: Principle, Process, and Politics* (2010), 59–62.

applies equally to applicants' counsel. Moreover, certain judges have opined that the standards of advocacy amongst civil servants who are not professionally trained advocates is poor—a phenomenon that potentially detracts from the efficacy of the Court and the interests of the respondent. Thus, it is suggested that the carte blanche given to respondents to organize and present their cases as they see fit free from the regulation of the Court is unsustainable in both principle and practice.

Were a code of conduct to be introduced, practical guidance should be provided to agents and counsel concerning the particular problems that each may face. For example, in the context of the Court's docket and indeed the historical background to representation before the Court, it should be emphasized that one of the duties of counsel is to act as a filtering mechanism for claims and defences. In other words, counsel are obliged to correctly advise their clients to ensure that meritorious applications and defences are advocated whilst others are handled through settlement or other means. Some issues, such as informing the Court about State compliance with judgments or of changes in representation, may particularly concern applicants' or respondents' representatives but others such as handling evidence or misleading the Court clearly concern both.

Concerning the key issue of the process of articulation of such a code, it is argued in Chapter 9 and elsewhere[98] that the Council of Bars and Law Societies of Europe (CCBE) would be the most logical drafting forum with appropriate input from the Strasbourg judiciary. This is based upon the comments made by judges and counsel in interviews concerning the issue as well as the quasi-federal nature of the CCBE for such a code to be adopted at the national level in a coordinated manner. Whilst the endeavour would have potential difficulties, they are not insurmountable.

[98] Sarvarian, 'Common Ethical Standards for Counsel before the European Court of Justice and European Court of Human Rights', 1012–13.

7

Investment Arbitration[1]

Having examined the practice and procedure concerning advocacy before traditional inter-State courts and arbitral tribunals represented by the ICJ as well as mixed-party regional courts in the ECJ and ECtHR, this chapter proceeds to address advocacy in investment arbitration. This field, which has been a growth area of international dispute settlement in recent decades, possesses its own peculiar jurisdictional and cultural features. It is also one of the most significant areas from the perspective of counsel ethics, in which a range of problems over a spectrum of complexity have arisen on an increasingly frequent basis. This phenomenon has prompted a correspondingly prominent debate in professional organizations and academia concerning the need for professional regulation for counsel as well as nascent efforts to articulate common ethical standards.[2]

Whilst 'international arbitration' has been employed, this chapter eschews that term in favour of 'investment arbitration' as a matter of terminological precision. The procedure and legal culture of the traditional 'public international law bar' that dominates inter-State arbitration and adjudication as explored in Chapter 4 differs considerably to that of the 'private international law bar' that practises in commercial arbitration. In this respect, the focus of this chapter upon investment arbitration—in particular, arbitration within the framework of the International Centre for the Settlement of Investment Disputes (ICSID)—not only conforms with the general focus of this book upon international adjudication (in which at least one of the parties is a State) but also serves as a convenient illustration of divergent ethical standards not only amongst 'national' but also 'international' bars.

Consequently, this chapter will focus principally upon the procedure and practice of ICSID arbitration with supplementary reference to the Iran-US Claims

[1] This chapter includes material previously published in the following article: Sarvarian, 'Problems of Ethical Standards for Representatives before ICSID Tribunals', 10(1) *LPICT* (2011), 67–134.

[2] Eg Benson, 'Can Professional Ethics Wait? The Need for Transparency in International Arbitration', 3(1) *DRI* (2009), 78–94; Mosk, 'Attorney Ethics in International Arbitration', 5 *BJILP* (2010), 31-37; Bishop and Stevens, 'The Compelling Need for a Code of Ethics in International Arbitration: Transparency, Integrity and Legitimacy' (2010), online: <http://www.josemigueljudice-arbitration.com/xms/files/02_TEXTOS_ARBITRAGEM/01_Doutrina_ScolarsTexts/ethics/ethics_in_int_arb_-_icca_2010_-_bishop.pdf> (Accessed: 28 April 2013); Rogers, 'The Ethics of Advocacy in International Arbitration' in Bishop and Kehoe, *The Art of Advocacy in International Arbitration* (2010), 49–66; Key, 'Draft Codes of Conduct for Practitioners in Investor-State and International Commercial Arbitration: From Brazil via Brussels to Beyond?', International Law Association British Branch Seminar Presentation (22 June 2011); Rogers, *Ethics in International Arbitration* (2013, forthcoming).

Tribunal, World Trade Organization (WTO) Dispute Settlement Body (DSB), and commercial arbitration. Whilst it will be of particular interest to specialists and practitioners in these fields, the abundance of practice and the growing interest amongst practitioners provides useful material for other courts and tribunals of the international judicial system. However, the procedural idiosyncrasies of the field—in particular, the relatively weak legal powers of arbitral tribunals vis-à-vis parties compared with international courts—should be factored in drawing upon arbitral practice.

Whilst there is a considerable body of opinion, gradually coalescing into a broad consensus, that there is a problem concerning divergent ethical standards in practice requiring attention, the process and solution are yet to be agreed. Early efforts to articulate common ethical standards have hitherto failed to gain traction in practice, at least in terms of formal citation and application by arbitrators who appear to be cautious in their handling of such matters and possibly reluctant to encourage what some believe to be a growing and potentially excessive tendency to challenge the participation of opposing counsel and to allege unethical behaviour. Another important factor is the absence of a text with sufficient authority to command widespread respect and inspire application in practice. In this respect, the International Bar Association Task Force on Counsel Ethics in International Arbitration[3] published its 'Guidelines on Party Representation in International Arbitration' on 25 May 2013. Whilst it is early to comment upon the potential impact of this text, it represents an important first step in addressing problems of real concern in practice.

7.1 Historical Background

The ICSID was created by the 'Convention on the Settlement of Investment Disputes between States and Nationals of other States' 1966 ('ICSID Convention') under the auspices of the World Bank. The Bank (created in 1945 as a lending institution for developing States) had initiated the project in 1961 due to its own ineffectiveness as an investment dispute settlement mediator over the course of the previous decade.[4] The typical investment dichotomy is a capital-rich investor from a so-called 'developed State' investing in a resource-rich 'developing State' (or 'host State'). The ICSID infrastructure is similar to that of the Permanent Court of Arbitration, in that it is not itself a court[5] but rather a facilitating institution for arbitration within a common procedural framework.[6]

The underlying purpose of the ICSID was 'to *depoliticize* the resolution of investment disputes by affording both States and investors access to a truly neutral

[3] The author is a member of the Task Force but is free to express his personal views concerning its work, subject to the confidentiality of internal deliberations.

[4] Nathan, *The ICSID Convention: The Law of the International Centre for Settlement of Investment Disputes* (2000), 47–50.

[5] Whilst the definitions of 'court' and 'tribunal' are not yet settled terms of art, one important criterion for distinguishing the two is the 'permanence' of a court contrasted with the 'temporariness' of a tribunal.

[6] Nathan, *The ICSID Convention*, 51–2.

forum'.[7] Thus, a crucial facet of ICSID arbitration is the removal of the judicial system of the host State from the dispute resolution process.[8] ICSID awards are binding upon national courts to a very high, if not absolute, degree.[9] Despite the existence of an internal mechanism for annulment of corrupt awards,[10] this necessarily places great pressure upon the procedural integrity of the arbitral process in order to justify the compulsoriness of its outcome.

The most important aspect of ICSID arbitrations is that the power to frame their procedural rules in large part lies with the parties. The sole source of binding positive law for all ICSID arbitrations is the Convention. The ICSID Arbitration Rules, drafted by the Administrative Council of the Centre,[11] may be varied by the parties to an arbitration except for the provisions that reflect the binding rules of the Convention.[12] Article 44 of the Convention provides:

> Any arbitration proceedings shall be conducted in accordance with the provisions of this Section and, except as the parties otherwise agree, in accordance with the Arbitration Rules in effect on the date on which the parties consented to arbitration. If any question of procedure arises which is not covered by this Section or the Arbitration Rules or any rules agreed by the parties, the Tribunal shall decide the question.

Thus, provisions of the Convention are binding and the default position is that the Arbitration Rules will be adopted, though the parties are free to amend those Rules as they please unless they reflect the Convention. The Tribunal, crucially, has the power to decide residual procedural issues. In considering the procedural regime of ICSID arbitrations, it is consequently necessary to bear in mind continuously the reality that although the Arbitration 'Rules' are for the most part optional,[13] unlike other international courts and tribunals,[14] an ICSID arbitral tribunal is placed in a relatively weak position vis-à-vis the parties in that it lacks the formal power to prescribe its own procedural rules.

7.2 Admission Requirements

The Convention is silent concerning the representation of parties in arbitral proceedings. Rule 18 of the Arbitration Rules, which is derogable, provides:

> Each party may be represented or assisted by agents, counsel or advocates whose names and authority shall be notified by that party to the Secretary-General, who shall promptly inform the Tribunal and the other party.

[7] Shihata, 'Towards a Greater Depoliticization of Investment Disputes: The Roles of ICSID and MIGA', 1 *ICSID Rev.-FILJ* (1986) 1–25, 4.
[8] ICSID Convention, Art 27(1).
[9] ICSID Convention, Art 53.
[10] ICSID Convention, Art 52.
[11] ICSID Convention, Art 6(1)(c).
[12] In particular, Arts 47–9, 56.
[13] Schreuer, *The ICSID Convention: A Commentary* (2001), 669, 672–3.
[14] The European Court of Justice (ECJ), however, may only propose amendments to its Rules that must be approved by the European Council.

For the purposes of these Rules, the expression 'party' includes, where the context so admits, an agent, counsel or advocate authorized to represent that party.

This rule goes further than those of the international courts previously examined in permitting all parties, State and non-State alike, to appoint whomever they wish as agents or counsel. Rule 18(1) requires the parties when notifying the Tribunal and the opposing party of the names of its representatives to also indicate clearly the scope of their authority.[15] Thus, there is no bifurcation of representation into privileged and unprivileged parties.

Although parties may consequently appoint professional or lay representatives as they wish, a leading commentator observes:

In practice, parties have nearly always been represented by lawyers. State parties have been represented by government lawyers, lawyers in private practice or a combination of both. Investors are nearly always represented by lawyers in private practice although representation by in-house counsel is not unheard of. Representatives are often specialists in arbitration with ICSID experience. The majority of lawyers representing parties have been from the United States and some from Europe but Latin American counsel have been retained increasingly in more recent cases.[16]

In light of what seems to be the standard practice of instructing professional counsel, a binding rule to that effect may not prove controversial. By amending Rule 18(1) or better still by amending the Convention to impose an admission requirement for representation by counsel who are members of national bars and presumably bound by professional ethics and discipline, current practice would be codified into the procedural rule.

One effect of this change would be to restrict the freedom of choice of parties. In principle, there are a number of justifications for doing so. First, parties should not be represented by lay representatives without professional qualifications or standards of conduct.[17] Secondly, minimal standards of competence are necessary for parties to be able to arbitrate on a reasonably equal footing. Thirdly, the increasing prevalence of challenges to counsel arising from alleged conflicts of interest prompts a need for transparent and principled standards to preclude unnecessary challenges. Fourthly, despite the greater party control over proceedings that is a cardinal feature of arbitration, the high stakes involved increase the importance of procedural efficacy.

[15] Schreuer, *The ICSID Convention: A Commentary*, 688 (para 66).

[16] Schreuer, *The ICSID Convention: A Commentary*, 688 (para 67).

[17] See, eg *Philippe Gruslin v Malaysia*. In two sets of proceedings, the Claimant was self-represented. The Claimant was self-represented against a legal team that included Elihu Lauterpacht, Freshfields solicitors, and so on. The Claimant went on to unsuccessfully apply for an annulment, refused to pay costs, and even sued the World Bank in Brussels whilst reporting ICSID and the World Bank to an international hotline for corruption. See also the fraudulent claim of an Iranian national, one Kaveh K Showrai, who successfully won an award posing as 'Mr Gordon Williams' in *Gordon Williams v Islamic Republic of Iran*, 271–2. However, the Federal Reserve Bank of New York, upon being ordered to pay out the award, discovered the fraud—Bederman, 'Nationality of Individual Claimants Before the Iran-United States Claims Tribunal' (1993) *ICLQ* 119–36, 120–1 (notes 11–12).

Two objections to these reasons come to mind. Some might, and do, argue that if parties engage academic or other lay representatives who do not have comparable advocacy experience to professional advocates of their seniority then the risk lies upon them. After all, it is their money and their case that they are hazarding. This objection may be discounted because it is based upon a premise that this book rejects, namely, a narrow view of due process involving only a passively impartial tribunal rather than one that actively ensures 'equality of arms' between the parties.[18] It is imperative to ICSID tribunals that their integrity not be doubted by parties or the public on the ground that one side or the other was unable to adequately argue its case owing to an inequality of arms. This applies *a fortiori* to vulnerable, poor and/or inexperienced parties who may, in effect, have to be protected from themselves.[19]

One experienced ICSID arbitrator wrote:

> Both States and Claimants may have difficulties in obtaining the quality of legal representation that the by-now highly specialized field of international investment arbitration requires. Ideally, the expertise deployed will include both public international law, international arbitration (and international judicial procedure in a wider sense), and comparative public/administrative law. It will go beyond rules and concepts that may be academically known and researchable, to include the much more arcane areas of the advocacy and politics of investment arbitration, e.g., arbitrator and chair selection; proclivities of appointment institutions; and personal, professional, institutional, and philosophical linkages and preferences. A party, Respondent, or Claimant not served by professionals experienced in this newly emerging field is quite likely to be at a considerable handicap. There are awards which indicate that one of the parties (or both) was unable to mount a reasonably competent claim or defense. This applies both to junior companies with no prior foreign investment experience (arguably the most frequent Claimants) and small developing countries with no prior Respondent experience.

[18] Wälde, '"Equality of Arms" in Investment Arbitration: Procedural Challenges' in Yannaca-Small, *Arbitration under International Investment Agreements* (2010), 161–88, 179–80. *Confer* the case of *European Communities—Regime for the Importation, Sale and Distribution of Bananas*, paras 4–12. Objection made to the representation of Saint Lucia by two private counsel was rejected on the ground that there was no rule restricting State representation and, moreover, 'we also note that representation by counsel of a government's own choice may well be a matter of particular significance—especially for developing-country Members—to enable them to participate fully in dispute settlement proceedings' (para 12).

[19] Eg a narrative given on Albania's first contact with the ICSID in the *Tradex* arbitration in Sands, *Lawless World* (2006), 118: 'This turned out to be Albania's first real contact with ICSID. In the heady days after the demise of Hoxha's regime, Albania had been persuaded to join ICSID and take steps to protect the tide of valuable foreign investments that were promised to be heading Albania's way. To encourage foreign investment, Albania was told it would be necessary to promulgate various national laws and investment protection treaties. Investors would not come to Albania if they had to go to the local courts, and they should have the right to arbitrate any disputes outside Albania and under the ICSID rules. In this way, so the theory ran, foreign investment would contribute to Albania's economic development. For a country that had had virtually no contact with the outside world for two generations, this was a rude change...The Albanian President was surprised—to say the least—that his country could be brought before an international tribunal. We had to explain that it was not he personally who was being sued. Plainly, no one had taken the trouble to explain to Albania exactly what it was signing up to, after nearly fifty years of isolation. Ironically, Albania was the first country to be sued at the International Court of Justice in the Hague...Albania lost, and the Corfu Channel case has remained engraved on the memories of Albanians as a great injustice, their last brush with international litigation until the Tradex case came along.'

Junior companies, in particular, will often have stumbled in their first foray abroad due to lack of international business experience. They may stumble equally when choosing advocates. Without sufficient funds for litigation, they may be limited to those firms or independent practitioners keen on but not prepared for international arbitration and therefore ready to accept contingent-fee arrangements. Governments can be handicapped when relying exclusively upon their internal legal services, in particular when, unlike the services of frequent Respondents such as, e.g., the United States, Iran, Canada, Mexico, Argentina, they lack experience.[20]

The connexion between competent representation and equality of arms is evident, as is the range of skills necessary to advocate effectively in investment arbitration.

Professor Wälde cites two compelling examples. In *Generation Ukraine*, the Claimant (a US company) was represented by Irish barristers whereas the Respondent was represented by employed government lawyers and private Ukrainian lawyers.[21] The following extract from the Tribunal's award is revealing:

Counsel for the Claimant has suggested that 'there's more documentation in this particular ICSID reference than has ever been in any previous ICSID reference.' The Tribunal is not certain that such an affirmation is verifiable; it is certainly true that the written evidence and submissions in this case have been voluminous. But the Claimant's written presentation of its case has also been convoluted, repetitive, and legally incoherent. It has obliged the Respondent and the Tribunal to examine a myriad of factual issues which have ultimately been revealed as irrelevant to any conceivable legal theory of jurisdiction, liability or recovery. Its characterisation of evidence has been unacceptably slanted, and has required the Respondent and the Tribunal to verify every allegation with suspicion. (For example, the Claimant's confident assertions of its mobilisation of necessary financing do not match the evidence of Crédit Lyonnais Ukraine's expression of interest…The fact that the author of that letter was announced as a witness, that a document purporting to be his written statement was produced, but that no signed version was forthcoming, and that he declined to appear before the Tribunal, has hardly helped matters.)

The Claimant's position has also been notably inconsistent. For example, it alleged that 'we established Heneratsiya in anticipation of the fact that the Bilateral Investment Treaty allowed us to function in Ukraine through a local subsidiary.' But Heneratsiya was formed in 1993, and Mr Laka ultimately, on the last day of his testimony, revealed that he had not become aware of the BIT until a U.S. Embassy official advised him about it at the time of preparing the Claimant's case before the Chamber of Independent Experts—which was in 1999.

Moreover, the Claimant's presentation of its damages has reposed on the flimsiest foundation…there is not one item of direct evidence of a single expenditure…the Claimant's approach to filling that evidentiary gap has been singularly unimpressive…And yet there are numerous documents in the file that refer to previous examinations of the Claimant's costs; somehow the relevant annexes, notwithstanding the plethora of the Claimant's documentation, are missing…

The Claimant's presentation has lacked the intellectual rigour and discipline one would expect of a party seeking to establish a cause of action before an international tribunal. This lack of discipline has needlessly complicated the examination of the claim.

[20] Wälde, '"Equality of Arms" in Investment Arbitration: Procedural Challenges', 161–88, 179.

[21] *Generation Ukraine, Inc v Ukraine*, para 2.

> Even at the stage of final oral submissions in March 2003, counsel for the Claimant relied on two ICSID awards without mentioning that they had been partially annulled. While the Tribunal was fortunately aware of that limitation on the pertinence of those awards, this was due to the happenstance of the arbitrators' personal knowledge. The Tribunal assumes in counsel's favour that he was unaware of the annulments; that is bad enough, and does no credit to the Claimant.[22]

This account suggests if not dishonesty then at least incompetence by the Claimant's representation. Additionally, the award in the *CDC Group* case[23] suggests that the Republic of the Seychelles was unable to adequately defend its interests.[24] In particular, its counter-memorial was sloppily drafted and had to be redrafted and refiled,[25] it made strange jurisdictional arguments that were later withdrawn,[26] and it called witnesses at the oral hearing who gave testimony adverse to its own case.[27] The Seychelles lost the case, with awards and costs in excess of £2,000,000.[28]

Such cases illustrate two practical needs: professional competence as an admission requirement to appear before an ICSID tribunal and a mechanism to provide poor or inexperienced parties with practical assistance to retain competent counsel. Such tools already exist at international criminal tribunals[29] and even, in a more limited fashion, at the ICJ.[30] The 'Advisory Centre on WTO Law' provides a third variant of legal aid, whereby internal or external counsel are provided to indigent States for advice and representation.[31] A 'list system' comprising professional counsel with competence in public international law, international investment law, international

[22] *Generation Ukraine, Inc v Ukraine*, para 24.

[23] *CDC Group Plc v Republic of the Seychelles* (Case No ARB/02/14), Award (17 December 2003).

[24] Its representative is named as its Attorney-General, thus indicating that it relied exclusively upon its internal legal service, whereas the Claimant (a British company) was represented by a solicitor from the highly experienced and expensive law firm of Allen & Overy—*CDC Group Plc v Republic of the Seychelles*, 1.

[25] *CDC Group Plc v Republic of the Seychelles*, 9 (paras 25–6).

[26] *CDC Group Plc v Republic of the Seychelles*, 9 (paras 21, 34).

[27] *CDC Group Plc v Republic of the Seychelles*, 9 (paras. 34–42).

[28] To contextualize such a sum in local economic terms, according to World Bank figures the government revenue of the Seychelles in the year 2007 was 38.6 per cent of a GDP of US $910,000,000, or US $351,260,000—'Seychelles at a glance', online: <http://devdata.worldbank.org/AAG/syc_aag.pdf> (Accessed: 8 September 2010).

[29] The vast majority of defendants before the ICTY, ICTR, SCSL, and ICC are indigent. Thus, they are reliant upon the 'list' system from which legal aid counsel may be selected. Additional admission requirements for these advocates are imposed beyond what is required of counsel privately retained by defendants, namely, 'established competence in criminal law and/or international criminal law/international humanitarian law/international human rights law' and 'at least seven years of relevant experience, whether as a judge, prosecutor, attorney or in some other capacity, in criminal proceedings'—Rule 45(B), ICTY Rules. The explanation for the additional requirements for legal aid counsel is likely to be found in the jurisprudence of the UN Human Rights Committee (UNHRC) interpreting Art 14(3)(d) ICCPR. Although there is some ambiguity in the Committee's reasoning, it has seemingly imposed a stricter standard upon parties to the ICCPR to ensure 'competent counsel' where they are provided by the State through legal aid as opposed to privately retained counsel—Joseph et al, *The International Covenant on Civil and Political Rights: Cases, Materials, and Commentary* (2005), 443–6.

[30] Namely, the 'Secretary-General's Trust Fund to Assist States in the Settlement of Disputes Through the International Court of Justice'—Zimmerman et al, *The Statute of the International Court of Justice: A Commentary* (2006), 1396–8.

[31] See the 'Agreement establishing the Advisory Centre on WTO Law' 2001 and the Advisory Centre website at <http://www.acwl.ch/e/about/about_us.html>.

procedural law, and international advocacy would be a potentially useful innovation. Additionally, a legal aid mechanism—perhaps combined with a pro bono requirement for counsel to undertake a percentage of cases for indigent clients at a subsidized rate—may assist in ameliorating inequality of arms.

The propriety of individuals serving as arbitrator in one arbitration whilst simultaneously serving as counsel in another is controversial.[32] There are two reasons for an admission requirement prohibiting serving and former arbitrators from serving as counsel. The first is that an appearance of inequality of arms emerges from the ability of parties to retain arbitrators as counsel because those arbitrators inevitably acquire—from their experiences *qua* arbitrator—'insider knowledge' concerning the mentalities and proclivities of fellow arbitrators. As seen in Chapter 4 concerning the ICJ, the perception, real or not, that parties will suffer a tactical disadvantage will lead to all parties seeking to retain arbitrators as counsel in a 'race to the bottom'. Such a practice would lead to allegations of nepotism or corruption. Moreover, arbitrators may well draw discomfort from having to address an individual as counsel in an arbitration who is contemporaneously serving with them as a colleague in another arbitration.

A second reason is the potential for 'issue conflicts'[33] whereby an arbitrator hearing argument on a legal issue in one arbitration may argue on the same issue as counsel in another arbitration. The possibility exists that the arbitrator-cum-counsel may appear to have manipulated his decision as arbitrator and/or his pleadings as counsel in order to benefit his client or his position as arbitrator. However, it is arguable that, where the arbitrator has not pronounced on the issue, his arguments qua counsel do not give rise to a conflict as they are made in the guise of counsel pursuant to the duty to represent the interests of his client without prejudice to his duty of neutrality qua arbitrator.

Regardless of one's view on the substantive issue, the prescription of admission requirements for counsel in investment arbitration is not only desirable but also necessary to address practical problems. Moreover, inequality of arms between parties requires redress. Article 44 of the ICSID Convention provides that the Arbitration Rules shall be adopted by default unless the parties decide to vary those provisions that are optional. Thus, amendment to Rule 18 to impose admission requirements for counsel would be unlikely to prompt major opposition as parties almost invariably retain professional counsel in current practice. Moreover, even without this change to the default position, parties to arbitral proceedings may amend Rule 18 to impose admission requirements *inter se* for their own arbitration. Since ICSID

[32] There is a good analogy to be drawn with the situation involving judges ad hoc before the ICJ, which led to the adoption of Practice Directions VII and VIII. See Chapter 4.

[33] Levine, 'Dealing with Arbitrator "Issue Conflicts" in International Arbitration', *DRJ* (Feb–April 2006); Wesler and Laird (eds), *Investment Treaty Arbitration and International Law* (2009), Part I. See, eg the participation of Mr Bernardo Cremades as counsel for the Claimant in *Compañia de Aguas and Vivendi Universal v Argentine Republic*. This case ostensibly concerned the same legal issue upon which Mr Cremades sat as arbitrator in *Lanco v Argentina*, which featured heavily in the *Vivendi* decision concerning jurisdiction. In essence, Mr Cremades was as counsel challenging his own findings as arbitrator. Although arbitral neutrality is the crux of the matter, it is his participation *as counsel* that engages it.

tribunals only have a residual power to decide procedural lacunae they cannot impose admission requirements upon parties without their consent.

7.3 Ethical Standards

As has already been observed, at present there are no common standards of conduct binding upon agents and counsel before ICSID tribunals. The purpose of this section is to demonstrate that this is an important lacuna that needs to be redressed. In examining experiences from practice, one may conclude that there is a real need for such standards to provide guidance equipping tribunals to more effectively address allegations of misconduct. The considerable financial and political stakes in arbitration can bring great pressure to bear upon counsel to achieve victory at all costs. Concordantly, standards of conduct can enable counsel to resist such pressures.

The following commentary indicates some of the types of misconduct that have already occurred, and why:

> While particular types of litigation misconduct may more frequently be engaged in by States, one needs to bear in mind that a good deal of such misconduct can be, and at times is, committed by private parties. Forgery and concealment of documents, illegal surveillance of communications (mail, phone, e-mail, and computer hacking), intimidation of the participants in arbitration (arbitrators, party representatives, counsel, experts and witnesses), lies, and false testimony are not reserved for States only. Arbitration against or between business oligarchs in countries with an underdeveloped system of 'rule of law' seems often to involve the use of private detectives to spy on and sometimes visibly follow arbitrators, either to intimidate them or to find evidence for suspected corruption; eavesdropping; threatening witnesses; and forgery, including forged 'evidence' of arbitrator corruption.
>
> But some governments, particularly in authoritarian systems with weak 'rule of law', find it difficult to refrain from using the many means at their disposal to frustrate the arbitration or steer it in their favor. Pierre Lalive noted that a State or State-controlled entity may have 'difficulties to accept a basic tenet of arbitral procedure, i.e. the principle of equality of the parties.' Politically, investment disputes are sensitive, and they may involve actions by a new government to disown or frustrate agreements made by prior governments and strong political condemnation of an earlier government's dealings with foreign businesses. They may involve the application of public policies important to the government. A loss of such an international arbitration claim can be, therefore, politically very embarrassing. The government, and the particular politicians and civil servants responsible, will therefore be under immense pressure not to lose—at least not during their tenure.
>
> Some governments are particularly prone to deploying the powers of the State in internal disputes, e.g., police, security services, government-controlled press and mass campaigning, tax auditing, environmental compliance control and permitting, travel restrictions, control over postal services, telephones, now Internet and e-mail, and the justice system (prosecution, courts, bailiffs). Accordingly, there is a certain political logic in the use of such services in investor disputes seen by the Respondent government as creating an internal or external political risk.[34]

[34] Wälde, '"Equality of Arms" in Investment Arbitration: Procedural Challenges', 162–3.

Thus, there is considerable temptation for certain parties to go to extreme lengths to subvert procedural fairness and integrity. The first compelling reason for the urgent introduction of rules of ethical conduct to ICSID arbitrations is to deter flagrant misconduct by counsel, namely, abuses that cannot be justified or excused under any system of justice. Furthermore, the harmonization of divergent standards of conduct is a practical need in light of the great diversity of counsel in investment arbitration.

7.3.1 Duties to the Client

7.3.1.1 Conflict of Interest

Conflicts of interest have become a prominent ethical issue in investment arbitration, particularly in relation to alleged links between counsel and arbitrators. As alluded to in the discussion concerning admission requirements above, the possibility for 'issue conflicts' have invited criticism[35] as well as multiple applications for the exclusion of counsel.[36] The sensitivity of the issue renders it likely that it will continue to feature in arbitral practice and that careful codification can assist in clarifying the rules of the game for all concerned. Counsel should disclose any personal links with the opposing party or with the Tribunal such as may give rise to an appearance of conflict and in certain cases should probably be obliged to refuse or withdraw from a case. Examples may include familial and romantic relationships.[37]

ICSID tribunals have recently had occasion to examine the problem of professional links between counsel and arbitrator. In the *Hrvatska* case,[38] the Respondent's representation (the English firm of Allen & Overy) informed the Tribunal and Claimant of the appointment of Mr David Mildon QC of Essex Court Chambers[39] as representative for the oral hearings.[40] Crucially, this appointment was made *after* the constitution of the Tribunal and the completion of the written stage of proceedings. The Claimant, upon learning that the President of the Tribunal (Mr David Williams QC) was also a member of Essex Court Chambers,[41] requested disclosure of the nature of the professional links between the two men. The Respondent's solicitors (Allen & Overy) resisted disclosure until the oral hearing itself, whereupon it emerged that they had approached Mr Mildon about instructing him some two months prior to their notification of his participation just before the oral hearing itself.[42]

[35] Levine, 'Dealing with Arbitrator "Issue Conflicts" in International Arbitration', *DRJ* (Feb–April 2006).

[36] Levine, 'Dealing with Arbitrator "Issue Conflicts" in International Arbitration'. Argentina mounted challenges in the cases of *Siemens v Argentina* and *Azurix v Argentina* against the same individual, both of which were unsuccessful. Subsequent initiatives have been taken within the ICSID system to broaden the duty of disclosure for arbitrators.

[37] For examples of sex scandals between counsel and arbitrators, see Hanotiau, 'Misdeeds, Wrongful Conduct and Illegality in Arbitral Proceedings', 1(5) *Oil, Gas and Energy Law* (2003), paras 10–15.

[38] *Hrvatska v Slovenia.*

[39] For a brief explanation of the relevant aspects of the English 'chambers' system, see *Hrvatska v Slovenia*, paras 17–19.

[40] *Hrvatska v Slovenia*, para 3.

[41] He is a 'door tenant', which is a member who does not maintain an office at the Chambers themselves.

[42] They did observe: 'we accept the point now made that it would have been sensible and prudent for us to have made that disclosure at that time'—*Hrvatska v Slovenia*, para 11.

The Claimant applied for Mr Mildon's exclusion on the ground that, had it known of his participation before the constitution of the tribunal, it would not have agreed to the President's appointment.[43] Being unfamiliar with the English Bar, it was uncomfortable with the idea that two members of the same chambers—though sharing no hierarchical relationship, being self-employed—could both appear in the same arbitration as arbitrator and counsel.[44] The Tribunal was confronted with the choice that, prompt disclosure having been precluded as a remedy by the Respondents' representatives' conduct, the only two ways to remove a risk of appearance of bias were the resignation of the President or the exclusion of the representative. Invoking an 'inherent power', considered in detail below,[45] the Tribunal opted for the latter course.

To demand the President's resignation—a course of action that neither party desired[46]—when his appointment long preceded that of the representative in question would have been both unfair and disruptive. The issue of disclosure or withdrawal due to appearance of bias arising from professional or personal links can be fairly solved with a temporal approach whereby the onus should lie upon the person appointed later, whether arbitrator or representative. A 'first come, first served' approach deals equally with both bench and bar and protects the most innocent individual concerned.

The issue reappeared recently in the *Rompetrol* arbitration,[47] in which objection was raised to the appointment of a representative (Mr Barton Legum) for the Claimant who was a former employee of a law firm of which an arbitrator had also been a member. The Claimant, through letters signed by Mr Legum himself,[48] denied any disclosure obligation.[49] The Tribunal, in denying the Respondent's application to exclude Mr Legum from the proceedings, interpreted the application as effectively an indirect challenge to the impartiality of the Tribunal.[50] In other words, the Tribunal considered that the application must be based upon an apprehension of bias on the part of the Tribunal member concerned towards his former colleague.

It is suggested that this premise was an incorrect one because there was no basis for a challenge to the arbitrator in question. This is due to the fact that Mr Legum was appointed as representative *after* the Tribunal had already been constituted. Each arbitrator is required to disclose the existence of any 'professional, business or other relationships...with the parties' upon appointment.[51] The arbitrator in question had already done so and, of course, there was at that time nothing to disclose. It was not the initial appointment of the *arbitrator* that created the conflict issue but rather the subsequent appointment of the *representative* who resisted disclosure and thereby prompted suspicions of close professional links such as would give rise to a

[43] *Hrvatska v Slovenia*, para 7.
[44] *Hrvatska v Slovenia*, para 10.
[45] Section 7.4.
[46] *Hrvatska v Slovenia*, para 16.
[47] *Rompetrol v Romania*.
[48] Itself a conflict of interest, as he should have suspended his own participation pending resolution of a procedural matter concerning him personally rather than his client.
[49] *Rompetrol v Romania*, para 6.
[50] *Rompetrol v Romania*, para 18.
[51] Arbitration Rules, Rule 6(2).

reasonable apprehension of bias.[52] The question of disclosure, withdrawal or exclusion consequently lay with him, not with the arbitrator.

Whilst it is certainly arguable that prompt and full disclosure on the part of the representative would have sufficed as the past professional links appear to have been tolerably remote, to interpret the entire issue as a surreptitious challenge to the integrity of the Tribunal is incorrect. The following statement from *Rompetrol* is interesting:

> If that be the regime applying to an arbitrator, the ICSID Convention contains nothing of a remotely similar kind in respect of the persons representing a Party in a dispute duly brought before the Centre, and remitted to a Tribunal under the Convention. Nor do either the Institution Rules or the Arbitration Rules. This silence cannot be accidental, and surely derives from the fundamentally different duties inherent in the roles of arbitrator and of counsel. The duty of the arbitrator is to judge independently and impartially, free from any influence other than the strength of the cases presented to him. Counsel, on the other hand, is not required to be 'impartial' at all, nor 'independent' in the sense demanded of an arbitrator, since counsel will by definition be retained, and paid, by one of the Parties. Counsel's duty is to present *his Party's* case, with the degree of dependence and partiality that the role implies, so long as he does so with diligence and with honesty, and in due compliance with the applicable rules of professional conduct and ethics.[53]

This author respectfully disagrees with this definition of counsel's role as dependent and partial, for the reasons described above. However, the reference to 'the applicable rules of professional conduct and ethics' is particularly difficult to understand since, with the exception of national rules for professional representatives whose national bars exercise extraterritorial jurisdiction for conduct before international courts and tribunals, there exist no such rules. Even more importantly, there exist no *common* rules that bind all representatives to uniform standards of professional conduct.

Conflicts of interest also entail contemporaneous representation of multiple clients whose legal interests clearly diverge, with differing national rules concerning whether such conflicts may be waived by the written consent of the client. The author inclines against such waiver on the ground that the conflict of interest concerns not just the client but also the court or tribunal, which has a duty to see justice done. The danger is that the interests of one client may be conflated by the advocate with the interests of the other client for private ends. Although this will most obviously manifest itself where both clients are party to the same proceedings, it may also occur where they are not, eg where their shared counsel conducts negotiations with a shared opponent in which he makes 'trade-offs' with their diverging cases.[54]

Finally, an interesting manifestation of a conflict of interest arose in the *RSM Production* case.[55] The subject matter of that claim concerned an allegation that the Attorney General of Grenada had been bribed by one 'Global Petroleum Group' ('Global') to award it an oil exploration contract whilst denying one to the

[52] For the test that the Tribunal adopted, see *Rompetrol v Romania*, para 15 (note 4).

[53] *Rompetrol v Romania*, para 19 (emphasis in original text).

[54] *Panel Report on the EC-Tariff Preferences*, paras 7.14–7.17.

[55] *RSM Production v Grenada*.

Claimant.[56] Before the Tribunal, the Claimant upon invitation from the Tribunal specifically refrained from requesting a finding that the person in question was corrupt.[57] However, some two years following the Merits Hearing, RSM Production applied to an ICSID ad hoc committee to make an order for disclosure by Grenada of 'the details of its relationship with Global Petroleum, beginning with disclosure of who is paying Freshfields' fees in the current annulment proceedings'. The basis for that request was an allegation that Global, the very same company that had allegedly bribed the Attorney General, was in fact financing Grenada's litigation costs.[58] Although the truth of that assertion was not determined, since the Committee denied the application, if true it constitutes a conflict of interest whereby a poor State was in effect being controlled by a powerful company whose legal interest in the proceedings clearly diverged.

7.3.1.2 Diligence

The duty of due diligence applies throughout the course of an advocate's representation. Not only should an advocate be required to acquire a sufficient level of professional competence in order to be admitted to appear before ICSID tribunals and only to accept briefs for which he has the requisite expertise and resources but, assuming that he meets both of those requirements, he should have a continuing duty of diligence in the performance of his duties. Thus, 'diligence' should not be confused with 'competence' as the concept assumes that an advocate has the ability to perform the task before him.

Diligence entails a failure to exert the necessary *effort* in order to represent his client to the requisite standard of competence. In the two cases of *Generation Ukraine* and *CDC Group* explored above, there appears to have been a difference. In the former case, it is ambiguous whether the counsel concerned were incompetent in the sense that they lacked the ability to perform their duties, they were dishonest in that they attempted to mislead the Tribunal and/or they were negligent in failing to exercise due diligence. By contrast, in *CDC Group* there it appears likelier that the representatives simply lacked the capability and expertise to competently represent their State as opposed to any question of professional negligence.

7.3.1.3 Loyalty

There has been concern in certain quarters of the international legal community at the unscrupulousness of certain powerful law firms that appear to successfully pressure their clients—small and inexperienced States—into unnecessary litigation in their own financial interests. Another scenario is that the law firm acts also for a wealthy company that has great influence as an investor in the State so that the firm represents the State in a manner that serves the interests of its wealthy—hence, more important—client. Clearly, such behaviour would violate a duty of

[56] *RSM Production v Grenada*, para 4.
[57] *RSM Production v Grenada*, paras 6–7.
[58] *RSM Production v Grenada*, para 13.

loyalty owed to one's client and, at a properly regulated bar, would consequently attract disciplinary sanctions.

7.3.1.4 Confidentiality

In the recent case of *Foresti*,[59] the Claimants, to whom counsel for the Respondent had disclosed confidential information belonging to his client and offered to assist in convincing his client to accept a settlement favourable to them in exchange for a bribe, did not inform their lawyers until a late stage about these proposals despite four meetings with the corrupt advocate. Once counsel were informed, to whom was their professional duty owed and to what action did that duty commit them? How were they to advise their clients to proceed and how were they to treat the confidential information which the latter had obtained from their 'mole' in their opponents' legal team? Specifically, is there a duty to disclose the existence of such a serious breach of fair trial to the Tribunal[60] or to the other side? Could counsel ethically utilize the confidential information about internal deliberations in order to frame their own legal strategy or were they obliged to redress an unfair advantage that would result? The powers of the Court to order disclosure of confidential information, never yet invoked, are alone insufficient to protect procedural integrity from such hazards. Only the advocates would be in a position to know of the

[59] See *Foresti and Others v South Africa* where counsel for South Africa (Mr Seth Nthai SC) was disbarred *in medias res* for breaching confidentiality by disclosing the internal deliberations of his legal team and offering to persuade his team to accept a settlement advantageous to the Claimants in exchange for a bribe. For a summary narrative of the incident, see the Award, paras 30–40. For documents relating to the disbarment proceedings, see online: <http://www.politicsweb.co.za/politicsweb/view/politicsweb/en/page71654?oid=171725&sn=Detail> (Accessed: 8 September 2010). Counsel for the Claimants was not informed by his clients of ongoing negotiations with Mr Nthai until a relatively late stage, whereupon they *advised* disclosure to the other side and to the arbitral tribunal—see 'Witness Statement of Mario Vittorio Marcenaro', paras 7.9, 7.30, 7.34–7.36. In *Thailand (Anti-Dumping Duties)*, paras 62–78, Thailand alleged in WTO proceedings that an amicus curiae brief submitted by the Consuming Industries Trade Action Coalition (CITAC) was made with knowledge of information concerning Thailand's case obtained through breach of confidentiality by Poland. Although the Appellate Body made no finding of such breach, Poland's own investigation revealed that its law firm (which had had access to Thailand's confidential material) had a member who had 'worked as a corporate lawyer' for CITAC upon which its representatives withdrew from the case.

[60] The English barristers who represented the Claimants were seemingly bound to keep the information secret until their clients consented to its disclosure—see English Code, para 702. The Tribunal's analysis in its Award (para 119) concerning the Claimants (but not their representatives) is telling: 'While understanding the Claimants' concern that they could not assume that an agreed compromise with the Respondent would be implemented and that the arbitration should not be definitively abandoned until the compromise was delivered by the Respondent in a legally-binding form, the Tribunal also considers that it is not established that the Claimants needed to wait as long as they did to inform the Respondent of the solicitation of a bribe by one of the Respondent's senior counsel, Seth Nthai, who continued to participate in the preparation of Respondent's pleadings while he was suggesting to the Claimants that he might secure the Respondent's agreement to settle the case without payment by the Claimants of the Respondent's costs. Similarly, the Claimants might have been able to inform the Respondent sooner than they were prepared to terminate the arbitration on a "with prejudice" basis. The Tribunal thinks that the Respondent's costs (and, indeed, the Claimants' costs) would have been smaller if the Claimants had indicated earlier their willingness to settle on a "with prejudice" basis, and if Mr Nthai's corrupt solicitations had been promptly disclosed. Accordingly, the Tribunal thinks it right that the Claimants should bear responsibility for a portion of the Respondent's costs.'

danger and only professional ethics would compel them to act upon it rather than tacitly accept the forbidden fruit.[61] As Professor Wälde put it:

> If one party is aware of all internal plans within the other party (identification of witnesses, experts, strengths and weaknesses, legal and factual strategy, remuneration arrangements, financial situation), it has an immense strategic advantage. It can persuade (or intimidate) experts and witnesses identified, it can manipulate the arbitration so that the other side reaches the bottom of its war chest and can exploit weaknesses discussed confidentially in the client-counsel relationship.[62]

In tracing the negotiating history of *Foresti*, it seems noteworthy in this respect that Seth Nthai disclosed sensitive internal information about his client's negotiating posture and internal divisions concerning a settlement.[63] Although there is no indication in the public documents that any further confidential information was disclosed by Nthai in at least three further face-to-face meetings as well as distance communication,[64] it seems plausible that such disclosures may have been offered by Nthai to 'prove his worth' to obtain agreement to his corrupt bargain.

7.3.2 Duties to the Tribunal

Examples of grave breach of duties to the Tribunal threatening procedural integrity include: bribery,[65] intimidation,[66] kidnapping,[67] espionage,[68] harassment,[69]

[61] Counsel for the Claimants were English barristers—Award, para 6; 'The State Attorney's Complaint against Seth Nthai', online: <http://www.politicsweb.co.za/politicsweb/view/politicsweb/en/page71654?oid=171738&sn=Detail>, para 2.6 (Accessed: 8 September 2010). Paragraph 608 of the Bar Code of Conduct states: 'A barrister must cease to act and if he is a self-employed barrister must return any instructions: (f) if having come into possession of a document belonging to another party by some means other than the normal and proper channels and having read it before he realises that it ought to have been returned unread to the person entitled to possession of it he would thereby be embarrassed in the discharge of his duties by his knowledge of the contents of the document provided that he may retire or withdraw only if he can do so without jeopardising the client's interests.'

[62] Wälde, "Equality of Arms" in Investment Arbitration: Procedural Challenges', 172.

[63] 'Witness Statement of Mario Vittorio Marcenaro', para 7.9.

[64] 'Witness Statement of Mario Vittorio Marcenaro', paras 7.25–7.30.

[65] *Foresti.*

[66] Wälde, '"Equality of Arms" in Investment Arbitration: Procedural Challenges', 167–71. Professor Wälde cites (at 169, note 29) the cases of *Sempra v Argentina* (para 31) and *Enron Corporation v Argentina* (paras 141–2) as examples of an 'intimidatory message [that] will come through a "nod and a wink," a telephone call, an inquiry about the expert or witness's involvement that appears on the face to be innocuous but carries a clear message'. See also *City Oriente Ltd v Ecuador* (paras 61–4) involving State use of criminal prosecution to intimidate the Claimant. Examples of alleged intimidation by 'private actors invisibly controlled by government services' include *Metalclad Corporation v Mexico* (para 46) and *Eureko BV v Poland* (paras 236–7). See also *Kensington v Congo*, where American lawyers were held to have attempted to intimidate witnesses in bad faith.

[67] See the abduction of an arbitrator by the State that appointed him in *Himpurna v Indonesia*. A summary of the incident appears in Werner, 'When Arbitration Becomes War: Some Reflections on the Frailty of the Arbitral Process in Cases involving Authoritarian States', 17 *Journal of International Arbitration* (2000), 97–103, 98–101.

[68] See discussions regarding alleged e-mail interception in *Libananco Holdings Co Ltd v Turkey* (paras 72–82); e-mail and telephone surveillance in *Europe Cement v Turkey* (paras 21–4, 35–6); and misuse of State or company intelligence assets to illegally procure 'evidence' in *Methanex Corporation v USA* (paras 54–60) and *Metalclad Corporation v Mexico* (para 46).

[69] See allegations in *Helnan International Hotels A/S v Egypt* (para 75); *Noble Ventures v Romania* (para 161); *Tokios Tokelés v Ukraine*, Award (para 51) and Procedural Order No 3 (18 January 2005);

document forgery, and witness tampering[70] or even assassination.[71] Not only must counsel not participate in such conduct, which in most cases would in any event be criminal, but he must not shut his eyes to his own suspicions of such behaviour nor consent to represent a party that he 'knows' (actual, reasonable, or constructive) to be engaging in it. Abusive litigation should not be dignified with the façade of professionalism.

7.3.2.1 Candour

Experienced counsel, in particular, may be able to skilfully skirt the line between zealous advocacy and dishonesty so that it is difficult for opposing counsel to allege dishonesty with compelling evidence.[72] This applies particularly to lies of omission and potential conflicts with the duty of client confidentiality.[73] For example, in the *Foresti* case above, the English counsel were bound by their domestic ethical rules to keep the fact that a grave breach of fair trial had occurred until their clients gave their permission to disclose its existence. This they were seemingly unwilling to do for quite some time, with the potential result that the Tribunal and opposing party would have remained ignorant of the infringement altogether. Counsel should be free, in these circumstances, to disclose the existence of such a serious threat to the integrity of the process without client consent.

The objection to this is that, since counsel were ignorant of the entire affair until their clients informed them, they would have likely been unable to persuade their clients to reveal the attempted bribery because the latter would have been unwilling to reveal such sensitive information knowing that their counsel would be free to disclose it. This argument clearly carries some force, in that the relationship of trust is what led the clients to convey the problem to counsel and led counsel to ultimately persuade the clients to 'do the right thing'. To untie counsel's hands would be to threaten that trust. Nevertheless, the possibility that tribunal awards can be jeopardized by such serious misconduct by parties or by their representatives and that counsel should be required by their professional duties to silently watch cannot be the best solution.

7.3.2.2 Documentary Evidence

In the adducing of evidence, there are not only the dangers of forgery and witness tampering—wilful attempts to manipulate and distort the veracity of evidence—but

Rumeli Telekom AS and Telsim Mobil Telekomunikasyon Hizmetleri AS v Kazakhstan (para 217); *Eureko BV v Poland* (paras 236–7).

[70] Eg allegations in *Tradex v Albania* (paras 34, 82).

[71] See an anecdote about an ad hoc arbitration in 1980 in Werner, 'When Arbitration Becomes War', 97–8.

[72] One may assert, for example, that the allegations of corruption made against the Claimant in *Luccheti v Peru* (paras 51, 60) concerning the averred bribery of a local judge were defamatory when there was no judicial finding to that effect, there are divergent legal definitions of bribery and the question was immaterial to the case.

[73] Eg if the ad hoc committee in *RSM Production v Grenada* had made an order for disclosure of what would have been confidential information.

also accidental contamination of evidence through improper handling. This of course largely derives from procedural law, which regulates the manner in which evidence may be adduced. Yet, as will be seen, there is a corresponding ethical dimension because courts and tribunals—and *a fortiori* ICSID investment arbitral tribunals—lack the capacity to omnisciently police the parties. Counsel should consequently act as autonomous facilitators of justice by shielding the tribunal from contaminated evidence and by ensuring through their own conduct that the evidence of their clients and opposing party may be fairly adduced and fairly tested.

The principal dangers arising from manipulation of documentary evidence are concealment and forgery. For example, governments may attempt to abusively invoke 'executive privilege' in order to conceal documents adverse to their cases.[74] A recent example of fraudulent evidence being adduced and of arguably unethical handling by counsel occurred in the *Gabay* arbitration[75] before the Iran-US Claims Tribunal. There, the Tribunal described counsel's conduct in the following terms:

> On the basis of the testimony of the Respondent's expert witness and of the Claimant's statements at the Hearing as well as other evidence, the Tribunal is convinced that the copy of the letter of 1 June 1983 submitted by the Claimant has been altered. Therefore, the Tribunal does not consider this document in determining the date on which the claim arose... On 13 July 1989, the Respondent offered to submit... the original carbon copy from which the Claimant's photographic copy of that letter was made, and it did so on 16 October 1989, more than eighteen months before the Hearing. Even before the Respondent's document had been submitted, the Claimant asserted that 'the production of the original false document will prove nothing', and the Claimant and his expert failed to examine the original until two days before the Hearing. The Claimant changed his position only at the Hearing, when his attorney conceded that the Claimant's document appeared to have been altered while the Respondent's copy appeared not to have been altered. The Tribunal disapproves of such behaviour on the part of the Claimant and of his attorney. Although it does not have the power to impose sanctions or disciplinary measures for presentation of false evidence, the Tribunal cannot pass over such abusive conduct in silence. The Claimant should have investigated the authenticity of his document before its presentation to the Tribunal and, at any rate, should have compared it to the original copy presented by the Respondent, and withdrawn his document and accusations of forgery against the Government of Iran soon after the latter's comments and evidence were filed.'[76]

Whilst this excerpt is also considered below in the context of the doctrine of inherent powers, the incident graphically illustrates the necessity for the professional regulation of counsel before international courts and tribunals in order to oblige advocates to, inter alia, shield the Tribunal from falsified evidence.

7.3.2.3 Testimonial Evidence

Testimonial evidence, involving human memory and candour, is particularly susceptible to tampering and contamination. With sufficient expertise, documentary

[74] Wälde, '"Equality of Arms" in Investment Arbitration: Procedural Challenges', 174–5.

[75] *Norman Gabay v Islamic Republic of Iran*, 40–8.

[76] *Norman Gabay v Islamic Republic of Iran*, 45–6 (para 13).

forgeries can usually be discovered. The memory of witnesses of fact and opinions of expert witnesses, however, are more easily corrupted. Concordantly, greater procedural safeguards are necessary to prevent not only tampering—a deliberate act—but also contamination, which is inadvertent. Since representatives play an important role in the adducing of evidence before ICSID tribunals, ethical rules have the potential to be impactful in order to homogenize divergent standards of behaviour in a critical area.

Tampering entails an intention to alter the substance of the evidence. Although this does not necessarily require a dishonest motive, fraudulence will be the dominant motive in the majority of cases. This essentially involves an overt act to encourage a witness to lie—whether overtly or by omission—such as persuasion, bribery, or intimidation.[77] It is unlikely that a proscription upon such activities in a putative ICSID code of conduct would prove controversial. As argued above, the removal from parties of the right to appoint their witnesses (particularly experts) as representatives and thereby exert greater control over their statements as well as insulate them from cross-examination should be removed.

A more intricate issue is evidence contamination, which entails the inadvertent corruption of evidence through inappropriate methods of preparing and interrogating witnesses. Appropriate procedure for the preparation of testimony (ie witness statements, depositions, and affidavits) and interrogation (witness coaching, extra-testimonial contacts, and suggestive questioning) vary greatly between common law and civil law systems on the one hand and within common law systems on the other. Whilst an outline of the procedural or *legal* differences is necessary in order to illustrate the points of contention, the *ethical* issues are uniform in that the underlying purposes to procedural safeguards are to prohibit counsel from manipulating—intentionally or accidentally—the substance of the evidence. Although the parties have a large degree of autonomy in selecting their procedures, this book suggests that strict ethical principles proscribing certain practices are vital in order to preclude avoidable complications for a tribunal's award. Such practices engage the human right to a fair trial and consequently, as argued below, empower tribunals to disregard parties' express wishes in procedure if they threaten the integrity of the process.

In light of the relative weakness of ICSID tribunals compared with national judges in common law and civil law systems alike, the application of the civil law regime in which the principal interrogator is the tribunal itself is inappropriate. The parties are necessarily closer to the evidence and the tribunal lacks powers of compulsion towards witnesses. A civil law safeguard—the prohibition upon pre-testimonial contact between counsel and witnesses—is consequently impractical. Since such contact is inevitable, it should be strictly regulated to prevent contamination. In the preparation of witness statements, for example, counsel should obviously be required to actively ensure that the statement accurately reflects the witness' own account by preparing it in a style that (while coherent and succinct) is as close as

[77] See, in particular, *Libananco* (para 72), *Europe Cement* (paras 21, 35) and *Tradex* (para 82).

practicable to the witness' own words, by requiring the witness to review and sign the statement and by avoiding in any way alterations to the evidence designed to manipulate the content in order to favour his client's case.[78]

7.3.3 Duties to Colleagues

A discrete category of 'duty to colleagues' is somewhat misleading, as it is really a subcategory of duties owed to the Tribunal. This is because each of the duties discussed impacts upon the ability of the Tribunal to conduct its proceedings with decorum and fairness. Given the lack of a centralized 'bar association' to which ethical complaints may be tendered, it will obviously be for the Tribunal to address such matters as they arise and to mete out sanctions. Such duties are, however, also owed to one's colleagues who thus have a right to demand their observance and complain at their infringement.

7.3.3.1 Confidentiality

Respect for the confidentiality of certain types of communication between counsel is critical. Although this applies most obviously in the matter of settlement negotiation, in which a 'without prejudice' rule[79] is required in order to barter freely, it is even more vital regarding the inappropriate acquirement of confidential information belonging to a party. This occurred in the *Foresti* case described above, where the corrupt advocate for the Respondent disclosed on at least one occasion confidential information concerning his party's attitude towards a settlement. Under the English legal ethics that applied to counsel for the Claimants in that case, an interesting paradox seemingly results whereby they were absolutely prohibited from utilizing such inappropriately obtained information whilst also forbidden from revealing that the leak had occurred.

There is a gap under that approach in that a barrister is required to withdraw from a case for 'professional embarrassment' only 'if having come into possession of a document belonging to another party by some means other than the normal and proper channels and having read it before he realises that it ought to have been returned unread to the person entitled to possession of it he would thereby be embarrassed in the discharge of his duties by his knowledge of the contents of the document provided that he may retire or withdraw only if he can do so without jeopardising his client's interest'.[80] This is an onerous test to satisfy, since it is difficult to see how withdrawal in most circumstances will not 'jeopardise a client's interest' and the rule only applies with respect to *documents* (which did not arise in *Foresti*) rather than knowledge of the *existence* of a leak.

[78] Eg *Generation Ukraine*.

[79] It should be noted that there is some divergence on this rule, as certain European jurisdictions recognize the confidentiality of such communications from their subject matter whereas other jurisdictions require that counsel make an express stipulation of confidentiality—CCBE Code, Commentary to Article 5.3. Thus, clarification is called for; the author favours a presumption of confidentiality from subject matter in order to avoid inadvertent prejudice.

[80] Code of Conduct of Bar of England and Wales, para 608(f).

7.3.3.2 Communication

A useful ethical rule is one that requires counsel to refrain from discussing the merits of the case with the opposing client without their colleagues' consent. This is obviously good practice to prevent misunderstandings and miscommunications from multiplying due to the involvement of a greater number of parties but also to preclude attempts at corruption. The *Foresti* incident is noteworthy in this respect in that the corrupt bargain was proposed in a meeting between an agent for the Claimants and Respondent counsel in the absence of Claimants' counsel. Whilst that meeting occurred with the permission of counsel on the understanding that it was a 'social meeting',[81] it illustrates the importance of contacts to be done only with caution.

7.4 Disciplinary Jurisdiction

There exist no prescribed disciplinary powers for ICSID tribunals. Still less is there any procedural framework for the fair imposition of such powers. Nevertheless, on the basis of the 'inherent jurisdiction' analysis below it is assumed that ICSID tribunals may exclude—and indeed have excluded—counsel from their proceedings in the interest of protecting procedural integrity and fair trial. Given that this is on the extreme end of potential disciplinary sanctions, it may be posited that more moderate sanctions—public admonishment, fines or 'personal costs orders', suspension from proceedings, or reporting to national bar authorities—are included within the range of sanctions that tribunals may mete out to counsel that infringe ethical principles.

However, a more sophisticated procedure is required in order to ensure that such powers are exercised wisely. Certain principles may be tentatively suggested for consideration. Representatives should have a right to a fair hearing before the Tribunal, with an opportunity to answer the allegations against them before any decision is taken concerning sanctions. Sanctions should be proportionate to the severity of the misconduct; excluding counsel on the basis of a minor infraction, particularly late in proceedings, would be prejudicial to justice. Such principles should apply *a fortiori* to ICSID tribunals because, unlike international criminal tribunals, there is no sophisticated disciplinary mechanism constructed especially for the handling of complaints against the professional conduct of counsel with—crucially—a right of appeal.

An important point is that the ICSID architecture is relatively primitive in dealing with such matters. Consequently, tribunals will have to build incrementally and apply even more than ordinary care. With appropriate caution (eg account taken of differences of procedure and jurisdiction), reference to the nascent doctrine being developed by other international tribunals—for example, in the criminal law field—would be useful. Although *ex post facto* application of ethical rules can

[81] 'Witness Statement of Mario Vittorio Marcenaro', para 7.9.

be safely done with flagrant examples of dishonesty or incompetence (eg *Foresti* or *Generation Ukraine*) this would be controversial upon particularly contentious ethical issues such as conflicts of interest, confidentiality or handling of evidence. Thus, a useful procedure for tribunals would be to require the representatives of all parties to sign and deposit a copy of a 'code of conduct' (eg the Hague Principles or some variation of them) at the commencement of proceedings. By putting representatives on notice of the standards of conduct expected of them, this would not only act as a deterrent upon flagrant misconduct and a clarification of the finer issues but would also provide tribunals with a textual basis for sanctions.

Other creative methods of improving tribunals' toolkits may be considered. A public admonishment delivered to a representative may, in a competitive legal services marketplace, be sufficient punishment for minor offences. The imposition of personal costs orders would potentially be useful, particularly in concentrating representatives' minds upon the need for succinctness in pleadings. Whilst parties may be punished through the existing costs regimes, it would be more just for representatives to bear the consequences of their own inefficiency or incompetence. The reporting of professional counsel to their national disciplinary authority, typically a bar association, could be a supplementary tool for particularly grave infractions because of the threat of disbarment.

An important issue to consider is the degree of reliance that can credibly be placed in individual arbitral tribunals to judiciously enforce breaches of ethical rules. Many arbitrators (and, indeed, judges of international courts), after all, have never themselves acted as professional counsel and consequently may not recognize the ethical issues that arise. Moreover, the assumption in relying upon arbitrators to fulfil this regulatory role is that they will themselves have the requisite degree of authority and integrity to do so with credibility. Regrettably, this is not always the case.[82] Whilst the current atmosphere indicates that such a move is premature, the creation of an external regulatory authority over counsel before international courts and tribunals (including ICSID tribunals) is both necessary and desirable.

If one accepts that practice suggests a pressing need for such initiatives, there remains the question of the jurisprudential basis for tribunals to do so. Whilst it appears accepted that there exist certain minimal standards of fair trial applicable to commercial arbitration that are binding upon the host State,[83] the situation concerning inter-State or investment arbitration is more complicated. This is due to the fact that before ICSID tribunals the possibility of external review by the judicial system of the host State is expressly excluded. Since the host State lacks jurisdiction to regulate either set of proceedings, it is not obliged to ensure that they conform to regional or universal standards of fair trial. Thus, the first question to be answered is whether fundamental standards of fair trial apply to arbitral proceedings.

[82] See, eg, accounts concerning the conduct of arbitrators in the early years of the Iran-US Claims Tribunal in Khan, *The Iran-United States Claims Tribunal: Controversies, Cases and Contribution* (1990), 41–7, 61–77.

[83] Petrochilos, *Procedural Law in International Arbitration* (2003), 109–65.

Perhaps understandably, in light of the nascent state of international human rights law in 1966, the ICSID Convention does not prescribe standards of fair trial. More surprisingly, the Arbitration Rules likewise omit any mention of impartiality and equality of arms as fundamental principles of procedural fairness.[84] Thus, except where conflicting with mandatory provisions of the Convention,[85] under positive law the parties are free to adopt any procedural rules they wish. One commentator, however, has written:

> An additional restriction on the choice of procedural rules by the parties arises, in our opinion, from the requirement that there be a minimum standard of procedural rules in any arbitration proceedings. From the provisions of the Convention . . . it can be seen that the arbitration proceedings at the Centre are to be conducted according to the provisions of the Convention and to the rules chosen by the parties (if they indeed make such a choice). We might, therefore, conclude that the provisions of the Convention satisfy the required minimum for the existence of fair arbitration proceedings. Examination of the above provisions reveals that this is not the case. For example, the Convention does not mention the obligation binding upon every tribunal to hear the arguments of both parties (or even to receive the pleadings in writing), nor the right of each party to know the arguments of the opposing side and to respond thereto, nor to the prohibition on the arbitrator against any delegation of his authority to decide the dispute to another person.
>
> These rules of procedure are essential to the conduct of any arbitration; they are inherent in any fair judicial proceedings, and it is surprising that they are not included in the provisions of the Convention. In most cases, the parties will choose procedural rules that grant them these basic rights. But one must ask whether a tribunal of the Centre would be bound to follow procedural rules that do not include these fundamental provisions. It seems to us that a tribunal is obliged to follow the most fundamental rules of procedure which ensure a fair hearing, even if the parties have not specified so in the arbitration rules, and even if the parties have specified the opposite in such rules. Any other answer could undermine one of the basic aims of the Centre (albeit one that is not mentioned explicitly in the Convention), which is to settle investment disputes between host states and foreign investors in a fair manner. To this we must add that the obligation imposed by the Convention upon all the contracting states to recognize and to enforce the arbitral awards of the Centre, also means that the awards must be rendered following fair arbitration proceedings, for otherwise, difficulties may arise in the enforcement proceedings in various states.[86]

Concerning the proposition that—irrespective of omission or contradiction in the parties' rules of procedure—an ICSID tribunal is bound by fundamental standards of impartiality and fair trial, this author respectfully agrees. However, despite

[84] Whilst Petrochilos, *Procedural Law in International Arbitration*, 144 (note 160) cites Rule 50(1)(c)(iii) in support of his proposition that equality is 'an imperative procedural rule in inter-state proceedings, which is to be found in all modern arbitration rules', Rule 50(1)(c)(iii)—itself an implementing provision of Article 52(1) of the ICSID Convention—does not expressly prescribe this principle: 'in an application for annulment [of an award] . . . the . . . grounds are limited to the following: that the Tribunal was not properly constituted; that the Tribunal has manifestly exceeded its powers; that there was corruption on the part of a member of the Tribunal; that there has been a serious departure from a fundamental rule of procedure; that the award has failed to state the reasons on which it is based.'

[85] In particular, Articles 47–9, 56.

[86] Hirsch, *The Arbitration Mechanism of the International Centre for the Settlement of Investment Disputes* (1993), 114–15.

the attractiveness of the argument that these principles are implied terms of the Convention, it is suggested that that positivist basis is insufficient in articulating more sophisticated standards of fair trial that have since come to be considered essential in human rights jurisprudence. As one tribunal has noted:

> The ICSID Convention and Rules do not…explicitly give the power to tribunals to exclude counsel. To the contrary, we readily accept that as a general rule parties may seek such representation as they see fit—and that this is a fundamental principle.[87]

On the contrary, the laissez-faire approach of the Convention to the representation of parties reflects precisely the opposite intention.

The pronouncements of the ICSID tribunals that have hitherto addressed the matter of inherent powers are inconsistent. The Tribunal in *Libananco* declared:

> These allegations and counter-allegations strike at principles which lie at the very heart of the ICSID arbitral process, and the Tribunal is bound to approach them accordingly. Among the principles affected are: basic procedural fairness, respect for confidentiality and legal privilege…the right of parties to seek advice and to advance their respective cases freely and without interference; and no doubt others as well. For its own part, the Tribunal would add to the list respect for the Tribunal itself, as the organ freely chosen by the Parties for the binding settlement of their dispute in accordance with the ICSID Convention. It requires no further recital by the Tribunal to establish either that these are indeed fundamental principles, or why they are. Nor does the Tribunal doubt for a moment that, like any other international tribunal, it must be regarded as endowed with the inherent powers required to preserve the integrity of its own process—even if the remedies open to it are necessarily different from those that might be available to a domestic court of law in an ICSID Member State. The Tribunal would express the principle as being that parties have an obligation to arbitrate fairly and in good faith and that an arbitral tribunal has the inherent jurisdiction to ensure that this obligation is complied with; this principle applies in all arbitrations, including investment arbitration, and to all parties, including States (even in the exercise of their sovereign powers).[88]

The Tribunal did not engage in detailed analysis and did not cite doctrine justifying these assertions. Whilst the remedies concerned did not directly concern counsel in that the orders sought were directed at controlling parties' conduct rather than that of counsel personally, the declaration is indirectly apposite because of the shared threat to procedural integrity.

The Tribunal in *Hrvatska* relied upon Article 44 of the ICSID Convention as providing a partial 'textual foothold' for the inherent powers doctrine.[89] Although Article 44 provides a positive power to prescribe for procedural lacunae—which

[87] *Hrvatska*, 10 (para 24). See also *Rompetrol*, para 14: 'It is common ground between the Parties that the rules governing the present arbitration proceedings, i.e. the ICSID Convention and the Arbitration Rules, contain no provision allowing in terms for a challenge to the appointment by a Party of counsel to represent it in an ICSID arbitration. Some other source for such a challenge must therefore be found, which the Respondent seeks to do by implication from the general tenor of the Arbitration Rules, and by invoking an inherent general power on the part of any tribunal to police the integrity of its proceedings.'

[88] *Libananco*, para 78.

[89] *Hrvatska*, paras 33–4.

will apply to many if not most ethical issues for counsel—it clearly does not assist in overcoming the problem of rules expressly selected by the parties that conflict with fair trial principles. Finally, the Tribunal in *Rompetrol* (one member of which was also a member of the panel in *Libananco*, though that arbitration was not cited) reserved its position with respect to the 'inherent powers' doctrine by rejecting the application on the ground that it was unjustified by the circumstances.[90] It is noteworthy, however, that that Tribunal seemingly grounded its 'inherent powers' in the right to a fair trial and acknowledged that these would be opposed to the statutory framework based upon the right of parties to nominate counsel.[91]

Ironically, parties (particularly States) in many if not most cases are likely to resist measures fettering what they perceive as their prerogatives in controlling the presentation of their cases. For some parties, such privileges better enable them to corrupt their representatives in order to attempt to gain any unfair advantage they can get away with in the proceedings.[92] For other parties, particularly States, this resistance is grounded in a fear that, if they 'lose control' of their cases, they are less likely to win.[93] In its analysis of ICSID cases in which ethical issues have arisen, this chapter seeks to demonstrate that not only is there a pressing need for robust regulation of representation of parties before the ICSID and that that need serves the interests not only of tribunals but, crucially, of those parties who wish only to be given a fair hearing with the opportunity to put their cases with equality and effectiveness.

Having set out the hypothesis that standards of due process apply to ICSID arbitral proceedings through the doctrine of inherent powers, the following question arises: who is responsible for ensuring that fair trial standards are observed in arbitral proceedings? The ICSID is vested with international legal personality.[94] It does not necessarily follow, however, that it is *ipso jure* vested with responsibility for the conduct of arbitral tribunals.[95] Whilst the Administrative Council of the Centre was tasked with adopting the ICSID Arbitration Rules,[96] the parties to a particular arbitration are permitted under the Convention to derogate from most of its provisions.[97] Therefore, on a strictly positivist legal analysis, since the Centre has no authority under the Convention to require arbitrating parties to observe such standards, it follows that it is not responsible for the conduct of arbitral tribunals nominally conducted under the ICSID framework.

[90] *Hrvatska*, paras 25–7.
[91] *Hrvatska*, paras 15–16, 20.
[92] Wälde, '"Equality of Arms" in Investment Arbitration: Procedural Challenges', 162–4.
[93] Wälde, '"Equality of Arms" in Investment Arbitration: Procedural Challenges', 162–4.
[94] ICSID Convention, Art 18: 'The Centre shall have full international legal personality. The legal capacity of the Centre shall include the capacity: (a) to contract; (b) to acquire and dispose of movable and immovable property; (c) to institute legal proceedings.'
[95] The responsibility of States and international organizations is, of course, a vast, complicated and developing field. However, for present purposes, the applicable proposition of the law of responsibility is that an international organization is only responsible for such acts as it has been vested with authority to perform. Thus, the Centre is only responsible to the extent that it is empowered under the Convention.
[96] ICSID Convention, Art 6(1)(c).
[97] Schreuer, *The ICSID Convention: A Commentary*, 669 (paras 11–12).

On the basis of the foregoing proposition that due process standards apply to ICSID proceedings and that they may be enforced through the doctrine of inherent powers, this conclusion is rejected. If one accepts that inalienable standards of fair trial apply to ICSID proceedings that override parties' freedom of choice with respect to arbitration rules and that tribunals have a duty to exercise their inherent powers to preserve the integrity of their proceedings, it follows that ICSID tribunals—whose actions for that purpose would presumably be attributable to the Centre, not to the parties[98]—are responsible for ensuring due process. This is most obviously manifested in the review procedure by ad hoc committees of awards made by tribunals.[99]

If to prioritize party control over the proceedings, a potential argument is that States that commit abuse in their capacity as parties to arbitral proceedings—for example, by assassinating, kidnapping, or attempting to intimidate an arbitrator, representative, witness, or other participant[100]—would thereby be held responsible for violating fair trial standards before domestic and international courts with jurisdiction.[101] Although fair trial provisions of human rights instruments are designed to apply to the exercise by States of their judicial powers or to their supervision of other entities (eg commercial arbitrations) exercising them on their territory, it is suggested that—if one accepts that party discretion trumps tribunal powers—the State, in framing rules of procedure for investment arbitrations and in acting as a litigant, is similarly exercising its 'jurisdiction' towards the other party in an equally impactful manner.

The second objection that may be made to the introduction of professionalism is that there is no need for it. In other words, that a tribunal has hitherto been able to adequately do its work without recourse to such rules they are *ipso facto* unnecessary. This argument may likewise be rejected for two reasons. First, it ignores the possibility of future scandal occurring such that would present a grave threat to the integrity of the Centre. Secondly, this chapter argues that it is disproved by practice. The reality is that tribunals have fairly often been forced to grapple with the two problems of counsel conduct that this chapter addresses, namely, dishonesty or incompetence and cultural differences of judicial procedure. Thus, it is proposed that the introduction of professionalism would be of great benefit in filling a serious lacuna in its procedure.

[98] International Law Commission Draft Articles on the Responsibility of International Organizations, Doc. A/CN.4/L.743 (2 June 2009), 61st Session, Art 4 ('General rule on attribution of conduct to an international organization'). See also Crawford, *The International Law Commission's Articles on State Responsibility* (2002), 310–11 (especially note 878); *Behrami and Saramati v France and others* (paras 133–49); *Al-Jedda* (per Lord Bingham of Cornhill, paras 18–25).

[99] See, however, the limitations discussed at note 89.

[100] See notes 70–6.

[101] In the European system, this would require a novel interpretation of the term 'jurisdiction' within Art 1 of the ECHR: 'The High Contracting Parties shall secure to everyone within their jurisdiction the rights and freedoms defined in Section I of this Convention.' Territoriality clearly would not apply due to the exclusion of the judicial system of the host State from the arbitral process. The meaning of jurisdiction under the Convention is primarily but not exclusively territorial in nature with other forms requiring special justification—see (in a very different context) the leading authority of *Bankovic* (paras 59–66).

A final problem concerning the regulatory jurisdiction of ICSID tribunals is that of 'double deontology' or conflicts of jurisdictions with national bars exercising extraterritorial jurisdiction over the conduct of their members before international courts and tribunals. It is obvious that, to command respect, the ethical rules of international tribunals must be supreme for their own purposes. Nevertheless, international criminal tribunals have encountered counsel who have—despite the supremacy of tribunals' codes, which counsel accept upon being admitted to proceedings—sought to invoke national rules in order to justify a particular course of conduct that they wish to pursue. Whilst the solution to this problem is the recognition by national bars of the primacy of the regulatory jurisdiction of international tribunals for their own proceedings, the primitive architecture before ICSID tribunals renders this impracticable in the near-term.

7.5 Conclusions

This chapter has examined the procedural and practical problems arising in connexion with advocacy in investment arbitration with ancillary reference to commercial arbitration, the Iran-US Claims Tribunal, and WTO dispute settlement. This survey has demonstrated that there is a practical need for stronger regulation of advocacy to address a range of ethical issues, such as conflicts of interest and dishonest pleadings. Whilst the principles concerned are common to the other international courts and tribunals examined in this book, the frequency of their occurrence in arbitration appears to be relatively great. Consequently, apart from preventing potential problems, promoting the image and reputation of the arbitral system and other rationales, the need to address existing problems in practice is compelling.

Whilst this chapter has not 'profiled' the investment arbitration bar in detail, it may be surmised that the relatively diverse nature of the practitioners involved—in contrast to the concentrated ICJ and ECJ de facto specialist bars—and the high financial stakes are two key factors. In addition, the even more lax and permissive culture of arbitration with its emphasis upon party consent underpinning the procedural powers of arbitrators contributes to a culture in which the regulation of conduct is weak. Although reputational consequences are presumably a deterrent to misconduct by counsel, practical experience suggests that this alone has proved to be an ineffective incentive.

The articulation of common standards of conduct, supported by admission requirements and disciplinary sanctions, is a sensitive and intricate problem in the specific context of investment arbitration. The permissive dynamics of the prevalent culture favour party autonomy and a wide discretion for counsel. The reconciliation of the existing mindset with the need for progressive reforms aimed at promoting procedural integrity and fairness presents not only technical but also political problems. However, it may be possible to strike compromises between these competing visions of the practice of advocacy in investment arbitration. In particular, the essential point is that the progressive professionalization of advocacy serves the interests of practitioners by eliminating costly procedural problems and promoting the legitimacy of the system by promoting parity and fairness amongst a diverse range of parties.

For example, the introduction of a 'list system' to vet counsel that provides for minimal requirements would not be contrary to prevalent practice but would serve to impose some measure of parity between parties. The provision of a legal aid mechanism along the lines of the WTO Legal Aid Centre to provide financial and practical support for parties lacking experience and resources would also be a useful means of promoting the legitimacy of the system and thereby strengthening the legal services market in investment arbitration. The provision of common standards of conduct aimed at eliminating potentially dangerous practices such as dishonesty and clarifying issues (eg conflicts of interest) upon which there are honest differences and considerable confusion in practice would reduce the cost of arbitration and make it a more efficient and attractive option to potential clients.

In this respect, the ongoing work of the International Bar Association Task Force on Counsel Ethics in International Arbitration, examined further in Chapter 9, is a project pregnant with potential. Whilst much depends upon the detail and the process by which any proposed reforms are introduced, the ability to achieve consensus amongst practitioners over the need for action in this field is a considerable achievement in itself in light of divergent views and legal cultures. The willingness of arbitrators to grapple directly with the ethical issues raised in practice and to address them in a principled and consistent fashion is also a key factor for the success of professionalization. In a field of law that, by its very nature, emphasizes a more informal and party-centric procedure in comparison with courts, the accomplishment of professionalization is likely to be one of the most challenging and intricate of all.

8

The International Criminal Court

This chapter considers ethical standards for counsel before the International Criminal Court (ICC). A distinguishing feature of the international criminal tribunals from civil tribunals is that they are expressly obliged through their statutes to ensure fair trial standards in their proceedings. Another important difference is that the criminal tribunals have more comprehensive regulatory systems for representation, particularly for defence counsel.[1] The criminal context, in particular the stricter fair trial standards in international human rights law, is an important reason for this. This is amplified by the Court's subject-matter jurisdiction, in that it was constructed to try 'the most serious crimes of international concern'.[2] This gravity demands the highest standards of fairness and integrity for the legitimacy of international criminal justice.

At first sight, the ethical issues that arise for counsel before international criminal tribunals differ considerably from those before 'civil' tribunals due to the distinctive nature of criminal procedure. For example, the prosecutorial discretion to indict and the disclosure of exculpatory evidence are issues that do not feature in civil procedure. An additional difference is that the ICC regulatory architecture for counsel is considerably more complex than before the ICJ and ECJ. However, the research presented in this chapter suggests that, despite these architectural and procedural differences, the essential principles (eg integrity, competence, and fair trial) that underpin the ethical issues are common to civil and criminal courts. The existence of universal principles of professional ethics, in turn, indicates that cross-fertilization between the various courts on these shared values would be appropriate, *mutatis mutandis*, in analogical cases.

The principal theme that has emerged in the early practice of the Court, particularly in its first trial, has seen a battle of wills between the Prosecutor and the judiciary. From the disclosure of potentially exculpatory evidence to the disclosure of intermediaries' identities to extrajudicial media statements, the Prosecutor has asserted his belief that, as a separate organ of the Court under the Rome Statute, he is a judicial officer of an equal status with the Chambers judges. By contrast, the Trial Chamber in *Lubanga* has treated the Prosecutor as an advocate who owes

[1] This chapter focuses upon prosecutors and defence counsel and omits the particular issues concerning victims' representatives, amici curiae and other advocates.

[2] Rome Statute, Art 1.

a duty of obedience to it. Additionally, precise scope of the role of ICC Prosecutor is as yet ill-defined.[3]

This chapter principally examines the ICC because it was created to be the sole permanent court for international criminal law and makes supplementary reference to the Nuremberg International Military Tribunal ('Nuremberg IMT'),[4] International Criminal Tribunal for the Former Yugoslavia (ICTY), International Criminal Tribunal for Rwanda (ICTR), and Special Court for Sierra Leone (SCSL).[5] Section 8.1 provides historical background concerning ethical standards for counsel before the Nuremberg IMT and the ICTY. Section 8.2 addresses the admission requirements, ethical standards, and disciplinary regimes applicable to Prosecutors. In analysing the ethical problems that have arisen concerning ICC Prosecutors, this chapter argues that the extension of the Court's regulatory superstructure for defence counsel to prosecutors would be a useful step to better handle ethical issues and raise standards.

8.1 Historical Background

The Nuremberg IMT and the ICTY that preceded the ICC provide three major historical themes concerning representation. The first is the regulatory dichotomy between prosecutors and defence counsel, whereby the former are internally self-regulating and the latter are externally regulated by the Tribunal. The second is the absence of common ethical standards for counsel caused by vague, terse, or absent ethical rules. The third is a culture of weak professional independence, whereby prosecutors and defence counsel during contentious procedural issues identified their first duty as to their clients. These themes have had a considerable impact upon the ICC infrastructure.

8.1.1 Nuremberg[6]

At the Nuremberg IMT, the regulatory architecture concerning representation was skeletal. As the first modern international criminal tribunal with representatives, judges, and tribunal officials from five jurisdictions there were considerable difficulties with conflicting national cultures and ethical standards. The Tribunal also disregarded several instances of questionable conduct on the part of individual

[3] For background, see Arbour, *The Prosecutor of a Permanent International Criminal Court* (2000).

[4] According to one Tribunal architect, it was not 'technically' international yet substantially so—Reuter, 'Nurnberg 1946: The Trial' 23 *NDL* (1947-1948), 76–97, 80–1. The Nuremberg trial is relevant due to the participation of counsel from five national jurisdictions in a mixed trial procedure.

[5] Although the 'international' character of the SCSL is disputed, it assists because counsel and judges come from various (albeit, common law) national jurisdictions.

[6] Calvocoressi, *Nuremberg* (1947); Harris, *Tyranny on Trial* (1954); Kranzbühler, 'Nuremberg Eighteen Years Afterwards' 14 *DLR* (1964–1965), 333–47; Smith, *Reaching Judgment at Nuremberg* (1977); Neave, *Nuremberg* (1978); Conot, *Justice at Nuremberg* (1983); Tusa and Tusa, *The Nuremberg Trial* (1983); Taylor, *The Anatomy of the Nuremberg Trials* (1993); Mettraux, *Perspectives on the Nuremberg Trial* (2008); Sarvarian, 'Ethical Standards for Prosecution and Defence Counsel before International Courts: The Legacy of Nuremberg' 10(1) *JICJ* (2012), 423-46.

counsel. They may have done so due to the absence of common standards and in the interest of preserving appearances.

For prosecutors, regulation by the Tribunal was non-existent. The Allied Powers had absolute discretion to appoint prosecutors, who were accountable to them.[7] There were no admission requirements, no ethical rules and no disciplinary powers in the London Charter or the Rules of Procedure. For defence counsel, the admission requirement of professional qualification to appear before a national court was inserted into the London Charter without debate 'to make the statute complete' by defining 'rights of the defense and the prosecution'.[8] The historical theme of regulatory dichotomy between prosecutors and defence counsel was thus created, though there were no prescribed ethical rules or disciplinary powers concerning defence counsel.

In this lax regulatory context, the second historical theme of lack of common ethical standards for counsel emerged with the result of conflicting national standards and questionable professional conduct. Prosecutors doubled as delegates to the London Conference that created the rules of the trial that they were to participate in, giving rise to a potential conflict of interest.[9] Certain applicants to serve as defence counsel offered to assist the Prosecution to secure the conviction of their putative clients.[10] Prosecutors failed to disclose pre-trial contacts with witnesses[11] and documents that they considered to be highly exculpatory to the defence.[12] For example, after his widely regarded humiliation in failing to effectively cross-examine Hermann Goering, Jackson:

> ...arranged a private meeting with Parker and Biddle and, in a 'wild' and 'uncontrolled mood,' he poured out all his complaints about the Court and its members. He accused Lawrence of always ruling against the Americans, blamed Biddle for undermining the morale of the prosecution, and in the end threatened to resign.[13]

Clearly, such actions had the potential to seriously compromise the integrity of the judicial process and thus detract from the legitimacy of the Tribunal.

The third theme of weak professional independence also emerged at the trial. For example, political pressure was brought to influence the prosecutorial discretion to indict, such as the Soviet attempt to falsely convict the accused for the Katyn Forest massacre that is now known to have been perpetrated by the Soviet Union[14] or British Admiralty pressure to remove Admiral Doenitz as a defendant to preclude examination of its own wartime practices.[15] Defence counsel also faced prejudicial instructions such as the exposition of irrelevant anti-Jewish propaganda[16] or

[7] London Charter, Arts 14, 23.
[8] Jackson, *The International Conference on Military Trials* (1949), 283.
[9] Tusa and Tusa, *The Nuremberg Trial*, 95.
[10] Conot, *Justice at Nuremberg*, 84.
[11] Conot, *Justice at Nuremberg*, 390–1.
[12] Conot, *Justice at Nuremberg*, 396.
[13] Smith, *Reaching Judgment at Nuremberg*, 109–10.
[14] Smith, *Reaching Judgment at Nuremberg*, 67, 452–5.
[15] Smith, *Reaching Judgment at Nuremberg*, 248–9.
[16] Conot, *Justice at Nuremberg*, 360, 364, 377, 385–6.

the intimidation of witnesses.[17] This close proximity between counsel and client, particularly for prosecutors, exposed the trial to the dangers of politicization and abuses carried out by counsel on client instructions.

8.1.2 ICTY

The ICTY was, after Nuremberg, the second influential forerunner to the ICC. As the first ad hoc international criminal tribunal, it provided a template for the ICTR and other tribunals that have since been created. It has also had occasion to address many of the most high-profile and sensitive procedural issues in its trials that engage counsel ethics. For procedural purposes, its practice provides an important background for the ICC.

The ICTY architecture concerning defence counsel is considerably more developed than at Nuremberg, largely attributable not only to the cautionary lessons of the Nuremberg precedent but also to the post-Nuremberg advent of the international human right to counsel for defendants in criminal trials.[18] The prescribed admission requirements, overseen by the Registry, go beyond the Nuremberg benchmark in demanding expertise in criminal law.[19] Defence counsel are bound by an ethical code of conduct and subject to a purpose-built disciplinary regime with procedural safeguards.[20] Thus, the Tribunal is considerably more active in regulating defence counsel and its Code of Conduct marks the first prescription of common ethical standards for counsel by an international criminal tribunal.

However, the three major themes concerning counsel identified in the Nuremberg trial have also emerged before the ICTY. The bifurcation of regulation between prosecutors and defence counsel has existed since the creation of the Tribunal. Apart from the Tribunal's contempt jurisdiction (which applies not only to counsel but to all participants in the trial process) and those national bars that exercise extraterritorial jurisdiction, prosecutors are professionally self-regulating. In two unreasoned decisions, Trial Chambers have decided that they lack jurisdiction to order a prosecutorial code of conduct or mete out disciplinary sanctions to prosecutors for professional misconduct.[21]

In the *Furundžija* trial, the Trial Chamber issued a decision in which it declared that, with reference to the Prosecution's handling of disclosure, it was 'appalled by what it considers to be conduct close to negligence in the Prosecution's preparation of this case'.[22] The Chamber then took the novel step of issuing a 'formal complaint', for which no express procedure existed in the Statute or the Rules, to the Chief Prosecutor in which it complained of 'a consistent pattern of non-compliance with the orders of the Trial Chamber, failure to comply with obligations imposed by the Rules...late and/or last minute filing of substantial motions and failure to provide the Trial Chamber with satisfactory reasons for such conduct' threatening

[17] Conot, *Justice at Nuremberg*, 248–9.
[18] ICTY Statute, Art 21(4)(d); ICCPR, Art 14(3)(d); ECHR, Art 6(3)(c).
[19] ICTY Rules, Rule 44(A).
[20] ICTY Code, Part III.
[21] *Kovačević*; *Furundžija* Formal Complaint, paras 11–12.
[22] *Furundžija* Decision, para 6.

'equal rights for all parties...and...the rights of the accused'.[23] The Chamber declared that it had made 'findings of misconduct on the part of the Prosecution' for which it issued its Formal Complaint.[24] It observed 'all Trial Chambers have the right to expect the highest standards of professionalism from counsel who appear before them' and that, whilst defence counsel were bound by their Code of Conduct, there exists no equivalent instrument for prosecutors.[25]

Whilst the Chamber considered the conduct of the counsel concerned was unprofessional, it considered that it did not arise to the level of contempt, reserved for 'the most extreme of cases where there has been interference with the course and administration of justice'.[26] Following an internal report, the Chief Prosecutor referred the Formal Complaint to the Lord Advocate and the Crown Agent of Scotland for external assessment who found that there had been 'an error of judgment in not disclosing, but no professional misconduct'.[27] Clearly, the Office of the Prosecutor (OTP) was sensitive to the potential conflict of interest arising from the Chief Prosecutor investigating her own deputies' professional conduct.[28] No disciplinary sanction was imposed by the Chief Prosecutor who, in defence of her deputies, considered that although they had been 'wrong' they had not been 'unprofessional' and criticized the Formal Complaint for having been 'made without notice to the lawyers involved...with no opportunity to respond to the allegations and no right of appeal against them'.[29]

There is force in the latter criticism because the Formal Complaint, as a public reprimand, may itself be regarded as a disciplinary sanction: a public admonishment would have had potential consequences for the professional reputations of the counsel concerned. Natural justice would require that counsel have an opportunity to defend themselves with adequate notice and a right of appeal (presumably to the Appeals Chamber). Paradoxically, the Formal Complaint supports the hypothesis that the ICTY has an inherent power to sanction prosecutors for professional misconduct.[30] Mme Arbour's call for the procedure to be prescribed or disapproved was not acted upon.[31]

However, it is suggested that Mme Arbour's view that professionalism entails a standard of honesty is wrong because it does not account for due diligence.[32] In her Response to the Formal Complaint, she wrote:

> I do not accept, however, that any aspect of the conduct of counsel for the prosecution constituted misconduct amounting to the wilful disobedience of court orders or deliberate and

[23] *Furundžija* Formal Complaint, para 2. See also the chamber's references to 'inaction, inefficiency, shoddiness and incompetence' in paras 6–10.

[24] *Furundžija* Formal Complaint, para 3.

[25] *Furundžija* Formal Complaint, para 4.

[26] *Furundžija* Formal Complaint, paras 11–12.

[27] Arbour, 'Legal Professionalism and International Criminal Proceedings' 4(4) *JICJ* (2006), 674–85, 681.

[28] *Furundžija* Response to the Formal Complaint, para 7.

[29] *Furundžija* Response to the Formal Complaint, para 7. See also Arbour, 'Legal Professionalism and International Criminal Proceedings', 677, 679, 682, 685.

[30] *Furundžija* Response to the Formal Complaint, para 23.

[31] Arbour, 'Legal Professionalism and International Criminal Proceedings', 685.

[32] See references to 'expedition' and 'diligence' in the UN Prosecutor Guidelines, Art 12 and UN Basic Principles, Art 14. See also *Furundžija* Response to the Formal Complaint, para 19.

improper withholding of relevant evidence from the trial process. My review of the way the prosecution was handled confirms that there were failings on the part of the prosecution team, that errors of judgement were made. I have found no suggestion of bad faith on the part of any member of staff involved in the case.[33]

The omission of due diligence may be found in her observation that:

There is no dishonour in being wrong, *assuming that one is otherwise diligent.* I believe that we can safely promote integrity, honesty and candour as universal trademarks of advocacy. I would suggest that the willingness to recognize errors and to correct them is the ultimate guarantee of justice. It should not be the hardest thing for a true professional to do, but it often is.[34]

The Trial Chamber's Formal Complaint was directed not at the integrity of the counsel concerned but rather at 'inaction, inefficiency, shoddiness and incompetence'.[35] The Chamber was complaining about diligence, not honesty.

The *Furundžija* Formal Complaint also demonstrates the second Nuremberg theme, namely, a lack of common ethical standards amongst counsel from divergent national cultures. Mme Arbour, understandably, relied heavily upon the jurisprudence of her home jurisdiction of Canada in her analysis of the ethical issues.[36] The two prosecutors concerned were English and American lawyers, each with their own national standards, to say nothing of the judges and defence counsel. In judicial proceedings with counsel from an even wider variety of national ethical cultures than the five present at Nuremberg, there is clearly difficulty in finding an 'international judicial culture'[37] with basic ethical standards concerning matters like honesty, courtesy, and diligence—to say nothing of even more contentious issues, such as conflicts of interest or client confession.

The ICTY has also engaged the third Nuremberg theme, namely, the principle of professional independence. For example, the decision by Chief Prosecutor Arbour to preliminarily investigate the alleged war crimes in the NATO bombing campaign of 1999 and her subsequent departure from her position gave rise to the question of political interference by UNSC Members in the activities of the OTP.[38] A sensitive problem for defence counsel has been withdrawal of assigned counsel from representation of unwilling defendants.[39] Such issues of professionalism formed a historical context in which the ICC was created.

[33] *Furundžija* Response to the Formal Complaint, para 13.

[34] Arbour, 'Legal Professionalism and International Criminal Proceedings', 685 (emphasis added).

[35] Note 22, *supra*.

[36] Arbour, 'Legal Professionalism and International Criminal Proceedings', 682–4.

[37] Harhoff, 'It is all in the Process', 78 *NJIL* (2010) 469–80, 479.

[38] Benvenuti, 'The ICTY Prosecutor and the Review of the NATO Bombing Campaign against the Federal Republic of Yugoslavia' 12(3) *EJIL* (2001) 503–29; Massa, 'NATO's Intervention in Kosovo and the Decision of the Prosecutor of the International Criminal Tribunal for the Former Yugoslavia Not to Investigate: An Abusive Exercise of Prosecutorial Discretion?' 24 *BJIL* (2006), 610–49, 634–8 and citations at 611 (note 7). Notably, Art 42(4) of the Rome Statute restricts the ICC Prosecutor to a single term of office.

[39] *Milošević*; *Barayagwiza*; *Taylor*, Official Transcript (Monday, 4 June 2007), 258–67; *Norman*; *Šešelj*.

8.2 Admission Requirements

8.2.1 Prosecutors[40]

Within that historical context, several of these issues have been addressed within the ICC framework to continue the progressive work of the ad hoc tribunals. Although the professional dichotomy between prosecutors and defence counsel has hitherto not been a central focus of criticism,[41] the role of the Prosecutor has been a topic of extensive debate since before the Rome Conference. This issue has been described as comprising two competing priorities: independence and accountability.[42] On the one hand, there should be safeguards to ensure the Prosecutor's freedom from undue influence. On the other hand, there should be checks to preclude abuse of prosecutorial powers. The problem is how to strike the right balance between those two needs.

However, the regulatory dichotomy has been narrowed under the Rome Statute. As before the ICTY, defence counsel are subject to admission requirements, a code of conduct and disciplinary regime. However, unlike at the ICTY the Prosecutor and Deputy Prosecutor are subject not only to admission requirements but are also professionally accountable to the Assembly of States Parties (ASP). Trial prosecutors are, subject to the Rome Statute, appointed, regulated, and disciplined by the Prosecutor. Thus, the bifurcation between prosecutors and defence counsel remains, in that: (1) prosecutors are professionally self-regulating, subject to the Prosecutor's professional accountability to a political organ; and (2) whereas defence counsel are subject to prescribed ethical rules, prosecutors are not. Thus, it is evident that the second historical problem of divergent ethical standards also persists. Although the third problem of professional independence has not yet been evident in practice, the ICC framework leaves open the possibility of future problems similar to those that have arisen before the ad hoc tribunals.

A key theme that emerged during the term of the first Prosecutor, Luis Moreno Ocampo of Argentina, was the status of the Prosecutor and his hierarchical status vis-à-vis the judiciary. The Prosecutor was criticized for overstepping his mandate as the OTP has clashed with Trial Chambers in *Lubanga* and other early trials and investigations. On the one hand, the judges with whom the OTP has disputed as well as the Office's critics believe that the Prosecutor and his subordinates are

[40] Arbour, *The Prosecutor of a Permanent International Criminal Court*; Jones, 'The Office of the Prosecutor' in Cassese et al, *The Rome Statute of the International Criminal Court* (2002) (Vol I), 269–83; Wouters et al, 'The International Criminal Court's Office of the Prosecutor' in Doria et al, *The Legal Regime of the International Criminal Court* (2009), 345–86; Schabas, *The International Criminal Court: A Commentary on the Rome Statute* (2010).

[41] See, however: International Bar Association, 'Counsel Matters at the International Criminal Court: A Review of Key Developments Impacting Lawyers Practising before the ICC' (November 2012), 17–18.

[42] Wouters et al, 'The International Criminal Court's Office of the Prosecutor', 345–86. See also Turone, 'Powers and Duties of the Prosecutor' in Cassese et al, *The Rome Statute of the International Criminal Court*, Vol II, 1137–80, 1139–43.

counsel and, as 'officers of the Court', are subordinate to the judiciary. On the other hand, the first Prosecutor and others believe that the OTP, as an independent organ of the Court, is equal to the judges and consequently subordinate only to the ASP.

These diametrically opposed conceptions of the Prosecutor's fundamental role may be described as a tension between the competing interests of independence and accountability.[43] In this context, the difficult problems encountered in *Lubanga* and other cases have illustrated the lack of prescribed ethical rules for prosecutors in their trial conduct. This regulatory void not only creates the problem of diverging ethical standards between prosecutors and defence counsel but also the danger of prosecutorial misconduct owing to a culture of self-accountability that prioritizes convictions over fair trial.

The Rome Statute does not expressly define the Prosecutor and his subordinates as 'counsel'.[44] Compounding this textual vagueness are two complications: (1) the hybrid nature of the role in combining diverging common law and civil law functions; and (2) the accountability of the Prosecutor to the ASP, which in practice is largely nominal. The Court's early activity—in particular, the *Lubanga* trial—has witnessed a power struggle between the judiciary and the OTP for control over the trial process. Thus, professional standards for prosecutors are not only important for the underlying philosophy of the Court but have also repeatedly arisen in practice.

As the Court evolves, greater clarity concerning the fundamental role and professional duties of the Prosecutor and his deputies would considerably assist in preventing future conflicts. Is the Prosecutor a magistrate in the civil law tradition, an advocate in the common law tradition, or some hybrid of the two? Since magistrates and advocates are subject to professional ethics and discipline under both systems, the question is not so much whether the Prosecutor ought to be subject to professional rules of conduct but rather how those rules should define his duties in light of his role in the ICC system. A supplementary question is whether the current disciplinary structure, in which the Prosecutor is accountable to the ASP and his deputies to him, is adequate. The early days of the Court suggest that these issues will continue to be highly topical and may well be considered for future reform.

The admission requirements for the Prosecutor and Deputy Prosecutors are prescribed in Article 42(3) of the Rome Statute:

> The Prosecutor and the Deputy Prosecutors shall be persons of high moral character, be highly competent in and have extensive practical experience in the prosecution or trial of criminal cases. They shall have an excellent knowledge of and be fluent in at least one of the working languages of the Court.

Despite being legal 'requirements', in practice they are exhortatory because the ASP could ignore them without the possibility of judicial review.[45] Since the Prosecutor bears wider political and administrative responsibilities than trial counsel, his

[43] Mégrét, 'International Prosecutors: Accountability and Ethics', *Leuven Center for Global Governance Studies*, Working Paper No 18 (December 2008), 9–10.

[44] Rome Statute, Art 42.

[45] Schabas, *The International Criminal Court: A Commentary on the Rome Statute*, 580.

appointment by the ASP seems appropriate. However, it remains the case that the Prosecutor is not only the head of the OTP but is also vested with the power to perform procedural acts for the Prosecution[46] and may also himself appear as trial counsel before the Court. To ensure that the requirements stipulated in Article 42(3) are observed, a useful reform has been the creation in 2011 of an ASP search committee for the nomination of the next Prosecutor.[47] However, the composition of the committee (three diplomats and two government lawyers) is not independent and there is no judicial review mechanism for future elections as a check upon the election of an unqualified candidate by the ASP.[48]

The requirement of 'high moral character' is vague, though it has been described as 'international law boilerplate for positions in judicial institutions'.[49] One possibility is that a candidate must have no record of dishonest or violent criminal offences. However, were a candidate to have committed a crime peculiar to one national jurisdiction, it would seem invidious to be thus disqualified. It is also questionable whether a candidate subject to ongoing criminal proceedings or alleged to have committed some lesser form of misconduct should be disqualified.

The requirement that the Prosecutor be 'highly competent in and have extensive practical experience in the prosecution or trial of criminal cases' is also vague, particularly in that it does not account for the managerial and political aspects of the role. The ICTY experience suggests that a variety of professional skills are required in the ideal candidate. Whilst the minimal requirement of ten years' experience in criminal trial work for defence counsel discussed below would be a rough starting point, an additional requirement of experience as the head of a major prosecution office with political and media relations aspects would seem appropriate.

Below the Prosecutor and Deputy Prosecutor are trial prosecutors within the 'Prosecutions Division' of the OTP.[50] Article 42 of the Rome Statute provides: 'The Prosecutor shall have full authority over the management and administration of the Office, including the staff facilities and other resources thereof.' This administrative autonomy was 'a considerable departure from previous practice at both the ICTY and ICTR, where the Registry has sometimes been alleged to have slowed down the recruitment and staffing process'.[51] Article 44 requires the Prosecutor to appoint 'such qualified staff as may be required' whilst ensuring 'the highest standards of efficiency, competency and integrity' and having regard, *mutatis mutandis*, to 'representation of the principal legal systems of the world', 'equitable geographical representation', and 'a fair representation of female and male [sexes]'.

46 Rome Statute, Arts 15, 42.

47 'Press Conference on Work of the ICC', online: <http://www.icc-cpi.int/NR/rdonlyres/443BD055-6EA6-4C97-B57A-C3D835B2A888/0/UNPressRelease201101MarENG.pdf> (Accessed: 6 October 2011).

48 One study has found that the election of ICC judges is primarily a question of politics rather than merit—Mackenzie et al, *Selecting International Judges: Principles, Process, and Politics* (2010), 173–5.

49 Schabas, *The International Criminal Court: A Commentary on the Rome Statute*, 580.

50 OTP Regulations, Reg 9(c).

51 Wouters et al, 'The International Criminal Court's Office of the Prosecutor', 345–86, 348.

The Prosecutor has paid particular attention to geography and gender in selecting his senior staff.[52]

Whilst the Prosecutor has been described as having 'a very wide margin of discretion' in his organization of the OTP, this 'is not totally unlimited since he has to respect the financial regulations and the staff regulations, which have been adopted by the Assembly of States Parties and... also provides for management oversight to the Prosecutor'.[53] Although 'management oversight' is prescribed by the Rome Statute and seems to envisage that the ASP may use 'budgetary tools'[54] to check Prosecutorial appointments that it dislikes, this is not specifically aimed at providing quality control to staff. The OTP has not published a document that sets out the criteria by which the Prosecutor recruits trial prosecutors but the 'selection criteria for prosecutorial counsel (especially at the higher levels) includes various levels of experience (ascending with the seniority of the post)' and some prosecutors are not members of national bars.[55]

A significant omission from the current arrangement is detailed requirements for the appointment of trial prosecutors as opposed to investigators or other staff members. It is arguable that the current setup may be improved by prescribing *external* requirements as already exist for defence counsel (eg membership of a national bar and criminal law expertise). However, it is conceivable that current prosecutors at the Office would resist the imposition of such requirements on the ground that a 'legitimate expectation' has been created for them to be able to plead before the Court. This could be addressed by prescribing transitional arrangements and applying new standards to future intakes.

8.2.2 Defence Counsel

An accused does not have an absolute choice of counsel.[56] Article 22(1) of the RoP prescribes admission requirements for defence counsel:

> A counsel for the defence shall have established competence in international or criminal law and procedure, as well as the necessary relevant experience, whether as judge, prosecutor, advocate or in other similar capacity, in criminal proceedings. A counsel for the defence shall have an excellent knowledge of and be fluent in at least one of the working languages of the Court. Counsel for the defence may be assisted by other persons, including professors of law, with relevant expertise.

All candidates who wish to appear before the Court as defence counsel must meet the requirements stipulated within Rule 22(1). Candidates must also furnish a

[52] 'Second Assembly of States Parties to the Rome Statute of the ICC: Report of the Prosecutor' (8 September 2003), online: <http://www.icc-cpi.int/NR/rdonlyres/C073586C-7D46-4CBE-B901-0672908E8639/ 143656/LMO_20030908_En.pdf> (Accessed: 3 April 2011).

[53] Wouters et al, 'The International Criminal Court's Office of the Prosecutor', 360.

[54] Wouters et al, 'The International Criminal Court's Office of the Prosecutor', 360. See Rome Statute, Art 112(2)(b).

[55] Interview with Mr Pubudu Sachithanandan, Associate Trial Lawyer, Office of the Prosecutor (20 August 2010), cited with permission.

[56] Schabas, note, 809. *Confer* Kay and Swart, 'The Role of the Defence' in Cassese et al, *The Rome Statute of the Internacional Criminal Court: A Commentary* (Vol II) (2002), 1421–37, 1430–2.

certificate from a national bar association confirming professional qualifications, right to practice and disciplinary standing,[57] thus clarifying an implied requirement in Article 22(1) that defence counsel must be a current member of a national bar. Counsel must have at least ten years' experience and not have been convicted of a 'serious' disciplinary or criminal offence.[58] The power to admit candidates to the list of counsel pursuant to these requirements is vested in the Registrar with review by the Presidency.[59]

An ambiguity within Rule 22(1) is the meaning of 'established competence in international or criminal law and procedure'. The literal meaning indicates that a counsel who is conversant with national criminal law and procedure will be admitted, notwithstanding that international criminal law and procedure is a discrete discipline. On the other hand, it is doubtful there is available expertise available in many jurisdictions, particularly in the home jurisdictions of 'situations'.[60] Experience before the ad hoc criminal tribunals suggests that a defence team comprising at least one 'foreign' counsel, who will presumably bring the requisite expertise in international and comparative criminal law and procedure, and one 'local' counsel who will bring knowledge of the local language(s), history, law, and politics. Setting an inordinately high bar would likely exclude local defence counsel at a time when the Court is particularly keen to engage more of them. However, a compelling counter-argument is that the professional competence of defence counsel is crucial in ensuring that the Court is able to function efficiently and that the rights of the accused are adequately represented.

Candidates for admission to the 'list of assistants to counsel' maintained by the Registry under regulation 125 must have 'either five years of relevant experience in criminal proceedings or specific competence in international or criminal law and procedure'.[61] Thus, the Court seemingly envisages that 'assistants to counsel' will either be specialist academic lawyers with expertise in international criminal law or a relatively junior criminal defence advocate with some advocacy experience. The distinguishing feature between 'counsel' and 'assistants to counsel' is the power to perform procedural acts on behalf of the defence, which requires a 'power of attorney' to be filed by counsel.[62] Thus, counsel are empowered to bind their clients during the proceedings by performing procedural acts on their behalf whereas assistants are confined to 'assist[ing] counsel in the presentation of the case before a Chamber'.[63]

A problem that has arisen concerning defence counsel has been former OTP staff members being appointed to defence teams.[64] In the cases of *Nourain*

57 Court Regulations, reg 69(2)(b).

58 Court Regulations, reg 67(1)–(3).

59 Court Regulations, regs 70, 72. A counsel not on the 'list of counsel' selected by an accused or assigned by the Court must be approved by the Registrar—Court Regulations, regs 75–6.

60 The 'Situation in Uganda', the 'Situation in the Democratic Republic of the Congo', the 'Situation in Darfur', and the 'Situation in the Central African Republic'.

61 Registry Regulations, regs 124–5.

62 Court Regulations, reg 75.

63 Court Regulations, reg 75.

64 IBA, Counsel Matters, 20–1 (para 2.4).

and Jerbo as well as *Kenya 2*, a former OTP staff member (Ibrahim Yillah) was appointed to defence teams. The Prosecution applied to the Trial Chamber to invalidate his appointment on grounds of conflict of interest including, inter alia, exposure to confidential material related to the case and situation. The Prosecution proposed a freezing period of one year on the appointment of former OTP lawyers to defence teams in cases that were being investigated while they were employed at the OTP.

Article 12(1)(b) of the Code of Conduct provides that counsel is barred from representing a client if he was 'involved or [was] privy to confidential information as a staff member of the Court relating to the case in which counsel seeks to appear'. The Appeals Chamber ruled that a conflict of interest based upon access to confidential information within the meaning of Article 12(1)(b) of the Code of Conduct requires that counsel have knowledge of any confidential information relating to the case in which counsel seeks to appear. Although the IBA has opined that 'it is not clear whether an amendment to the Code would further clarify the law in this area',[65] it may be useful to amend Article 12 of the Code to codify the test laid down by the Appeals Chamber in its judgment. The OTP proposal of a blanket freezing period also merits further consideration, though a one-year ban may be too short in light of the length of ICC cases.

8.3 Ethical Standards

8.3.1 Prosecutors

The bifurcation between prosecutorial and defence counsel is evident in that there exists a code of conduct for the latter but not the former. In 2002, a draft 'Code of Professional Conduct for Prosecutors of the International Criminal Court'[66] was developed by the International Association of Prosecutors and the Coalition for the International Criminal Court but was never adopted.[67] As an IBA report relates:

> The issue concerning whether the Code of Conduct [applicable to defence counsel] should apply to prosecution counsel has been raised in several contexts at the ICC. Allegations of inappropriate public statements by the OTP in the *Lubanga* case and the Libya situation among others, has created angst among some defence counsel, who opine that the provisions on misconduct in the Rome Statute should be supplemented by some behavioural code for prosecution counsel. In the case of Laurent Gbagbo, following an order by Pre-Trial Chamber III for the parties to file a joint proposal on a Protocol for the handling of confidential information, the defence proposed the insertion of a clause that the Code of Conduct should be extended beyond its specific terms to apply to prosecution counsel. This was vehemently opposed by the OTP.[68]

[65] IBA, Counsel Matters, 21.
[66] Online: <http://www.amicc.org/docs/prosecutor.pdf> (Accessed: 9 February 2011).
[67] IBA, Counsel Matters, 17 (para 2.3).
[68] IBA, Counsel Matters.

There is a belief that, as 'international civil servants',[69] prosecutors are different from defence counsel:

> The common sentiment in the Office is that, unlike the duties of defence counsel, prosecutors have duties of confidentiality imposed upon them upon joining the Office. The Prosecutor has adopted a middle road of imposing certain duties through the [OTP] Regulations in order to emphasise predictability, consistency and transparency as priorities.[70]

From the administrative perspective, prosecutors clearly differ from defence counsel in that they are more integrally a part of the Court.[71] However, from the litigious perspective the Prosecution and Defence are strictly equal—requiring equal regulation.[72]

In the absence of a code of conduct, prosecutors are externally bound only by the broad provisions of the Staff Regulations and Staff Rules, which provides:

> By accepting appointment, staff members pledge themselves to discharge their functions and regulate their conduct with the interest of the Court only in view. Loyalty to the aims, principles and purposes of the Court, as set forth in the Rome Statute, is a fundamental obligation of all staff members by virtue of their status as international civil servants.[73]

Prosecutors are also bound by the Regulations of the OTP, Article 17 of which provides: 'the Office shall ensure compliance with the Staff Rules and Regulations and Administrative Instructions of the Court in order to ensure that its staff members uphold the highest standards of efficiency, competence and integrity.'

However, these provisions do not provide clarity concerning potential conflicts that may arise between the interests of the Court, ASP, victims, witnesses, and procedural justice. This vagueness may be explained by a duality in the role of the Prosecutor whereby he may be considered a judge or a counsel. According to one commentator:

> [M]ore or less the same standards are required of judges and prosecutors alike throughout the Rome Statute. This would seem to imply that the Prosecutor and Deputy Prosecutors are considered to be judicial officers, possessing the same qualities and conduct as that of judges. In England and Wales, this would fit in with the notion of the prosecution counsel as an officer of the court whose task is to present the facts of the case, not to do his utmost to secure a conviction and of whom independence and impartiality may be required. In other jurisdiction—for example the United States—the prosecutor, or district attorney, fulfils a more partisan role, however, and the notion that he must be impartial might be regarded as bizarre.[74]

[69] Staff Regulations, reg 1.1(a).
[70] Interview with Mr Sachithanandan.
[71] Rome Statute, Art 34(c).
[72] Rome Statute, Art 67(1).
[73] Staff Rules, reg 1.2(e).
[74] Jones, 'The Office of the Prosecutor', 271. See also Schabas, *The International Criminal Court: A Commentary on the Rome Statute*, 582–3; English Code, Written Standards for the Conduct of Professional Work, para 10.1.

In a departure from the ad hoc tribunals, the Prosecutor is required to be neutral in the civil law tradition.[75] During pre-trial investigations his duties resemble those of a *juge d'instruction* who impartially investigates both incriminatory and exculpatory evidence.[76] Adding to this confusion is the role of the Pre-Trial Chamber, which was originally created to be 'the reasoned gatekeeper' for a 'zealous' Prosecutor.[77]

Whilst it may consequently appear logical to treat the Prosecutor as a judicial magistrate, a key difference is that he is not bound by the ICC Code of Judicial Ethics whereas, in France, prosecutors and *juges d'instruction* are bound by judicial ethics.[78] Additionally, early practice has followed the common law model of the Prosecution as partisan against the accused.[79] It is arguable that the concept of the Prosecutor as a neutral judge rather than a partial advocate during litigation is not realistic in that, having decided to indict, he is committed to seeking a conviction with no duty of continual review.[80] Although an advocate may be required to be objective, a judge cannot be required to be partial.

In principle, there is no convincing justification for the bifurcation of prosecutorial and defence counsel. Both are advocates: both perform the essentially identical function of advocacy, albeit representing opposing parties. Even if their procedural roles diverge in detail, they are grounded in identical principles. As the IBA has commented, prescribing codes of conduct for both is as much about perception as it is about practicalities:

> What then is the added value of a Code of Conduct for the Prosecution at the ICC? Codes of conduct are more than just a disciplinary mechanism; they are a set of mores that govern counsel's day-to-day practice. They are also a clear articulation of common ethical and professional standards against which all counsel at the Court can be equally judged. Lawyers who work in the OTP come from equally diverse legal and cultural backgrounds as other counsel appearing before the Court and thus the professional and ethical standards to which they adhere may vary. Unfortunately, the absence of a code of conduct for the OTP may create the unfortunate and inaccurate impression that defence and victims' counsel require more ethical guidance than the counsel in the OTP.[81]

This author favours the approach of the SCSL in applying a uniform code of conduct with appropriate modalities for each side of the courtroom over that of the ICTY and ICTR in prescribing separate codes. This is to reinforce the principle of equality of parties and, in particular, the subordination of prosecutors to the authority of the Court as a whole. The approach of the ad hoc tribunals has the specific weakness of the prosecutors' code being internally prescribed and enforced, not externally. This should be avoided at the ICC to enhance the independence of the standards prescribed from those to whom they apply.

[75] Wouters et al, 'The International Criminal Court's Office of the Prosecutor', 378;

[76] Rome Statute, Arts 42(7)–(8), 45, 54(1)(a).

[77] Rome Statute, Arts 53(3), 56, 57–8, 61; Stahn and Sluiter, *The Emerging Practice of the International Criminal Court* (2009), 585–97, 586.

[78] French Magistrates Code of Conduct, Art b.16.

[79] Doria et al, *The Legal Regime of the International Criminal Court*, 1439–93, 1477.

[80] Rome Statute, Arts 54(1)(a), 61(1), 61(4), 61(9); ICC Rules, Rule 104. *Confer* OTP Regulations, Regs 29(4), 35(4), 60.

[81] IBA, Counsel Matters, 18.

8.3.1.1 Discretion to Investigate and to Indict

The discretion to investigate and to indict is one of the Prosecutor's most important powers. Criticism of the Prosecutor bringing a charge of genocide against President Omar al-Bashir of the Sudan demonstrates that the criteria in the exercise of this discretion are sensitive and topical.[82] The policy factors driving the exercise of the discretion and the process by which the decision is made are crucial in defining the fundamental philosophy of the Office. Concordantly, the absence of an ethical code defining precise limits is suggested to be a weakness in the Court's procedure.[83]

Article 53(1) of the Rome Statute provides that 'the Prosecutor shall…initiate an investigation unless he or she determines that there is no reasonable basis to proceed under this Statute'. The Prosecutor must consider whether there is a reasonable basis to believe that a crime has been committed within the Court's jurisdiction, the case would be admissible and 'taking into account the gravity of the crime and the interests of victims, there are nonetheless substantial reasons to believe that an investigation would not serve the interests of justice'. The same test applies for the discretion to prosecute under Article 53(2). Not only does the negative phrasing of Article 53 create a presumption in favour of investigation or prosecution by requiring the Prosecutor to justify any negative decision, but Article 53(3)(b) empowers a Pre-Trial Chamber to review a negative decision if taken according to the 'interests of justice' criterion.

Although much of Article 53 is progressive, particularly the advent of judicial review of negative decisions, ambiguity remains.[84] From the ethical perspective, the crucial issue is the decision-making process. There is a case for an ethical duty to consider only such apolitical factors as the sufficiency of the evidence and the law to support an investigation or indictment coupled with the concept of 'gravity' to focus the necessarily limited resources of the Office upon the serious crimes that it was created to pursue.[85] Experience at Nuremberg and the modern ad hoc tribunals not only shows the need for prosecutorial independence from external pressure but the Prosecutor and his deputies could also face individual pressures to prioritize extraneous considerations over the merits (eg re-election or re-appointment).

The nature of international criminal prosecution necessarily engages a political dimension to refrain from pursuing suspects on the ground that it would derail reconciliation processes ('the interests of peace'). The Prosecutor, subject to judicial review, could decide not to investigate or prosecute in the 'interests of justice'. It is

[82] *Al Bashir* Decision; *Al Bashir* Appeal Judgment; *Al Bashir* Second Decision. See also Rodman, 'Is Peace in the Interests of Justice? The Case for Broad Prosecutorial Discretion at the International Criminal Court', 22(1) *LJIL* (2009), 99–126; Goldston, 'More Candour About Criteria: The Exercise of Discretion by the Prosecutor of the International Criminal Court', 8(2) *JICJ* (2010), 383–406; Stahn and Sluiter, *The Emerging Practice of the International Criminal Court*, 183–280.

[83] However, it is not as broad as that of the ICTY Chief Prosecutor—Goldston, 'More Candour About Criteria: The Exercise of Discretion by the Prosecutor of the International Criminal Court', 390–3.

[84] Schabas, *The International Criminal Court: A Commentary on the Rome Statute*, 659–70.

[85] Schabas, *The International Criminal Court: A Commentary on the Rome Statute*, 660–6; Stahn and Sluiter, *The Emerging Practice of the International Criminal Court*, 209–17, 229–46.

suggested that 'justice' should take the meaning of procedural justice, namely, to promote the integrity of judicial proceedings and fair trial. The integrity of judicial proceedings necessarily entails the blindness of justice to political considerations. Equality before the law, as a component of the rule of law, demands that no one be exempted from investigation or prosecution. This commitment to consistent and impartial justice, the antithesis of political prosecutions or non-prosecutions, should be expressed not only as a legal duty but also as an ethical one.

8.3.1.2 Documentary Evidence

As before the ad hoc tribunals, both the scope and implementation of prosecutorial disclosure duties is a major issue before the Court. In the *Lubanga* trial, the first before the Court, the disclosure of confidential exculpatory evidence opposed the Prosecutor and the Trial Chamber to one another. The resulting standoff provoked criticism of the Prosecutor and general support for the Trial Chamber.[86] Whilst the lack of clearly prescribed ethical duties for prosecutorial counsel has precluded discussion of the ethical duties of prosecutorial counsel, the language employed by the Trial Chamber in its criticism of the Prosecution supports the need for a prosecutorial code of conduct.

In *Lubanga*, the accused was surrendered by the DRC government on 17 March 2006 and made his first appearance before the Pre-Trial Chamber on 20 March 2006. His trial commenced on 26 January 2009—a span of 1,046 days in pre-trial detention. Even by the relatively slow standard of international criminal tribunals, such an extensive period of pre-trial detention arguably infringes the right of an accused to an expeditious trial 'without undue delay'.[87] Whilst allowing for the fact that *Lubanga* is the Court's first trial, the disclosure dispute engaged not only equality of arms but also expeditious trial issues. The Prosecutor is required to 'as soon as practicable, disclose to the defence evidence in [his] possession or control which he... believes' to be exculpatory.[88] This disclosure duty is subject to an exception by which the Prosecutor may enter into agreements not to disclose 'documents or information that [he] obtains on the condition of confidentiality and solely for the purpose of generating new evidence, unless the provider of the information consents'.[89] The Trial Chamber is empowered to decide procedural matters during trial, such as ordering additional documentary disclosure.[90]

86 Rozenberg, 'Why the World's Most Powerful Prosecutor Should Resign: Part I', *The Telegraph* (3 July 2008); Stuart, 'The ICC in Trouble', 6(3) *JICJ* (2008), 409–17; Ambos, 'Confidential Investigations (Article 54(3)(E) ICC Statute) vs. Disclosure Obligations: The Lubanga Case and National Law', 12(4) *NCLR* (2009), 543–68, 567–8; Katzman, 'The Non-Disclosure of Confidential Exculpatory Evidence and the Lubanga Proceedings', 8 *NUJIHR* (2009), 77–101, 100–1; Anoushirvani, 'The Future of the International Criminal Court', 22 *PILR* (2010), 213–40, 221–2.

87 Rome Statute, Art 64(2), 67(1)(c).

88 Rome Statute, Art 67(2); ICC Rules, Art 77.

89 Rome Statute, Art 54(3)(e); ICC Rules, Art 82(1).

90 Rome Statute, Art 64(6); Schabas, *The International Criminal Court: A Commentary on the Rome Statute*, 762–8.

A major cause for the delay to the *Lubanga* trial was the refusal by the Prosecution to disclose exculpatory documents because Article 54(3)(e) confidentiality agreements had been concluded with the UN and other organizations in order to 'protect staff members' working on the ground.[91] On 10 June 2008, the Prosecution informed the Trial Chamber that 207 documents provided under such agreements had not been disclosed due to provider refusal.[92] Although the Prosecution considered that certain documents could 'in principle' materially impact upon the proceedings, it argued that there was 'no doubt' that 'in fact' they would not.[93]

Despite a judicial confidentiality undertaking, the providers refused to permit their disclosure to the Chamber to evaluate their exculpatory nature. The Prosecution proposed that, for 33 of the documents, it would evaluate their exculpatory effect following which 'elements of information' would be disclosed without the actual documents.[94] The Chamber rejected this proposal, noting that its effect would be to render it dependent upon the Prosecution's evaluation.[95] Staying the trial, the Chamber held that the Prosecution's interpretation of Article 54(3)(e) was 'broad and incorrect' because it had been used to gather 'evidence "*for use at trial*" contrary to the provision's intended meaning of permitting confidentiality to gather "information or documents *which are not for use at trial*"' and characterized it as 'a wholesale and serious abuse' resulting in 'the trial process [being] ruptured to such a degree that it is now impossible to piece together the constituent elements of a fair trial'.[96] Following appellate confirmation of the stay, the Prosecution disclosed the documents and the stay was lifted.[97]

The principal ethical issue concerns the handling of evidence in a manner that respects procedural justice. The need to protect informants is immaterial in that Article 54(3)(e) requires confidential documents to be used '*solely* for the purpose of generating *new evidence*'. Rather, the problem arose from a culture by which it was considered acceptable to use such agreements routinely to selectively adduce confidential documents as *evidence* whilst refusing to allow the Court to evaluate them.[98] The need for judicial scrutiny is amplified by the fact that many documents were collated second-hand by unprofessional persons,[99] increasing the risk of mishandling. Another issue is the Prosecutors' decision to resist the Chamber's disclosure orders and statutory role.[100]

91 *Lubanga*, Decision on Non-Disclosure, paras 3–5, 26.
92 *Lubanga*, Decision on Non-Disclosure, paras 19, 63.
93 *Lubanga*, Decision on Non-Disclosure, para 22.
94 *Lubanga*, Decision on Non-Disclosure, para 67.
95 *Lubanga*, Decision on Non-Disclosure, paras 68–9.
96 *Lubanga*, Decision on Non-Disclosure, paras 71–6, 93–5.
97 *Lubanga*, Decision on Release; *Lubanga*, Decision on the Request of the Prosecutor; *Lubanga*, Redacted Version of Decision; *Lubanga*, Judgment on the appeal of the Prosecutor 2008, paras 17, 37–55, 74–101; Separate Opinion of Judge Georghios M Pikas, paras 30–5; *Lubanga*, Status Conference, 1–4.
98 Stuart, 'The ICC in Trouble', 413; Ambos, 'Confidential Investigations (Article 54(3)(E) ICC Statute) vs. Disclosure Obligations', 567–8; Katzman, 'The Non-Disclosure of Confidential Exculpatory Evidence and the Lubanga Proceedings', 98–101. See also *Katanga*, paras 10–12, 46, 52, 56, 102 and 123.
99 Stuart, 'The ICC in Trouble', 414–15.
100 *Lubanga*, Decision on Non-Disclosure, paras 44–5, 72.

8.3.1.3 Testimonial Evidence

Concerning the ethics of testimonial evidence, the problem of 'witness proofing' has also arisen during the *Lubanga* trial.[101] Despite the fact that this is an issue of procedural importance upon which there exist diverging national rules, it is absent from the ICC texts.[102] Whilst the Pre-Trial and Trial Chambers in *Lubanga* diverged from the practice of the ad hoc tribunals by prohibiting witness proofing as unacceptably hazardous to evidential integrity, the lack of precise rules governing counsel's contacts with witnesses remains a lacuna in the Court's procedure.

In *Lubanga*, the Prosecution applied for leave to conduct 'witness proofing' which it defined according to ICTY jurisprudence as the 'practice whereby a meeting is held between a party to the proceedings and a witness, before the witness is due to testify in Court, the purpose of which is to re-examine the witness's evidence to enable more accurate, complete and efficient testimony'.[103] The Prosecution cited jurisprudence from major common law jurisdictions as well as that of the ad hoc tribunals. However, as the Trial Chamber noted, not only is there definitional variation amongst common law jurisdictions concerning witness proofing but no civil law jurisdiction was cited—thus precluding the existence of a 'general principle based on established practice of national legal systems'.[104] Whilst the Chamber accepted that witness proofing as defined by the Prosecution was a generally accepted practice before the ad hoc tribunals, it did not consider itself bound by Article 21 of the Rome Statute to apply those precedents.[105]

The decision consequently turned upon policy arguments. The Prosecution submitted that witness proofing assists in the discovery of the truth by 'furnishing all involved with a complete picture of the case' and enabling 'a more accurate and efficient presentation of evidence'.[106] However, the Trial Chamber rejected the Prosecution's proposal to meet with the witness prior to testimony in order to discuss the topics to be dealt with in court and to show the witness exhibits for comments on the grounds that it would created an unavoidable danger of 'rehearsal of in-court testimony' and 'may diminish what would otherwise be helpful spontaneity during the giving of evidence by a witness' that 'can be of paramount importance to the Court's ability to find the truth'.[107] Thus, whilst allowing the practice of 'witness

[101] *Lubanga*, Pre-Trial Chamber Decision on Witness Proofing; *Lubanga*, Trial Chamber Decision on Witness Proofing. See also Karemaker et al, 'Witness Proofing in International Criminal Tribunals', 21(3) *LJIL* (2008), 683–98; Ambos, '"Witness Proofing" Before the International Criminal Court: A Reply to Karemaker, Taylor and Pittman', 21(4) *LJIL* (2008), 911–6; Karemaker et al, 'Witness Proofing in International Criminal Tribunals: A Response to Ambos', 21(4) *LJIL* (2008), 917–23; Stahn and Sluiter, *The Emerging Practice of the International Criminal Court*, 599–614; Vasiliev, 'Proofing the Ban on "Witness Proofing"', 20(2) *CLF* (2009) 193–261; Jordash, 'The Practice of "Witness Proofing" in International Criminal Tribunals', 22(3) *LJIL* (2009), 501–23.

[102] *Lubanga,* Trial Chamber Decision on Witness Proofing, para 36.

[103] *Lubanga,* Trial Chamber Decision on Witness Proofing, para 7.

[104] *Lubanga,* Trial Chamber Decision on Witness Proofing, paras 39–41.

[105] *Lubanga,* Trial Chamber Decision on Witness Proofing, paras 43–5.

[106] *Lubanga,* Trial Chamber Decision on Witness Proofing, para 46.

[107] *Lubanga,* Trial Chamber Decision on Witness Proofing, paras 51–2.

familiarisation', the Trial Chamber prohibited the practice of 'witness proofing' as defined by the Prosecution.[108]

The *Lubanga* decisions, by expressly rejecting the permissive policy of the ad hoc tribunals, have prompted a re-evaluation of the merits of pre-testimonial communication between counsel and witness in which the substance of the witness' testimony is reviewed. The ensuing debate has addressed not only the desirability of such contacts for the integrity of the judicial process but has only briefly examined the corresponding ethical issues.[109] Leaving to one side the interpretation of the Rome Statute, on the policy arguments, Karemaker and others on the one hand assert that the advantage of witness proofing (namely, ensuring completeness of testimonial evidence) outweighs the risk of improper influencing of evidence by counsel that may be mitigated by cross-examination, the judiciary and ethical rules prohibiting manipulation of evidence.[110] Ambos, on the other hand, argues that the serious risks of manipulation involved in the witness proofing process outweigh the supposed benefits in that a distinction between 'familiarisation' and 'coaching' does not work in practice and mitigation of the risks is doubtful.[111]

The invocation by one side or the other of the ethical duties of counsel[112] prompts closer examination of those duties. The ICC instruments are silent on the issue, in addition to the ethical handling of witness statements, pre-testimonial communication, witness examination or extra-testimonial communication with a witness under oath. The Trial Chamber's decision in *Lubanga* was beneficial not only in clarifying the terminology but also in emphasizing the danger of a witness' evidence being improperly influenced by counsel and the need to preserve the spontaneity of witness interrogation in order to assess credibility. A 'proofed' witness insulated from this and (intentionally or not) alerted to evidentiary weaknesses by counsel necessarily removes that possibility.[113] Based upon this assumption, ethical rules should prohibit counsel from conducting pre-hearing rehearsal of testimony with a witness and any communication with a witness under oath. The common law rules upon leading, designed to preserve testimonial integrity, should be adopted. A general rule prohibiting counsel who has drafted the witness statement from later interrogating that witness may also be a useful safeguard.

8.3.1.4 Loyalty

In the *Lubanga* trial, on 28 January 2009 the first prosecution witness dramatically recanted his original statement by alleging that an intermediary for the Prosecution

[108] *Lubanga*, Trial Chamber Decision on Witness Proofing, paras 53–7.

[109] Vasiliev, 'Proofing the Ban on "Witness Proofing"', 260–1.

[110] Karamaker et al, 'Witness Proofing in International Criminal Tribunals', 694–8.

[111] Ambos, '"Witness Proofing" Before the International Criminal Court: A Reply to Karemaker, Taylor and Pittman', 913–16.

[112] Karamaker et al, 'Witness Proofing in International Criminal Tribunals', 697–8; Ambos, '"Witness Proofing" Before the International Criminal Court: A Reply to Karemaker, Taylor and Pittman', 916–7; Vasiliev, 'Proofing the Ban on "Witness Proofing"', 252–8.

[113] *Confer* Karemaker et al, 'Witness Proofing in International Criminal Tribunals', 694.

had coached his statement.[114] However, when the witness resumed his testimony two weeks later following a break requested by the Prosecution, he affirmed his original statement and withdrew the allegations. At this stage, the principal issue appears to have been whether intermediary 321 had unduly influenced the witness' evidence. An ancillary ethical issue, assuming that the witness remained under oath during the two-week break, is what contact prosecutors had with the witness in question. Although this was not an issue in *Lubanga*, in future cases it is potentially sensitive to allegations of counsel influencing a witness under oath (particularly where a witness dramatically changes his evidence) and is a matter upon which the ICC texts are silent. Whilst Laurel Baig of the ICTY Office of the Prosecutor suggests that 'the first witness in the first ICC trial...experienced a number of problems that might have been ameliorated if he had been better prepared by the prosecution',[115] it may also be argued that the dangerous revelations of the first witness and others may never have been discovered if prosecutors had been allowed to coach him—thus vindicating the earlier decision on proofing.

Subsequently, another prosecution witness recanted his original statement and alleged that the OTP's intermediary coached him to change his testimony in order to 'get rich'.[116] On 27 January 2010, the Defence in its opening statement declared that it would prove that the Prosecution's witnesses were manipulated into lying and were in fact never child soldiers.[117] On 2 February, Defence witness Joseph Maki Dhera then testified that intermediary 321 had coached him to falsely claim that he was a child soldier in order to get money.[118] The following day, the Trial Chamber instructed the Prosecution by email to provide it with 'comprehensive information on all the intermediaries'.[119]

Subsequently, a Defence witness and a recalled Prosecution witness both alleged that intermediaries had sought to coach them to falsely claim that they were child soldiers by offering money and other incentives.[120] On 15 March 2010, the Trial Chamber ordered disclosure of the names of the intermediaries to the Defence.[121] However, the Prosecution argued, inter alia, that it had a duty of care toward its intermediaries and witnesses, that the risk of harm to the intermediaries and witnesses is high, and that their identities should accordingly not be disclosed to the Defence 'unless there is the most pressing reason'.[122] It submitted that 'any action by the Court that chills the ability of the Prosecution to protect their identities and securities will chill the Prosecution's ability to obtain assistance by other intermediaries in future cases'.[123] In response, the Defence emphasized the importance of the

[114] *Lubanga*, Redacted Decision on Intermediaries, paras 7–10.
[115] Baig, 'International Criminal Law and Legal Ethics: The Need for Shared Expectations' 103 *ASILP* (2009), 255–67, 257–8.
[116] *Lubanga*, Redacted Decision on Intermediaries, paras 21–2.
[117] *Lubanga*, Redacted Decision on Intermediaries, para 25.
[118] *Lubanga*, Redacted Decision on Intermediaries, paras 26–9.
[119] *Lubanga*, Redacted Decision on Intermediaries, para 30.
[120] *Lubanga*, Redacted Decision on Intermediaries, paras 36, 39.
[121] *Lubanga*, Redacted Decision on Intermediaries, para 41.
[122] *Lubanga*, Redacted Decision on Intermediaries, para 58.
[123] *Lubanga*, Redacted Decision on Intermediaries, para 58.

intermediaries' role to the defence case[124] and submitted that disclosure of their identities would be unlikely to endanger the safety of those involved or impair the work of the OTP.[125] The Defence 'contend[ed] that there is an issue as regards the intermediaries' commitment to the integrity of the judicial process and there needs to be a thorough investigation of their identities, any links with external authorities and their approach towards witnesses'.[126]

The Trial Chamber, acknowledging that the intermediaries' issue had become important in the trial, held that there was a 'real basis for concern as to the system employed by the prosecution for identifying potential witnesses' and that 'there was extensive opportunity for the intermediaries, if they wished, to influence the witnesses as regards the statements they provided for the prosecution' so that 'it would be unfair to deny the defence the opportunity to research this possibility with all the intermediaries used by the prosecution for the relevant witnesses in this trial, where the evidence justifies that course'.[127] The Chamber ordered the Prosecution to, inter alia, disclose the identity of intermediary 143 and call intermediaries 316 and 321.[128]

On 3 June 2010, the Trial Chamber was informed that the VWU was confident that it would be able to implement protective measures for intermediary 143 preparatory to identity disclosure.[129] However, the intermediary subsequently changed his mind about the adequacy of the security arrangements.[130] Following submissions, on 6 July 2010 the Trial Chamber ruled that disclosure be confidentially made to the Defence. The Prosecution 'unsurprisingly immediately indicated that the Chamber's order was understood and would be implemented'.[131] On 7 July, the Chamber again ordered disclosure to be effected that day.[132] The Prosecution did not comply with that order but instead applied to the Chamber to reconsider it on the basis that the Chamber's order would have placed intermediary 143 at risk of being killed.[133] The Chamber rejected this application and re-ordered disclosure.

The Prosecution, again not complying with the Order, filed an urgent application to delay the time limit for disclosure or alternatively stay the proceedings in which it argued that the OTP had an autonomous duty under the Rome Statute to protect witnesses and that 'the Prosecution considers it indispensable that prior to any disclosure being effected, the Prosecution be satisfied that it is acting in compliance with it specific duties under the Statute and the Rules'.[134] The Prosecutor declared:

> The Prosecution is sensitive to its obligation to comply with the Chamber's instructions. However, it also has an independent statutory obligation to protect persons put at risk on account of the Prosecutor's actions. It should not comply, or be asked to comply, with

[124] *Lubanga*, Redacted Decision on Intermediaries, paras 74–9.
[125] *Lubanga*, Redacted Decision on Intermediaries, para 80.
[126] *Lubanga*, Redacted Decision on Intermediaries, para 82.
[127] *Lubanga*, Redacted Decision on Intermediaries, para 138.
[128] *Lubanga*, Redacted Decision on Intermediaries, paras 141–7, 150.
[129] *Lubanga*, Redacted Decision on the Prosecution's Urgent Request, para 3.
[130] *Lubanga*, Redacted Decision on the Prosecution's Urgent Request, para 6.
[131] *Lubanga*, Redacted Decision on the Prosecution's Urgent Request, para 8.
[132] *Lubanga*, Redacted Decision on the Prosecution's Urgent Request, paras 10–11.
[133] *Lubanga*, Redacted Decision on the Prosecution's Urgent Request, para 12.
[134] *Lubanga*, Redacted Decision on the Prosecution's Urgent Request, para 13.

an Order that may require it to violate its separate statutory obligation by subjecting the person to foreseeable risk. The Prosecutor accordingly has made a determination that the Prosecution would rather face adverse consequences in its litigation than expose a person to risk on account of prior interaction with this Office. This is not a challenge to the authority of the Chamber, it is instead a reflection of the Prosecution's own legal duty under the Statute.[135]

The Prosecutor suggested that his Office was 'torn between competing obligations' and that it was endeavouring to resolve the dilemma by obtaining an expeditious response from the VWU 'to make sure that measures are in place that will protect all interests in the proceedings'.[136] On 8 July, the VWU informed the Trial Chamber that the disclosure of intermediary 143's identity did not threaten his safety.[137]

The Trial Chamber considered that the Prosecution believed that it had an autonomous power to comply with or disregard Chamber orders depending upon its own interpretation of its duties under the Rome Statute.[138] The Chamber found that Article 68 of the Rome Statute obliged the Prosecutor to take protective measures whilst investigating and prosecuting crimes but that 'those responsibilities do not give him licence, or discretion, or autonomy to disregard judicial orders because he considers the Chamber's decision is inconsistent with his interpretation of his obligations'.[139] It held:

No criminal court can operate on the basis that whenever it makes an order in a particular area, it is for the Prosecutor to elect whether or not to implement it, depending on his interpretation of his obligations. The judges, not the Prosecutor, decide on protective measures during the trial, once the Chamber is seized of the relevant issue... These are issues for the Court, and the Court alone, to determine, having heard submissions and having considered all the information the judges consider necessary and relevant. The Prosecutor now claims a separate authority which can defeat the orders of the Court, and which thereby involves a profound, unacceptable and unjustified intrusion into the role of the judiciary.

...

Therefore, the Prosecutor has elected to act unilaterally in the present circumstances, and he declines to be 'checked' by the Chamber, In these overall circumstances, it is necessary to stay these proceedings as an abuse of the process of the Court because of the material non-compliance with the Chamber's orders of 7 July 2010, and more generally, because of the Prosecutor's clearly evinced intention not to implement the Chamber's orders... Whilst these circumstances endure, the fair trial of the accused is no longer possible, and justice cannot be done, not least because the judges will have lost control of a significant aspect of the trial proceedings as provided under the Rome Statute framework.[140]

On 9 July, the Trial Chamber issued the following warning:

Under Rule 171 of the Rules of Procedure and Evidence, we hereby give the Prosecutor and the Deputy Prosecutor an oral warning of sanctions in the event of any continuing breach

[135] *Lubanga*, Redacted Decision on the Prosecution's Urgent Request, para 14.
[136] *Lubanga*, Redacted Decision on the Prosecution's Urgent Request, para 16.
[137] *Lubanga*, Redacted Decision on the Prosecution's Urgent Request, para 17.
[138] *Lubanga*, Redacted Decision on the Prosecution's Urgent Request, para 21.
[139] *Lubanga*, Redacted Decision on the Prosecution's Urgent Request, para 24.
[140] *Lubanga*, Redacted Decision on the Prosecution's Urgent Request, paras 27–8, 31.

of our orders; the Deputy Prosecutor on 8 July 2010 having identified those members of the Bar as the individuals responsible for the refusal to comply with the Chamber's orders.[141]

The reference to 'members of the Bar' is intriguing, since it identifies the Prosecutor and Deputy Prosecutor as counsel before the Trial Chamber. On 15 July, the Chamber ordered the unconditional release of the accused, finding that the uncertainty over trial resumption and the length of custody made it unfair to continue to hold him.[142]

On 8 October 2010, the Appeals Chamber reversed the Trial Chamber's decisions to stay the proceedings and release the accused. In his appeal against that decision, the Prosecutor argued, inter alia, that 'he did not refuse to comply with the orders of the Court but instead exercised rights available to him as a party'[143] and that the Trial Chamber 'erred by concluding that it has a monopoly of protective functions'.[144] The Appeals Chamber observed:

> The Prosecutor's non-compliance was deliberate. The Appeals Chamber finds that such wilful non-compliance constituted a clear refusal to implement the orders of the Chamber. To characterise such wilful non-compliance as anything other than refusal, as the Prosecutor does in his Document in Support of the Appeal, is, at best, disingenuous. At worst, it is an expression of what the Trial Chamber correctly described as 'a more profound and enduring concern', namely that the Prosecutor may decide whether or not to implement the Trial Chamber's orders depending on his interpretation of his obligations under the Statute.[145]

However, the Appeals Chamber found that the imposition of a stay was an unjustified remedy in that the Trial Chamber should have first used sanctions under Article 71 of the Statute, the purpose of which 'is not merely, as the Prosecutor suggests, to punish the offending party, but also to bring about compliance'.[146]

On the same day, the OTP 'by courtesy' disclosed the identity of intermediary 143 to the Defence.[147] It also, in its view, effected full disclosure compatible with the Trial Chamber's 12 May decision though this was disputed by the Defence.[148] Presiding Judge Fulford invited the parties to resolve the disclosure issues amongst themselves in the first instance and specifically invited the Prosecution to consider meeting the Defence requests on a courtesy basis.[149] He also declared that, following the Appeals Chamber judgment, 'nothing more [would] be said or done about' the Rule 171 warning.[150]

On 7 March 2011, the Trial Chamber rejected a Defence application for a permanent stay of the proceedings and immediate release of the accused due to prosecutorial abuse of process arising from its use of the intermediaries.[151] It found that the

141 *Lubanga*, Verbatim Record (9 July 2010), 22–3.
142 *Lubanga*, Judgment on the appeal of the Prosecutor 2010, paras 12–3.
143 *Lubanga*, Judgment on the appeal of the Prosecutor 2010, para 32.
144 *Lubanga*, Judgment on the appeal of the Prosecutor 2010, para 33.
145 *Lubanga*, Judgment on the appeal of the Prosecutor 2010, paras 46–8, 54.
146 *Lubanga*, Judgment on the appeal of the Prosecutor 2010, para 59.
147 *Lubanga*, Verbatim Record (11 October 2010), 2.
148 *Lubanga*, Verbatim Record (11 October 2010), 7–9.
149 *Lubanga*, Verbatim Record (11 October 2010), 12, 15–6.
150 *Lubanga*, Verbatim Record (11 October 2010), 21.
151 *Lubanga*, Redacted Decision on Defence Application for Permanent Stay.

Defence accusations even 'taken at their highest' were insufficient to meet the legal test that it would be 'repugnant' or 'odious' to continue the trial.[152] However, it specifically reserved its definitive findings concerning the allegations that the Prosecution 'failed in its duty to ensure that it was submitting reliable evidence' for the end of the proceedings.[153]

In its judgment, the Trial Chamber devoted some 167 pages of analysis to the topic: 'The Development of the Prosecution's Investigation.'[154] In assessing the impact of the investigative methods adopted by the Prosecution upon the credibility of the testimonial evidence adduced before the Court, in particular concerning the 'intermediaries' technique, the Chamber concluded:

> The Chamber is of the view that the prosecution should not have delegated its investigative responsibilities to the intermediaries in the way set out above, notwithstanding the extensive security difficulties it faced. A series of witnesses have been called during this trial whose evidence, as a result of the essentially unsupervised actions of three of the principal intermediaries, cannot safely be relied on. The Chamber has spent a considerable period of time investigating the circumstances of a substantial number of individuals whose evidence was, at least in part, inaccurate or dishonest. The prosecution's negligence in failing to verify and scrutinise this material sufficiently before it was introduced led to significant expenditure on the part of the Court. An additional consequence of the lack of proper oversight of the intermediaries is that they were potentially able to take advantage of the witnesses they contacted. Irrespective of the Chamber's conclusions regarding the credibility and reliability of these alleged former child soldiers, given their youth and likely exposure to conflict, they were vulnerable to manipulation.
>
> ...These individuals may have committed crimes under Article 70 of the Statute. Pursuant to Rule 165 of the Rules, the responsibility to initiate and conduct investigations in these circumstances lies with the prosecution. Investigations can be initiated on the basis of information communicated by a Chamber or any reliable source. The Chamber hereby communicates the information set out above to the OTP, and the Prosecutor should ensure that the risk of conflict is avoided for the purposes of any investigation.

In assessing this aspect of the *Lubanga* trial, two distinct ethical issues arise: (1) obeying the orders of the Trial Chamber; and (2) protecting the integrity of evidence. The alleged failures by Prosecutors to protect the integrity of their testimonial evidence through the use of intermediaries are difficult to ethically assess due to the lack of a prescribed standard. The battle of wills between the Trial Chamber and the Prosecutor and the Prosecutor's assertion of an 'autonomous duty' overriding his duty to implement judicial orders is a manifestation of the Prosecutor's ambiguous role. However, the Trial Chamber's appellation of the Prosecutor as counsel is the more convincing because the Prosecutor's approach would endanger the neutrality of the trial process by undermining the authority of the judges.

[152] *Lubanga*, Redacted Decision on Defence Application for Permanent Stay, paras 200–6.

[153] *Lubanga*, Redacted Decision on Defence Application for Permanent Stay, para 204.

[154] *Lubanga*, Judgment (14 March 2012), 63–230.

8.3.1.5 Media Statements

Another issue that has arisen has been the propriety of public statements made by prosecutors to the press concerning pending proceedings. This is a topic that is not specifically addressed in any of the ICC instruments (apart from confidentiality provisions[155]). It is also one upon which national approaches significantly diverge. For example, rule 3.6(a) of the ABA Model Rules provides:

> A lawyer who is participating in or has participated in a criminal or civil matter shall not make an extrajudicial statement that the lawyer knows or reasonably should know will be disseminated by means of public communication and will have a substantial likelihood of materially prejudicing an adjudicative proceeding in the matter.

Additionally, rule 3.8(f) of the ABA Model Rules states:

> [E]xcept for statements that are necessary to inform the public of the nature and extent of the prosecutor's action and that serve a legitimate law enforcement purpose, refrain from making extrajudicial comments that have a substantial likelihood of heightening public condemnation of the accused and exercise reasonable care to prevent investigators, law enforcement personnel, employees or other persons assisting or associated with the prosecutor in a criminal case from making an extrajudicial statement that the prosecutor would be prohibited from making under Rule 3.6 or this Rule.

Thus, the ABA Model Rules clearly provide a stricter standard for prosecutors than for defence counsel. This is likely due to a perceived need to restrain prosecutors from conducting 'media trials'[156] of an accused.

The English Bar Code of Conduct, more broadly, provides: 'A barrister must not in relation to any anticipated or current proceedings or mediation in which he is briefed or expects to appear or has appeared as an advocate express a personal opinion to the press or other media or in any other public statement upon the facts or issues arising in the proceedings.'[157] Neither the CCBE Code nor the French CPP nor the Paris Code addresses the issue. However, the Brussels Order has frowned upon interviews given by *avocats* concerning their cases and, in a specific resolution, prescribed strict circumstances in which *avocats* may communicate with the press on public acts of procedure.[158]

Thus, the position of statements to the media about ongoing proceedings in national ethical codes seemingly ranges from the silent (in France) to the very detailed (in the USA). There is consequently a lack of uniformity amongst national jurisdictions about the permissibility of media statements so that an international judicial standard needs to be found. In the criminal context, this is particularly relevant because of the gravity of the alleged crimes and the potential consequences

[155] Eg Rome Statute, Arts 64(6)(c), 64(7); ICC Rules, Rule 6; ICC Code, Art 8(2).

[156] ABA Annotated Rules, 352. See also Phillips and McCoy, *Conduct of Judges and Lawyers* (1952), 213–14.

[157] English Code, para 709.1.

[158] Brussels Code, 274.

to human rights. In the *Lubanga* trial, the Trial Chamber has disapproved of media statements made by prosecutors. Early in the trial, Presiding Judge Fulford 'gave a very firm indication that the Judges did not expect to see satellite litigation in the press with the issues which we are considering being the subject of some kind of debate, with commentators on one or both sides seeking to litigate the issues in this trial in a different forum' and indicated 'that this is an inappropriate activity, particularly for the Prosecutor to undertake'.[159]

However, on 17 March 2010 the Trial Chamber had occasion to address an interview given by Ms Béatrice Le Fraper Du Hellen (then head of the Jurisdiction, Complementarity and Cooperation Division of the OTP).[160] A central theme of that interview, with reference to the emerging issue of the intermediaries, was 'that the intermediaries are very committed persons who are very supportive of international justice'.[161] The Trial Chamber took issue with several specific comments.[162] For example, concerning the intermediaries, she remarked that 'they are fantastic and committed people...I do not think that we should try to affect the reputation of those intermediaries'.[163] Addressing the possibility (later eventuated) of a defence abuse-of-process application, she said:

> There was absolutely no abuse of process. Prosecutor Moreno-Ocampo is a very accurate and fair prosecutor...So this is just talk...I understand the defence entirely...it's their last chance but nothing is going to happen. Mr Lubanga is going away for a long time.[164]

Concerning the child witnesses heard in closed session, she commented:

> But Lubanga knows who they are, and frankly I am amazed at the courage of the children. They actually were in the courtroom with Lubanga and you know, Mr Lubanga, he is making signs to the audience, he is smiling, he is doing a lot of body language—it is very terrifying for the children to testify in front of him. So they have been very courageous but we definitely cannot show their identities to the public.

The Trial Chamber, declaring itself to be 'extremely disturbed' by the interview, directed the Prosecution to serve all evidence upon which 'those very clear and unequivocal indications' of the intermediaries' characters were based, comment upon the propriety of her comment that 'Mr Lubanga is going away for a long time' in light of the Trial Chamber's role in determining the guilt or innocence of the accused, and the sentence (if any) that he should receive and adduce evidence to sustain her extrajudicial allegation that the accused had been behaving in a way 'terrifying for children' in the courtroom—reflecting, in the Trial Chamber's view, upon its own handling of the trial.[165]

The Prosecution denied that it had a fresh disclosure obligation arising out of the interview remarks on the intermediaries and that 'the Rome Statute does not

[159] *Lubanga*, Verbatim Record (17 March 2010), ICC-01/04-01/06, 5.
[160] *Lubanga*, Verbatim Record (17 March 2010), 1.
[161] *Lubanga*, Verbatim Record (17 March 2010), 2.
[162] *Lubanga*, Decision on the press interview, paras 3–9.
[163] *Lubanga*, Decision on the press interview, para 4.
[164] *Lubanga*, Decision on the press interview, para 8.
[165] *Lubanga*, Verbatim Record (17 March 2010), 2–5.

prevent either party from making the kind of comments in issue'.[166] In particular, it 'argued that the Bench, unlike a jury, is unlikely to be influenced by remarks of the kind that were made'.[167] On the matter of the accused's courtroom conduct, the Prosecution averred that 'Ms Le Fraper du Hellen did not suggest that the accused had deliberately taken steps to terrify the witnesses, but instead she merely observed that they had been courageous notwithstanding having to testify in his presence' and accepted that the accused had not behaved in a way that called for judicial censure.[168] It asserted that it would be unacceptable to 'hamper the Office of the Prosecutor's ability to affirm publicly its moral authority to perform its role', 'there are no legal reasons to require silence by the Prosecution in the face of public attacks against its repute' and that 'when [its] integrity is publicly attacked' by an abuse of process application it is entitled to publicly respond.[169]

On 12 May 2010, the Trial Chamber issued a written decision on the interview. It observed that 'none of the provisions of the Rome Statue framework address the relationship between the parties and the press, and public statements outside the courtroom are in this sense unregulated'.[170] After describing the general principle of public trials, which for security reasons had been displaced to a 'very considerable' extent in the *Lubanga* trial, the Trial Chamber observed:

> Most particularly in these circumstances, the public needs to be able to trust the published statements of those involved in the case, as reflecting, in a suitably balanced way, the evidence that has been heard and the decisions that have been made. It is important that in media statements there is a clear and accurate description as to whether issues that are reported have been decided or are still unresolved. Most importantly, and as a matter of professional ethics, a party to proceedings is expected not to misrepresent the evidence, to misdescribe the functions of the parties or the Chamber, or to suggest or imply without proper foundation that anyone in the case, including the accused, has misbehaved.[171]

After finding that 'in essence, the prosecution has accepted that it should abide by these principles', the Chamber declared that 'respecting the Chamber, the judicial process and the other participants involves speaking publicly about the proceedings in a fair and accurate way, and avoiding any comment about issues that are for the Chamber to determine'.[172] The Chamber found that Ms Le Fraper du Hellen's remarks during the press interview 'breached these restrictions in a manner that is prejudicial to the ongoing proceedings (in the sense that they tend to prejudice the public's understanding of the trial), which tends to bring the Court into disrepute'.[173] Finally, the Chamber declared:

> The Chamber is wholly uninfluenced by these misleading and inaccurate remarks, but it deprecates the prosecution's use of a public interview, first, to misrepresent the evidence and

[166] *Lubanga*, Decision on the press interview, paras 17–21.
[167] *Lubanga*, Decision on the press interview, para 21.
[168] *Lubanga*, Decision on the press interview, para 22.
[169] *Lubanga*, Decision on the press interview, para 28.
[170] *Lubanga*, Decision on the press interview, para 34.
[171] *Lubanga*, Decision on the press interview, para 39.
[172] *Lubanga*, Decision on the press interview, para 40.
[173] *Lubanga*, Decision on the press interview, para 41.

to comment on its merits and weight, and including by way of remarks on the credibility of its own witnesses in the context of a trial where much of the evidence has been heard in closed session with the public excluded; second, to express views on matters that are awaiting resolution by the Chamber, thereby intruding into the latter's role; third, to criticise the accused without foundation; and, finally, to purport to announce how the Chamber will resolve the submissions on the abuse of process application, and, moreover, that the accused will be convicted in due course and sentenced to lengthy imprisonment at the end of the case.

Although on this occasion the Chamber does not intend to take any action beyond expressing its strongest disapproval of the content of this interview, if objectionable public statements of this kind are repeated the Chamber will not hesitate to take appropriate action against the party responsible.

Ms Le Fraper du Hellen left her position within three weeks of these comments.[174]

However, the matter of public statements arose again in the *Lubanga* trial. The Defence complained that a novel published by Mr Gil Courtemanche (a consultant for the OTP from April 2008 to November 2009) called *Un lizard au Congo* allegedly 'call[ed] into question the rights of the accused and the entire judicial process, including the Judges of the Chamber'.[175] The Defence asserted that the fact that the author was an OTP consultant and 'worked very closely with Mr Ocampo, for whom he drafted numerous speeches, and that in addition this book talks not about Mr Lubanga but about Mr Kabanga and that this individual is the first accused before the ICC and that the charges levelled against him are exactly the same as those levelled against the Accused' breached the Prosecution's duty of impartiality.[176] In response, the Prosecution contended that the complaint, against 'a work of fiction' written in a private capacity, was 'frivolous' and 'a catastrophic waste of Court time'.[177] Whilst the Trial Chamber found that the publication of the novel did not meet the test of 'odious' or 'repugnant' to justice for a permanent stay of proceedings, it did not at that time make any merits findings.[178]

Other media statements by OTP members have been criticized for breaching the Prosecutor's duty of impartiality by prejudging facts or guilt in pending investigations or encroaching upon Trial Chambers' function to determine the guilt or innocence of an accused. For example, comments at the outset of investigations have definitively referred to 'the crimes committed' rather than 'alleged crimes'.[179] The Prosecutor has also been criticized for media statements concerning the Kenya situation, such as his remark that 'in the next year and a half, there are 15 elections

[174] Rozenberg, 'ICC prosecutors should not be grandstanding on their own cases' *The Guardian* (18 August 2010).

[175] *Lubanga*, Verbatim Record (11 October 2010), 17.

[176] *Lubanga*, Verbatim Record, 18.

[177] *Lubanga*, Verbatim Record, 19.

[178] *Lubanga*, Redacted Decision on Defence Application for Permanent Stay, para 222.

[179] Eg 'Statement by the Prosecutor Related to Crimes Committed in Barlonya Camp in Uganda' (23 February 2004), online: <http://www.icc-cpi.int/NR/rdonlyres/47964D88-93C8-4E71-9119-4DA540EF5EE2/143705/PIDSOTP0022004EN2.pdf> (Accessed: 3 April 2011); 'Statement of the Prosecutor...to the Security Council on 29 June 2005 Pursuant to UNSCR 1593 (2005)', online: <http://www.icc-cpi.int/NR/rdonlyres/47964D88-93C8-4E71-9119-4DA540EF5EE2/143705/PIDSOTP0022004EN2.pdf> (Accessed: 3 April 2011).

in Africa…Kenya will send a signal to all these elections: if you commit crimes, you go to The Hague'.[180] The Kenyan government reportedly wrote to the UNSC to request a deferral to the trials on the ground that the Prosecutor had stigmatized the so-called 'Ocampo Six' by naming them publicly before the pre-trial confirmation hearing.[181] As the Pre-Trial Chamber observed:

> The Chamber is cognizant of the concerns of the Applicant with respect to the prejudice suffered due to the public disclosure of his name made by the Prosecutor. However, the Chamber is not of the view that such publicity caused could ground a construction of the proceedings of article 58 of the Statute in adversarial terms, contrary to the legal instruments of the Court. While it is not the Chamber's role to comment and advise the Prosecutor on his interaction with the press and media, the Chamber nevertheless is concerned if his actions have the potential to affect the administration of justice and the integrity of the present proceedings before the Chamber. In this respect, the Chamber expresses its deprecation regarding the Prosecutor's course of action in the present case, as it has unduly exposed the Applicant to prejudicial publicity before a determination of the Chamber pursuant to article 58 of the Statute has even been made.[182]

An article[183] published in the British newspaper *The Guardian* on 15 July 2010 (three days after the Pre-Trial Chamber's 'Second Decision on the Prosecution's Application for a Warrant of Arrest') about the Darfur situation has formed the basis for legal challenges to the indictments against Sudanese President Omar al-Bashir. In that article, the Prosecutor wrote:

> The genocide is not over. Bashir's forces continue to use different weapons to commit genocide…the court found that Bashir's forces have raped on a mass scale in Darfur. They raped thousands of women and used these rapes to degrade family and community members. Parents were forced to watch as their daughters were raped.
>
> The court also found that Bashir is deliberately inflicting on the Fur, Masalit and Zaghawa ethnic groups living conditions calculated to bring about their physical destruction…He has officially denied the genocide, the rapes, the camp conditions and his responsibility for them…He is also laying the groundwork for new crimes against Darfuris and against the south of Sudan. Bashir used Ahmad Harun, as minister of state for the interior, to co-ordinate genocidal attacks on villages; he later used Harun, as minister of state for humanitarian affairs, to control genocidal conditions in the camps. Harun's current role as governor of South Kordofan could indicate an intention to continue using him as a future crimes co-ordinator.

The ad hoc defence counsel assigned by the Court for the accused applied to the Pre-Trial Chamber for an order condemning the Prosecutor's statements and 'taking appropriate measures concerning the Prosecutor' on the ground that the Prosecutor

[180] 'ICC Prosecutor in Nairobi to probe post-election violence' (8 May 2010), online: <http://www.france24.com/en/20100508-kenya-icc-prosecutor-nairobi-probe-post-election-violence-hague> (Accessed: 3 April 2011).

[181] Leftie, 'Kenya: ICC Censures Ocampo, Rejects Ali's Plea' (12 February 2011), online: <http://allafrica.com/stories/201102140018.html> (Accessed: 3 April 2011).

[182] *Kenya Situation*, Decision on Application for Leave to Participate (11 February 2011), paras 21–2.

[183] Moreno-Ocampo, 'Now end this Darfur denial' (15 July 2010), online: <http://www.guardian.co.uk/commentisfree/libertycentral/2010/jul/15/world-cannot-ignore-darfur> (Accessed: 3 April 2011).

had irreparably prejudiced a fair trial of the accused by declaring that the accused was already guilty of the alleged crimes before he had been tried for them, thus, inter alia, violating his duty of impartiality towards the accused and undermining the legitimacy and credibility of the Court.[184] This application was declared inadmissible by a single judge for falling outside the scope of the functions of the ad hoc defence counsel.[185] Another application by the 'Office of Public Counsel for the Defence' also failed.[186]

These criticisms demonstrate the potential for unregulated matters of professional ethics to seriously affect the integrity of judicial proceedings. The propriety of extra-judicial public statements by counsel is an issue upon which the ICC instruments are silent and yet have arisen repeatedly and in a serious way. The challenges raised by defence counsel and the criticisms made by judges and commentators of the Prosecutor's recourse to media statements illustrates the dangers of such comments—particularly for the Prosecutor because of his judicial duty of impartiality during the investigative phase. It may be argued that there is a need for clear ethical rules and a strict standard concerning media comments (particularly in light of national differences).

8.3.2 Defence Counsel

The defence Code of Conduct was drafted by the Registry in consultation with national bars.[187] An interesting anomaly in the drafting and amendment process is that the Prosecutor is consulted.[188] This is ironical in that the Prosecutor is himself not bound by a similar code of conduct and that during the trial process he is the 'opponent' of defence counsel. Unlike the ICTY Association of Defence Counsel, there is no equivalent ICC body through which defence counsel may contribute their views concerning the Code.[189]

For defence counsel, unlike Article 3(iv) of the ICTY Code of Conduct, which prescribes anarchical duties to Tribunal and to client, and Article 8(A) of the SCSL Code of Conduct, which mandates an overriding duty to the Court over the client, the ICC Code is silent on the matter of their fundamental duties.[190] This lack of a clear statement of first principles may be seen in the tendency within several provisions to require counsel to act 'in conformity with the Statute, the Rules of Procedure and Evidence and the Regulations of the Court'.[191] This necessarily assumes clarity and certainty within those instruments, which may be absent

[184] *Al Bashir*, Application for an Order.
[185] *Al Bashir*, Decision on the Application for an Order.
[186] *Al Bashir*, Decision on the 'OPCD Request for authorization'.
[187] 'Proposal for a draft Code of Professional Conduct for counsel', ICC Doc No ICC-ASP/3/11/Rev.1 (27 August 2004); 'Report of the Bureau on the draft Code of Professional Conduct for counsel', ICC Doc No ICC-ASP/4/21 (10 October 2005); *Official Records of the Assembly of States Parties*, Report on Fourth Session, ICC Doc No ICC-ASP/4/L.32 (28 November–3 December 2005), para 32.
[188] Code of Conduct, Art 3(2).
[189] Kay and Swart, 1430, 1432.
[190] Kay and Swart, 1429–30.
[191] Code of Conduct, Arts 7(3), 8(1), 9(3), 14(2)(a), 16(1), 18(2), 31(a).

(eg media statements, witness contacts, or witness proofing). Thus, in omitting a clear foundation of principle underpinning the professional role of defence counsel the Code necessarily leaves ambiguity both on issues where it expressly prescribes and on those where it is silent. This vagueness pervades much of the Code, diluting its authoritativeness concerning such difficult ethical problems as confessions of guilt or assignment to an unwilling accused.

The IBA has proposed a revision of the Code of Conduct to clarify terminology and update it to bring it into conformity with judicial developments in the first decade of ICC practice.[192] This would be a useful exercise, as the Code does not currently address the variety of problems that have arisen in practice. It would also be valuable even beyond the need to keep the Code fresh, in that a periodic time of reflection and consultation would reveal potential issues that can be redressed in advance at reduced expense rather than on an ad hoc basis during the course of litigation.

8.3.2.1 Confessions of Guilt

The ethical problem of confessions of guilt by an accused is one of the most intricate in the criminal field and vividly illustrates the potential conflict between the interests of justice, court, and client. It is also the subject of the famous dinner-table question: 'How can you represent a client whom you know to be guilty?' The ethical consequences of an express confession of guilt may be divided into two questions, namely, whether counsel should continue to represent the client in the event of the client's insistence upon a 'not guilty' plea; and whether confessions of guilt should be protected by counsel's ethical duty of confidentiality.

Although there has been no precedent in which a confession of guilt to counsel has been famously controversial,[193] national practice is illustrative of the potential for reputational damage to the judicial system and to the legal profession amongst the wider public. In England, the *Courvoisier* trial of 1840[194] witnessed a confession of guilt in mid-trial by the accused who refused to change his plea. Faced with an ethical dilemma, the barrister (Charles Phillips) informed Baron Parke (assisting the presiding judge) *in camera* of his situation but was instructed to continue his representation of the accused by 'us[ing] all fair arguments arising on the evidence.'[195] Following robust cross-examinations of prosecution witnesses, in his closing speech Phillips was reported in the press as claiming that 'no one but God knows who committed this crime'. The defendant was acquitted, but publicly confessed to his crime just days after his conviction whereupon Phillips' actions were made public. Phillips was widely condemned in the lay press as an example of a counsel lying for a fee. His summing-up statement, which he denied having made, was particularly criticized. An even more controversial confession occurred

[192] See IBA, Counsel Matters, 16–17,

[193] Eg Combs, *Guilty Pleas in International Criminal Law: Constructing a Restorative Justice Approach* (2007).

[194] Mellinkoff, *The Conscience of a Lawyer* (1973), 41–7, Asimow and Weisberg, 'When the Lawyer Knows the Client is Guilty: Client Confessions in Legal Ethics, Popular Culture, and Literature', 18 *Southern California Interdisciplinary Law Journal* (2009), 229–58;

[195] Mellinkoff, *The Conscience of a Lawyer*, 140.

in the *Reid* trial of 1847, in which a co-accused was unjustly convicted when it emerged that the acquitted defendant had confessed to his counsel before the trial. The lay press and some barristers attacked these defence counsel as deceitful men saving the guilty, whereas the professional press defended their conduct by arguing that the right of an accused to counsel must be absolute.

In the United States, the *Westerfield* case is a modern example of the problem in which, during plea bargaining, the defendant apparently suggested to the prosecutor that he knew where the murder victim's body was located.[196] Following the collapse of the plea bargain when the police independently found the body, the defence counsel (Steven Feldman) defended his client at trial by suggesting that another person might have killed the victim, introducing expert evidence to support an alibi defence and declaring in his opening statement that 'we have doubts as to who left [the victim] where...she remained. And we have doubts as to who took her'. When Feldman's role leaked to the press, there was public outrage and widespread condemnation of his actions but was defended by some colleagues and ethics experts.[197] In an interview, he defended his professionalism:

> 'Whether or not an individual is guilty or not guilty is not my issue,' he said. 'I don't care. My job is to evaluate the case and assist the person as best as I possibly can. That is the ethical requirement of the criminal defense lawyer.'
>
> Feldman said he views his job as keeping the prosecution honest. He said he never assumes his client is guilty regardless of what the client says, adding that clients often lie to their lawyers or accidentally misstate the facts.'

Whilst there was apparently no express confession of guilt subsequently made public, the condemnation of the defence counsel rested upon his awareness of highly incriminating evidence suggesting that he knew the case that he was putting to be false.

The second limb of the guilty confessions dilemma is the counsel's duty of confidentiality to his client. In Canada, a defence counsel's refusal to disclose the existence of incriminating video evidence with which he had been entrusted by his client resulted in his being charged with obstruction of justice.[198] He was ultimately acquitted on the ground that he had an honest belief that his suppression of the evidence was lawful.[199] Subsequently, disciplinary proceedings that had been suspended pending the termination of the criminal trial were dropped in deference to the judge's verdict and the Law Society of Upper Canada announced: 'the public interest would be better served by the clarification of lawyers' professional responsibilities when confronted with such a dilemma than by the continuation of disciplinary proceedings against Mr. Murray.'[200] The Society formed a committee

[196] Asimow and Weisberg, 'When the Lawyer Knows the Client is Guilty', 233.

[197] Roth, 'Attorney breaks his silence on defending Westerfield', *San Diego Union-Tribune* (1 December 2002), online: <http://legacy.utsandiego.com/news/metro/danielle/20021201-9999_1m1feldman.html> (Accessed: 10 April 2011).

[198] Clemmer, 'Obstructing the Bernardo Investigation: Kenneth Murray and the Defence Counsel's Conflicting Obligations to Clients and the Court', 1 *Osgoode Hall Review of Law and Policy* (2008), 137–97.

[199] Clemmer, 'Obstructing the Bernardo Investigation', 154.

[200] Clemmer, 'Obstructing the Bernardo Investigation', 155.

to consider the issues from the case and consider new ethical rules. Its proposal, a compromise between duties to justice and to client, met with opposition as a continued mandate for suppression of evidence and was dropped.[201]

National standards significantly diverge on the guilty confessions problem, upon which international tribunals' codes of conduct are silent:

> [In] considering matters such as confessions of guilt, the [SCSL] Code of Conduct is brief when compared with national provisions. In Germany, for example, counsel is bound likewise to put a negative defence but no more than that. Counsel must not present positive evidence. In some jurisdictions, however, counsel would be bound to withdraw from the case. Thus, there are lacunas in the Code which national codes and understandings must fill. This creates the problem of conflicting national ethics.[202]

The modern ethical rule in England and Wales[203] and, apparently also in Germany,[204] is that counsel, in a case of a confession of guilt, counsel are to continue representation whilst putting only a 'negative defence'. Counsel may scrutinise the prosecution's case and compel it to discharge its burden of proof but may not put a positive case, such as an alibi defence or an alternate theory of the crime. However, in the United States the rule appears to be a looser one by which counsel are allowed individual discretion 'to choose…depending on the dictates of the lawyer's conscience, the lawyer's perception as to what would be a just result, the interests of third parties, and the specific facts with which only the lawyer is conversant.'[205] A lawyer seemingly 'cannot be subjected to professional discipline for the difficult decision (which sometimes arises unexpectedly during trial) of whether to take a strong or a weak approach'.[206]

At first sight, the ICC Code adopts the American relativistic approach in its rule on withdrawal from representation: 'With the prior consent of the Chamber, counsel may withdraw from the agreement in accordance with the Regulations of the Court if…the client insists on pursuing an objective that counsel considers repugnant.'[207] The reference to 'pursuing an objective *that counsel considers* repugnant' clearly vests counsel with discretion to determine 'repugnance'. However, this is tempered by the requirement of the Trial Chamber's prior consent. Since the Trial Chamber is both the tribunal of law and the tribunal of fact, it is impossible for counsel to disclose the reason for his withdrawal without condemning his client and violating confidentiality. According to one ICTY judge on the guilty confessions problem:

> I would understand if counsel were to invent another reason for their withdrawal. On the question of negative defences, by challenging the prosecution's case, this may also be done.[208]

[201] Clemmer, 'Obstructing the Bernardo Investigation', 185–9.
[202] 'Interview with Justice Teresa Doherty and Mr Simon Meisenberg (Senior Legal Officer)', Special Court for Sierra Leone (20 August 2010), cited with permission.
[203] English Code, Written Standards for the Conduct of Professional Work, para 12.
[204] The rule does not appear in the terse German Code.
[205] Asimow and Weisberg, 'When the Lawyer Knows the Client is Guilty', 237.
[206] Asimow and Weisberg, 'When the Lawyer Knows the Client is Guilty', 238.
[207] ICC Code, Art 18(1)(a).
[208] Interview with Judge Fausto Pocar, ICTY (17 August 2010), cited with permission.

For counsel to lie to the Court in order to withdraw from an uncomfortable position cannot be a satisfactory solution. Moreover, the relativistic approach may be criticized as a failure to set clear parameters on a difficult issue. For example, a straightforward confession as in *Courvisier* may be considered to substantially differ from a situation in which counsel strongly suspects his client's guilt owing to discovery of incriminating evidence (of whatever weight), as in *Westerfield.* It is significant, in this respect, that the withdrawal of the counsel in the *Bernardo* case was directly prompted by his suppression of the incriminatory video evidence.[209]

The implied position under the international codes of conduct seemingly allows counsel to withdraw according to their individual conscience, subject to the permission of the Trial Chamber, whilst obliging them to preserve strict confidentiality.[210] The lack of an express provision or prioritization of basic duties under the ICC Code, coupled with diverging national standards, creates the risk that the legitimacy of the ICC could be seriously threatened by the handling of a counsel following his individual conscience in what would (given the ICC's jurisdiction) inevitably be a sensitive trial. In a difficult case, counsel would be likely be exposed to serious reputational and disciplinary consequences regardless of his course of action. Without a textual rule to invoke in his defence, he would be damned whatever he does. In addition to these potential consequences to the Court and the individual counsel (to say nothing of the defendant and the victims), a clear ethical rule is necessary to sharpen the philosophy of the Court.

The guilty confessions dilemma is illustrative of conflicts between duties to justice, court and client and engages fundamental and ancient problems of the criminal justice process. A puritanical prioritization of substantive justice, or objective truth, would require counsel to ultimately withdraw from representation and to disclose incriminating evidence (including confessions) as a witness of fact. This approach entails an exception to the confidentiality principle and would necessarily incentivize the concealment by clients of incriminatory evidence from their counsel. Additionally, it rests upon counsel's duty to refrain from misleading the Court by positing a defence which he knows to be false or, more broadly, concealing material evidence.

The prioritization of a duty to the court would entail an obligation to solicit and follow the court's direction: this could be an order to continue, as in *Courvoisier*, or an order to withdraw. This course (particularly in a judge-only system, as at the ICC) would require a mechanism whereby counsel could solicit that direction without fear of prejudicing his client's interests before the tribunal of fact. No such interlocutory mechanism currently exists at the ICC outside of the Trial Chamber, which is clearly ineligible as the tribunal of fact. This solution is unsatisfactory because, instead of providing a principled rule, it merely passes the decision to the judiciary which, without a textual basis, would be in no better position than counsel to provide a legitimate solution. Also, the necessity for secrecy would likely worsen the legitimacy of the decision.

[209] Clemmer, 'Obstructing the Bernardo Investigation', 155.

[210] ICTY Code, Arts 9(B)(2), 13(A), 25; ICTR Code of Conduct for Defence Counsel, Arts 4(2)(a), 8(1); SCSL Code of Conduct, Arts 12(A)(3), 17(A), 18(C)(ii).

The duty to the client, if prioritized, would require counsel to use 'all expedient means'[211] to zealously defend his client's interests even if that entailed putting a false case. The rationale for this approach is that all defendants, even guilty ones, should have the right to counsel. This stems from an overriding conception of procedural justice over substantive truth, with the presumption of innocence, the prosecution's burden of proof and the right to avoid self-incrimination taking precedence. It also rests upon the argument that it is the duty of defence counsel to defend and the duty of the Trial Chamber to determine his guilt. Whilst these principles are enshrined in the Rome Statute,[212] the argument that procedural justice should take precedence over the substantive truth of the case is contestable on the ground that the judicial process is, first and foremost, a forensic and normative search for the truth.

Thus, it may be that a new exception to the confidentiality principle for incriminatory evidence should be considered. One risk inherent in any weakening of the strict confidentiality principle is that a corrupt counsel may try to blackmail his client by threatening to falsely testify to a confession or otherwise disclosing incriminatory evidence. However, this danger is mitigated by the Court's inquisitorial role in ensuring that guilty confessions are voluntarily made and supported by the facts.[213]

8.3.2.2 Withdrawal of Assigned Counsel

As indicated above, a sensitive ethical area for defence counsel before the ad hoc tribunals has been their assignment by the Tribunal to unwilling accused. One reason why this has yet to become a live issue is that the ICC jurisdiction is based upon a multilateral treaty rather than (for the ICTY and ICTR) a UNSC resolution or (for the SCSL) a bilateral UN-Sierra Leone treaty. However, though no accused has yet sought to boycott their trial or self-represent before the ICC, there is no structural reason precluding it from occurring in a particularly sensitive case in future (eg in the unlikely event of the apprehension of Omar al-Bashir).

Counsel may be either retained by the client or, as for legal aid, assigned by the Court to a client.[214] Where counsel is assigned, he may only be discharged not by the client but by the Court.[215] Article 9 of the ICC Code prescribes for withdrawal in the following circumstances:

(B) Counsel may terminate or request, if applicable subject to the provisions of the Directive, withdrawal of his representation of a client if such termination or withdrawal can be accomplished without material adverse effect on the interests of the client, or if:

(i) the client has used counsel's services to perpetrate a crime or fraud, or persists in a course of action involving counsel's services that counsel reasonably believes is criminal or fraudulent;

[211] In 1820, Henry Brougham articulated the so-called 'doctrine of all expedient means' in the *Queen Caroline Trial* as a political threat which has been subsequently misinterpreted as a professional duty of absolute loyalty that counsel owe to their clients—Patterson, 'Legal Ethics and the Lawyer's Duty of Loyalty', 29 *Emory Law Journal* (1980), 909–70, 909.

[212] Rome Statute, Arts 66–7, 74.

[213] ICC Code, Art 65(1).

[214] ICC Code, Art 11.

[215] ICC Code, Art 11.

(ii) the client insists upon pursuing an objective that counsel considers repugnant or imprudent;
(iii) the client fails to substantially fulfil an obligation to counsel regarding counsel's services and has been given reasonable warning that counsel will terminate or request withdrawal of his representation unless the obligation is fulfilled; or
(iv) other good cause for termination or withdrawal exists.

A general point to be made concerning this provision is its lack of precision concerning, in particular, sub-paragraphs (ii) and (iv) of 'repugnance', 'imprudence' and 'good cause'. Specifically, the language of sub-paragraph (ii) ('that *counsel considers*') suggests that the rule is subjective to the professional judgement of counsel whereas that of sub-paragraph (iv) ('other good cause...*exists*') indicates an objective test. This tension is borne out in practice, in that:

There is a tension between the Bench and counsel. Defence counsel may say 'I've done all that I can, I must withdraw' but the Tribunal may think otherwise. Counsel may be supported by the client and replacement counsel but the Tribunal refuses. Thus, counsel needs to understand that they are 'not in complete control' but subject to the Tribunal.[216]

Thus, there appears to be a tension between the personal judgement of counsel and that of the Registrar or Trial Chamber who decide upon applications for withdrawal.[217]

Before the ICTY, counsel from the English criminal defence bar have resisted assignments to unwilling defendants on the ground that their first loyalty is to their client. In so doing, they have (despite the supremacy of the ICTY Code,[218] which they accepted upon becoming counsel) sought to rely upon their interpretations of domestic bar rules in order to support applications for permission to withdraw from assigned representation of unwilling defendants. In doing so, certain counsel have even resorted to unilateral withdrawal.

The most well-known example of this occurred during the *Milošević* trial, in which the accused at his arraignment chose to self-represent and, when cautioned by the presiding judge (Judge May) to 'consider carefully whether it's in [his] own best interests not to be represented [by counsel]', declared:

I consider this Tribunal [to be] a false tribunal and the indictment a false indictment. It is illegal being not appointed by the UN General Assembly, so I have no need to appoint counsel to [an] illegal organ.[219]

Thus, from the beginning the accused adopted a strategy of challenging the lawfulness of the Tribunal and his decision not to appoint counsel was made expressly for that purpose. The ICTY Appeals Chamber rejected the challenge to the lawfulness of the ICTY's creation in the *Tadić* case.[220] Although that judgment is not binding upon future cases,[221] the extreme unlikelihood of a different outcome in an interlocutory

[216] Interview with confidential source (on file with author).
[217] ICTY Rules, Rule 46(A)(ii); ICTY Directive on the Assignment of Counsel, Art 20.
[218] ICTY Code, Art 4; ICTR Code, Art 19; SCSL Code, Art 3(B); ICC Code, Art 4.
[219] *Prosecutor v Milošević* (IT-02-54), Trial Transcripts (3 July 2001), 1–2.
[220] *Prosecutor v Dusko Tadić* (IT-94-1), Decision on the Defence Motion for Interlocutory Appeal on Jurisdiction (2 October 1995), paras 9–40. *Confer* the Separate Opinion of Judge Sidhwa, paras 32–6 especially para 34.
[221] ICTY Statute, Art 25.

appeal on jurisdiction negated Milošević's aim as a legal, as opposed to political, strategy. This is important because, in considering the ethical position of assigned counsel, the issue is whether counsel should be required to represent an unwilling accused in the latter's best *legal* interests or whether the client's (however legally ill-advised) wishes must be paramount.

The procedural history of Milošević's representation must be set out in some detail in order to contextualize the ethical problem. On 30 August 2001, the Trial Chamber rejected a Prosecution application that counsel be assigned to the accused—declaring that 'the accused has a right to counsel, but he also has a right not to have counsel'.[222] On 6 September 2001, the Registrar appointed three counsel as amici curiae. The trial commenced on 12 February 2002. On 10 April 2002, the Trial Chamber granted the defence application for privileged communications with Mr Zenko Tomanovic and Mr Dragoslav Ognjanovic (both Serbian lawyers) as his 'legal associates'.[223] On 8 November 2002 the Prosecution again applied for the assignment of defence counsel, citing the ill-health of the accused and the trial delays.[224] On 18 December 2002, the Trial Chamber rejected the motion but reasoned differently from its previous ruling, declaring:

> Defence counsel will not be imposed upon the accused against his wishes in the present circumstances. It is not normally appropriate in adversarial proceedings such as these. The Trial Chamber will keep the position under review.[225]

On 25 March 2003, the Tribunal adjourned the trial due to the defendant's ill-health.[226]

On 4 April 2003, the Trial Chamber denied another prosecution motion for the assignment of defence counsel. The Prosecution argued: 'the public interest demands a comprehensive prosecution of the indictment and that neither the international community nor the Prosecution could accept the curtailment of the case in a situation where the Accused, by declining to avail himself of the benefit of counsel, has exacerbated his health problems.'[227] By contrast, the amici curiae submitted that the right of self-representation is absolute: '*any* imposition of counsel upon the Accused against his wishes would constitute a breach of his guaranteed rights.'[228] Crucially, they argued:

> ... the Prosecution's examples of mandatory provision of defence counsel are drawn from inquisitorial systems where the functions of defence counsel in a trial are very different from those in the adversarial form of trial adopted at the International Tribunal. For instance, the obligation of 'putting a case', which is required of the defence in the adversarial system, is impossible for an advocate to achieve without instructions from the Accused as to the

[222] *Milošević*, Reasons for Decision on the Prosecution Motion Concerning Assignment of Counsel (4 April 2003), para 3.

[223] *Prosecutor v Milošević* (IT-02-54), para 5.

[224] *Prosecutor v Milošević* (IT-02-54), para 7.

[225] *Prosecutor v Milošević* (IT-02-54), para 8.

[226] Noting the reported refusal of the accused to take prescribed medication—*Milošević* (IT-02-54), Order on Adjournment of Proceedings (25 March 2003).

[227] *Prosecutor v Milošević* (IT-02-54), para 10.

[228] *Prosecutor v Milošević* (IT-02-54), para 14 (emphasis added).

nature of the defence. Therefore, the *Amici Curiae* submit, 'no meaningful trial would be possible if the advocate was not instructed by the Accused.' The *Amici Curiae* note that in England and Wales, where an accused expresses a desire to conduct his own defence, he should be allowed to do so and counsel should not be assigned to him against his will.[229]

The Trial Chamber, citing the Faretta case and its recounting of the history of the common law right of self-representation,[230] accepted the amici curiae submissions.[231] The Chamber laid particular emphasis upon the distinction between the adversarial and inquisitorial functions of the judiciary and the impossibility of defence counsel putting the defendant's case to witnesses without instructions in 'reject[ing] the suggestion that defence counsel should be imposed on an accused against his will in proceedings that are essentially adversarial'.[232]

Whilst leaving the door slightly ajar for exceptions,[233] the Trial Chamber interpreted the right to self-representation as virtually absolute. However, delays caused by Milošević's ill-health continued.[234] Following the commencement of his case on 31 August 2004, the Trial Chamber invited the parties and amici curiae to make oral submissions on medical reports and the assignment of counsel.[235] Building upon their previous arguments, the Prosecution cited the ill-health of the Accused and further alleged 'obstructionist behaviour'[236] whilst the amici curiae made the self-contradictory submission that the right to self-representation is absolute because '...the interests of justice do not require the assignment of counsel, which would deprive the Accused of his right to conduct his own defence'.[237] They proposed that the accused, if not fit to represent himself fully, should receive 'assistance' rather than 'have his decision-making powers completely removed'.[238]

In a departure from its previous ruling, the Chamber held that the right to self-representation could be removed by a Tribunal where there would be a 'material risk' of the defendant not receiving a fair trial on the grounds of illness or where there exists a 'real prospect that [the trial] will be disrupted and the integrity of the trial undermined that it will not be conducted fairly'.[239] The Chamber held that '[f]airness is...the overarching requirement of criminal proceedings' and that '[t]he right to represent oneself must therefore yield when it is necessary to ensure that the trial is fair'.[240] Re-examining the precedents, the Tribunal also cited an exception of 'serious and obstructionist misconduct' in *Faretta*.[241] However, the

[229] *Prosecutor v Milošević* (IT-02-54), para 16. The amici curiae cited case-law from the English Court of Appeal (*R v Woodward* [1944] KB 118) and the US Supreme Court (*Faretta v California* 422 US 806 (1975)

[230] *Prosecutor v Milošević* (IT-02-54), para 22.

[231] *Prosecutor v Milošević* (IT-02-54), paras 18–41.

[232] *Prosecutor v Milošević* (IT-02-54), paras 24–5 (emphasis in original).

[233] *Prosecutor v Milošević* (IT-02-54), paras 36, 37.

[234] *Milošević*, Reasons for Decision on Assignment of Defence Counsel (22 September 2004), paras 9-18.

[235] *Prosecutor v Milošević* (IT-02-54), para 1.

[236] *Prosecutor v Milošević* (IT-02-54), paras 19-23, 26.

[237] *Prosecutor v Milošević* (IT-02-54), para 25.

[238] *Prosecutor v Milošević* (IT-02-54), para 26.

[239] *Prosecutor v Milošević* (IT-02-54), paras 32–3.

[240] *Prosecutor v Milošević* (IT-02-54), paras 29, 34.

[241] *Prosecutor v Milošević* (IT-02-54), para 45.

Chamber based its decision not upon obstructionism but upon the ill-health of the accused and 'real danger that this trial might last for an unreasonably long time or, worse yet, might not be concluded should the Accused continue to represent himself without the assistance of counsel'.[242] Crucially, in its Order on the modalities of assignment of counsel, the Chamber declared:

> Should the Accused fail to cooperate with counsel, the trial will nonetheless proceed. If such failure on the part of the Accused results in material which is actually relevant to the Accused's case not being presented, then the Accused must bear responsibility for that and cannot plead injustice.[243]

Thus, in an almost complete reversal of its earlier rulings, the Chamber assigned Mr Steven Kay QC and Miss Gillian Higgins of the English Bar as defence counsel.

The assigned counsel attempted to secure the attendance of defence witnesses but only five from a list of one hundred and forty agreed to testify, all the rest refusing to attend because they disagreed with the Trial Chamber's decision to assign counsel.[244] Following this, the assigned counsel applied to the Registrar to withdraw. Citing Articles 8–12 and 14 of the ICTY Code of Conduct, they submitted that: 1) in the absence of instructions from and communications with the accused they could not discharge their professional duties; 2) representation of the accused against his will comprised a conflict of interest between his instructions and the Tribunal's assignment breaching the ethical duty of loyalty; and 3) the Tribunal assignment constituted an external pressure to compromise professional integrity in violation of the ICTY Code and the English Bar Code of Conduct with complaints made to the Dutch Bar against lead counsel by the accused.[245] Finally, the assigned counsel declared: 'Should their application for leave to withdraw be refused, counsel may in any event unilaterally terminate their assignment as defence counsel on the basis that good cause exists for them to do so.'[246]

By contrast, the Prosecution argued, inter alia:

> that court assigned counsel are perfectly able to act in the best interests of the Accused, because those interests are forensic, and court assigned counsel should be able to deduce them from the statements and cross-examination of the Accused. They argue further that the codes of conduct relied upon by court assigned counsel do not effectively cover the assignment of counsel on an unwilling accused, that reliance on provisions concerning a conflict of interest are misplaced in the context of these circumstances, and that the jurisprudence of the ICTY is that, in circumstances where an accused unjustifiably resists legal representation from assigned counsel, counsel's professional obligation to continue to represent the accused remains.[247]

In rejecting the motion, the Trial Chamber held that a failure to communicate with or take instructions from an unwilling client does not ethically give rise to a

[242] *Prosecutor v Milošević* (IT-02-54), paras 64–5.
[243] *Prosecutor v Milošević* (IT-02-54), para 70.
[244] *Milošević*, 'Decision on Assigned Counsel's Motion for Withdrawal' (7 December 2004), para 2.
[245] *Milošević*, para 5.
[246] *Milošević*, para 5.
[247] *Milošević*, para 8.

conflict of interest or otherwise give rise to a cause for withdrawal.[248] The Chamber rejected the argument that the inability to take instructions prejudiced his defence, declaring that '[w]hat is required of counsel is that they act in what they perceive to be the best interests of the Accused...it is all that can be reasonably expected of counsel in such circumstances'.[249]

The practical problem that assigned counsel complained of was their inability to take instructions from their client concerning the presentation of his case. Although this would have limited the scope for their presentation of the defence case, counsel would have had material from which to extrapolate Milošević's defence. Thus, counsel were not operating in a fog. If necessary, they certainly would have been equipped to mount, minimally, a 'negative defence' by which they could present rebutting evidence in order to create 'reasonable doubt' without presenting an alternative factual theory. Concerning the objection that the vast majority of Milošević's planned witnesses would not cooperate with counsel, the value of those witnesses is questionable and in any event there was the possibility of recourse to subpoena orders.[250] Moreover, it may be questioned whether Mr Milošević's best *legal* interests were being served by his insistence upon representing himself where he was in ill-health, not legally trained and pursuing a questionable trial strategy.[251]

The senior assigned counsel (Mr Steven Kay QC) said at the time:

> He does not want us as counsel and it is our duty to fight for that for him. It doesn't change because the court appoints you that they can somehow override his rights, your duties to him, because you're a court-appointed lawyer. What would they have made of that in Nuremberg? For God's sake, it just doesn't make sense, it's humpty-dumpty.[252]

The statement illustrates the view of assigned counsel that his first loyalty was owed to the client and to his *instructions* rather than to his *legal interests*. It should be noted that counsel cited the Code of Conduct of the English Bar despite the supremacy of the ICTY Code and the fact that that Code does not address the specific question of assignment of counsel to an unwilling defendant[253] but does prescribes a hierarchically superior duty to the court over the duty to the client.[254] The threat to unilaterally withdraw in the event of the refusal of their application, although justifiable in extreme circumstances where a court or tribunal acts in a manner patently offensive to justice, was unjustified in light of the Trial Chamber's at the least defensible, at the most inevitable, decision (after much patience) to finally assign counsel.

[248] *Milošević*, paras 17–18.
[249] *Milošević*, para 19.
[250] ICTY Rules, Rule 54.
[251] Note.
[252] Note 121.
[253] English Code, Written Standards for the Conduct of Professional Work, paras 13–16.
[254] English Code, paras 302–3. Counsel also must not withdraw from representation where his client's interests would be prejudiced—para 610(d).

Although the Appeal Chamber, in effect, reversed the Trial Chamber's order as 'disproportionate' by restoring the right of the Accused to 'take the lead' in the presentation of his case,[255] from the ethical perspective the episode serves to illustrate the fundamental importance of an ethical code that prioritizes the overriding duty of counsel to justice where conflicting (as they did there) with the wishes of the tribunal and/or those of the client. Counsel must independently weigh the best legal interests of his client as well as the need for expedition and procedural integrity in the trial within an overall test of fairness. In so doing, an advocate serves the interests of justice.

Similar problems concerning attempts by defence counsel to unilaterally withdraw from assigned representation have arisen before both the ICTR and the SCSL. In the *Barayagwiza* case,[256] Canadian and American counsel from the bars of Québec and the State of Washington applied to withdraw on the ground that their client (who was boycotting the Tribunal) had given them an instruction to do so but were ordered by the Tribunal to continue because its international code of conduct prevailed and, citing Strasbourg precedent to the effect that boycotting accused have a continuing right to representation as part of their human right to a fair trial, it held:

> In the present case, Mr Barayagwiza is actually boycotting the United Nations Tribunal. He has chosen both to be absent in the trail and to give no instructions as to how his legal representation should proceed in the trial or as to the specifics of his strategy. In such a situation, his lawyers cannot simply abide with his 'instruction' not to defend him. Such instructions, in the opinion of the Chamber, should rather be seen as an attempt to obstruct judicial proceedings. In such a situation, it cannot reasonably be argued that Counsel is under an obligation to follow him, and that not do so would constitute grounds for withdrawal.[257]

Additionally, at the outset of the *Taylor* case[258] before the SCSL counsel for a defendant (an English barrister, Mr Karim Khan) applied to withdraw without notice[259] from his assignment as counsel to Mr Charles Taylor on the ground that his client (who at the time was not participating in his trial) had terminated his representation.[260] Following the Court's rejection of his application to withdraw, Mr Khan rejected its authority to rule against his application to withdraw as counsel by ultimately departing from the courtroom without permission.[261] The Court did not impose any disciplinary sanction (for example, an official finding of misconduct

[255] *Milošević*, Decision on Interlocutory Appeal of the Trial Chamber's Decision on the Assignment of Defense Counsel (1 November 2004), paras 17–20.

[256] *The Prosecutor v Jean-Bosco Barayagwiza* (Case No ICTR-97-19).

[257] *The Prosecutor v Jean-Bosco Barayagwiza* (Case No ICTR-97-19), 'Decision on Defence Counsel Motion to Withdraw' (2 November 2000),

[258] *The Prosecutor of the Special Court v Charles Ghankay Taylor* (Case No SCSL-2003-01-T).

[259] Interview with Judge Teresa Doherty (appointed to deal with disciplinary matters concerning counsel) and Mr Simon Meisenberg (Senior Legal Officer) of the SCSL, 20 August 2010 (cited with permission).

[260] Official Transcript (Monday, 4 June 2007), 258–67.

[261] See Art 18(B) on the applicable provision for withdrawal by Court-appointed counsel. Mr Khan sought to invoke not only *Milošević* but also the so-called 'doctrine of all expedient means' articulated by Lord Brougham LC in 1820—Official Transcript (Monday, 4 June 2007), 266. National ethical rules, of course, are inapplicable before SCSL proceedings in any event for the purposes of those proceedings—SCSL Code, Art 3(B).

combined with a fine and complaint to the Bar Standards Board) for counsel's failure to observe his overriding duty to the Court.[262] This example of misconduct by counsel may be contrasted with the observance of appropriate procedure by counsel in the *AFRC* case who made a confidential, written application for withdrawal that was approved by the Court.[263]

8.3.2.3 Courtesy

The ethical duty of courtesy in the Court is straightforward and uncontroversial.[264] There have been cases of discourtesy offered by defence counsel before the SCSL. In the only misconduct hearing thus far before the SCSL, Mr Yada Williams (defence counsel in the *CDF* case[265]) was sanctioned by the Court for having orally and physically assaulted[266] a Court staff member.[267] In the *Taylor* trial, Mr Karim Khan unilaterally left the courtroom after his application for withdrawal was rejected by the Trial Chamber.[268]

Later in the *Taylor* trial, the lead Defence counsel (Mr Courteney Griffiths QC) insulted a Prosecutor by referring to him as a 'boy' and commanding him to 'sit down' whilst banging upon his lectern.[269] Counsel agreed to apologize to the Court but repeatedly refused to apologize to the Prosecutor until he was temporarily denied rights of audience. The Defendant separately apologized to both the Court and prosecutor through his junior counsel, citing the Code of Conduct, for the behaviour of his senior counsel. Mr Griffiths was reinstated when he obeyed the Court's direction to apologize to the Prosecutor whom he insulted. A delay of approximately one hour was caused by Mr Griffiths' gratuitous insult and stubborn refusal to apologize. In light of what must have been a significant financial cost, and for future deterrence, a fine[270] may have been appropriate.

Subsequent events in the *Taylor* trial arguably support this. On 14 January 2011, Mr Griffiths violated a Court order (after the application of the Defence for additional time was rejected) by not filing the final trial brief and declining to accept service of the Prosecution final trial brief, 'on Mr Taylor's instructions', on the ground that it would not be in the defendant's best interests.[271] On 7 February,

[262] Note 152.

[263] *The Prosecutor v Brima, Kamara and Kanu (AFRC Case)*(Case No SCSL-04-16-T), 'Decision on the Confidential Joint Defence Application for Withdrawal by Counsel for Brima and Kamara and on the Request for Further Representation by Counsel for Kanu' (20 May 2005).

[264] ICC Code, Art 7(1); ICTY Code, Art 27(1); ICTR Code, Art 17(1); SCSL Code, Art 7. Discourtesy could also constitute 'misconduct' as a 'disruption of proceedings' under the Rome Statute, Art 71; Rules of Procedure, Rule 25.

[265] *Norman.*

[266] The term 'assault' is taken from the Code of Conduct hearing, although in the English common law the physical contact would be termed 'battery'.

[267] SCSL Decision (10 November 2005), Code of Conduct Hearing.

[268] Notes 292–3.

[269] *Taylor*, Transcript (12 August 2010), 46092–103.

[270] SCSL Rules of Procedure and Evidence 2010, Rule 46(C).

[271] *Taylor*, Transcript (8 February 2011), 49139–40.

the Trial Chamber rejected by majority a defence application to file a late brief.[272] The following day, Mr Griffiths on the instructions of the defendant unilaterally withdrew from the courtroom in protest, defying a Court order to remain.[273] On 3 March, the Appeals Chamber reversed the Trial Chamber order on the ground that the silence of the defendant concerning Mr Griffiths' actions did not constitute a knowing waiver of his procedural rights and that the Trial Chamber should have inquired beyond Mr Griffiths' representations to satisfy itself 'that the Accused fully understood and agreed with his lawyer's actions and representations and that he was aware that the consequences of that agreement included the possibility that his right to be heard at the conclusion of the case could be considered waived'.[274]

The Trial Chamber granted the request of Mr Griffiths to hold a special Code of Conduct hearing into the matter of his walkout. On 25 March, the hearing was held but adjourned in bizarre circumstances. Justice Julia Sebutinde refused to attend the hearing on the ground that she disagreed with the Trial Chamber's citation of Mr Griffiths.[275] Following a dispute concerning whether the Trial Chamber was properly constituted in the absence of Justice Sebutinde with a reserve judge present, the presiding judge adjourned the hearing.[276] The matter was resolved when Mr Griffiths publicly apologized to the Trial Chamber and resumed his duties at the next hearing.

On the final day of the trial, he defended his walkout:

> Now, on the 25th of February of this year I walked out of this Court despite your request, Madam President, that I remain. I make it clear, I did not leave through anger, but principle, because I am enjoined by the code of conduct of the Bar of England and Wales, and I quote, 'To promote and protect fearlessly and by all proper and lawful means the lay client's,' that's Mr Taylor's, 'best interests and do so...without any regard to my own interests or to the consequences either to myself or to any other person.'
>
> However, if it is felt that I have been disrespectful to this Court, then I am willing to make a formal apology to this Court, in order to draw a line finally underneath these proceedings and bring it to an amicable end. We have always treated this tribunal and these proceedings with respect and will continue to do so.[277]

The Trial Chamber accepted his apology and declared the matter closed.[278] However, this 'apology' was more of a justification. Not only are national bar rules immaterial before the Court under the code of conduct to which Mr Griffiths expressly promised to adhere upon applying to be admitted as an SCSL counsel,[279] but the English Bar Code of Conduct itself provides that a barrister: 'must in all his professional activities be courteous and act promptly conscientiously diligently and

272 *Taylor*, 'Decision on Late Filing of Defence Final Trial Brief' (7 February 2011).

273 *Taylor*, Transcript (8 February 2011), 49137–45.

274 *Taylor*, 'Decision on Defence Notice of Appeal and Submissions Regarding the Decision on Late Filing of Defence Final Trial Brief' (3 March 2011), paras 57–67, 61.

275 *Taylor*, Transcript (25 February 2011), 49316.

276 *Taylor*, Transcript (11 March 2011), 49317–8.

277 *Taylor*, Transcript (11 March 2011), 49621.

278 *Taylor*, Transcript (11 March 2011), 49622.

279 SCSL Rules of Procedure and Evidence, Rule 44(B); SCSL Code of Conduct, Art 4.

with reasonable competence and take all reasonable and practicable steps to avoid unnecessary expense or waste of the Court's time and to ensure that professional engagements are fulfilled.'[280]

Not only is it difficult to envisage how gratuitously antagonizing the Trial Chamber (save through publicity) would promote his client's legal interests but it is similarly difficult to imagine that Mr Griffiths would have got away with a walkout in an English court. In this respect, discourtesy not only detracts from the dignity and smoothness of its proceedings but also arguably invites counsel to treat an international court with less respect than they would their own national courts. Discourtesy can also occur in subtler ways. As one ICTY judge explains:

> Fifth, the lack of a *coherent system of criminal legal procedure* at the international level implies the pace of the trials is often slowed down by the high frequency of motions submitted by the parties for clarification of a number of procedural issues. This is associated with the wider lack of a fully developed *international judicial culture* which not only includes rules of procedure but also an understanding by the parties of how to play the game in the courtroom and a consensus on basic standards for ethical and professional conduct. That takes time as well.[281]

When questioned on the meaning of 'international judicial culture', he elaborated:

> It entails diligence in pursuing issues, a way of speaking to one another, a way of putting argument. For example, one counsel, not one of the best counsel but a decent counsel, recently raised a *tu quoque* argument. There was an objection from the Bench but the counsel carried straight on without taking notice. Another counsel spent three hours in cross-examination recently. The Bench was reluctant to cut on time for witness examination but he spent much of it on irrelevant historical material. He was interrupted repeatedly to be questioned on the relevance of his questions but he gave evasive answers to the judges and carried on. In domestic proceedings, counsel would never get away with it but some counsel think that before the Tribunal they are at large to handle their examinations as they see fit. These sorts of issues one cannot put onto paper in the Rules of Procedure but there is a 'margin of appreciation' in the culture.[282]

Thus, it may be seen that courtesy—in the sense of respectful and dignified address – naturally overlaps or leads into a duty of diligence in pursuing meritorious argumentation. Persisting irrelevant evidence or arguments that irritate the Bench not only entails a lack of diligence in advancing the client's legal interests but is also discourteous towards the Tribunal. It may be argued that this sort of discourtesy is not unethical but merely bad advocacy. However, it is suggested that bad advocacy of this type—entailing not ineffective oratory, rhetoric, or use of evidence but rather discourtesy towards the Bench—should, if sufficiently grave, be considered professional misconduct, not least to the potential prejudice of the client's cause.

280 English Bar Code of Conduct, para 701.

281 Harhoff, 'It's all in the Process: Reflections on the Relation between International Criminal Trials and International Humanitarian Law', 78 *NJIL* (2010), 469–80, 479 (emphasis in original).

282 Interview with Judge Harhoff.

On this point, the ICC Code provides:

> Counsel is personally responsible for the conduct and presentation of the client's case and shall exercise personal judgement on the substance and purpose of statements made and questions asked.
>
> Counsel shall represent the client expeditiously with the purpose of avoiding unnecessary expense or delay in the conduct of the proceedings.[283]

However, developing a culture of efficiency and courtesy also requires a certain activism on the part of the Bench to both firmly indicate to counsel that a certain line of argument is irrelevant or frivolous culminating, if necessary, in an order or direction to that effect and sanctions for serious infractions.

8.3.2.4 Confidentiality of Judicial Proceedings

In the *Taylor* trial, Mr Griffiths has been implicated in Rule 77 contempt of court proceedings concerning the alleged leak of confidential material.[284] It was alleged by the Prosecution that Mr Griffiths 'knowingly and wilfully' and/or 'recklessly' disclosed the identities of seven Prosecution witnesses by publicly filing the Defence Final Brief in violation of a judicial confidentiality order providing for protective measures for those witnesses and that, in addition, testimony that had been given *in camera* was disclosed to a third party (Professor William Schabas) who then published it on an internet blog.[285]

In response, the Defence 'accept[ed] and apologiz[ed] for the fact that the identities of the seven protected witnesses were inadvertently disclosed in the public Table of Contents' and that 'viewed objectively, it [was] understandable given the considerable time pressure and work load the defence was under'.[286] On 12 June, Justice Teresa Doherty (the SCSL Disciplinary Judge) sitting as a single judge ruled that the undisputed fact of disclosure 'is sufficient to constitute "reason to believe" that Defence Lead Counsel, who signed the document that was filed, disclosed information in violation of an order of the Chamber directing that the names of witnesses provided with protective measures safeguarding their privacy and security shall not be disclosed' may be in contempt of court and directed that a Status Conference be held to determine the procedure to hear the matter.[287]

Whilst the matter is currently being dealt with under the rubric of contempt of court, should a code of conduct hearing be held into the matter, the applicable

[283] ICC Code, Arts 24(2), 24(5).

[284] *Taylor*, 'Decision on Confidential with Confidential Annexes A-E Prosecution Motion for the Trial Chamber to Summarily Deal with Contempt of the Special Court for Sierra Leone and for Urgent Interim Measures', Trial Chamber II (24 March 2011); *Taylor*, 'Decision on Confidential with Confidential Annexes A-E Prosecution Motion for the Trial Chamber to Summarily Deal with Contempt of the Special Court for Sierra Leone and for Urgent Interim Measures', Trial Chamber II (19 June 2012).

[285] *Taylor*, 'Decision on Confidential with Confidential Annexes' (24 March 2011), paras 4–5.

[286] *Taylor*, para10.

[287] *Taylor*, 'Decision on Confidential with Confidential Annexes' (19 June 2012), paras 10–11.

provision would appear to be Article 10(A)(i) of the SCSL Code of Conduct for Counsel:

> subject to the Rules of Procedure and Evidence, preserve confidentiality, and not disclose information which may jeopardise the privacy, safety and security of, in particular, those witnesses who have been afforded protective measures under Rule 69 or Rule 75 of the Rules.

The standard appears to be one of strict knowledge, whereby the mere fact of disclosure is sufficient to constitute a breach of the Code. Consequently, the state of knowledge of defence counsel (i.e.—whether he intentionally, recklessly or inadvertently disclosed) is immaterial to the determination of the existence of a breach, save perhaps as a mitigating or aggravating factor. Whilst one may question the strictness of this standard, it appears to be appropriate in light of the potentially grave consequences not only to procedural integrity but to personal safety in the event of breach of confidentiality orders.

8.4 Disciplinary Jurisdiction

8.4.1 Prosecutors

The disciplinary regime for prosecutors is complex and reflects several competing priorities. First and foremost, there is a sensitivity concerning the mutual independence of each of the organs of the Court. Secondly, there is an acknowledged need for public confidence in the disciplinary process to preclude allegations of conflict of interest or bias. Thirdly, a distinction is drawn between the Prosecutor and Deputy Prosecutor—as elected officials—and trial counsel, as appointed staff, in their accountability. Following the creation by the ASP of the 'independent oversight mechanism' (IOP) in 2010, investigative jurisdiction for misconduct by elected officials and appointed staff is vested in a single organ. However, disciplinary jurisdiction remains split whereby the Prosecutor is accountable to the ASP whilst trial prosecutors are accountable to him.

Unlike the ICTY and ICTR, there exists an external disciplinary system for the Prosecutor which makes him professionally accountable to the ASP. However, this accountability has been, in practice, largely nominal.[288] Whilst the role of the ASP in the appointment and removal of the Prosecutor and Deputy Prosecutor has a clear rationale in that both offices are politically important and also have considerably wider responsibilities attached to them than those of trial counsel, its power to impose disciplinary sanctions for professional misconduct arising from their functions as counsel is problematic because the ASP is not a professional but a political body.

Three sanctions may be applied to the Prosecutor on an absolute majority of the ASP on any combination according to seriousness: (1) reprimand; (2) fine;

[288] Stahn and Sluiter, *The Emerging Practice of the International Criminal Court*, 247–79, 259.

and (3) removal from office.[289] There are also detailed procedural rights for the Prosecutor, though no right of appeal.[290] Whilst Articles 24 and 25 of the Rules provide examples of 'less serious'[291] and 'serious'[292] misconduct, the language is broad. The legitimacy of disciplinary sanctions is potentially diluted because there is no prior notice of the precise ethical standards to be applied. For example, the application of disciplinary sanctions to the Prosecutor or his subordinates for extra-judicial media statements prejudicing the integrity of the judicial process would be open to the criticism of arbitrariness because there are no rules prescribing precise professional standards regulating such statements.

The second disciplinary system concerns trial counsel within the Prosecution Division, who are accountable to the Prosecutor.[293] This system of internal discipline, as illustrated by the *Furundžija* case discussed above,[294] creates potential problems of conflict of interest, transparency, and fairness. The outsourcing of the investigation in that case reflects the sensitivity of the head of the Office disciplining her subordinates, which is arguably a latent conflict of interest.

An investigation of the Prosecutor for sexual misconduct and the Prosecutor's summary dismissal of the whistleblower revealed problems within the disciplinary system. On 20 October 2006, Mr Christian Palme (then an OTP Media Relations Officer) filed an internal complaint against the Prosecutor in which he alleged with corroborating evidence that he had committed rape and requested his removal from office.[295] The Presidency appointed a panel to determine whether the complaint was 'manifestly unfounded'. The panel considered the complaint *in camera* and interviewed the alleged victim and the Prosecutor—who both 'firmly denied the allegations'[296]—and produced a confidential report.[297] On 8 December 2006, the Presidency accepted the panel's recommendation that the internal complaint be set aside as manifestly unfounded and ordered the surrender for destruction of all the corroborating evidence.[298]

On 13 April 2007, the Prosecutor summarily dismissed the complainant for serious misconduct in having 'falsely alleged, with obvious malicious intent, to damage the professional and personal reputation of the Prosecutor'.[299] A Disciplinary Advisory Board recommended reversal of the dismissal on the ground, inter alia,

[289] Rome Statute, Arts 46–7; ICC Rules, Arts 26(2), 29(4), 30(2), 31–2.

[290] ICC Rules, Art 27.

[291] Eg interference in official functions or repeatedly failing to comply with or ignoring requests made by the Presidency or Presiding Judge.

[292] Eg breach of confidentiality, concealment of important information, gross negligence, knowing failure to request excusal, or repeatedly causing unwarranted delay to proceedings.

[293] Staff Regulations, Reg 1.1(c).

[294] Note 20, *supra*.

[295] *Palme*; Palme, 'Complaint against ICC Prosecutor', para 2, online: <http://www.innercitypress.com/ocampocomplaint.pdf> (Accessed: 9 February 2011).

[296] Rozenberg, 'Why the world's most powerful prosecutor should resign: Part 2', *Daily Telegraph* (14 September 2008).

[297] *Palme*, 3.

[298] *Palme*, 2.

[299] *Palme*, 3.

that it was procedurally flawed due to the Prosecutor's participation. However, the Prosecutor confirmed his decision to summarily dismiss because 'the fact that the "serious misconduct concerned [him] personally [was] not enough to call into question his impartiality"' and that there was 'an obvious malicious intent' to damage the Prosecutor's reputation.[300] On 9 July 2008, an ILO Administrative Tribunal found that the complainant had not acted maliciously and that the Prosecutor had violated 'a fundamental aspect of due process that a person should not take a decision in a matter in which he or she has a personal interest'.[301] It set aside the decision and awarded compensation and 'moral damages' of €25,000 plus costs.[302]

This case demonstrated the need for external investigation and judgement of alleged misconduct in order to ensure the observance of fundamental fair trial principles. On 4 December 2008, the Bureau of the ASP appointed a facilitator to report upon the issue of establishing an 'independent oversight mechanism' for the staff members of the Court.[303] With the assistance of a Working Group, the facilitator reported:

> There was agreement on the merit of establishing an enhanced professional investigative capacity situated within the Court's existing internal disciplinary structures, since investigations conducted by staff members not professionally trained for this function could compromise the legitimacy of the process, especially given that their recommendations could lead to summary dismissals.[304]

On 26 November 2009, the ASP adopted a resolution to create an 'independent oversight mechanism' (IOM) based upon Article 112(4) of the Rome Statute with a 'professional investigative unit' to operate 'in support of the existing disciplinary structures of the Court to conduct investigations on allegations of misconduct and to ensuring effective and meaningful oversight thereof'.[305] On 10 December 2010, the ASP adopted a resolution on the IOM setting out its framework to investigate reports of misconduct by elected officials, staff, and contractors.[306]

The aim of the IOM is to promote the legitimacy of the disciplinary process by transferring investigative powers to an independent body created for the purpose. Given the criticisms which may be made about the disciplinary proceedings concerning the Prosecutor and Mr Palme, this effort would appear to be justified. However, the reforms have not been wholly welcomed by the Prosecutor, who has perceived the IOM as an interference with his authority over the Office:

> I welcome the possibility to have a tool to investigate misconduct of the Office's staff. However, the IOM mandate proposed includes the possibility to replace the authority of

300 *Palme*, 3–4.

301 *Palme*, 11–13 (paras 13–17), 14 (para 19).

302 *Palme*, 15.

303 'Report of the Bureau on the establishment of an independent oversight mechanism', ICC-ASP/8/2 (15 April 2009), para 1.

304 'Report of the Bureau on the establishment of an independent oversight mechanism', para 14.

305 'Establishment of an independent oversight mechanism', ICC-ASP/8/Res.1 (26 November 2009), Annex, para 7, online: <http://www.icc-cpi.int/iccdocs/asp_docs/ASP8/OR/OR-ASP8-Vol.I-ENG.Part.II.pdf> (Accessed: 5 April 2011).

306 'Independent Oversight Mechanism', ICC-ASP/9/Res.5 (10 December 2010), Annex, para 2, online: <http://www.icc-cpi.int/iccdocs/asp_docs/ASP9/OR/ICC-ASP-9-20-Vol.I-Part.III-ENG.pdf> (Accessed: 5 April 2011).

the Prosecutor to start investigations and provides it for the IOM, a subsidiary body of the ASP. This proposal creates the risk of undue interference with the judicial activities of the Office. As explained in our legal memoranda, the Statute establishes that the Prosecutor is accountable before the Assembly, and to protect their independent work, the Office staff is under the full authority of the Prosecutor... As a matter of policy, the Office never received an explanation as to why the Prosecutor could be trusted to investigate Heads of State, but not to investigate the staff of the Office.[307]

In light of the experiences in *Furundžija* and *Palme*, it is arguable that the external enforcement of a prescribed prosecutorial code of conduct (or, better still, the extension of the existing Code of Conduct to prosecutorial counsel, as at the SCSL) instead of the status quo of self-regulation. Additionally, the generality of the confidentiality rule on disciplinary proceedings is problematic in that there is a public interest, as well as those of concerned parties, in knowing the details of such investigations. The general rule should be one of transparency with discretion to preserve confidentiality in exceptional cases and to the minimum necessary.

8.4.2 Defence Counsel

The disciplinary procedure for defence counsel is contained within Chapter 4 ('Disciplinary regime') of the Code of Conduct. Complaints concerning the conduct of defence counsel may be made by a Chamber, the Prosecutor or '[a]ny person or group of persons whose rights or interests may have been affected by the alleged misconduct'.[308] A Commissioner with 'established competence in professional ethics and legal matters' is appointed by the Presidency to investigate with the principal task of investigating allegations of professional misconduct under the Code.[309] The Commissioner may summarily dismiss unfounded complaints or investigate well-founded complaints, for which he may seek to find an amicable settlement (presumably between the complainant and the impugned counsel) or submit a report of his investigative findings to the Disciplinary Board.[310]

The Disciplinary Board is composed of three members, two permanent and one ad hoc, elected by 'all [defence] counsel entitled to practise before the Court... from amongst persons with established competence in professional ethics and legal matters'.[311] The Disciplinary Board hearings are generally in public but may be held *in camera*, in particular to preserve 'confidentiality of information in the report of the Commissioner or to protect victims and witnesses'.[312] The Board has evidence-gathering powers but is required to respect prescribed procedural rights of impugned counsel, including right of appeal.[313] The sanctions available to the Board

[307] Moreno-Ocampo, 'Address to the ASP' (6 December 2010), 8, online: <http://www.icc-cpi.int/NR/rdonlyres/F7EB40D9-77A5-456C-BFAD-4724D442DB18/282780/LMOspeech_06122010.pdf> (Accessed: 5 April 2011).
[308] Code of Conduct, Art 34.
[309] Code of Conduct, Art 33.
[310] Code of Conduct, Art 39.
[311] Code of Conduct, Art 36(4).
[312] Code of Conduct, Art 39(6).
[313] Code of Conduct, Art 40.

are any combination of (presumably private) admonishment, public reprimand with an entry in counsel's personal file, a fine of up to €30,000, suspension of practice before the Court for up to two years and a permanent ban on practising.

This disciplinary regime for defence counsel may be favourably compared with that for prosecutors. There are greater prescribed procedural rights for the impugned counsel, such as the right of appeal.[314] There is a greater variety of disciplinary sanctions and direct links with the impugned counsel's national bar. A better balance between the competing demands of transparency and confidentiality is struck, in that the report of the Disciplinary Board must be made public and its hearings are generally public. The IBA has considered the possibility of revising this mechanism to render it more 'pro-active' and external.[315] This ensures that the public and private interests in knowing the details of the proceedings are met whilst providing a power to protect sensitive areas. Crucially, the impugned counsel is investigated and judged by persons who are required to be competent in professional ethics. This is contrasted by the new IOM for prosecutorial counsel, which in any event only has the power to investigate alleged misconduct and make recommendations. Trial prosecutors remain ultimately accountable to the Prosecutor, who has an inherent conflict of interest and who is not necessarily an expert in counsel ethics. Reform of the IOM to bring it to the same procedural standard as for defence counsel would not only be inherently beneficial but would also eliminate one of the imbalances between counsel.

8.4.3 Double Deontology

The problem of double deontology, or conflicts between the prescriptive and disciplinary jurisdictions of national bars and international courts, does not at first sight appear to arise concerning the conduct of prosecutorial counsel owing to their status as 'international civil servants'. However, it is conceivable that members of the Prosecution Division who are also members of national bars may face double deontology were they to be subjected to a complaint at their home bar concerning their conduct at the Court. There is no mechanism available to solve such problems, whether for conflicts between prescriptive or disciplinary jurisdictions.

By contrast, some attempt has been made to address the issue for defence counsel. For prescriptive conflicts, the Code provides that it prevails 'in respect of the practice and professional ethics of counsel when practising before the Court'.[316] However, this does not ensure that national bars that have reserved extraterritorial applicability of their own ethical rules[317] with respect to this provision. As seen in the *Taylor* and *Milošević* trials, for example, English barristers have on multiple occasions ignored supremacy clauses in international codes of conduct by invoking national rules to justify their conduct. On the other hand, the Code does not follow the ICTY

[314] Code of Conduct, Art 42(1).
[315] *ILA*, 27–30.
[316] ICC Code, Art 4.
[317] Eg English Code, Annexe A ('International Practice Rules'), para 2; ABA Model Rules, Rule 8.5. *Confer* Brussels Code, 5.

approach in providing mitigation for counsel acting pursuant to their national rules who infringe the ICTY Code.[318]

Concerning conflicts of disciplinary jurisdiction, the Code states that its disciplinary regime 'is without prejudice to the disciplinary powers of any other disciplinary authority that may apply to counsel subject to this Code'.[319] Whilst one may think it obvious that the ICC can do nothing to prevent national bars from asserting a parallel jurisdiction, it is conceivable that the Court could invoke parties' general duty of cooperation by making a request that national governments take measures to abolish that jurisdiction.[320] A useful provision is that the ad hoc members of ICC Disciplinary Boards serve as contact points with the relevant national bars for communication and consultation.[321] The Code provides that Disciplinary Boards shall suspend their own proceedings pending the completion of ongoing national proceedings unless: (1) the national bar does not respond to communications with the ad hoc member within a 'reasonable time'; (2) the Disciplinary Board considers that the information received is not satisfactory; or (3) the Disciplinary Board considers that, in light of the information received, the national bar is unable or unwilling to conclude the disciplinary procedure.[322]

Thus, in attempting to resolve the problem of conflicting national and international disciplinary jurisdictions, the Code seemingly gives first pass to national bars to apply their own disciplinary procedure whilst reserving its own. This is problematic because the ICC is better-placed both geographically and technically to speedily and effectively conduct disciplinary hearings. It will in most cases have better access to the requisite evidence and be able to better contextualize the allegations owing to greater familiarity with its own procedures. Moreover, the provisions preserve the conflict of jurisdiction because the Board's acceptance of the national bars' decisions is subject to its own evaluation. This preserves the possibility of counsel being subject to conflicting disciplinary jurisdictions, judging according to diverging standards. This is clearly a systemic weakness that promotes uncertainty and vagueness.

One concrete example of the double deontology problem in practice arose at the ICTY when the Serbian Bar Association (SBA) ordered all of its members, including those appearing before the Tribunal, to strike over a taxation dispute with the Serbian government.[323] Serbian defence counsel were understandably reluctant to appear before the ICTY due to the threat of disciplinary proceedings, which would paradoxically affect their continued good standing before the ICTY itself.[324] Consequently, the two counsel concerned failed to appear before the Trial Chamber. Although the temporarily assigned counsel proposed that the Tribunal remind Serbia of its duty of cooperation under Article 29 of the ICTY Statute as well as the supremacy of the ICTY Code of Conduct and order the defence counsel

318 ICTY Code, Art 47(E).

319 ICC Code, Art 30.

320 Rome Statute, Arts 86–7.

321 ICC Code, Art 38(2).

322 ICC Code, Art 38(4)–(5).

323 *Zupljanin*, Transcript (10 November 2009), 2846.

324 *Zupljanin*, 2842, 2845–6.

to appear,[325] the Chamber decided to temporarily allow counsel to withdraw until the strike elapsed.[326] As one of the judges relates:

> I recall that in the *Stanisić and Zupljanin* cases in November 2009, the Serbian counsel applied to withdraw because their home bar had instructed them that they were going on strike due to a dispute about legal pay with the Serbian Government. Any lawyer who did not go on strike was threatened with disbarment. The Chamber told counsel that this was unacceptable because a private body does not have extraterritorial jurisdiction to impose such an order. Counsel telephoned Belgrade requesting permission to continue but were ordered to strike or be disbarred. The Tribunal decided to accept their temporary resignation for one or two days and appointed standby counsel, Mr Karim Khan, for the interim period. However, the Tribunal expressly refused to allow its trials to be stopped just because of a Serbian strike. Not only did the Tribunal not accept the extraterritorial jurisdiction of the Serbian bar, but it also considered that the right of the accused to counsel could not be disturbed by reasons foreign to the appearance of the particular counsel before the Tribunal. Conduct considered to be unethical under the Serbian Code would engage the jurisdiction of the Serbian Bar Association but only insofar as conduct is concerned—any other matter would not be acceptable to the Tribunal.[327]

Although the Chamber doubted it could take practical action against a private entity such as the SBA, it is possible that it could have invoked its contempt powers.[328] Regardless, the case illustrates the difficulty of the double deontology problem not only for the international tribunal concerned but for the counsel caught in the middle.

8.5 Conclusions

This chapter has illustrated some of the principal themes concerning counsel ethics before international criminal tribunals, particularly the ICC. In certain respects, the ICC regulatory system concerning counsel is considerably more developed than was the case at Nuremberg. However, there remains a bifurcation between prosecutors and defence counsel, lack of common ethical standards, and independence issues. Whereas defence counsel are externally regulated by admission requirements, a code of conduct and a disciplinary regime, prosecutors remain largely self-accountable apart from the essentially theoretical oversight of the ASP over the Prosecutor and the contempt powers of the judiciary. This difference causes a significant imbalance in the procedural standing of the parties in practice.

Most of the early ethical issues that have arisen thus far have concerned prosecutors. Imprecise definition of the fundamental role of the Prosecutor, whether as investigating magistrate or as advocate or a hybrid of the two, has caused considerable difficulties in the *Lubanga* trial and elsewhere. On the one hand, the Prosecutor considers himself to be a judge of equal standing with the members of the Chambers.

[325] *Zupljanin*, 2842–3.
[326] *Zupljanin*, 2848; Interview with Judge Harhoff (17 August 2010), cited with permission.
[327] Interview with Judge Harhoff.
[328] ICTY Rules, Rule 77(A)(v).

On the other hand, the Trial Chamber in *Lubanga* has treated him as a counsel of equal standing with defence counsel. The battle of wills that arose in the term of the first Prosecutor between the two may be attributed to the lack of precision concerning the role of the Prosecutor and, in particular, to the lack of clear ethical standards governing his conduct.

In addition to the *Lubanga* trial concerning the perennial problem of disclosure of exculpatory evidence as well as obedience of judicial orders, other ethical issues that have arisen in the early days of the Court include appropriate communications with the media and the moral character of the Prosecutor due to alleged criminal misconduct unconnected to the performance of his duties. These episodes illustrate the potential utility of common ethical standards for prosecutors and defence counsel alike to provide transparency, equality and consistency in handling such matters in practice.

The bifurcation between prosecutors and defence counsel is also connected to the divergent ethical standards between them. Although the Code of Conduct for defence counsel is an incomplete and imprecise document, there are no externally prescribed ethical rules for prosecutorial counsel at the ICC level that deal with the nuanced issues of forensic advocacy. Moreover, certain ethical issues (such as media statements or contacts with witnesses) are not addressed for either prosecutors or defence counsel and have created procedural problems. As the ICC prepares to elect the next Prosecutor and progress to a new phase, useful work could be done to solve these problems.

The chapter has also shown that, in comparison with other international courts, the regulatory architecture of the Court concerning counsel (particularly defence counsel) is considerably more detailed and sophisticated. For example, the integration of national bars into the procedure of the ICC disciplinary system concerning defence counsel is a useful mechanism (though not a complete solution) concerning the problem of double deontology. The experiences of the ad hoc tribunals, particularly those of the ICTY, illustrate the importance of developing such tools to ensure that inevitable problems concerning counsel conduct can be effectively addressed. As the Court continues to accumulate experience and encounter new procedural challenges in its work, the perennial importance of professional ethics for counsel and the inculcation of an international judicial culture for the smooth, efficient, and fair conduct of international criminal trials has been underscored by its early experiences.

9

Developing Common Ethical Standards before International Courts

The test identified in Chapter 1 in the debate regarding professionalization is whether it is desirable and feasible. The comparative study of international courts and tribunals in Chapters 4 to 8 suggests that there is a real need for normativity in the area of professional ethics for counsel. However, the question remains whether it is feasible to articulate common ethical standards for counsel despite considerable differences amongst national jurisdictions. In addressing this issue, this chapter examines the articulation of ethical principles for advocacy as proto-codes of conduct by professional organizations and the application of those texts by international courts. That application can be in the form of prescription as codes of conduct integrated into the courts' procedural rules or in that of ad hoc application for courts to resolve ethical problems.

Through examination of this nascent process, two preliminary propositions are advanced. The first is that it is possible to identify universal or quasi-universal ethical principles that are both common to all of the major legal traditions of forensic advocacy and of general application to international courts and tribunals. The second is that the search for uniformity in professional ethics is of limited effectiveness because of major philosophical divisions amongst national ethical traditions. Consequently, in cases of divergent national views a selective approach on a given ethical issue (eg witness proofing) is necessary in order to provide textual clarity.

This chapter is divided into two halves. In the first half, it addresses the question of the feasibility of the articulation of common ethical standards. In the second half, it examines the question of the practicability of enforcement of such standards by international courts. Section 9.1 analyses the regulatory jurisdiction of international courts, including the problems arising in the jurisprudence and their practical competence. Section 9.1.1 examines whether international courts have the legal power to exercise regulatory jurisdiction towards counsel. Section 9.1.2 considers whether international courts have the practical competence to enforce ethical standards, with particular reference to the expertise of judges and registrars as well as the challenge of harmonizing the disciplinary jurisdiction of international courts with that of national bars.

Section 9.2 examines the nascent efforts to articulate common standards by professional organizations. In particular, it considers the challenges concerning the key issues of balancing textual integrity with consent in articulating authoritative texts. Section 9.2.1 analyses the new principles proposed by the International Law Association (ILA), section 9.2.2 explores the ongoing work of the International Bar Association (IBA), and section 9.2.3 examines the potential of the Council of Bars and Law Societies of Europe (CCBE). Sections 9.2.4 and 9.2.5 scrutinize the obstacles concerning the equally crucial issue of enforcement. Through this analysis, it is suggested that there are considerable challenges for professionalization that can be overcome with care, flexibility, and ingenuity. An incremental approach based upon a pragmatic acknowledgement of the practical issues and systemic needs rather than a dogmatic clash of national legal cultures is likely to yield greater success and enable international courts and tribunals to regulate counsel in an effective and fair manner.

9.1 Regulatory Jurisdiction of International Courts

In this section, the first question considered is whether international courts have the legal power to regulate counsel by prescribing and enforcing common ethical standards to protect the integrity of their proceedings. Interview responses from nine judges[1] from non-criminal[2] international courts suggest that this question is contentious in relation to the regulation of State representatives. Judges at inter-State courts are clearly sensitive to 'State sovereignty' concerns and judges at mixed courts are also alive to the potential jealousy of States over their control over agents. The majority of the four judges interviewed from the criminal courts[3] likewise expressed divergent views about the regulation of prosecutors. Overall, nearly every interviewee acknowledged that the power to regulate counsel is an unresolved issue.

Regulatory powers towards counsel, comprising prescriptive and enforcement elements, exist in three forms: (1) admission requirements; (2) ethical rules; and (3) disciplinary sanctions. Although the unfairness of *ex post facto* law generally calls for courts to prescribe, those courts that have not done so (or that otherwise encounter a lacuna in their procedural rules) may be compelled to nevertheless invoke an enforcement power where the seriousness of the professional misconduct outweighs that of retrospection. It has already been suggested that there the occurrence of procedural problems in practice arising from divergences in ethical standards; the question that arises is how judges should handle them when they do.

One possibility is to discreetly admonish the advocates in question. This has the virtues of ease and tact by enabling the court to proceed rather than become sidetracked by incidental matters. This approach may be appropriate for disposing of difficult and nuanced problems on which procedural texts are silent or for allowing

[1] Judge Cot (ITLOS), Judge Keith (ICJ), Judge Higgins (ICJ), Judge Koroma (ICJ), Judge Edward (ECJ), Judge Forwood (EU General Court) and Judge Fora (ECtHR). Two other judges agreed to be interviewed on condition of anonymity.

[2] The power to regulate prosecutors is also an issue before the criminal courts due to judicial concerns about the appearance of undue proximity between the judiciary and the prosecution.

[3] Judge Harhoff (ICTY), Judge Pocar (ICTY), Judge Doherty (SCSL) and Judge Fulford (ICC).

a degree of leeway for junior or inexperienced counsel. Moreover, there is an important human dimension to trials in that there will be a practical need to calm tensions (which may stem from misunderstandings or personality clashes) in order to enable the trial to smoothly proceed. In the words of one experienced judge:

> Ultimately, it is easy to talk tough on [enforcement], but in real-life situations the real need is for a nuanced approach. The authority of the Court is often enhanced by dealing with egregious behaviour with a firm but moderate response. The Court is likely to attract respect by showing restraint rather than judicial bad temper, expressed in the heat of the moment.[4]

Thus, it is arguable that tactful and restrained admonishment is a useful judicial method of preventing rather than curing problems.

However, it could also be argued that this method is alone inadequate to uphold strict ethical standards. In serious cases, judges are compelled to publicly reprimand counsel to preserve procedural integrity and clearly disapprove of such conduct. As described in Chapter 8, an ICC trial chamber criticized a media interview given by a prosecutor:

> The point needs to be made publicly and directly whenever necessary. Imposing a stay on the proceedings was, in a way, an indirect and substantial sanction because of the public nature of the reprimand. Again, I repeat this was not the object of the exercise, given the Chamber was focussing on the alleged abuse of process. Furthermore, the Trial Chamber's criticisms of Ms le Fraper du Hellen were so clearly expressed that the Chamber's authority would not have been enhanced by the addition of a fine. It could have been seen as rather petty to have gone further. I agree that there is a need to be firm and to control behaviour but more often than not these situations can be disposed of without resort to formal sanctions. It should also be emphasised that some judges believe that resorting to penalties involves, in some degree, admitting failure because a judge should be able to exercise control over the proceedings by detecting and dealing with problems early—'nipping them in the bud'. Although judges are not in control of everything that counsel does, they are in a position to give early and firm warnings to counsel, to avert problems at the outset.[5]

Hence, a public reprimand can be an effective judicial tool to deal with inappropriate conduct without resorting to formal disciplinary procedures.

However, there is a drawback to this approach, namely, that since a public reprimand is itself a sanction there is a clear need not only for natural justice to be observed in handling the conduct (eg allowing the impugned counsel the opportunity to defend himself prior to public criticism) but also for prescribed standards to preclude *ex post facto* law. Without prescribed standards, a court may feel compelled to merely issue a warning without reprimanding the counsel in question. However, this is clearly unsatisfactory because some counsel may draw the conclusion that they can exploit the lack of common standards and counsel in general will be left without clear direction on a host of difficult ethical issues.

[4] Interview with Judge Sir Adrian Fulford, ICC (8 July 2011), cited with permission.

[5] Interview with Judge Sir Adrian Fulford.

Consequently, from the judicial viewpoint, a code of conduct is a useful tool to provide a normative framework within which to handle ethical issues. Paradoxically, prescribed standards may result in fewer disciplinary cases:

> There is a definite need for a code of conduct for all counsel so that there is something in black and white that applies across the board. This provides certainty and a fair level playing field, and it avoids the impression that individual judges are making up the rules as they go along. That said, most experienced judges ensure that situations of difficulty do not arise, and they rarely need to refer to a written code. Nevertheless, a definitive document is necessary in order to deal with extreme cases.[6]

Thus, it is arguable that the lack of prescribed standards causes ethical issues to assume greater importance in practice whereas articulated rules diminish their importance by better enabling courts to deal with professional conduct.

However, there may be serious cases in which formal disciplinary procedures prove necessary. In this respect, the question arises whether international courts can exercise disciplinary jurisdiction. An attractive recourse for judges is to refer the matter to a national bar by writing formally to inform it of the alleged misconduct. As seen in Chapters 5 and 8, the ECJ and ICC have prescribed rules specifically empowering judges to do so. Alternatively, a more subtle approach could entail public judicial criticism or the relevant bar authority being discreetly informed by a judge from its jurisdiction. The attractiveness of this solution is that it enables the trial judges to proceed with the proceedings whilst also ensuring that they have raised the issue with an authority specifically created to investigate such matters.

However, there are also disadvantages to this approach. First, the alleged misconduct may be so grave that it will prove impossible to avoid it without injustice. Secondly, there is no guarantee that the bar authority in question will investigate the alleged misconduct—particularly where it is permitted or disputed according to its own standards. Thirdly, this solution does not solve the problem of divergent ethical standards: as has been seen, many counsel do not belong to a national bar. It is unfair to hold professional counsel to one standard and amateur counsel to another simply by virtue of the fact that the former happen to hold a licence to practice. Fourthly, even if the national bar sanctions the misconduct, the deterrent effect is likely to be negligible. Consequently, for the immediate future it appears inevitable that international courts will continue—in the absence of a unified international bar authority, examined in Chapter 10—to be confronted with problems arising from divergent ethical standards in their practice. Thus, assuming that the prescription and enforcement of common ethical standards by international courts is desirable, two discrete issues arise: (1) whether international courts have the legal power to regulate counsel; and (2) whether they have the requisite expertise and resources to do so fairly.

9.1.1 Powers to Regulate Counsel

No international court is vested with express powers to regulate all representatives equally. Practice hitherto suggests that the legal basis for a particular power varies

[6] Interview with Judge Sir Adrian Fulford.

from court to court. Some powers are expressly conferred upon the court through its statute,[7] other powers are implicitly conferred through a broad statutory power to frame rules of procedure[8] and still other powers have been prescribed by courts invoking an inherent jurisdiction in procedural rules or ad hoc decisions.[9] Several international courts[10] have yet to engage with the regulation of counsel in either their procedural rules or cases whereas others[11] have done so to varying degrees. The overall picture is further complicated by the political relationship of each court with its constituency, particularly the autonomy of the court to control its own procedures. Thus, there is a live question of whether international courts have the legal power to regulate counsel.

Hitherto, the practice of international courts has been mixed and inconsistent. In 1992, a Chamber of the Iran-US Claims Tribunal held that the Tribunal 'does not have the power to impose sanctions or disciplinary measures for the presentation of false evidence' by counsel.[12] However, this should not be treated as authoritative since it was the unreasoned comment of one Chamber and the possibility cannot be excluded that the Tribunal, invoking its broad power to Article 15(1) of its Rules of Procedure,[13] would exclude a representative from proceedings for fraudulent or otherwise abusive misconduct. It is also inconsistent with other jurisprudence by the Tribunal in which it invoked an inherent jurisdiction concerning revision of awards based upon 'forged documents or perjury',[14] ordering a party to stay parallel domestic litigation[15] and jurisdiction and provisional measures orders.

In two ICTY cases,[16] the Trial Chambers held that they did not have inherent jurisdiction to prescribe a code of conduct or exercise disciplinary jurisdiction for prosecutors. However, those unreasoned decisions are inconsistent with the broader power of contempt of court that the Tribunal expressly based upon inherent jurisdiction.[17] It is illogical to invoke an inherent jurisdiction to prescribe a crime for procedural abuses whilst denying a jurisdiction to prescribe professional standards and sanctions for similar, if less severe, procedural misconduct. Consequently, these decisions are unpersuasive.

[7] Eg Rome Statute, Arts 15, 42, 46–7; ECJ Rules, Art 35.

[8] Eg Rome Statute, Art 51; ICC Rules, Rules 8, 22.

[9] Eg *Hrvatska*; Sarvarian, 'Problems of Ethical Standards for Representatives before ICSID Tribunals' 10(1) *LPICT* (2011), 67–134, 96–9, 128–9, 96–7.

[10] Eg the IACtHR, AUCJ, PCA, WTO DSB, Ir-USCT, and ITLOS.

[11] Eg the ICJ, ECJ, ECtHR, ICSID tribunals, ICTY, ICTR, SCSL, and ICC.

[12] *Gabay*, 40–8.

[13] 'Subject to these Rules, the arbitral tribunal may conduct the arbitration in such manner as it considers appropriate, provided that the parties are treated with equality and that at any stage of the proceedings each party is given a full opportunity of presenting its case.'

[14] *Ram*, 383–92, 387–8 (paras 16–17).

[15] *E-Systems*, 51-64, 59.

[16] *Kovačević*; *Furundžija*, paras 11–12.

[17] ICTY Rules, Rule 77(A); Buteau and Oosthuizen, 'When the Statute and Rules are Silent: The Inherent Powers of the Tribunal' in May and McDonald, *Essays on ICTY Procedure and Evidence* (2000), 65–84, 75–8. It is also implicitly inconsistent with the criminal courts' regulatory jurisdiction over defence counsel, which lacks an express statutory basis. Eg Rome Statute, Art 112(2); ICC Rules, Rule 8.

Three recent decisions concerning the application of inherent jurisdiction to the regulation of counsel have been rendered by ICSID tribunals.[18] In the *Libananco* arbitration, allegations of espionage by Turkey prompted an application to exclude it from proceedings. The tribunal declared:

> These allegations and counter-allegations strike at principles which lie at the very heart of the ICSID arbitral process, and the Tribunal is bound to approach them accordingly. Among the principles affected are: basic procedural fairness, respect for confidentiality and legal privilege... the right of parties to seek advice and to advance their respective cases freely and without interference; and no doubt others as well. For its own part, the Tribunal would add to the list respect for the Tribunal itself, as the organ freely chosen by the Parties for the binding settlement of their dispute in accordance with the ICSID Convention. It requires no further recital by the Tribunal to establish either that these are indeed fundamental principles, or why they are. Nor does the Tribunal doubt for a moment that, like any other international tribunal, it must be regarded as endowed with the inherent powers required to preserve the integrity of its own process—even if the remedies open to it are necessarily different from those that might be available to a domestic court of law in an ICSID Member State. The Tribunal would express the principle as being that parties have an obligation to arbitrate fairly and in good faith and that an arbitral tribunal has the inherent jurisdiction to ensure that this obligation is complied with; this principle applies in all arbitrations, including investment arbitration, and to all parties, including States (even in the exercise of their sovereign powers).[19]

Whilst the case only indirectly concerned counsel[20] in that the orders sought were directed at controlling parties' conduct, it is analogous because of the nature of the misconduct, the similar remedy of exclusion, and the rationale of procedural integrity.

In the *Hrvatska* decision of 6 May 2008, an ICSID tribunal (Mr David Williams QC, Mr Jan Paulsson, and the Honourable Charles Brower) relied upon Article 44 of the ICSID Convention[21] as providing a partial 'textual foothold' for the inherent powers doctrine.[22] However, this is a conflation of discrete grounds for the existence of a regulatory power. Whereas an implied power would require a 'textual foothold', an inherent jurisdiction does not because it exists to fill textual lacunae. Significantly, the tribunal cited ICTY jurisprudence on contempt in support of its assertion that '[m]ore broadly, there is an "inherent power of an international court to deal with any issues necessary for the conduct of matters falling within its jurisdiction"; that power "exists independently of any statutory reference" '.[23] Thus, this precedent may be construed either as the application of an implied power under the ICSID Convention or of a freestanding inherent jurisdiction.

[18] Sarvarian, 'Problems of Ethical Standards for Representatives before ICSID Tribunals', 128–9.

[19] *Libananco*, para 78.

[20] *Libananco*, para 79.

[21] 'Any arbitration proceeding shall be conducted in accordance with the provisions of this Section and, except as the parties otherwise agree, in accordance with the Arbitration Rules in effect on the date on which the parties consented to arbitration. If any question of procedure arises which is not covered by this Section or the Arbitration Rules or any rules agreed by the parties, the Tribunal shall decide the question.'

[22] *Hrvatska*, paras 33–4.

[23] *Hrvatska*, para 33 (note 17).

In the *Fraport* decision of 18 September 2008, an ICSID ad hoc committee (Judge Peter Tomka of the ICJ, Judge Dominique Hascher of the *Cour d'Appel de Paris*, and Professor Campbell McLachlan QC) denied the Respondent's request in the *Fraport* arbitration to exclude Mr Eric Schwartz of Dewey & LeBoeuf from proceedings for a conflict of interest arising from the contested prior representation of the Respondent in a related proceeding. Mr Schwartz was dually admitted as a California attorney and Paris *avocat* and the Committee heard submissions on the ethical rules of both bars as well as the CCBE Code. Whilst no submissions were heard on ICSID or international jurisprudence,[24] the Committee relied upon Article 44 of the ICSID Convention (with the agreement of the impugned counsel and the Respondent) to decide the application.

The Committee relied upon the 'functional justification' of protecting fairness and equality, which included the 'power and obligation to make sure that generally recognized principles relating to conflict of interest and the protection of the confidentiality of information imparted by clients to their lawyers are complied with'.[25] The Committee observed that questions concerning representation affects the rights of both parties but emphasized that, as it lacked 'deontological responsibilities', it '[had] no power to rule on an allegation of misconduct under any such professional rules as may apply' so that 'its concern [was] therefore limited to the fair conduct of the proceedings before it'.[26] Whilst the Committee specifically asserted that it was not relying upon any specific set of ethical standards, it ultimately rejected the application on the factual ground of lack of evidence of a real risk of the disclosure of confidential information.[27]

Thus, the legal basis for the *Fraport* decision was an implied power to regulate counsel within the Article 44 express power to decide procedural questions. Despite the lack of argumentation concerning prior international jurisprudence on the doctrine of inherent jurisdiction, this is a convincing basis upon which to decide the application that was clearly connected to the functional justification. Whilst the consent of the parties and the impugned counsel is practically useful, it is not determinative. However, the Committee's assertion that its decision had no deontological implications is unpersuasive because an exclusion of counsel from proceedings for conflict of interest, or even factual findings, has reputational implications for that counsel in the legal services marketplace.

In the *Rompetrol* decision of 14 January 2010, an ICSID tribunal (Sir Franklin Berman QC, Mr Donald Donovan, and the Honourable Marc Lalonde QC) reserved its position on inherent jurisdiction but rejected an application to exclude counsel for conflict of interest due to professional links with an arbitrator on factual grounds.[28] The Tribunal grounded the doctrine in the right to a fair trial and acknowledged that these would be opposed to the statutory framework based upon the right of parties to choose their own legal representation.[29] Whilst the Tribunal cast doubt on the doctrine, it did not disapprove of the *Hrvatska* decision but distinguished it with respect to the degree of potential prejudice caused by the alleged

[24] *Fraport*, para 36. [25] *Fraport*, para 37. [26] *Fraport*, paras 38–9.
[27] *Fraport*, paras 41, 54–5. [28] *Rompetrol*, paras 25–7. [29] *Rompetrol*, paras 15–16, 20.

conflicts of interest.[30] Thus, the view of the Tribunal appeared to be that the inherent jurisdiction doctrine may apply to the regulation of counsel but that it was not yet settled and should in any case be exercised sparingly. There was no analysis of Article 44 or of the *Libananco* and *Fraport* decisions.

This survey of the jurisprudence suggests that there is as yet no general consensus amongst international courts concerning the applicability of inherent jurisdiction to the regulation of counsel. Since the legal source of the doctrine has yet to be authoritatively determined, international courts have often cited a broad statutory power to decide procedural questions as their legal basis for the regulation of counsel. Whilst this is a logical and persuasive foundation, the language of implied power should be clearly distinguished from that of inherent jurisdiction. Whereas an implied power grounded in the treaty provides a set of powers, including the regulation of counsel, the doctrine of inherent jurisdiction exists to fill specific and narrow procedural gaps.

In considering the nature of the doctrine of inherent jurisdiction, a comprehensive analysis is found in the recent works of Dr Chester Brown.[31] In examining the jurisprudence, he concludes that its origin principally lies in common law jurisdictions and that its rationale for international courts is 'the need to ensure the carrying out of the functions that have been expressly conferred upon them'.[32] He argues that this functional justification stems from the jurisprudence concerning the administration of justice, particularly the prevention of procedural abuses by parties.[33] He asserts that the doctrine is circumscribed by courts' statutes and 'the relationship between each particular international court and the parties'.[34] Whilst this book generally endorses these conclusions, they may be further developed by connecting the doctrine to the duty of procedural integrity.

Although international courts have generally not grounded their invocations of inherent jurisdiction in a source of law, scholarship has offered four potential sources: (1) the functional justification; (2) the doctrine of implied powers; (3) the general principle of law recognized by common law jurisdictions; and (4) the identity of international courts as judicial bodies. In examining these four bases, it is suggested that the doctrine of inherent jurisdiction is based either upon a general principle of law deriving from national jurisdictions or upon natural law empowering international courts to discharge their duty to protect procedural integrity. Neither the functional justification, doctrine of implied powers nor the identity of international courts as judicial bodies provides a satisfactory legal basis for inherent jurisdiction.

The functional justification provides a convincing rationale for the doctrine because its original purpose in common law jurisdictions and subsequent adoption

[30] *Rompetrol*, paras 22–7.

[31] Brown, 'The Inherent Powers of International Courts and Tribunals', 66 *BYIL* (2005), 195–244; Brown, *A Common Law of International Adjudication* (2007), 55–82. See Brown (2005), 197 (note 11) for others.

[32] Brown (2007), 71.

[33] Brown (2007), 71

[34] Brown (2007), 80.

by international courts has been to safeguard the integrity of the judicial process.[35] This purpose is consistent with the identity of international courts as judicial bodies bound by duties of impartiality, integrity, and independence. However, the functional justification, though compelling, does not provide the legal basis for inherent jurisdiction.

An implied power is rooted in a statutory provision as a logical assumption or outcome of it. An inherent jurisdiction need only be invoked in cases where an international court is faced with a procedural problem for which no express or implied power exists. Consequently, it is a subsidiary basis for an international court to solve procedural dilemma and may *only* be invoked to fill lacunae.[36] It is displaced by an express or implied power and may not be invoked to justify a wider discretion than prescribed under that power. Thus, the necessity to invoke an inherent power derives from a gap concerning a procedural matter in the statute of the court or tribunal.

The first plausible source for inherent jurisdiction is its commonality to national jurisdictions, particularly in the common law world.[37] On this approach, the doctrine derives from the judicial process, which accords with its historical origin and expressly recognizes its functional rationale to protect the integrity of that (national or international) process. The applicability of the doctrine to international advocacy is particularly persuasive because of the analogy between party-led adversarial procedure and the practical dependence of international courts upon parties. The need for safeguards to protect procedural integrity makes inherent jurisdiction a practical necessity.

However, it is arguable that there are two key differences between national and international jurisdictions. First, national courts have asserted their powers within constitutional frameworks that operate upon different theoretical foundations to those of international courts. The lack of a comparable constitutional mandate to exercise such judicial powers, it could be argued, renders the claim of international courts to exercise the same regulatory powers tenuous. However, this objection may ultimately be discounted as a distinction without difference because, functionally, national and international courts are both tasked with adjudication.

Secondly, at least one party in any international litigation must be a State, which is not the case before national courts. On this argument, States may vest their own courts with inherent jurisdiction whilst denying it to international courts and thereby amplify their own influence as parties. Since the international judicial system historically developed out of a laissez-faire, party-centred procedure, therefore, international courts may only regulate advocacy to the extent that they are statutorily empowered to do so. This argument may also be discounted as it not only fails to account for international courts' accepted invocation of inherent jurisdiction in other procedural contexts but it also ignores the possibility of procedural lacunae. As this book has shown, States from the PCA and PCIJ onwards generally scrutinized the issue of representation scantly in negotiations for international court statutes, often leaving the matter over for international courts to decide.

[35] Brown (2007), 205–8. [36] Brown (2005), 239–40. [37] Brown (2005), 231.

In this context, the following propositions may be advanced: (1) international courts with broad powers to prescribe procedural rules possess an implied power to regulate counsel; (2) the legal source of inherent jurisdiction is a general principle of law deriving from national jurisdictions; and (3) the doctrine is applicable to the regulation of counsel due to the clear connection between the role of counsel and the procedural integrity. In the absence of a contrary express statutory provision, the applicability of inherent jurisdiction to the regulation of counsel is supported by the contempt powers that the criminal tribunals have claimed and the connexion between its functional rationale and the procedural role of counsel. Thus, international courts may invoke either an implied power or, in its absence, the doctrine of inherent jurisdiction to enable themselves to regulate counsel in order to discharge their duties of fairness, equality, and procedural integrity.

9.1.2 Practical Ability to Regulate Counsel

Assuming that international courts have jurisdiction to regulate counsel in their proceedings to protect procedural integrity, the next question is whether they are practically capable of effectively exercising that jurisdiction. This raises two issues: (1) the qualifications of international judges and registrars; and (2) the regulatory architecture of international courts. In examining these two points, the competence of international courts to regulate counsel is linked to the ongoing debate concerning the qualification standards applicable to judicial candidates as well as the ability of the courts to construct a transparent disciplinary system that safeguards natural justice rights of hearing and defence for impugned counsel. In order to enlist the cooperation and support of practitioners in the professionalization process, it is imperative that adequate assurances of fairness be offered to preclude the arbitrary exercise of the jurisdiction.

The qualifications of candidates for international judges and the systems of election have been criticized as at times being inadequate and deleterious to judicial independence.[38] Clearly, this issue concerning the general integrity and competence is connected to that of professionalization of counsel because practitioners are unlikely to support their regulation by judges elected under a questionable system with questionable results. The consequences of the exercise of disciplinary jurisdiction by international judges can be potentially devastating to the professional livelihoods of counsel, which accordingly demands that it be exercised by persons of integrity and competence observing natural justice standards. Even the criticism of counsel in public is arguably a form of sanction.[39]

In addition to the question of the general integrity and competence of successful candidates for judicial office and the transparency of the electoral systems, there is an issue concerning their expertise to regulate counsel. International judges come from a variety of professional backgrounds; those who have primarily been diplomats, academics, government officials or career judges have often never been professional

[38] Mackenzie et al, *Selecting International Judges: Principles, Process, and Politics* (2010), 173–5.

[39] Eg *Furundžija* and *Lubanga*, Chapter 6.

advocates. It is questionable whether such persons are in a position to competently regulate counsel without firsthand experience of the realities of advocacy. In the course of 14 interviews with serving or former international judges,[40] a rough difference could be detected on whether international courts should regulate counsel between those judges with a background as practitioners and those without: the former group was generally in favour of regulation whereas the latter group was generally against.

This pattern cut across geographical and jurisdictional lines. Although the majority of those in favour of regulation were from common law jurisdictions and the majority against were from civil law jurisdictions, virtually all of those interviewees asserted that their views were not based upon systemic differences. Moreover, there is a logical explanation for this pattern, namely, that in the common law world the great majority of judges are recruited from senior counsel whereas in the civil law world counsel and judges are recruited separately. Interviewees also cited the institutional culture of each court as a major factor with the inter-State courts even more wary of 'State sovereignty' than the mixed courts. The criminal court judges, by contrast, were readier to regulate counsel.

Thus, it is suggested that this pattern amongst common law and civil law judges is predominately attributable to professional rather than jurisdictional background. As one interviewee expressed it:

> There is undoubtedly a real advantage for this court in having a certain number of judges who have previously been advocates or judges, thereby having gained a real understanding of the problems that will occur once they come to the ICC, and how to solve them. In the field of ethical problems as regards court proceedings, you only really learn the rights and wrongs of how to react from practice and experience rather than by reading a book. The balance between those judges who have experience of judging or criminal trials versus ex-diplomats, academics etc, is a real question in our institution.
>
> To some degree, at the ICC the judges have engaged with the regulation of counsel through Chapter IV of the Regulations of Court. Personally, I have no difficulty in dealing with these issues given my background and experience. I believe that national origins have no real bearing on this. Those who have been judges or criminal advocates, wherever they come from, are familiar with the issues that come up in practice. I believe that the shyness of certain judges concerning these difficulties, in the main, comes from their inexperience.[41]

The link between professional background and willingness to regulate counsel was also noted by another interviewee from a civil law country and former practitioner:

> Absolutely correct [that it will be difficult for judges who have not served themselves as practising counsel to detect or fully understand the sorts of problems that arise for counsel], and this seems to me to be self-evident. For example, I have an advantage in this area over those of my colleagues who have principally been academics, for example, in that I have sometimes had to explain how counsel is fairly charging a certain amount of money in fees

[40] Namely: Judges Higgins (UK—ICJ), Keith (NZ—ICJ), Koroma (SIE—ICJ), Cot (FRA—ITLOS), Forwood (UK—EU General Court), Jaeger (LUX—EU General Court), Edward (UK—ECJ), Fora (SWE—ECtHR), Fulford (UK—ICC), Harhoff (DEN—ICTY), Pocar (ITA—ICTY) and Doherty (UK—SCSL). Two other judges were interviewed on condition of anonymity.

[41] Interview with Judge Fulford.

for documents which they say is only X number of pages in length. However, I can explain that, as a counsel, it is actually quicker to produce a document that is many times longer than that short document but to produce a concise document that is well-drafted for the judges to read takes many more hours. For these types of matters, it is important that judges called upon to deal with disciplinary matters concerning counsel have the background necessary to see all of the issues.[42]

Whilst those judges who expressed sceptical views concerning regulation are not uniformly non-practitioners and raised cogent arguments concerning jurisdiction, necessity, and enforceability, the divide between practitioners and non-practitioners remained striking. It is likely that lack of experience is a factor for scepticism.

Since there is no express qualification requirement for international judges to be competent to regulate counsel, there is a practical question concerning their practical ability to do so. One way to address this is to ensure that judges with practical experience as counsel are appointed as the presiding judges of trials to ensure that an experienced hand manages the advocates and deals with ethical issues that may arise. Another technique utilized at the Special Court for Sierra Leone (SCSL) is to appoint former practitioners with expertise in counsel ethics as disciplinary judges of the court.

These techniques necessitate a minimal number of judges on the bench who are able to assume these roles. Whilst it is pragmatic for at least a percentage of judges serving at international courts at any one time to be experienced practitioners, there are no requirements in the system of judicial election to that effect. In the absence of statutory reform to admission requirements, one method may be for the serving judges to publicly request (eg through an annual address by the President of the Court) that States nominate candidates with, inter alia, experience as practitioners. Whilst it is possible that informal lobbying already occurs in judicial elections, a more transparent and formalized procedure would lead to a more legitimate and meritocratic process. These considerations also apply to registrars who often have more frequent and closer contact with counsel than judges and play a regulatory role. However, the efficacy of these tools will clearly vary from court to court. Whereas permanent infrastructure of international courts proper (eg the ICJ, ITLOS, ECJ, and ECtHR) provide greater continuity, arbitral institutions like ICSID, the PCA, and NAFTA may struggle to regulate parties' choice of arbitrator.

Architectural reform raises not only the question of judicial qualifications but also that of the disciplinary process. There is a need to avoid the arbitrary exercise of discipline due to the potentially drastic consequences for the professional livelihoods of impugned counsel. Natural justice rights of hearing, appeal, and neutrality are critical to instil confidence in the justice of the disciplinary jurisdiction. Whilst trial judges have a duty to maintain the discipline of the courtroom, which in turn requires that they have sanctions at their disposal, the construction of an external disciplinary board to consider referrals from the court would clearly be advantageous. A particularly useful technique is the creation of a formal link between the disciplinary board and the home bar of the impugned counsel.

[42] Interview with Judge Elisabet Fora (ECtHR), 15 October 2010 (cited with permission).

As suggested in Chapter 10, the true solution to the double deontology problem is the relinquishment by national bars of extraterritorial disciplinary jurisdiction for conduct before international courts. This, however, will only be possible upon the harmonization of international courts' and national bars' disciplinary jurisdictions. The supremacy of the disciplinary jurisdiction of the international court over that of national bars is vital to ensure that counsel are not subjected to double jeopardy, divergent national ethical standards are not applied to judge identical conduct, and that the disciplinary body is able to hear the complaint promptly with access to evidence.

9.2 Articulation of Common Ethical Standards

The second core issue that this chapter examines is the feasibility of articulating common ethical standards for counsel before international courts. There are a number of challenges facing this task. First, there is the problem of harmonizing divergent national standards that conflict with each other. Clearly, there are times when harmonization through compromise is impossible because the degree of divergence is too great. In addition, it is impossible to 'agree to disagree' before shared proceedings—ruling out the transnational conflict-of-laws approach.

Secondly, there is the problem of prescribing standards based upon shared ideology and values such as justice and the rule of law that, even if universally accepted, are neither uniformly understood nor universally applied to the same standard. For example, positing an 'overriding duty to justice' over the client or the State as a fundamental ethical principle for counsel is more readily harmonious to jurisdictions with traditions of professional independence and a relatively weak market ideology. Amidst pressures for a more client-oriented or State-oriented philosophy, the identification of common ground for the basic identity of the international bar is challenging and vital.

Thirdly, there is the problem of striking the appropriate balance between the incisiveness necessary to ensure that common standards are practically effective and the consensus needed to instil confidence in them. Standards that please everyone are necessarily so banal and anodyne as to be practically useless. Standards that offend everyone will not be applied for want of a mandate. Careful and pragmatic drafting that identifies this delicate balance is required to ground common standards in the realities and needs of international litigation rather than a dogmatic national approach.

9.2.1 ILA Hague Principles

During the twentieth century, there were no common ethical standards for counsel before international courts which (with the partial exception of the ICC and the ad hoc criminal tribunals) still lack them to the present day. One reason for this has been the perceived difficulty of identifying universal principles common to the various national traditions discussed in Chapter 2. Today, some argue that the regulation of representatives by international courts and tribunals according to prescribed ethical principles is futile owing to differences of national culture.

As explored in Chapter 3, even in the days of the PCIJ and increasingly in the late twentieth century individual commentators (notably international judges) were identifying ethical standards for counsel as a practical problem and calling for the establishment of an 'international bar' to address them. To address this gap, the ILA Study Group on the Practice and Procedure of International Courts and Tribunals ('the Study Group') decided on 12 June 2009 to take up the matter.[43] On 18 August 2010, the Study Group proposed the 'Hague Principles on Ethical Standards for Counsel Appearing before International Courts and Tribunals'[44] ('the Hague Principles') at the 74th ILA Conference in the Hague.

The ILA is an organization whose mission is 'the study, clarification and development of international law, both public and private, and the furtherance of international understanding and respect for international law'.[45] The Study Group was created in 2001 with the mandate of inquiring into contemporary, procedural problems within international courts and tribunals. This is significant for two reasons: (1) its authoritativeness in the area of international advocacy is enhanced by the expertise of its membership and its focus upon the international judicial procedure; and (2) its mandate is limited by the fact that ILA does not have a direct relationship with national bars.

Significantly, the Study Group's first topic of inquiry was the ethical standards of judges in international courts and tribunals which culminated in the proposition of the 'ILA Burgh House Principles on the Independence of the International Judiciary'.[46] One factor behind the Study Group's decision to select counsel ethics as its second topic was the desire expressed by judges who assisted it in the formulation of the Burgh House Principles that ethical standards for counsel also be addressed.[47] Thus, there is an important connection between ethical standards for judges and for counsel which affects the prospect of international judges regulating counsel.

The Study Group held three working meetings over the course of one year with the aim of drafting a text of common ethical principles for counsel before international courts. Its meetings, conducted under the 'Chatham House Rule' of confidentiality, included a range of individual views. Besides a core group of members participating in the working meetings, the Study Group had the benefit of input from several overseas members as well as serving and former members of the international judiciary as advisers. The composition of the Study Group—including practitioners

[43] The author served as co-rapporteur to the Study Group throughout the drafting process of the Hague Principles. The views expressed in this book are entirely the author's own and do not necessarily reflect those of any individual member of the Study Group or of the Study Group as a whole.

[44] 10(1) *LPICT* (2011) 6–15. For commentary by Study Group members, see Sands, 'The ILA Hague Principles on Ethical Standards for Counsel before International Courts and Tribunals', 10(1) *LPICT* (2011), 1–5; Kazazi, 'Commentary on the Hague Principles on Ethical Standards for Counsel Appearing before International Courts and Tribunals', 10(1) *LPICT* (2011), 17–23; Cot, 'The Hague vs. Burgh House', 10(1) *LPICT* (2011), 25–9.

[45] Online: <http://www.ila-hq.org/en/about_us/index.cfm> (Accessed: 4 May 2011).

[46] Online: <http://www.ila-hq.org/en/committees/study_groups.cfm/cid/1012> (Accessed: 19 July 2011).

[47] ILA Study Group, Summary Report of First Meeting (12 June 2009), on file with author.

and academics from a variety of jurisdictions and professional backgrounds[48]—was intended to bring together a diverse range of views concerning these issues in order to produce a balanced and informed text. At the formal presentation of the Hague Principles at the ILA Conference in August 2010, the Study Group benefited from the criticism offered by a mixed panel by regional and professional background comprising Professor John Dugard of South Africa and Judge Kamal Hossein of Bangladesh.[49]

The Study Group, conscious of its limited mandate, intended the Hague Principles to be a first step in sparking debate and future development by addressing 'gaps' and recurring issues in practice on a general level rather than draft a comprehensive 'code of conduct'.[50] This cautious approach emphasizing consensus can be detected throughout the text. As Professor Dugard observed, they 'clearly reflect the "lowest common denominator" of a large committee with many compromises and few risks taken on the serious issues'. Additional criticisms included the omission of issues arising in criminal practice, the assumption of a self-regulated rather than externally-regulated 'international bar', a naive assumption of counsel 'independence' towards clients, the omission of the 'cab rank rule', and the tolerance of 'witness proofing'.[51] Anonymous comments from interviewees also suggest that some judges felt that they had had insufficient input into the Principles. Finally, the drafting process was relatively short (one year) with uneven participation from the Study Group members and no consultation with national bars. The aims of the Study Group were accordingly modest.

The Principles adopt a conservative or vague position on several sensitive issues upon which there exist national and philosophical divisions.[52] For example, Principle 2.1 declares that 'counsel has a duty of loyalty to his or her client consistent with a duty to the international court or tribunal to contribute to the fair administration of justice and the promotion of the rule of law'. This statement, virtually identical to Article 3(iv) of the ICTY Code of Conduct, adopts a neutral position between conflicting duties to justice, court, and client and suggests differences between the ' "realists" principally including those who regularly appear as counsel and the "ethical" school who emphasised due process and duties to justice'.[53]

This sort of compromise is significant because it is indicative of the difficulty that will be encountered during the articulation of common ethical standards, namely, the resistance from a client-oriented culture to its displacement by

[48] A list of the Study Group members is appended to the Hague Principles. The Study Group lacked members from international criminal tribunals and from African and Asian jurisdictions.

[49] International Law Association, *Report of the Seventy-Fourth Conference* (2010), 956–60.

[50] Sands, 'The ILA Hague Principles on Ethical Standards for Counsel before International Courts and Tribunals', 3; Kazazi, 'Commentary on the Hague Principles on Ethical Standards for Counsel Appearing before International Courts and Tribunals', 21.

[51] ILA Report (2010), 956–7.

[52] Eg the admission of non-members of national bars (Principle 1.1); 'double deontology' between national and international standards (Principle 1.3); prioritisation of fundamental duties (Principle 2.1); the scope of confidentiality (Principles 2.4, 3.4); and withdrawal from representation (Principle 3.6).

[53] ILA Report (2010), 960.

justice-oriented values. In the words of a former judge who spoke on condition of anonymity:

> I would say that it is difficult to write it all down given the very wide diversity of national approach. Almost certainly this entails trying to prescribe rules preventing lawyers from obeying client instructions, which is quite a big step to take. This lies at the heart of this entire discussion and the real source of difficulty is the diversity of views concerning the fundamental duties of lawyers.

The creation and inculcation of an 'international judicial culture' is not something that can happen through enacting a code of conduct or in a few years of practice. However, prescribed standards can provide a platform upon which advocates and judges can build until the accumulation of practice incrementally coalesces into a justice-oriented professional culture. Thus, the articulation of an overriding duty to justice is vital as a declaration of intent and of the fundamental values of the new culture being created.

Moreover, there are also matters upon which the Principles are largely or wholly silent.[54] They largely serve to illuminate existing problems rather than to solve them. Whilst they represent the agreement of individual counsel, judges, and academics from diverse national and professional backgrounds, their conservative and consensual nature largely does not offer solutions to those politically sensitive problems. Without further work, this largely dilutes from the utility of the Principles to solve the practical problems they avoid. To create ethical standards that will solve those problems, the dynamic of consensus must give way to the imposition of justice-based values.

Clearly, this is an exercise that can only be undertaken by the international judiciary vested with the requisite authority. Whilst several judges interviewed for this book expressed a preference for counsel to prescribe their own standards rather than judges to impose them, the Principles illustrate that the 'lowest common denominator' is the inexorable outcome of this consensual dynamic. Although the Principles represent an attempt to spark debate on this important practical topic, they also demonstrate the limitations of their own methodological approach. Moreover, the Study Group's express recognition[55] of an inherent jurisdiction for international courts is a clear call by counsel for greater activity by the judiciary to regulate the bar. Thus, the Hague Principles both expressly and implicitly demonstrate the necessity for a compulsory, not only consensual, dynamic to gradually create an international judicial culture that prioritizes justice and the rule of law over the narrow, tactical interests of parties seeking to win cases at all costs.

[54] Eg the standard of 'reasonable knowledge' (Principles 3.2, 3.6, 4.1, 4.3.1, 4.3.3, and 6.1); acceptance of briefs to address prejudice towards clients (Principle 3.5); witness examination, particularly extra-testimonial contacts during testimony and interrogation technique; enforcement of the Principles, including reporting misconduct by counsel, judges or officials; and the reasonableness of fees.

[55] ILA Hague Principles, Preamble.

9.2.2 IBA Guidelines

The IBA is an organization of national bars with the aim of 'supporting the establishment of law and the administration of justice worldwide'.[56] Its membership now comprises more than 40,000 individual lawyers and 197 bar associations and law societies spanning all of the continents,[57] providing its activities with a uniquely global scope. In 2008, the IBA Arbitration Committee formed a Task Force on Counsel Ethics in International Arbitration[58] ('the Task Force') for the purpose of studying the different ethical and cultural norms, standards, and disciplinary rules that may apply to counsel in international arbitration.[59] The mandate of the Task Force is 'to investigate whether the lack of international guidelines and conflicting norms in counsel ethics undermines the fundamental protections of fairness and equality of treatment and the integrity of international arbitration proceedings'.[60] Although this book has examined the practice of three international courts rather than that of international investment tribunals in the ICSID and NAFTA organizations in order to more accurately compare their experiences with one another, the field of international arbitration is an area in which the problem of divergent ethical standards has become increasingly prominent.[61]

The ethical standards that the IBA has already produced[62] are formally exhortatory but can be applied in practice due to their acceptance by the international arbitration community. This suggests that formally exhortatory ethical guidelines can nevertheless be practically effective. In this respect, the IBA Guidelines on Party Representation in International Arbitration 2013 represent a modest first step of potential practical utility.

However, there are obstacles in the path of professionalization over and above the problems that apply to international courts generally. Chief amongst these is the problem of enforcement, which is particularly acute in the arbitral context. This is due to its party-controlled procedure, the flexibility of which is one of its hallmark features. This militates against that of individual tribunals to control procedure and, by extension, advocacy. It is arguable that, unless a way can be found to ground the enforcement of common ethical standards in party consent, the imposition of such standards by arbitral tribunals would potentially damage the arbitration market by negating one of its most attractive features.

[56] Online: <http://www.ibanet.org/About_the_IBA/About_the_IBA.aspx> (Accessed: 5 July 2011).

[57] Online: <http://www.ibanet.org/About_the_IBA/About_the_IBA.aspx> (Accessed: 5 July 2011).

[58] The author has been a member of the Task Force since August 2011. The views expressed in this book are entirely the author's own and do not necessarily reflect those of any individual member of the Task Force or of the Task Force as a whole.

[59] 'IBA Task Force on Counsel Ethics in International Arbitration Survey', online: <http://www.ibanet.org/Article/Detail.aspx?ArticleUid=610bbf6e-cf02-45ae-8c3a-70dfdb2274a5> (Accessed: 5 July 2011).

[60] 'IBA Task Force on Counsel Ethics in International Arbitration Survey', online: <http://www.ibanet.org/Article/Detail.aspx?ArticleUid=610bbf6e-cf02-45ae-8c3a-70dfdb2274a5> (Accessed: 5 July 2011).

[61] Sarvarian, 'Problems of Ethical Standards for Representatives before ICSID Tribunals', 69 (note 5).

[62] The Guidelines on Conflicts of Interest in International Arbitration 2004, the Rules on the Taking of Evidence in International Arbitration 2010, the Rules of Ethics for International Arbitrators and the International Principles on Conduct for the Legal Profession 2011.

On the other hand, it is arguable that the death of international arbitration would be an exaggerated outcome of professionalization. First, by rectifying existing practical problems and thereby strengthening procedural integrity, parties may react favourably to a regulatory framework requiring *all* representatives to observe strict ethical standards based upon principles of fairness, integrity and equality. Secondly, the authority of arbitral tribunals to regulate counsel can be based upon party consent. For example, this could be achieved for institutional arbitration by amending standard arbitral rules on representation.[63] Another way to engage party consent (particularly important for ad hoc arbitral tribunals[64]) is to require counsel to adopt a code of conduct at the outset of proceedings whilst permitting them to amend optional provisions by common consent. Whilst another alternative is for national bars to prescribe a common code for international arbitration, this would necessarily be inapplicable to those representatives who are not members of national bars and so must be rejected as inadequate.

Alternatively, it is possible that the momentum for professionalization in international arbitration can be provided by the adoption of common ethical standards by international courts with a clear mandate to do so. The permanent international courts are, *mutatis mutandis*, in this respect better-placed to take the lead in doing so. Although the problems arising from divergent ethical standards have not yet attracted the same degree of attention before these courts as in the investment arbitration context, they nevertheless exist. Since the mandate provided by the participation of national bars in the legislative process is vital to the success of the professionalization project, another organization with the potential to undertake the task is the CCBE.

9.2.3 CCBE

The CCBE is an organization comprising national bars and law societies from forty-one European States with the principal aim of representing the interests of its members in dealings with EU and other international institutions.[65] The founding of the CCBE in 1960 was sparked by the creation of the EEC through the Treaty of Rome 1957, which raised fears of a threat to the independence of European lawyers amongst the presidents of national bars.[66] The CCBE's membership includes the bar associations of all twenty-seven EU members alongside those of fourteen States that are members of the Council of Europe. Only six bar associations of Council of Europe members are not members.[67]

[63] Eg ICSID Arbitration Rules, Rule 18; PCA Optional Rules for Arbitrating Disputes between Two States, Art 4.

[64] Eg UN Convention on the Law of the Sea 1982, Annex VII, Art 5.

[65] 'Objectives', online: <http://www.ccbe.org/index.php?id=16&L=0/index.php%3Fid%3D1> (Accessed: 20 December 2011).

[66] 'History', online: <http://www.ccbe.org/index.php?id=15&L=0> (Accessed: 20 December 2011).

[67] Andorra, Azerbaijan, Bosnia and Herzegovina, Monaco, Russia, and San Marino.

In 1988, the CCBE created the 'Code of Conduct for European Lawyers', which has been integrated into the national rules of all forty-one members.[68] Its provisions, backed by disciplinary sanctions at the national level, are binding upon some seven hundred thousand European lawyers.[69] Whilst the CCBE Code applies to transnational legal services throughout the Common Market—which does not apply to the ECJ or ECtHR—it has nevertheless indirectly been influential as a source of inspiration for ethical standards for international courts (eg the ILA Hague Principles). Its authoritativeness stems not from its textual provisions, which are highly anodyne,[70] but rather from its bindingness based upon the consent of a wide range of national bars.

In considering this precedent, the possibility arises whether the CCBE can play a role in the development of codes of conduct for the ECJ and ECtHR. It is conceivable that such a code, based upon the consent of the national bars in consultation with the Courts, would be a relatively straightforward first step in the professionalization of the international judicial system. One of the functions of the CCBE is the articulation and development of professionalism and its mandate is particularly powerful. Moreover, the CCBE maintains a permanent delegation to the ECJ as well as a committee on its relationship with the ECtHR. Crucially, a code adopted by the organization in plenary would be binding upon its members.[71] Such a code could be adopted *ex proprio motu* by the ECtHR and would be likely to be adopted by the EU Council for the ECJ.

However, there are also obstacles that should be taken into account. One is the divide between the bars of States that are members of both the EU and the CoE and those that are members of the CoE only. The former group of States are full CCBE members with voting rights whereas the latter are associate members without voting rights.[72] In this respect, a code of conduct for the Strasbourg Court would be problematic if it did not also have the approval of the associate members. It may in any case prove controversial since six CoE members do not have membership in the CCBE—most notably Russia. Thus, it may be politic to begin with a relatively straightforward code of conduct for the ECJ and subsequently articulate one for the ECtHR.

A second problem involves reconciling the need for consensus for textual integrity. Whilst this is a key issue for the professionalization process in general, it may particularly apply to the CCBE context because of the failure of a recent initiative to prescribe a code of conduct for international arbitration. The history of this project is not generally known in the public domain,[73] though it appears to be

[68] 'Status of the CCBE Code of Conduct at a national level' as of 26 May 2009, online: <http://www.ccbe.org> (Accessed: 20 December 2011).

[69] 'CCBE President's Letter to Commissioner McCreevy', 10 March 2009, online: <http://www.ccbe.org/fileadmin/user_upload/NTCdocument/Letter_to_Commission1_1239952825.pdf> (Accessed: 20 December 2011).

[70] Terry, 'An Introduction to the European Community's Legal Ethics Code Part I' 7 *GJLE* (1993-1994), 1–87.

[71] CCBE Statutes 2009, Art VI(b).

[72] CCBE Statutes 2009, Art IV.

[73] There is no reference to it on the CCBE website—online: <http://www.ccbe.org/index.php?id=25> (Accessed: 12 July 2011).

common knowledge amongst European lawyers working in the arbitration field. On 22 May 2010, the CCBE Plenary decided to appoint a working group 'to prepare some recommendations/guidelines with regard to the function, training, ethics, liability and other aspects of lawyers acting in [international arbitration]'.[74] The terms of reference included 'monitor[ing] developments in the field of arbitration at EU and international level', 'reply[ing] to EU and international consultations affecting the role of European lawyers in the field of arbitration as arbitrators, counsel or experts', and 'draw[ing] up ethical recommendations/guidelines for the use of European lawyers in arbitration'.[75]

This was, by any standard, an ambitious undertaking. It was also based upon a questionable premise, namely, that the standards produced by the Working Group for use by European lawyers in international arbitration would assist in the harmonization of ethical standards worldwide. Since European lawyers represent only one regional group amongst arbitration practitioners, a binding code of conduct would arguably have at best had a marginal effect in harmonizing standards or even have exacerbated the problem by holding European lawyers collectively to a higher standard than other counsel. Moreover, voluntary guidelines would likely have been ignored in practice unless they were exceptionally well-drafted and intrinsically authoritative. In addition to these obstacles, it appears that the Working Group was hampered by lack of expertise and interest with very few members actively participating in the research and drafting process and the bulk of the work being done by only a few individuals.

Despite these difficulties, a 'final draft' of exhortative guidelines was produced by the Working Group after less than a year of work. However, certain arbitral institutions have registered strong objections to the draft, the German CCBE delegation has called for a motion to be passed by the CCBE Standing Committee requiring the project to be stopped, and the Standing Committee appears to be in favour of stopping it.[76] In reading the draft guidelines,[77] it is easy to see why this occurred. It shows the marks of hasty drafting with verbose and imprecise language,[78] a broad remit[79] and a weak grip on the subject matter. Since it would not only be of dubious practical utility but even, due to the bindingness of CCBE rules, detrimental to European practitioners, the termination of the project would be sensible.

[74] Paul Key, 'Draft Codes of Conduct for Practitioners in Investor-State and International Commercial Arbitration: From Brazil via Brussels to Beyond?', ILA British Branch Lecture (22 June 2011).

[75] Paul Key, 'Draft Codes of Conduct for Practitioners in Investor-State and International Commercial Arbitration: From Brazil via Brussels to Beyond?', ILA British Branch Lecture (22 June 2011).

[76] Paul Key, 'Draft Codes of Conduct for Practitioners in Investor-State and International Commercial Arbitration: From Brazil via Brussels to Beyond?', ILA British Branch Lecture (22 June 2011).

[77] On file with the author.

[78] Eg CCBE Working Group 'Ethical guidelines for lawyers serving in arbitration proceedings' (on file with author), Art 4.1.1 ('Corporate spirit of the profession'): 'The corporate spirit of the profession requires a relationship of trust and co-operation between counsels for the benefit of their clients and in order to avoid unnecessary litigation and other behaviour harmful to the reputation of the profession. It can, however, never justify setting the interests of the profession against those of the client.'

[79] The Guidelines address the role of lawyers acting as arbitrators, counsel, witnesses and administrative secretaries and assistants to tribunals.

Although this experience concerns a narrow subject, it nevertheless illustrates the danger of hasty and over-ambitious drafting. Since the professionalization project is particularly dependent upon the authoritativeness of ethical standards for success and that authoritativeness depends in large part upon the strength of its drafting, a putative code of conduct for the European Courts would require exceptionally well-considered draftsmanship not only to gain the support of the European bars and the Courts but also to be of practical utility. Clarity, succinctness, logic and pragmatism are imperative to transcend the national differences towards uniformity based upon practical demands and an overarching ideal of professionalism. To achieve this outcome, the drafting committee must have eminent and expert membership, adequate time and sufficient outside consultation (eg from the judiciary and institutions).

Given these conditions, it is likely that a code of conduct could be achieved that would mark a major milestone in the professionalization project. By showing that the articulation of common ethical standards is feasible, the European Courts could take the lead in inspiring other international courts. The relatively greater homogeneity of the European bars (compared with that of all bars worldwide) and, in particular, the existence of the CCBE Code is an important advantage in this respect. Although there is considerable variation amongst European bars on ethical issues, there are also important commonalities that provide a philosophical and cultural foundation for harmonization. Through a spirit of pragmatism, flexibility, and creativity it is probable that a drafting committee could produce a useful set of common ethical standards for the European Courts.

9.3 Conclusions

This chapter has focused upon the question of the feasibility of the professionalization project. In that respect, it has addressed two critical issues, namely, the articulation of common ethical standards and their enforcement through the disciplinary jurisdictions of international courts. Obstacles have been identified that would hinder professionalization, such as the difficulty of balancing consensus with textual integrity in the prescriptive process and the need for safeguards to ensure that the judges and registrars who would enforce ethical standards are qualified to do so and observe natural justice rights for impugned counsel. However, this chapter has also suggested that the obstacles are surmountable through a pragmatic, flexible and creative approach that is sensitive to national differences and competing interests and priorities.

The politics and practicalities of professionalization are dependent upon a process that is respectful of the various interests involved yet capable of constructing an architecture that imposes justice-based values to justify the exercise. Whereas it is clearly sensible to utilize professional organizations' expertise and powers to articulate ethical standards, the input of the judiciary and institutions is also imperative. The authoritativeness of codes of conduct depends not only upon the care and rigour of the drafting process but also upon their incisiveness in addressing the very practical problems that prompted them in the first place. In this challenging process, compromise and pragmatism are called for in lieu of dogmatic and inflexible postures. In addition, international courts should be prepared to assert their regulatory jurisdictions as required to provide predictability and transparency rather than ad hoc, reactive decisions. This necessarily requires international courts to ensure that they are practically capable of discharging this task in terms of personnel and procedure.

The ILA Hague Principles have shown that common ethical standards are, to an extent, feasible for general application and the international criminal tribunals have provided templates for architectural reforms that can meet these demands. This chapter has offered two bases for international courts to assert regulatory jurisdiction over counsel, namely, an implied statutory power within a broad express power to frame procedural rules and, alternatively, the doctrine of inherent jurisdiction. Through its analysis, it has offered an answer to the legal objection to professionalization that international courts lack the power to regulate counsel. However, the policy consideration of whether international courts should exercise that jurisdiction depends upon the ability of the court to do so with competence and basic fairness. In that respect, the adoption by international courts of codes of conduct should be accompanied by architectural reforms to instil confidence in the integrity of the system and thereby propel the professionalization process forward.

10

Towards an International Bar

This chapter examines two questions: (1) the feasibility of self-regulation by the international bar; and (2) the potential consequences of the professionalization of advocacy in the international judicial system. In Chapter 9, the regulation of advocacy by international courts was explored as one avenue to professionalization whereby the onus would principally be upon the various courts to individually prescribe and enforce admission requirements, ethical standards, and disciplinary powers. Assuming that the individual court has the jurisdiction and expertise to do so, this creates the basic conditions of professionalism. As previously discussed, this appears to be the most feasible regulatory option in the near-term.

However, as explained in Chapter 1, professionalization does not require self-regulation as an architectural model. Beyond the minimal conditions for a profession, there are practical and political factors to be considered in the construction of a permanent regulatory structure. One such factor is the ability and willingness of the judiciary to regulate counsel—even if the desirability of regulation is accepted. There are legitimate doubts about this with splits of opinion amongst the judiciary and de facto bar. Interviews conducted for this book with the international judiciary suggest that the majority of the interviewed judges would prefer advocates to regulate themselves rather than to assert regulatory jurisdiction over them. The chief reason for this appears to be a desire to increase the distance between bench and bar by promoting the independence of the latter from the former.

Hence, there is a body of judicial opinion that would prefer self-regulation over the regulation of counsel by the courts. There are advantages to be offered by self-regulation, including the creation of a tangible forum for collective discussion and representation of the bar's common interests and the promotion of collective responsibility for the conduct of its members. The legitimacy of the regulatory process would also presumably be enhanced by counsel applying agreed standards to themselves rather than having imposed standards by judges who may or may not have personal experience as counsel. On this reasoning, this is best achieved through advocates regulating themselves. Thus, there are potential advantages to self-regulation not only to raise standards but also to provide a permanent forum within which to address other matters of common concern to advocates.

As also indicated in Chapter 1, the consequences of professionalization for the practice of advocacy in the international judicial system stem from the degree of incisiveness that is generated by the process. For example, centralization into an international bar would presumably have a profound effect upon the independence, transparency, and professional accountability of advocacy. By contrast, the less radical step of international courts setting up their own regulatory infrastructure may be less impactful. Although professionalization would change the realities of litigation, its success in creating an independent bar depends upon the incisiveness and utility of its standards and the efficacy of their enforcement mechanisms.

In this context, this chapter examines the prospects for the creation of a centralized regulatory authority for the international bar. In the absence of experience, this is a necessarily speculative exercise that is nevertheless valuable as a means of evaluating an alternative model for professionalization. Section 10.1 addresses the various degrees of centralization that are possible within the international judicial system. Section 10.2 examines the possibility of national enforcement of international standards. Section 10.3 considers the creation of an international bar authority, which would be mandated to create admission standards, ethical standards, and/or a standing disciplinary organ. Section 10.4 sets out the possible consequences of professionalization for the practice of advocacy in the international judicial system. Finally, section 10.5 concludes the chapter by reflecting upon the competing themes and dynamics involved in the professionalization of advocacy.

10.1 Centralization of Regulatory Authority

The creation of an international organ to regulate counsel before international courts engages two dynamics, namely, the centralization of regulatory authority over licensed practitioners and the expansion of that authority to cover non-practitioners. Centralization comprises the transfer of national bars' powers to regulate licensed practitioners before international courts to the international authority. Expansion entails the extension of regulation to counsel who are not licensed to practise law by a national bar (eg academics and diplomats). The aim of centralization would be to ensure the uniform application of common standards for the practice of advocacy.

However, it is questionable whether centralization is necessary to achieve the professionalization of advocacy. It may also be argued that uniformity is a chimera in that the diversity of national standards is too great. The practical obstacles to the creation of a supranational bar authority to regulate counsel are considerable, particularly conflicts of jurisdiction. Considering the disparate and centrifugal nature of the international judicial system, the success of centralization depends upon its degree.

Commonality necessarily entails an element of centralization by reconciling differences. If one accepts the need for commonality, one necessarily accepts the need for a degree of centralization. However, there is a considerable difference between 'harmonization' and 'uniformity'. Harmonization suggests the acceptability of a degree of divergent standards within a common framework whereas uniformity requires identical standards. Thus, an important dynamic in considering the professionalization of international advocacy through architectural centralization is this tension between divergence and centralization.

Thus, centralization entails numerous possibilities. First, it could denote the divergent enforcement of common ethical standards by national bars. This would be the weakest solution in that it would preserve the centrifugal structure of the existing system, leaving the greatest scope for divergence. Secondly, it could signify regulation by international courts. As explored in Chapter 9, this is a pragmatic solution for the near-term that would not create an 'international bar' in a unitary sense but rather several 'international bars' attached to each court. Thirdly, it could involve the creation of a supranational authority mandated by international courts and national bars. This could take the form of a standing disciplinary committee at a professional organization such as the International Law Association. Fourthly, it could involve the federalization of national bars into a single supranational authority such as a strengthened International Bar Association. This would be the most radical and far-reaching solution in scale and consequently the most practically difficult to achieve.

Paradoxically, a peculiar strength of the complex and diffuse nature of the international judicial system is that it provides considerable scope for creativity and ingenuity. Whereas in national jurisdictions the presence of an overarching State superstructure may inhibit the ability of the bar to unilaterally reform itself, no comparable, centralized public authority exists at the international level. For example, the creation of a supranational bar authority does not require a State mandate to function. The centralization of regulatory authority engages three key actors: (1) senior members of the de facto international bars; (2) the international judiciary; and (3) the national bars. The test for the success of professionalization lies in the ability to mobilize these three actors and to reconcile their priorities and jurisdictions within a common framework.

10.2 National Enforcement of Ethical Standards

As explored in Chapter 9 in relation to the CCBE, one method for the professionalization of advocacy entails the enforcement of common ethical standards by national bars. The attractiveness of this solution is twofold. First, it is relatively cheap in terms of effort in that no major architectural reform would be required to achieve it. Secondly, it seemingly precludes the double deontology problem by vesting disciplinary jurisdiction firmly with the national bars. Hence, on this approach the principal challenge to professionalization is the articulation of common standards acceptable to the various national bars.

This solution is also practicable for certain organizations and jurisdictions that provide a framework for the compulsory integration of common standards into national codes of conduct. The CCBE Code of Conduct is the principal example of this method whereby common standards were articulated at the supranational level and, following adoption in plenary, were required to be integrated at the national level. In principle, the same procedure could be utilized to articulate codes of conduct for the ECJ and ECtHR with the addition of judicial consultation to ensure the subsequent adoption of the codes by those Courts. All four judges from those two courts interviewed for this book supported this idea.[1] On this approach, the principal actors driving the process would be national bars with the support of judges and senior counsel.

However, it is questionable whether the same process would work for the articulation of common standards for other international courts that are not jurisdictionally defined by the European region. For other regional courts (eg the IACtHR) there is no equivalent organization to the CCBE to provide a mechanism for this bar-driven process. For international courts with a wider territorial jurisdiction (eg the ICJ or ICC), the only organization with a similar forum for this technique is the IBA. However, unlike the CCBE, IBA texts are not required to be adopted by national bars.[2]

Even if the articulation and adoption of common standards by national bars through the IBA is feasible, there remain significant weaknesses inherent in this technique. First, there would remain divergent enforcement of the common standards. National bars are highly diverse with different standards, cultures, and resources. Since the law is a process that does not stop at its articulation and enactment but continues into its interpretation and application, it is probable that on divisive issues requiring normativity there would be divergent application of the common standards in line with national cultures. This would defeat the principal objective of professionalization to harmonize divergent standards within common standards.

Secondly, common standards would not apply to non-practitioners because international courts lack the power to subject them to the discipline of national bars. The 'common' standards would consequently apply only to counsel who are already subject to national standards through their practising licences. This would defeat another important objective of the exercise: to ensure the application of common ethical standards to *all* counsel. For reasons explored below, the adoption of an admission requirement by all international courts that advocates should be practitioners would be insufficient to ensure that all counsel are subject to common standards.

Thirdly, a process driven principally by national bars does not require practitioners to assume principal responsibility for their collective conduct in their advocacy before international courts. This runs counter to the spirit of the professionalization project to create an 'international judicial culture' based upon the specific requirements and procedures of international courts and drawing upon national traditions for inspiration. The history of national bars explored in Chapter 2 suggests that, as a sociological phenomenon, an important facet of professionalization is an awakening of corporate identity. The organization of the international bar can only really be done by the practising advocates themselves to ensure its independence and begin to construct its collective identity rooted in common philosophical principles like truth, justice, and

[1] Interview with Judges Jaeger and Forwood, EU General Court (14 October 2010); Interview with Judge Elisabet Fura, ECtHR (15 October 2010), cited with permission. Another judge spoke anonymously.

[2] The IBA has a highly anodyne 'International Code of Ethics', which has not been incorporated at the national level.

the rule of law. Thus, it is vital for the creation of a common culture that the organization of the international bar be undertaken principally by the international bar.

This is not to say that the national adoption of common ethical standards before international courts is not an important part of the project. The engagement of national bars, as collectively one of the key actors in the process, is critical to preclude double deontology and provide the international bar with an important mandate for its work. For example, the adoption of common standards by the CCBE (for the ECJ and ECtHR) and by the IBA (for the ICSID) would provide a strong mandate for the adoption and application of those standards by those international courts. Indeed, as noted in Chapter 8, the IBA played an important role in the drafting of the ICC Code. However, an equally important facet is the assumption by international advocates of responsibility for their own regulation. Whilst self-regulation is not a precondition for professionalism, it is arguably the most effective way of inculcating common standards by centralizing regulation in a supranational authority.

10.3 International Bar Authority

A second option for the professionalization of international advocacy entails the creation of an international bar authority mandated to regulate counsel appearing before international courts. Whilst the salient feature of this option is self-regulation, its architecture may significantly differ from a national bar. The lack of an overarching State superstructure providing a constitutional framework demands different tools to ensure that international bar is accountable in its task of self-regulation.

Today, the CCBE is the organization that most closely resembles an international bar. Due to ideological differences concerning federalization, there is no consensus concerning the degree of centralization that might occur in future. As one ECtHR judge, who was previously active in the organization, relates:

> Certainly, it is very premature to speak of this. When we cannot even create a 'European bar' as such, we probably would struggle to create an even more inclusive, unified bar. However, the ILA Hague Principles are a very useful idea in that they provide ideas and suggestions for the various Courts to consider and adapt to their own circumstances.[3]

Consequently, if feasible at all, the creation of a self-regulating international bar with the full range of regulatory and representational functions of a national bar is a long-term prospect. In the nearer term, it may be more plausible to establish of a standing disciplinary committee with a specific remit. The success of its self-constitution would depend upon the recognition by international courts and national bars of its authority, which in turn would require a strong structure and leadership by the most eminent international lawyers. The historical emergence of the oldest national bars (eg the Massachusetts colonial bar) explored in Chapter 2 indicates that the support

[3] Interview with Judge Fora.

of the judiciary is the most crucial factor in establishing the authority of a new bar through a monopoly over rights of advocacy.

10.3.1 Bar Admission

The creation of an international bar, like any other organization, raises the question of membership rules. In a historically decentralized legal services market concerning advocacy before international courts, this exercise is especially difficult due to the diffuse and centrifugal nature of international law education. However, closer examination of various options reveals that the creation of objective admission criteria is practicable even in the absence of a centralized system of legal education. This is due to the existence of a number of de facto requirements that have been asserted by the market rather than by a regulatory authority, which provides a degree of natural continuity. Additional requirements that the market has not yet imposed can be created to raise standards.

In determining the expertise that an international law advocate should have, the following broad elements are suggested: (1) a strong academic foundation with a speciality in public international law; (2) advocacy skills, including a command of international procedure, evidence, litigation strategy, and rhetoric; (3) a mastery of one of the two official languages of English or French; and (4) good moral character including integrity, industry, and temperance. In the first place, it is clear that the market demands a period of academic study. This takes the form of a national foundation in the initial bachelor of laws degree programme, typically varying between three and five years, to obtain a grounding in a national legal system with the possibility of an introduction into the study of public international law (typically in the later years of study). Moreover, a period of academic specialization has become increasingly standard through a master of laws degree (of one or two years' duration) and a doctorate (three to five years). Thus, academic requirements of a law degree combined with at least two or three years of specialized study in public international law would appear to be straightforward.

More difficult is the question of quality control, namely, a qualitative assessment of an applicant's academic qualifications. There is a clear interest in asserting such control in light of the multiplicity and diversity amongst higher educational institutions and the corporate interest of the image of the bar. A published and annually updated list of academic institutions whose degree certifications are recognized may be one method to provide consistency.[4] Additionally, the attainment of degree results of a minimal standard (eg the equivalent a 'B' grade of the European Credit Transfer and Accumulation System[5]) would provide an additional control. Due to the difficulty in comparing higher educational standards, a sufficient geographical representation amongst the standard-setters at the bar is vital to ensure accuracy and fairness.

[4] Although there is an inevitable element of subjectivity in this exercise, the specialized nature of international law assists in identifying the strongest law faculties.

[5] The Bologna Process, aimed at harmonizing higher education standards within the European Higher Education Area, is a useful guide, though geographically limited.

Another potential requirement is that candidates be members of a national bar in good standing. Although this appears to be the minimal requirement imposed by those international courts that have admission standards, it is potentially contentious because of its exclusion of academic lawyers.[6] The principal advantages that this requirement would bring would be subjection to professional ethics and discipline at the national level and the implied addition of practical training in advocacy and civil procedure that membership of a national bar theoretically entails. However, these benefits are in practice unlikely to be substantial because the entire point of creating an international bar is to provide common ethics and discipline and national training standards differ widely in quality and focus. Moreover, in light of the traditional predominance of academics in the discipline their exclusion would arguably deprive the bar of necessary expertise.

However, it is also illogical to exclude from the membership requirements of a guild of advocates any training or experience of advocacy. There are two possible solutions to this. First, a training institute could be created to provide a course in the practical skills that international law advocacy requires (eg civil procedure, written pleading, evidence, litigation strategy, and oratory). This would clearly be an expensive, and the consequently more difficult, option. Secondly, candidates could be required to prove their expertise in these skills through proof of practical experience (eg three years) and/or other forms of advocacy training.

Clearly, either option would exclude academics with no advocacy expertise from admission.[7] This, on balance, would be a healthy development in forcing the market to raise standards by requiring all advocates to have at least a basic foundation (however subjectively defined) in advocacy. Despite the traditionally academic character of public international law, it is indefensible in both principle and practice that individuals with no training or experience in these skills should be admitted to the bar. Whilst this would clearly run counter to the interests of some international lawyers, transitional provisions can ensure that the bar is gradually raised and provide notice and a 'generational shift'. Another potential method to test the qualifications (academic, practical, or both) of candidates is by bar examination. Although this has the attraction of consistency, it may be difficult and onerous to design and apply. It may also be superfluous by overlapping with examinations already given for academic degrees and admission to national bars. It would also be logistically more complicated, requiring an examinations board to manage the process, than setting degree and vocational requirements.

Knowledge of one of the two working languages of English or French is vital to the international judicial system. Whilst exceptions can be made for individual cases, as a general rule the efficiency of the system depends upon keeping translation costs within acceptable limits. In addition, the historical foundations of the system render knowledge of at least one of the two languages indispensable with

[6] The ECJ and ICC require that counsel generally be members of national bars but have exemptions for academics—see Chapters 5 and 8. The ECtHR has a membership requirement but no academic exemption—ECtHR Rules, Rules 35–6.

[7] See discussion in Chapter 4.

knowledge of both a significant advantage.[8] Despite the clear predominance of English, there are compelling reasons for the retention of French as the second language including representativeness of the 'other' major legal tradition, accessibility and historical value. It is doubtful that assessment of proficiency would be a difficult problem.

The final admission requirement would be that candidates be of good moral character,[9] which is commonly demanded by national bars. This is potentially more complicated than may appear at first sight, particularly in light of cultural differences concerning the relevance of a candidate's private life to their professional character. Whilst it seems plain that personal adherence to principles of justice, integrity and the rule of law are vital to the professional character of an advocate, it is difficult to draw the line clearly in all cases. One basic requirement may be that a candidate has no unspent criminal convictions, though this may be more difficult in cases of convictions unrelated to honesty, the administration of justice, or violence. For example, a conviction for a 'political offence' (eg participating in a violent public protest or a violation of demonstration laws) or private character (eg adultery or tax evasion) arguably impact upon professional character to the extent that an advocate's respect for the rule of law or honesty. However, the national laws, fair trial standards, and cultural perspectives on such offences makes criminality problematic as the professional standard for moral character.

Furthermore, moral standards are difficult to determine in more subtle qualities like sobriety or good judgement. For example, a candidate may have a history of making intemperate statements against opposing counsel, improper media statements or a history of professional negligence lawsuits. On the one hand, such behaviour could be disruptive to the fair conduct of proceedings or otherwise bring the profession into disrepute. On the other hand, it is arguable that pugnacious advocates can be effective. Thus, it may ultimately be a subjective exercise to assess moral character in light of the candidate's circumstances. A final requirement may be knowledge of either English or French, as required by the ECJ, ECtHR, and ICC.

10.3.2 Code of Conduct

The second regulatory aspect of an international bar entails the enactment of a code of conduct. Whilst it is conceivable that the disciplinary jurisdiction of the bar authority could be exercised by applying multiple codes of conduct for the various courts, simplicity and consistency would demand that a single code be used for all members of the bar. Despite the fact that different provisions of the code will apply to different courts according to their procedures,[10] such provisions would naturally not apply to those courts that do not require them. Thus, the uniformity of ethical standards for all courts has no practical detriment.

[8] *The International Judge.*

[9] Described as 'boilerplate' for international institutions—Chapter 8.

[10] Eg ad hoc judges at the ICJ, issue conflicts at ICSID, or the prosecutorial discretion at the ICC.

However, this is clearly predicated upon the recognition of the international bar authority and its prescribed standards by international courts. Assuming that the judiciary is regularly consulted in the drafting process and able to directly address the bar on matters of common concerns (eg at bar colloquia), a code of conduct agreed amongst advocates would presumably be a welcome development to the judiciary:

> It is up to counsel to set up an international bar and the Court should not interfere in this endeavour. Formally, the establishment of a bar could be achieved through the creation of a disciplinary committee comprising experienced people at the bar to engage with ethical issues. The International Bar Association or the International Law Association may be the organisations that are able to address this project. The problem with the ICJ setting up a bar is that there is a question concerning the relationship with national bars. The English Bar, for example, has extraterritorial jurisdiction—though this is not perhaps the case with other bars.[11]

Thus, though Chapter 9 sets out the professionalization of advocacy by international courts as the more practicable near-term variant it is arguable that self-regulation is the more politic solution for the independence of the bar from the bench. However, the degree to which judges should be distant from the bar depends also upon the development of the international judiciary (eg recruitment of judges from senior advocates).

10.3.3 Standing Disciplinary Panel

In creating a supranational regulatory authority, a standing committee of a professional organization could be designed to assume disciplinary jurisdiction over alleged misconduct before international courts. Whilst this organ could be created as part of an entirely new organization dedicated to the regulation of the international bar, there is no practical advantage to this approach. Rather, the pragmatic variant would be to create this disciplinary organ within an existing organization with an established reputation and the ability to create the essential links with the judiciary and national bars. Its composition and procedures must be harmonized with those key actors to establish its authority.

The two principal candidates for this role are the IBA and the ILA.[12] These organizations have different missions, memberships, and activities. The former, based in North America, more closely resembles the CCBE as an organization with direct links to national bars and extensive involvement in the development of professional ethics worldwide. The latter, based in the Hague, is devoted to the study of international law and does not have links to national bars—though it counts many judges at international courts as members. Whereas the IBA does not have direct links to international courts, the ILA lacks direct links to national bars.

As explored above, the ideal disciplinary mechanism would entail international law advocates assuming primary responsibility with links to both national bars

[11] Interview with Judge Abdul Koroma (4 August 2011), cited with permission.
[12] See Chapter 9.

and the international judiciary. Of the two organizations, the ILA may be the better choice within which to create a permanent disciplinary mechanism. First, the ILA is specifically devoted to the study and development of international law with international lawyers in its membership. If international lawyers are to constitute an international bar to self-regulate, the ILA would be the more logical forum. Secondly, there are practical benefits to the location of the disciplinary mechanism in the Hague. Thirdly, it would be politically easier to achieve agreement to constitute and operate the organ amongst international law advocates and judges than between national bars. Finally, the participation of national bars in the disciplinary mechanism can be achieved through the creation of a link with the bars directly or through the IBA.

On the other hand, the IBA offers certain advantages. First, it has a strong tradition of activity in the field of professional ethics with an architecture for addressing them. Secondly, its direct links to national bars are a great advantage. Thirdly, it is the better-known of the two organizations as it claims to represent the legal professions worldwide. The principal disadvantages are the lack of an international law tradition (outside of the international criminal law and arbitration spheres) and the possibility of the initiative becoming overly politicized; specifically, through the national bars. As a great deal would depend upon the political will and resources, the author expresses no firm view about the prospects of either organization assuming this role.

The membership and procedures of the disciplinary committee would need to conform to the demands of natural justice. The ICC disciplinary mechanism for defence counsel provides a useful template.[13] Initial investigation should be conducted by a standing ombudsman elected by the committee for that purpose. Members of the disciplinary board should be required to have expertise in comparative professional ethics and international procedural law. There should be rights to be heard, to representation by counsel and to appeal. One member of the panel should be of the impugned advocate's nationality. To preclude double deontology and provide a national perspective, the national bar or university should be invited to provide one member of a three-person disciplinary panel. One member should come from the referring international court in the form of a judge or registrar not of the advocate's nationality and not the complainant. The third member should come from a list of senior international law practitioners.

The efficacy of a disciplinary organ of this kind mostly depends upon the strong support of international courts. Those courts without an existing disciplinary mechanism of their own would need to recognize the authority of the ILA committee to adjudicate alleged misconduct before them, subject to their inherent jurisdiction to do so themselves where the interests of justice require it (eg to exclude an advocate from ongoing proceedings to prevent prejudice). This category of courts includes the ICJ, ITLOS, WTO DSB, ECJ, ECtHR, IACtHR, and ACJ. Although it would be ideal to centralize disciplinary jurisdiction for these courts into a single entity,

[13] ICC Code—Chapter 8.

pragmatism may demand an exception for the ECJ and ECtHR by vesting their jurisdiction into the CCBE.

However, this centralization may be more difficult for institutional and ad hoc arbitral tribunals to do owing to their impermanence and generally greater weakness in relation to the parties.[14] Courts in this category include the Iran-US Claims Tribunal, ICSID, NAFTA, UNCLOS Annex VII tribunals, and PCA. Whilst individual tribunals could invoke their inherent jurisdiction to refer alleged misconduct to the disciplinary committee, it would be preferable for the institution to provide them with an express power to do so. Were a referral to be made pursuant to an inherent jurisdiction and the impugned advocate decline to participate in the proceedings, the authority of an *in absentia* decision would depend upon the tribunal. For example, a decision to impose a fine would depend upon the tribunal declining admission until the advocate paid it. However, the tribunal would still have discretion to back the decision or not. A tribunal that disagreed with the finding, the international bar's jurisdiction or its own inherent jurisdiction may decline to do so. Similarly, the ultimate sanction of 'disbarment' would have only reputational effect unless backed by the authority of all the tribunals.

A third category of courts comprises the criminal courts, which already have their own disciplinary structures. Whilst Chapter 8 reveals that those structures have scope for further improvement, particularly in extending them to prosecutors, there is a strong argument for the exclusion of the ICC, ICTY, ICTR, SCSL, and STL from the international bar authority. This argument is on the grounds of unnecessary duplication and the procedural and cultural differences between civil and criminal proceedings. According to one judge:

> [It is necessary] to treat each international court separately, as what is true for the ICC for example may not be true for the ICJ. Each Court naturally has a separate and different culture. For example, the ICTY can sanction counsel for contempt but the ICJ does not have such a provision.[15]

The most important difference is in the higher fair trial standards that apply in the latter, which in turn require counsel to observe stricter ethical standards.

However, this may be countered by the need for consistency in the application of ethical standards before all international courts. This argument is predicated upon the commonality of those standards in criminal as well as civil proceedings. Whilst it is arguable that there are procedural differences between the two that can give rise to ethical issues peculiar to themselves,[16] these issues derive from universal ethical standards. After all, national bars apply their standards to civil and criminal proceedings alike while acknowledging their differences by prescribing specific rules to address particular issues.[17] Moreover, there are a variety of ethical

[14] See arbitral decisions in Chapter 7.

[15] Judge Koroma, Interview.

[16] Eg prosecutorial discretion, confessions of guilt, and disclosure of exculpatory evidence are embedded within a distinctive international criminal procedure.

[17] Eg paras 9–16 of the English Bar 'Written Standards for The Conduct of Professional Work' contain 'Standards Applicable in Criminal Cases'.

standards[18] which apply identically to both civil and criminal proceedings. From this viewpoint, the creation of an international judicial culture amongst counsel depends upon the uniformity of application of these universal standards throughout the international judicial system.

On balance, the arguments for the complete centralization of jurisdiction in a single international bar for all international courts are compelling in the interests of creating common culture through consistent application of uniform ethical standards. However, the complexity of the architectural issues involved and the delicacy of centralization argue for an incremental approach. In the near-term, the most practical option is the creation of an international bar to regulate counsel before those international courts that currently lack such regulation. Once the bar authority is functional and has settled after overcoming the early challenges that inevitably accompany a new and transformative institution, its jurisdiction may thereafter be gradually extended to the arbitral tribunals and ultimately the ICC.

In this way, the obstacles confronting the creation of an international bar authority may be confronted gradually from the easier towards the more difficult. A catalyst for the success of the project may thereby be created by picking the low-hanging fruit, namely, the construction of a regulatory jurisdiction to address problems of ethical standards for those courts that currently lack it. The resulting momentum can be sustained so that the architectural problems attendant to each particular court may be solved with due deliberation. Concerning the practicality of (eventually) integrating the criminal courts into the international bar, realistically this only applies to the ICC in light of the advanced stage of the ad hoc tribunals' work. This would entail amendment to the Rules of Procedure and Evidence by the ASP in order to abolish the current disciplinary system and tie its jurisdiction to the international bar authority. Thus, the ultimate integration of the ICC into the unified international bar may not prove as difficult as it may first appear.

10.4 Consequences of Professionalization

As explained in Chapter 1, the principal rationale for the professionalization of advocacy is to protect the integrity of the international judicial process. This phenomenon is best understood as a reaction to divergent standards amongst professional advocates bound by conflicting national rules as well as non-professionals bound by no comparable standards. Consequently, the most important potential consequence of professionalization is increased protection for the procedural integrity of the international judicial system. Potential secondary consequences include: increased independence for counsel, reduced party control over case presentation, exclusion of non-professionals, and enhanced image of international adjudication.

[18] Eg conflicts of interest, misleading the Court, the submission of false documentary evidence, witness contacts, witness examination, contacts with judges, or professional courtesy.

10.4.1 Procedural Integrity

The effect upon procedural integrity is likely to be beneficial. The harmonization of national standards through the prescription of uniform standards applied at the supranational level would eliminate dangers to procedural integrity arising from those conflicts. Where national standards are so far apart as to render impossible their hybridization, harmonization may nevertheless be achieved through selectivity.[19] A case in point is the standards of France, the USA, and England and Wales on witness proofing. Despite the impossibility of hybridizing these standards, a single rule on witness proofing for international litigation could nevertheless be achieved through a selective approach that prioritizes the standard that is the most suitable to protect procedural integrity.[20] Thus, harmonization of national standards for international litigation is achievable through a selective approach on their respective merits.

Although the effect upon procedural integrity is likely to be beneficial, a more contestable point is the impact upon procedural efficiency. A useful example is the recent propensity for challenges to the participation of counsel in ICSID arbitrations on grounds of conflicts of interest.[21] On the one hand, it is arguable that uniform standards on conflicts would reduce challenges in ICSID proceedings by providing a clear normative framework. On the other hand, it is plausible that prescribed standards would encourage more challenges by providing a platform. It is suggested that well-articulated standards are likelier to promote rather than detract from procedural efficiency for three reasons. First, challenges already happen in the absence of a clear normative framework. Secondly, the current absence of any standards to guide arbitrators and counsel complicates the handling of conflicts. Thirdly, challenges that are made in the future can be addressed more simply and quickly under a single and relatively clear framework rather than through argumentation on the array of national and international standards.[22]

An important factor for realizing the potential benefits of professionalization for procedural integrity is the authoritativeness of the common standards. This depends upon several factors, including sufficient consensus amongst the legal community, the incisiveness of the standards in deftly addressing recurrent problems on which national standards differ, their sensitivity and understanding of those national differences, and their succinctness and clarity. For example, the omission of witness proofing from the ICC procedural framework prompted two procedural decisions with extensive argumentation in *Lubanga*. Where hybridization of national standards is impossible due to the degree of divergence, harmonization requires selection. Whereas parties may favour proofing because it increases their control over the testimony to support their cases, the truth-seeking process of justice is objective. In such cases, lax ethical standards are unlikely to be effective in discharging their rationale of protecting procedural integrity.

[19] See Chapter 9.

[20] Eg *Lubanga*, Trial Decision on Witness Proofing in Chapter 8.

[21] Sarvarian, 'Problems of Ethical Standards for Representatives in ICSID Proceedings', 10(1) *LPICT* (2011), 67–134, 95–100.

[22] Eg *Fraport*, in Chapter 7.

As explored in Chapter 9, early efforts by study groups to articulate common standards have provided some important lessons. First, lack of incisiveness to make choices between conflicting standards that produce in a text that is too cautious and anodyne will not be effective. Secondly, excessive ambition in attempting to articulate a wide-ranging text without the requisite time, effort or expertise can be more dangerous than beneficial by resulting in a draft that lacks a sufficient consensus or produces incoherent or weak standards. Thirdly, an incremental and progressive approach that anticipates the accumulation of practice to address and rectify ethical dilemma is better than a comprehensive approach that can fail at the committee stage. The *Lubanga* decisions are now ICC precedents that have provoked subsequent criticism by the ICTY and in academia which would likely feature in a review of ICC Rules. Thus, the optimal method of professionalization entails the initial construction of a professional framework within which these matters can be addressed. Whilst a degree of incisiveness is essential for articulated standards to be practically effective, resolution of particularly difficult problems can occur gradually through the accretion of practice.

10.4.2 Counsel Independence

The increased practical independence for counsel from their clients is an important potential consequence of professionalization, which is also connected to party control over case presentation. It extends to party control over the composition of their legal teams in that admission requirements would limit the pool of counsel. There would be less incentive for parties to retain, as they can now, incompetent or dishonest counsel when a framework exists for challenge, investigation, and sanction. Hence, even without admission requirements that impose legal training upon potential counsel this added deterrence can be expected to naturally exclude 'pettifoggers'.

The independence of counsel vis-à-vis clients may also cause another beneficial effect, namely, increased protection for inexperienced parties from dishonest practitioners. For example, counsel acting in pursuit of their own private interests in their representation of their clients[23] could face disciplinary proceedings. Similarly, counsel failing to respect opposing counsel during the course of proceedings[24] could be fined. Before the civil courts, it is only through costs orders (paid by the client, not counsel personally) through which the cost to the court resulting from such misconduct can currently be recovered. Professionalization could result in independent counsel who engage in inefficient advocacy being subject to fines.[25] Furthermore, since admission requirements would compel parties to engage professional counsel it is conceivable that fees and legal aid[26] would become subject to regulatory oversight.

[23] Eg *Grand Prince* and *DRC v Uganda*, Declaration of Judge Oda in Chapter 4.

[24] Eg *Taylor* in Chapter 8.

[25] Sarvarian, 'Problems of Ethical Standards for Representatives in ICSID Proceedings', 76–80.

[26] Sarvarian, 'Problems of Ethical Standards for Representatives in ICSID Proceedings', 80. See also Chapter 7.

10.4.3 Party Control over Case Presentation

The prescription of common ethical standards designed to promote the independence of counsel in order to protect procedural integrity would necessarily reduce party control over the presentation of their cases. Professionalism often entails empowering and obliging counsel to say the word 'no' to their clients. Those counsel who are bound by no professional standards at the national level, forbidding them from making use of information that their clients provide to them through covert surveillance[27] of the bench or the other side, will be able to do so with relatively low risk. Since professional standards would oblige them to refrain from using such information, the risk to counsel agreeing to participate in such practices would rise considerably. Parties would have less incentive to engage in such misconduct without the cooperation of their counsel.

For government officials, this is a potentially sensitive area. As seen in Chapters 5 to 7, the bifurcation between privileged and non-privileged litigants concerning the appointment of their counsel entails greater control for the former over their cases. Agency is an important manifestation of this imbalance whereby only States may appoint agents and agents are outside of the court's regulatory jurisdiction. This clearly provides an advantage for government officials who are willing to exert pressure upon agents to compel them to engage in dubious tactics to win cases. Officials who wish to submit false documentary evidence[28] or to refuse to disclose adverse evidence on false grounds[29] or without explanation[30] will find it easier to do so if they do not need to persuade independent counsel to participate.

10.4.4 Exclusion of Non-Professionals

Another potential consequence of professionalization is the removal of certain categories of amateurs or non-professionals from advocacy or otherwise restricting their role in litigation. As indicated above, to some degree this would inevitably happen as the incentives shift in the market to adapt to the new regulation. However, even minimalistic admission requirements would be likely to be prescribed by the courts as part of the process. Whilst this would restrict the choice of parties to appoint whomever they wish as counsel, that restriction would be more beneficial than detrimental by ensuring that only persons with at least some legal training appear as advocates before the courts.[31]

Categories of persons who may currently appear as counsel but would likely be excluded are: experts,[32] diplomats and politicians,[33] and other laymen with no legal training or qualifications. This would be accomplished through the requirement that

[27] Sarvarian, 'Problems of Ethical Standards for Representatives in ICSID Proceedings', 86–7. See also Chapter 7.
[28] Eg *Behring Fur Seals*, *Qatar v Bahrain*, *List D*, *Società Italiana Vetro*, *Gabay* in Chapters 4 to 7.
[29] Eg *Corfu Channel* in Chapter 5.
[30] Eg *JI Case v Iran*.
[31] On the problems arising from representation by non-lawyers, see in particular Chapter 4.
[32] Eg *Pulp Mills* in Chapter 4.
[33] Eg *DRC v Uganda*. See, however, the agency discussion in Chapter 3.

counsel be members of national bars, which is standard before the ECJ, ECtHR, and ICC. However, as discussed in Chapter 4, academic lawyers who are specialists in international law are unlikely to be excluded before the inter-State courts and, in any case, exceptions are prescribed for them within the rules of the aforementioned courts. Whilst this requirement is insufficient in itself to ensure the competence of counsel, it would at least eliminate some of the problems that have arisen in practice such as experts making statements as counsel rather than witnesses or government officials making references to personal knowledge in the course of statements as agents. Whilst the price for professionalization is consequently to restrict the pool of potential counsel, this can hardly be considered detrimental.

10.4.5 Formation of a Collective Bar

A final consequence of professionalization is the formal constitution of the existing de facto bars.[34] Currently, there is no normative nexus that binds counsel from different national traditions into a collective. The de facto bars are founded more upon personal and collegial relationships built through shared educational and occupational experience rather than a common ideal. The articulation of common ethical standards necessitates a common purpose, which creates in its turn a common culture. In the current 'golden age' of international adjudication, the need for an 'international judicial culture' to fill that normative void has become increasingly evident. The ideals of justice and the rule of law have important practical consequences for the integrity and legitimacy of international courts and thus for the willingness of parties to use them.

It is no longer sufficient to simply regard international courts as cloistered institutions that deal with abstruse and largely trivial matters. Where the ICJ once dealt with one or two cases a year, now it has a full docket. Where the ECJ and ECtHR were once obscure, now they have become increasingly prominent in the public eye of Europe. Where international criminal law was a completely theoretical area with no prospect for practical implementation, now there are the ad hoc and mixed tribunals and a permanent court. Where international investment arbitration was once relatively peripheral, the explosion of bilateral investment treaties has rendered it one of the most important and dynamic areas of the law. In short, the explosion in the scale and prominence of international litigation has necessitated a reassessment of the collective identity of its practitioners. The articulation of common values through professionalization would be an important step in that process.

10.5 Conclusions

This chapter has explored possibilities for centralization into a self-regulating international bar authority. As this has never before been attempted and is not on the current agenda of the international legal community, only tentative observations

[34] Eg the 'mafia' of international law professors at the ICJ in Chapter 5.

can be offered concerning this necessarily speculative analysis. Certain dynamics can be identified as important to the success of such a bar authority should one day the idea garner significant support. The creation of a supranational regulatory authority has hitherto been discussed by international lawyers at an informal level and there are practical difficulties to its manifestation.

First, centralization is a variable concept. This particularly applies to the fragmented international judicial system, which lacks a formal superstructure to ensure consistency and certainty. Centralization requires support from a significant majority of senior international law practitioners, the major national bars, and international courts. It is suggested that these interests can be made mutually compatible through a disciplinary framework that integrates national bars into a supreme international jurisdiction.

Secondly, the option of delegation of regulatory authority to the national bars offers more disadvantages than advantages. Although it is architecturally the easiest option, it does not solve the essential problem of divergent ethical standards that currently complicates the practice of international advocacy. Since the law entails both its articulation and application, the prescription of a common text is alone inadequate to create an international judicial culture. Standards are defined and raised not only through words but also through inculcation, requiring a common forum and a common discipline.

Thirdly, the rationale for self-regulation is the independence of advocates from other authorities and the collective responsibility of the bar over its members, which raise ethical standards in practice. Although the judiciary would likely welcome a self-regulating international bar, natural justice rights and the participation of national bars in the disciplinary process would be necessary. Double deontology would need to be solved through national bars' recognition of the international bar's jurisdiction.

Fourthly, the support of the international judiciary is crucial because the establishment of the new bar's authority practically depends upon the recognition and application of its jurisdiction by the courts. As an initiative by the bar itself to independently tackle these issues, it is politically likely to attract the support of those judges who are reluctant to regulate. This requires the consensus of the senior members of the de facto bar but also the support of the courts.

Fifthly, it is suggested that the more pragmatic approach towards the creation of an international bar authority would be incremental rather than comprehensive. The bar would initially exercise its jurisdiction over advocacy before those international courts that currently do not have regulatory structures of their own. Once the authority is smoothly functioning, the desirable unification of the bar could gradually be achieved through the extension of the authority's jurisdiction to the arbitral tribunals and the ICC.

Finally, the consequences of professionalization depend upon its incisiveness. An incremental approach would likely see minimal and anodyne standards created initially that would accumulate through practice. The aim of protecting procedural integrity would be achieved through increased independence of counsel and reduced control of parties. A useful step would be taken towards the creation of an international judicial culture founded upon the fundamental ideals of justice and the rule of law.

Conclusions

In summary, the central conclusion of this book is that the professionalization of advocacy before international courts and tribunals is both desirable and feasible. In reaching this conclusion, this chapter proceeds according to the structure of the book. First, it explains the rationale for professionalization in Chapter 1. Secondly, it gives reasons for its desirability as explored in Chapters 3 to 7. Thirdly, it analyses its feasibility in Chapters 9 and 10. Fourthly, it sets out its potential consequences as examined in Chapter 10. Finally, it offers recommendations for action to successfully implement professionalization on the basis of the principal themes identified in the book.

As set out in Chapter 1, the rationale identified in this book for the professionalization of advocacy is to ensure the greatest possible protection of the integrity of the judicial process, including the fundamental elements of fair trial. This rationale is consistent with the historical emergence of professional advocacy in Europe as a reaction to the perceived need for competent counsel who meet the highest standards of integrity and professionalism. Similarly, the inherent jurisdiction of national courts to regulate counsel existed to prevent procedural abuses.

Consequently, it is necessary to address the question whether professionalization is desirable as a matter of practice and policy. Since the price paid for professional advocacy may be the entrenchment of elites with exclusive rights of hearing before international courts, in a manner that constrains accessibility to the general public, the price must be justified by the advantages that may be obtained as a consequence of changing and raising standards that professionalism is designed to create. It must be shown not only that inclusive, non-professional advocacy leads to lower standards that may raise difficulties, but also that professional advocacy produces higher standards. In addressing the former, this implies that misconduct (intentional or otherwise) needs to be identified in addition to problems arising from honest but conflicting national standards of professional advocacy.

The professionalization of advocacy would reduce the power of parties (particularly States) over their counsel. Restricted rights of hearing to professionals coupled with ethical standards requiring counsel to comply with rules (backed by disciplinary sanctions) designed to protect procedural integrity clearly has the potential to shift the balance of power between parties and courts. By creating autonomous intermediaries with duties not only to the client but also to the court, parties lose a degree of control. In exchange, all concerned are intended to benefit from the raised standards of integrity, competence, and fairness in the judicial process.

As set out in Chapter 1, the desirability of professionalization is based both upon its necessity with reference to existing practice and to its benefit with regard to the image of the international judicial system. Necessity is prompted by two phenomena, namely, divergent ethical standards and low standards caused by a lack of regulation that threaten the integrity of the judicial process. Image benefit derives from the public legitimacy and confidence that professionalism aims to provide courts as an ideology intended to safeguard fundamental principles of fairness and integrity.

As explored in Chapter 2, national standards of advocacy do diverge depending upon the procedural and judicial systems of the jurisdiction. In common law jurisdictions, the role of the advocate has been historically larger than in civil law jurisdictions. Since common law counsel have a larger role in the judicial process, the impact of professional misconduct upon the process is greater. Consequently, the ethical standards imposed have been stricter in line with that role. The various jurisdictions also have their own histories, philosophies, and contemporary challenges. Younger bars that operate within authoritarian political systems and/or in cultures historically sceptical of professional advocacy clearly struggle to inculcate high standards. The older bars also face modern pressure to instil a competitive ethos potentially detrimental to the traditional value of independence.

As set out in Chapter 2, the role of legal adviser is particularly important due to the formative 'diplomatic tradition' of nineteenth-century advocacy that relies upon government lawyers as agents rather than external counsel. Although the British and American legal advisers are generally qualified practitioners, the efficacy of the regulatory jurisdiction of the national bars over their conduct is doubtful. For those governments that utilize career diplomats (who may not have a legal background) or academic lawyers, there is clearly no external regulator. Thus, the independence of legal advisers relative to external counsel is questionable.

Chapter 3 explained the origins of the laissez-faire system of representation that continues before the PCA, ICJ, ITLOS, and the Iran-US Claims Tribunal. Ironically, although the PCIJ declined to regulate counsel on the ground that States could not act dishonourably, the historical record shows that arbitral tribunals and the Court itself were periodically compelled to regulate counsel. Indeed, problems that have arisen before the modern Court (eg experts acting as counsel, false evidence, and incompetence) appeared in PCIJ practice. Whilst this historical record disproves the argument that international courts lack jurisdiction to regulate counsel, the PCIJ narrative shows that they may decline to exercise it as a policy matter.

Chapters 4 to 8 principally addressed whether professionalization is desirable. Although the broad conclusion is that it is desirable, the conclusion varies according to the particular circumstances of different courts. For the ICJ, practice suggests that common ethical standards are necessary in light of divergent and inadequate standards. Although there are clearly eminent and respectable counsel who are members of the de facto bar, this bar does not have a complete monopoly over rights of hearing. Consequently, the laissez-faire policy of the Court in leaving representational matters generally to the parties allows parties greater control over case presentation and their counsel. Practice suggests that this has provided scope for some counsel to be appointed who have arguably not acted in accordance with professional standards of independence, integrity, and competence.[1] Interviews with judges have shown that there is a conservative camp that believes that the Court cannot or should not regulate counsel and a progressive view that advocates such regulation to protect the Court's procedural integrity.

By contrast, Chapter 5 has shown that there has been remarkably little practice concerning counsel conduct before the ECJ. This is attributable to the more limited, review-based jurisdiction of the Court as well as the relative homogeneity of the six founding members. However, the chapter further illustrates that even before the ECJ there have been periodic issues concerning the conduct of counsel. For example, sharp differences regarding the independence of employed lawyers amongst national jurisdictions have been topical and in rare cases there has been questionable handling of documentary evidence. Notably, all of the latter cases have concerned the conduct of agents representing governments and the EU Commission. This suggests that, contrary to the Victorian argument that States could not act dishonourably, government lawyers and diplomats are equally prone to misbehaviour. Consequently, this renders the bifurcation between privileged and non-privileged litigants dubious from the perspective of fairness, integrity, and equality.

By contrast, Chapter 6 illustrated that there are considerably more examples of problems concerning counsel conduct arising in practice before the ECtHR. This is due not only to the greater prominence of factual issues before the Court but also to the even greater diversity of national traditions whence counsel hail. Particular problems manifested before the Court include the overarching backlog issue, attempts to mislead the Court, and the generally poor standards of advocacy—particularly amongst agents.

Chapter 7 examined the topical field of investment arbitration with supplementary reference to commercial arbitration. It demonstrated that there are substantial examples of challenges to the participation of counsel, allegations of misconduct, and public criticism by arbitrators of counsel. The relatively weak posture of arbitral tribunals compared with permanent courts towards parties, compounded by the high financial stakes, would appear to account for growing concern about the status quo of unregulated advocacy in this area.

Chapter 8 focused upon the practice of the ICC concerning prosecutors who, unlike defence counsel, are self-regulating before all of the international criminal tribunals apart from the SCSL. Its examination revealed that multiple problems of a serious nature (eg obeying court orders, handling of testimonial and documentary evidence, and prejudicial media statements) have arisen concerning the professional conduct of prosecutors. Although the concern of the judiciary to maintain an appropriate distance between itself and the prosecutors is sustainable, the dichotomy between self-regulating prosecutors and defence counsel regulated by the Court is not. Indeed, the fact that hitherto most of the controversy has emanated from prosecutors rather than defence counsel suggests that there is a pressing need for both sides of the courtroom to be subject to common ethical standards. The

[1] Eg *Corfu Channel*, *DRC v Uganda*, *ELSI*, *Preah Vihear*, *Qatar v Bahrain*, *Pulp Mills*, *Grand Prince*—see Chapter 5.

unreasoned ICTY decisions finding that it lacked jurisdiction to regulate prosecutors are unconvincing. They are not only inconsistent with that Tribunal's invocation of inherent jurisdiction to prescribe the broader contempt powers for itself but also lack an express statutory basis for the regulation of defence counsel.

Chapters 4 to 8 examined the feasibility of professionalization as a subsidiary issue, principally concerning the legal power of the respective courts to regulate. However, feasibility was the principal focus of Chapters 8 and 9. Although the conclusion of these analyses is that professionalization is feasible, important problems have been identified. Although the creation of a unified international bar authority to regulate counsel is not impossible, it is suggested that regulation by international courts is more practicable in the medium-term.

In Chapter 9, the possibility of regulation by international courts was considered through analysis of two issues. First, the legal authority of the courts to regulate counsel was considered. It was suggested that the power to do so derives from the doctrine of implied powers, whereby those courts with a broad express power to frame rules of procedure can by implication lay down rules concerning representation by counsel. Alternatively, it was argued that those courts lacking such a broad statutory power could invoke the doctrine of inherent jurisdiction. It was suggested that this doctrine derives from national judicial systems, particularly common law systems, for the prevention of procedural abuses. It was argued that the jurisprudence of international courts is inconsistent on the doctrine's applicability to the regulation of counsel but that the decisions against are not persuasive.

Secondly, the practical ability of the courts to regulate counsel was examined. A link was made between the system of judicial election and the courts' regulation in that there is currently no method of ensuring that judges are themselves sufficiently expert in counsel ethics. Interviews with judges confirmed that there is a clear difference between those judges who have experience as practising counsel and those who have been primarily diplomats or academics. It was argued that there is a need for architectural mechanisms that ensure the observance of natural justice standards in the disciplinary systems of the courts in order to instil confidence amongst practitioners in their fairness. These standards are also necessary to resolve the problem of double deontology by establishing the prescriptive and disciplinary supremacy of international courts. National bars that claim jurisdiction over their members' conduct before international courts must be persuaded to relinquish it in the interests of providing certainty for their members and upholding the courts' authority.

Chapter 10 examined two questions, namely the possibility of self-regulation by counsel through the creation of an international bar authority and the potential consequences of professionalization. Whilst the centralization of regulatory authority required for self-regulation by counsel is possible, it is suggested that the decentralized nature of the international judicial system allows for it to be manifested to varying degrees. The option of delegating the enforcement of common ethical standards to national bars is suggested to be undesirable because it allows for variable application according to national standards, thus unravelling the uniformity of the common standard.

Although the creation of a common regulatory authority (eg an ILA disciplinary panel or an association of national bars such as the CCBE) is theoretically possible and is favoured by some judges, the experience of the CCBE suggests that it may not yet be politically feasible. Its principal advantages are that it creates distance between the bench and the bar as well as a forum for the inculcation of common standards and the collective representation of the bar. However, the principal obstacles are the lack of consensus and momentum for the creation of such an authority and the potential unwillingness of national bars to relinquish their own regulatory jurisdiction concerning their members' conduct before international courts.

In addition, were the creation of an international bar authority to be pursued in the future, it is suggested that the support of the international courts for its jurisdiction would be indispensible for its success. This would likely be a gradual process rather than comprehensive, whereby the bar authority could be constructed to serve one international courts (eg the ICJ) and subsequently expand to cover other courts. Although the centralization of regulatory authority across the international judicial system has the potential advantages of strengthening the applicability of common standards and fostering a common identity and ideology, there are strong arguments for the segregation of those courts with their own infrastructure. This would principally comprise the ICC and other criminal tribunals and the ECJ and ECtHR, which already have the CCBE as a potential forum.

Chapter 10 also considered the potential consequences of professionalization for the international judicial system. It was suggested that the articulation of common ethical standards, if done effectively, would have a beneficial impact upon the integrity of the judicial process by ameliorating differences amongst divergent national standards and imposing ethical duties upon non-professionals. This would have a number of potential secondary effects: (1) the promotion of the independence of counsel from the client; (2) reduction of party control over case presentation, leading to a rebalancing of authority between parties and courts; (3) the exclusion of non-professionals through admission requirements, thus creating a formal bar; and (4) the formation of a collective bar that would undertake regulatory and/or representational functions. These potential consequences depend upon the degree and effectiveness of the professionalization measures undertaken.

Based upon the research and analysis described above, this book makes the following recommendations for the achievement of professionalization. First, it is proposed that common ethical standards be prescribed by international courts as codes of conduct for counsel. Although these standards must be enacted by the courts to achieve practical effectiveness, they should be articulated by international law practitioners through professional organizations with links to the respective courts as well as national bars. Courts like the ICJ and ITLOS could enact codes of conduct. The IBA Task Force is seized with the topic and could produce standards for adoption by both national bars and the ICSID. The CCBE could articulate standards for adoption by the ECJ and ECtHR in consultation with the judiciaries of those Courts. The ICC could extend its Code of Conduct, currently only applicable to defence counsel, to prosecutors and update it to tighten standards in light of the problems that have arisen in its early jurisprudence.

Secondly, it is suggested that the articulation of those common standards be done in a careful, deliberate, and pragmatic fashion. Notwithstanding divergences amongst national jurisdictions, the fundamental values of the profession should be recognized as justice and the rule of law. There should be informed acknowledgement of conflicting national standards and a willingness to harmonize them through hybridization and selectivity in accordance with the practical demands of international litigation. Selecting national standards should not be done dogmatically but rather pragmatically according to their function in promoting procedural justice.

Thirdly, it is recommended that international courts assert the supremacy of their regulatory jurisdictions over counsel in order to eliminate the double deontology problem. This entails both the textual supremacy of their codes of conduct over national standards (an invariable provision of the criminal courts' codes) but also the supremacy of their disciplinary jurisdictions over those of national bars. The effectiveness of an international jurisdiction and the need for counsel to have regulatory certainty demand that national courts relinquish their jurisdictions in support of international courts. National bars should be integrated into the international courts' jurisdictions by inviting them to participate in the prescription of codes of conduct and in the courts' disciplinary procedures.

Fourthly, it is proposed that admission requirements be imposed by international courts for both agents and counsel in order to exclude non-lawyers from rights of hearing. As seen in this book, this principally applies to the inter-State tribunals and arbitral tribunals. The basic admission requirements applicable before the international criminal courts alongside the ECJ and ECtHR are membership of a national bar and familiarity with one of the official languages of the court. Whilst academic lawyers of proven expertise should be exempted from the requirement of membership of a national bar, they should be required to comply with the same standards as practitioners. This would beneficially exclude diplomats, politicians, and other non-lawyers from acting as advocates. Whilst the exclusion of government lawyers may be sensitive, it is argued on the basis of *Akzo Nobel* reasoning as discussed in Chapter 6, as well as cases involving alleged agent misconduct in Chapters 4 to 6 that government lawyers are insufficiently independent from their employers.

Fifthly, it is suggested that the possibility of creating an authority that could assume regulatory and representational functions for the international bar should be examined. Whilst the current circumstances indicate that this is a long-term project and is not necessary to achieve professionalization, it is nevertheless of potential benefit in inculcating a common identity amongst international law practitioners. This would promote the creation of an international judicial culture grounded in solidarity, mutual understanding, and respect for universal values of justice and the rule of law.

Bibliography

BOOKS AND ARTICLES

1908. Convention Relative to the Establishment of an International Prize Court. (Suppl.) *AJIL* (2), 174–202.

1908. Convention for the Establishment of a Central American Court of Justice. (Suppl.) *AJIL* (2), 231–43.

1914. Regulations of the Central American Court of Justice. (Suppl.) AJIL (8), 179–94.

1914. Ordinance of Procedure of the Central American Court of Justice. (Suppl.) *AJIL* (8), 194–213.

Abel, R. 1989. *American Lawyers*. New York: Oxford University Press.

——1999. The Politics of Professionalism: the Transformation of English Lawyers at the End of the Twentieth Century. *Legal Ethics* (2), 131–47.

Abel, R. and Lewis, P. 1995. *Lawyers in Society: An Overview*. Berkeley: University of California Press.

Abghari, *Introduction to the Iranian Legal System and the Protection of Human Rights in Iran* (2008)

Al-Arayed, J. 2003. *A Line in the Sea: The Qatar v. Bahrain Border Dispute in the World Court*. Berkeley: North Atlantic Books.

al-Eshaikh, 'Human Rights and the Trial of the Accused', 193

Al-Ghadyan, 'The Judiciary in Saudi Arabia', *13*(3) *ALQ* (1998), 235–51

al-Hubayshi, *Legal System and Basic Law in Yemen* (1988)

al-Jarbou, 'Judicial Independence: Case Study of Saudi Arabia', 19(1) ALQ (2004), 5–54

Ambos, K. 2008. 'Witness proofing' before the International Criminal Court: a reply to Karemaker, Taylor and Pittman. *LJIL* (21), 911–6.

——2009. Confidential Investigations (Article 54(3)(E) ICC Statute) vs. Disclosure Obligations: The Lubanga Case and National Law. *NCLR* (12), 543–68.

Anderson, D. and Demetriou, M. 2002. *References to the European Court*. London: Sweet & Maxwell.

Ando, N., McWhinney, E. and Wolfrum, R. 2002. *Liber Amicorum Judge Shigeru Oda*. The Hague: BRILL.

Anoushirvani, S. 2010. The Future of the International Criminal Court: The Long Road to Legitimacy Begins with the Trial of Thomas Lubanga Dyilo. *PILR* (22), 213–40.

Antoine, A. 1953. La Cour de Justice de la C.E.C.A. et la Cour internationale de Justice. *RGDIP* (57), 210–61.

Arbour, L. 2000. *The Prosecutor of a Permanent International Criminal Court*. Berlin: Freiburg im Breisgau.

——2006. Legal Professionalism and International Criminal Proceedings. *JICJ* (4), 674–85.

Aristotle, 2005. *Politics*. Translated by: Rackham, H. Cambridge: Harvard University Press.

Arnull, A., Tridimas, T. and Eeckhout, P. 2008. *Continuity and Change in EU Law: Essays in Honour of Sir Francis Jacobs*. Oxford: Oxford University Press.

Austin, J. 1968. *The Province of Jurisprudence Determined*. London: Weidenfeld and Nicholson.

Bablitz, E. 2007. *Actors and Audience in the Roman Courtroom*. London: Routledge.

Baig, L. 2009. International Criminal Law and Legal Ethics: The Need for Shared Expectations. *ASILP* (103), 255–67.

Baker, J. 1969. Counsellors and Barristers: an Historical Study. *CLJ* (27), 205–29.

Bannelier, K., Christakis, T. and Heathcot, T. (eds), Due Diligence, Self-Help and the Rise of International Law: The Continued Relevance of the Corfu Channel Judgment 60 Years On. London: Routledge.

Bayer, A. 2003. Litigators at Community patent proceedings—whose representation is it? *IRIPCL* (34), 361–73.

Bederman, D. 1993. Nationality of individual claimants before the Iran-United States Claims Tribunal *ICLQ* (42), 119–36.

Beignier, B., Blanchard, B. and Villacèque, J. 2002. *Droit et déontologie de la profession d'avocat*. Paris: Presses Universitaires France.

Benson, C. 2009. Can Professional Ethics Wait? The Need for Transparency in International Arbitration. *DRI* (3), 78-94;

Bentham, J. 1982. *An Introduction to the Principles of Morals and Legislation* (1982), London: Methuen.

Benvenuti, P. 2001. The ICTY Prosecutor and the Review of the NATO Bombing Campaign against the Federal Republic of Yugoslavia. *EJIL* (12), 503–29.

Bilder, R. 1962. The Office of the Legal Adviser. *AJIL* (56), 633–85.

Bingham, T. 2010. *The Rule of Law*. London: Penguin Group.

Bishop, C. 1931. *International Arbitral Procedure*. Washington, D.C.: J. Byrne & Co.

Bishop, R. and Kehoe, E. 2010. *The Art of Advocacy in International Arbitration*. New York: Juris Net.

Bodde, D. and Morris, C. 1967. *Law in Imperial China: Exemplified by 190 Ch'ing Dynasty Codes*. Cambridge: Harvard University Press.

Bodin, J. 1962. *The Six Bookes of a Commonweale*. Translated by: McRae, K. New York: Arno Press.

Bonner, R. 1927. *Lawyers and Litigants in Ancient Athens: The Genesis of the Legal Profession*. Chicago: University of Chicago Press.

Boon, A. and Levin, J. 2008. *The Ethics and Conduct of Lawyers in England and Wales*. Oxford: Hart Publishing.

Boudant, J. 2005. *La Cour de justice des Communautés Européennes*. Paris: Dalloz.

Boulton 1953. *A Guide to Conduct and Etiquette at the Bar of England and Wales*.

Brady, J. 1982. *Justice and Politics in People's China: Legal Order or Continuing Revolution?* New York: Academic Press.

Brown, C. 2005. The Inherent Powers of International Courts and Tribunals. *BYIL* (66), 195–244.

——2007. *A Common Law of International Adjudication*. Oxford: Oxford University Press.

Brown, L. and Kennedy, T. 2000. *The Court of Justice of the European Communities*. London: Sweet & Maxwell.

Brownlie 1995. 'International Law at the Fiftieth Anniversary of the United Nations', *Recueil des Cours*, (255), 9–228

Brundage, J. 2008. *The Medieval Origins of the Legal Profession*. Chicago: University of Chicago Press.

Buergenthal, T. 2001. 'Proliferation of International Courts and Tribunals: Is it Good or Bad?', *LJIL* (14), 267–75.

Bulsara 1937. *The Laws of the Ancient Persians*.

Burrage, M. *Revolution and the Making of the Contemporary Legal Profession: England, France and the United States*. Oxford: Oxford University Press.

Bustamente, A. 1925. *The World Court*. London: Macmillan.

Byers, M. 1997. Conceptualising the Relationship between *Jus Cogens* and *Erga Omnes* Rules. *NJIL* (66), 211–39.

Calhoun, S. 2008. Globalization's Erosion of the Attorney-Client Privilege and What U.S. Courts Can Do to Prevent It. *TxLR* (87), 235–65.

Caloyanni, M. 1931. The Judicial Policy for the Settlement of International Disputes. *TGS* (17), 85–111.

——1931. L'organisation de la Cour permanente de justice. *RdC* (1931), 651–786.

Calvocoressi, P. 1947. *Nuremberg: The Facts, the Law and the Consequences*. London: Chatto and Windus.

Carty, A. 2004. The Corfu Channel case—and the Missing Admiralty Orders. *LPICT* (3) 1–35.

Cassese, A., Gaeta, P. and Jones, J. 2002. *The Rome Statute of the International Criminal Court*. Oxford: Oxford University Press.

Chavrier, 2003. L'avocat devant les jurisdictions européennes. *L'observateur de Bruxelles* (52), 21–31.

Ch'en, P. 1979. *Chinese Legal Tradition under the Mongols: the Code of 1291 as Reconstructed*. Princeton: Princeton University Press.

——1981. *The Formation of the Early Meiji Legal Order: The Japanese Code of 1871 and its Chinese Foundation*. Oxford: Oxford University Press.

Chen, J., Li, Y. and Otto, J. 2002. *Implementation of Law in the People's Republic of China*. New York: Kluwer Law International.

Chinkin, C., Nouwen, S. and Ward, C. 2010. *Report of the Seventy-Fourth Conference*. London: International Law Association.

Clark, G. 2008. An Introduction to the Legal Profession in China in the Year 2008. *SULR* (51), 833–50.

Cocks, R. 1983. *Foundations of the Modern Bar*. London: Sweet & Maxwell.

Cohen, H. 1929. *A history of the English Bar and attornatus to 1450*. London: Sweet & Maxwell.

Charney, J. 1997. Book Review: International Law Decisions in National Courts. *AJIL* (91), 394–6,

Cicero. 1942. *De Oratore: Books 1-II*. Translated by: Sutton, E. Edited by: Rackham, H. Cambridge: Harvard University Press.

Clayton, R. and Tomlinson, H. 2009. *The Law of Human Rights*. Oxford: Oxford University Press.

Conot, R. 1983. *Justice at Nuremberg*. London: Weidenfeld and Nicolson.

Cot, J. 2011. The Hague vs. Burgh House. *LPICT* (10), 25–9.

Council of Europe, 1972. *Bringing an Application before the European Commission of Human Rights (Procedure and Practice of the Commission)*. Strasbourg: European Commission of Human Rights.

——1975. *Collected Edition of the Travaux Préparatoires concerning the European Convention on Human Rights and the first protocol 1949–52*. The Hague: Council of Europe.

Cranston, R. 1995. *Legal Ethics and Professional Responsibility*. Oxford: Oxford University Press.

Crawford, J. 2006. *The Creation of States in International Law*. Oxford: Oxford University Press.

——2006. *The International Law Commission's Articles on State Responsibility*. Cambridge: Cambridge University Press.

——'Ian Brownlie: 1932-2010', online: <http://www.lcil.cam.ac.uk/Media/lectures/Brownlie_British_Academy.pdf> (Accessed: 12 November 2012),

Crook, J. 1967. *Law and Life of Rome*. Ithaca: Cornell University Press.

Delvaux, L. 1956. *La Cour de Justice de la Communauté Européenne du Charbon et de l'Acier.* Paris: J. Duculot.

De Meyer, 1974. La situation des 'personnes physiques', 'organisations non gouvernmentales', et 'groupes particuliers' dans la procédure devant la Cour européenne des droits de l'homme. *Annales de droit: revue trimestrielle de droit belge* (34), 65–74,

De Richemont, J. 1954. *Communauté européenne du charbon et de l'acier: La cour de justice, code annoté guide pratique.* Paris: Libraire du journal des notaires et des avocats.

Dezalay, Y. and Garth, B. 1996. *Dealing in Virtue: International Commercial Arbitration and the Construction of a Transnational Legal Order.* Chicago: University of Chicago Press.

Dicks, A. 1989. The Chinese Legal System: Reforms in the Balance. *CQ* (119), 540–76.

Diez, E., Monnier, J. Müller, J. et al. *Festschrift für Rudolf Bindschedler.* Bern: Stämpfli.

Doria, J., Gasser, H. and Bassiouni, C. 2009. *The Legal Regime of the International Criminal Court: Essays in Honour of Professor Igor Blishchenko.* The Hague: Martinus Nijhoff.

Edward, D. 1990. Different Assumptions—Different Methods. *S.S.C. Biennial Lecture 1990.* Edinburgh: Society of Solicitors in the Supreme Court of Scotland.

Edwards 1964. *The Law Officers of the Crown.*

Eissen, M.A. 1977. La présentation de la preuve dans la jurisprudence et la pratique de la Cour européenne des Droits de l'Homme in *La presentation de la preuve et la sauvegarde des libertés individuelles.* Brussels: Émile Bruylant.

Evans, M. 2003. *International Law* (2003). Oxford: Oxford University Press.

Evetts, J. 1999. Professionalisation and professionalism: issues for interprofessional care. *JIC* (13), 119–28.

Feldbrugge, F. 1992. *The Emancipation of Soviet Law.* New York: St. Martin's Press.

Forsyth, W. 1849. *Hortensius: or, The advocate: an historical essay.* London: J. Murray.

Fujikura, K. 1996. *Japanese Law and Legal Theory.* Aldershot: Dartmouth Publishing.

Gawalt, G. 1979. *The Promise of Power: The Emergence of the Legal Profession in Massachusetts.* Westport: Greenwood Press.

Gellhorn, W. 1987. China's Quest for Legal Modernity. *JCL* (1), 1–22.

Glendon, M. 1994. *A Nation Under Lawyers: How the Crisis in the Legal Profession is Transforming American Society.* New York: Farrar, Straus and Giroux.

Goh, B. 2002. *Law without Lawyers, Justice without Courts: On traditional Chinese mediation.* Aldershot: Ashgate.

Goldschmidt, L. 1874. Projet de Règlement pour Tribunaux Arbitraux Internationaux. *RdDI* (6), 421.

——1875. Procédure arbitrale internationale. *RdDI* (7), 418–26.

Goldhaber, M.D. 2009. *A People's History of the European Court of Human Rights.* London: Rutgers University Press.

Goldston, J. 2010. More candour about criteria: the exercise of discretion by the Prosecutor of the International Criminal Court. *JICJ* (8), 383–406.

Goodman, C. 2008. *The Rule of Law in Japan: A Comparative Analysis.* Leiden: Kluwer Law International.

Gormley, W.P. 1966. *The Procedural Status of the Individual before International and Supranational Tribunals.* The Hague: M. Nijhoff.

Guillaume, G. 2004. 'Advantages and Risks of Proliferation: A Blueprint for Action', *JICJ* (2), 300–3.

Guyomar, G. 1973. *Commentaire du règlement de la Cour internationale de justice: interprétation et pratique.* Paris: A. Pendone.

Haley, J. 1991. *Authority without Power: Law and the Japanese Paradox*. Oxford: Oxford University Press.
Halsbury's Laws of England (1954) (3rd edn) (Vol VII).
Hanotiau, B. 2003. Misdeeds, Wrongful Conduct and Illegality in Arbitral Proceedings. *Oil, Gas and Energy Law* (1).
Harding, A. 2002. *Medieval Law and the Foundations of the State*. Oxford: Oxford University Press.
Hardinge, S. and Mackay, J. 2008. *Halsbury's Laws of England*. London: LexisNexis.
Harhoff, F. 2010. It is all in the Process: Reflections on the Relation between International Criminal Trials and International Humanitarian Law. *NJIL* (78), 469–80.
Harris, W. 1954. *Tyranny on Trial: The Evidence at Nuremberg*. Dallas: Southern Methodist University Press.
Hazard, G. and Dondi, A. 2004. *Legal Ethics: A Comparative Study*. Palo Alto: Stanford University Press.
Henkin, L. 1993. The Mythology of Sovereignty. *ASIL Newsletter*, 1.
Hicks, F. 1908. The Equality of States and the Hague Conferences. *AJIL* (2), 530–61.
Higgins, A. 1908. The Papacy and International Law. *JSCL* (9), 252–64.
Higgins, R. 2001. Respecting Sovereign States and Running a Tight Courtroom. *ICLQ* (50), 121–32.
——2010. Ethics and International Law *LJIL* (23), 277–89.
Hilderbrand, R. 1990. *Dumbarton Oaks: The Origins of the United Nations and the Search for Postwar Security*. Chapel Hill: University of North Carolina Press Books.
Hirsch, M. 1993. *The Arbitration Mechanism of the International Centre for the Settlement of Investment Disputes*. Martinus Nijhoff: London.
Hobbes, T. 1947. *Leviathan*. London: J.M. Dent.
Honoré, T. 1998. *Law in the Crisis of Empire 379-455 AD: the Theodosian Dynasty and its Quaestors*. Oxford: Clarendon Press.
Hu, J. 2000. *The development of the Chinese legal profession since 1978*. Durham: University of Durham.
Hudson, M. 1932. The Central American Court of Justice. *AJIL* (26), 759–86.
——1943. *The Permanent Court of International Justice 1920–1942*. New York: The Macmillan Company.
——1946. The Twenty-Fourth Year of the World Court. *AJIL* (40), 1–52.
Hull, W. 1908. Obligatory Arbitration and the Hague Conferences. *AJIL* (2), 731–42.
Ipp, D. 1998. Lawyers' Duties to the Court. *LQR* (114), 63–107.
Jackson, R. 1949. *Report of Robert H. Jackson, United States Representative to the International Conference on Military Trials*. Washington, D.C.: Government Printing Office.
Jeantet, F. 1954. Les intérêts privés devant la Cour de Justice de la Communauté Européenne du Charbon et de l'Acier. *RDP* (70), 684–713.
Jiménez de Aréchaga, E. 1973. The Amendments to the Rules of Procedure of the International Court of Justice. *AJIL* (67), 1–22.
Johnson, T. 1972. *Professions and Power*. London: Palgrave Macmillan.
Joint Committee on the Role of the Legal Adviser of the Department of State. 1991. The Role of the Legal Adviser of the Department of State. *AJIL* (85), 358–71.
Jordash, W. 2009. The practice of 'witness proofing' in international criminal tribunals. *LJIL* (22), 501–23.
Joseph, S., Schultz, J. and Castan, M. (eds). 2005. *The International Covenant on Civil and Political Rights: Cases, Materials, and Commentary*. Oxford: Oxford University Press.

Kalshoven, F., Kuyper, P., van Panhuys, H. and Lammers, J. 1980. *Essays on the Development of the International Legal Order*. The Hague: Martinus Nijhoff.

Kaplan, W. and McRae, D. 1993. *Law, Policy, and International Justice* (1993). Quebéc City: McGill-Queen's University Press.

Karpik, L. 1999. *French Lawyers: a study in collective action 1274 to 1994*. Oxford: Oxford University Press.

Katzman, R. 2009. The Non-Disclosure of Confidential Exculpatory Evidence and the *Lubanga* Proceedings: How the ICC Defense System Affects the Accused's Right to a Fair Trial. *NUJIHR* (8), 77–101.

Karemaker, R., Taylor, B. and Pittman, T. 2008. Witness proofing in international criminal tribunals: a critical analysis of widening procedural divergence. *LJIL* (21), 683–98.

——2008. Witness proofing in international criminal tribunals: a response to Ambos. *LJIL* (21), 917–23.

Kawashima, Y. 1986. *Puritan Justice and the Indian: White Man's Law in Massachusetts*. Connecticut: Wesleyan University Press.

Kazazi, M. 2011. Commentary on the Hague Principles on Ethical Standards for Counsel Appearing before International Courts and Tribunals. *LPICT* (10), 17–23.

Keith, R. 1994. *China's Struggle for the Rule of Law*. London: Macmillan.

Kelsen, H. 1946. *General Theory of Law and State*. Oxford: Blackwell.

Khan, R. 1990. *The Iran-United States Claims Tribunal: Controversies, Cases and Contribution* (1990). Martinus Nijhoff: London.

Kirby, J. 2011. Witness Preparation: Memory and Storytelling. *JIntA* (28) 401–6.

Koh, H. and Zelinsky, A. 2009. Practising International Law in the Obama Administration. *YJIL* (35), 1–13.

Konstantinov, E. 1997. Procedure of the New Permanent European Court of Human Rights. *EEHRR* (3) 101–16.

Kranzbühler, O. 1964-1965. Nuremberg Eighteen Years Afterwards. *DLR* (14), 333–47.

Krüger, H.C. 1980. The European Commission of Human Rights. *HRLJ* (1), 66–87.

Lagrange, M. 1954. La Cour de Justice de la Communauté Européenne du Charbon et de l'Acier. *RDP* (70), 417–35.

——1978. La Cour de Justice des Communautés Européennes: du Plan Schuman à l'union Européenne. *RTDE*, 2–17.

Lambert, P. 2009. L'avocat devant la Cour européenne des droits de l'homme in *Liber Amicorum Jean-Pierre Cot: le procès international*, 171–84. Brussels: Emile Bruylant.

Lasok, K. 1984. *European Court of Justice: Practice and Procedure*. London: Butterworths.

Leach, P. 2009. On reform of the European Court of Human Rights. *EHRLR* (6), 725–35.

——2011. *Taking a Case to the European Court of Human Rights*. Oxford: Oxford University Press.

League of Nations Advisory Committee of Jurists. 1920. *Draft Scheme of the Committee with Reports to the Council of the League of Nations and Resolutions by the Council Relating to It*. Geneva: League of Nations.

——1920. *Procès-verbaux of the Proceedings of the Committee*. League of Nations: the Hague.

Leng, S. 1967. *Justice in Communist China: A Survey of the Judicial System of the Chinese People's Republic*. Dobbs Ferry: Oceana Publications.

Leonard 1996. 'Attorney Ethics and the Size of the Japanese Bar' in Fujikura, *Japanese Law and Legal Theory*, 504

Leubsdorf, J. 2001. *Man in His Original Destiny: legal ethics in France*. London: Ashgate.

Levine, J. 2006. Dealing with Arbitrator 'Issue Conflicts' in International Arbitration, *DRJ*.

Lewis, J. 1982. *The Victorian Bar*. London: Hale.

Li 1970. 'The Role of Law in Communist China', *CQ* (44), 66–111.

Lubman, S. 1995. Introduction: The Future of Chinese Law. *CQ* (141), 1–21.

Mackenzie, R., Malleson, K., Martin, P. and Sands, P. 2010. *Selecting International Judges: Principle, Process, and Politics*. Oxford: Oxford University Press.

Mackenzie et al, *The Manual on International Courts and Tribunals* (2010)

Mahoney, P. 1984. Developments in the Procedure of the European Court of Human Rights: the Revised Rules of Court. *YEL* (3) 127–68.

——2008. The International Judiciary—Independence and Accountability. *LPICT* (7), 313–49.

Malintoppi, L. 2008. Remarks on Arbitrators' Independence, Impartiality and Duty to Disclose in Investment Arbitration. *LPICT* (7), 351–6.

Mallat 2007. *Introduction to Middle Eastern Law.*

Malleson, K. 2000. Judicial Bias and Disqualification after Pinochet (No 2). *MoLR* (63), 119–27.

Marston, G. 2000. Falsification of Documentary Evidence before International Tribunals: An Aspect of the *Behring Sea* Arbitration, 1892-3. *BYIL* (71), 357–73.

Massa, A. 2006. NATO's Intervention in Kosovo and the Decision of the Prosecutor of the International Criminal Tribunal for the Former Yugoslavia Not to Investiate: An Abusive Exercise of Prosecutorial Discretion? *BJIL* (24), 610–49.

Matheson, M. 2002. Practical Aspects of the Agent's Role in Cases before the International Court. *LPICT* (1), 467–79.

Matscher, F. and Petzold, H. (eds). Protecting Human Rights: The European Dimension, 159–69.

May, A. 2003. *The Bar and the Old Bailey*. Chapel Hill: University of North Carolina Press.

May, R., Tolbert, D. Hocking, J. et al. 2000. *Essays on ICTY Procedure and Evidence in honour of Gabrielle Kirk McDonald*. The Hague: Martinus Nijhoff.

McDowell, D. 1986. *Spartan Law*. Edinburgh: Scottish Academic Press.

Mégrét, F. 2008. International Prosecutors: Accountability and Ethics. *Leuven Center for Global Governance Studies*, Working Paper No. 18.

Mendelson, M. 2001. The Curious Case of *Qatar v. Bahrain* in the International Court of Justice. *BYIL* (72) 183–212.

Mérignhac, A. 1895. *Théorique et pratique de l'arbitrage international: le rôle du droit dans le fonctionnement actuel de l'institution et dans ses destinées futures*. Paris: L. Larose.

Mettraux, G. 2008. *Perspectives on the Nuremberg Trial*. Oxford: Oxford University Press.

Mikaelsen, L. 1980. *European Protection of Human Rights*. Alphen aan den Rijn: Sijthoff and Noordhoff.

Mohammadi 2008. *Judicial Reform and Reorganization in 20th Century Iran.*

Monconduit, F. 1965. *La Commission Européenne des Droits de l'Homme*. Leyden: A.W. Sijthoff.

Monnet, J. 1976. *Mémoires*. Paris: Fayard.

Moore, J. 1898. *History and digest of the international arbitrations to which the United States has been a party*. Washington, D.C.: Government Printing Office.

——1929. *International Adjudications, Ancient and Modern*. Oxford: Oxford University Press.

Morcom, C. 2009. 'Representation of parties before the European Court of Justice—is there a need for reform?' *EIPR* (31), 223–6.

Mosler, H. 1964. 'The Protection of Human Rights by International Legal Procedure', *Georgetown Law Journal* (52), 800–23.

——1969. La procédure de la Cour Internationale de Justice et de la Cour Européenne des Droits de l'Homme. Observations à l'occasion de la nouvelle procédure interne de la Cour Internationale de Justice in *René Cassin Amicorum Discipulorumque Liber I: Problèmes de protection internationale des droits de l'homme*. Paris: A. Pedone.

Mosk, R. 2010. Attorney Ethics in International Arbitration. *BJILP* (5), 31–37;

Mouton, J. and Soulard, C. 2004. *La Cour de justice des Communautés Européennes*. Paris: Presses Universitaires France.

Müller, D. 2005. Procedural Developments at the International Court of Justice. *LPICT* (4), 141–63.

Nathan, K. 2000. *The ICSID Convention: The Law of the International Centre for Settlement of Investment Disputes*. New York: Juris Publishing.

Neave, A. 1978. *Nuremberg*. London: Hodder and Stoughton.

Nichibenren 2010. 'White Paper on Attorneys', online: <http://www.nichibenren.or.jp/library/en/about/data/WhitePaper2010.pdf> (Accessed: 30 November 2011)

Nicholson, D. and Webb, J. 2004. Lawyers' Duties, Adversarialism and Partnership in UK Legal Ethics. *Legal Ethics* (7), 133–40.

Nys, E. 1912. *Droit international*. Paris: Libraire des sciences politiques sociales.

O'Boyle, M. 1992. Procedure before the European Court of Human Rights. *AEHRY* (2), 93–104.

Oppenheim, L. 1912. *International Law*. London: Longmans.

Orakhelashvili, A. 2006. *Peremptory Norms in International Law*. Oxford: Oxford University Press.

Owada, H. 1971. What Future for the International Court of Justice? *AJIL* (65) 268–74.

Papakonstantinou, Z. 2008. *Lawmaking and Adjudication in Archaic Greece*. London: Duckworth.

Pearce 2004. 'Soskice, Frank, Baron Stow Hill (1902-1979)', *Oxford Dictionary of National Biography*, OUP, online: <http://www.oxforddnb.com/view/article/31703> (Accessed: 10 March 2011).

Peck, C. and Lee, R. 1997. *Increasing the Effectiveness of the International Court of Justice*. The Hague: Martinus Nijhoff.

Peerenboom, R. 1998. *Lawyers in China: Obstacles to Independence and the Defense of Rights*. USA: Lawyers Committee for Human Rights.

Pellet, A. 2006. Remarks on Proceedings before the International Court of Justice. *LPICT* (5), 163–82.

——2008. The Anatomy of Courts and Tribunals. LPICT (7), 275–87.

Petrochilos, G. 2003. *Procedural Law in International Arbitration*. Oxford: Oxford University Press.

Philip, C. 1983. *La Cour de Justice des Communautés Européennes*. Paris: Presses Universitaires de France.

Phillips, O. and McCoy, P. 1952. *Conduct of Judges and Lawyers: A Study of Professional Ethics Discipline and Disbarment*. Los Angeles: Parker and Co.

Phillipson, C. 1911. *The International Law and Custom of Ancient Greece and Rome*. London: Macmillan & Company.

Pocar, F. 2004. 'The Proliferation of International Criminal Courts and Tribunals: A Necessity in the Current International Community' *JICJ* (2), 304–8.

Prest, W. 1981. *Lawyers in Early Modern Europe and America*. New York: Holmes and Meier.

——1986. *The Rise of the Barristers: A Social History of the English Bar 1590-1640*. Oxford: Clarendon Press.

Pue, W. and Sugarman, D. 2003. *Lawyers and Vampires: Cultural Histories of the Legal Professions*. Oxford: Hart Publishing.

Rabinowitz, R. 1956-1957. The Historical Development of the Japanese Bar. *HLR* (70), 61–81.

Radhi 2003. *Judiciary and Arbitration in Bahrain.*

Raeder, A. 1912. *L'Arbitrage international chez les Hellenes.* Oslo: Kristiania.

Ralston, J. 1910. *International arbitral law and procedure.* Boston: Ginn & Co.

——1929. *International Arbitration from Athens to Locarno.* Palo Alto: Stanford University Press.

Reid, K. 2008. *A Practitioner's Guide to the European Convention on Human Rights.* London: Sweet & Maxwell.

Reuter, P. 1947-1948. Nurnberg 1946: The Trial. *NDL* (23), 76–97.

——1952. Le Plan Schuman. *RdC* (81) 523–628.

——1953. *La Communauté Européenne du Charbon et de l'Acier.* Paris: Institut des hautes études internationales.

Revon, M. 1892. *L'Arbitrage international.* Paris: Lévy.

Reydams, L. 2005. The ICTR Ten Years On: Back to the Nuremberg Paradigm? *JICJ* (3) 977–88.

Rhode, D. 2000. *In the Interests of Justice: Reforming the Legal Profession.* New York: Oxford University Press.

——2004. *Access to Justice.* Oxford: Oxford University Press.

Riese, O. 1953. Die Verfahrensordnung des Gerichtshofes der Europäischen Gemeinschaft für Kohle und Stahl. *Neue Juristische Wochenschrift* (6), 521–5.

Robertson, A. 1957. Legal Problems of European Integration. *RdC* (91), 105–211.

——1961. *The Law of International Institutions in Europe: being an account of some recent developments in the field of international law.* Manchester: Manchester University Press.

Rodman, K. 2009. Is peace in the interests of justice? The case for broad prosecutorial discretion at the International Criminal Court. *LJIL* (22), 99–126.

Romano, C. 1998-1999. The Proliferation of International Judicial Bodies: The Pieces of the Puzzle, *NYUJILP* (31), 709–52.

Rogers, C. 2009. Lawyers without Borders. *UPILR* (30), 1035–86.

——2013. *Ethics in International Arbitration.* Oxford: Oxford University Press.

Rosenne, S. 1985. *The Law and Practice of the International Court.* Leiden: Martinus Nijhoff.

——2002. International Court of Justice: Practice Directions on Judges ad hoc; Agents, Counsel and Advocates; and Submission of New Documents. *LPICT* (1), 223–45.

——2005. *The Law and Practice of the International Court 1920-2004.* Leiden: Martinus Nijhoff.

Roxburgh, R. 1968. *The Black Books: Vol. V A.D. 1845-A.D. 1914.* London: The Honourable Society of Lincoln's *Inn.*

Sandifer, D. 1975. *Evidence before International Tribunals.* Charlottesville. University Press of Virginia.

Sands, P. 2005. *Lawless World.* London: Penguin Books.

——2011. The ILA Hague Principles on Ethical Standards for Counsel before International Courts and Tribunals. LPICT (10), 1–5.

Sarvarian, A. 2011. Problems of Ethical Standards for Representatives before ICSID Tribunals. LPICT (10), 67–134.

——2012. Ethical Standards for Prosecution and Defence Counsel before International Courts: The Legacy of Nuremberg. *JICJ* (10), 423-446.

——2012. Common Ethical Standards for Counsel before the European Court of Justice and European Court of Human Rights. EJIL (23), 991–1014.

Schabas, W. 2010. *The International Criminal Court: A Commentary on the Rome Statute.* Oxford: Oxford University Press.

Schaffer, M. 1988. *L'avocat et l'Europe des 12 et des 21.* Strasbourg: Centre de formation professionnelle des avocats d'Alsace.

Schreuer, C. 2001. *The ICSID Convention: A Commentary*. Cambridge: Cambridge University Press.

Schulz, F. 1946. *History of Roman Legal Science*. Oxford: Clarendon Press.

Schulze, R. and Hoeren, T. 2000. *Dokumente zum Europaischen Recht Bandz Justiz (bis 1957)*. Berlin: Springer.

Schuman, R. 1963. *Pour l'Europe*. Paris: Nagel.

Scott, J. 1908. The Proposed Court of Arbitral Justice. *AJIL* (2), 772–810

——1920. *The Proceedings of the Hague Peace Conferences*. New York: Oxford University Press.

SFDI. 2004. *La Pratique et le droit international*. Paris: Pedone.

Shelton, D. 2008. *The Regional Protection of Human Rights*. Oxford: Oxford University Press.

Shihata, I. 1986. Towards a Greater Depoliticization of Investment Disputes: The Roles of ICSID and MIGA. *ICSID Rev.-FILJ* (1), 1–25.

Smith, B. 1977. *Reaching Judgment at Nuremberg*. London: Andre Deutsch.

Spiermann, O. 2003. Who Attempts to Do Too Much Does Nothing Well: The 1920 Advisory Committee of Jurists and the Statute of the Permanent Court of International Justice. *BYIL* (73), 187–260.

Stahn, C. and Sluiter, G. 2009. *The Emerging Practice of the International Criminal Court*. Leiden: Martinus Nijhoff.

Stephen 1936. *Digest of the Law of Evidence*.

Stuart, H. 2008. The ICC in trouble. *JICJ* (6), 409–17.

Tams, C. 2005. *Enforcing Obligations Erga Omnes in International Law*. Cambridge: Cambridge University Press.

Taylor, T. 1993. *The Anatomy of the Nuremberg Trials*. London: Bloomsbury.

Teitelbaum, R. 2007. Recent Fact-Finding Developments at the International Court of Justice. *LPICT* (6), 119–58.

Terris et al 2007. *The International Judge*.

Terry, L. 1993-1994. An Introduction to the European Community's Legal Ethics Code Part I: An Analysis of the CCBE Code of Conduct. *GJLE* (7), 1–87.

Thorne, S. 1985. *Essays in English Legal History*. London: Hambledon Press.

Toth, A. 1978. *Legal Protection of Individuals in the European Communities*. Amsterdam: North Holland Publishing Company.

Tusa, A. and Tusa, J. 1983. *The Nuremberg Trial*. London: Macmillan.

Tyrrell, A. and Yaqub, Z. 1996. *The Legal Professions in the New Europe*. London: Cavendish.

Usher, J. 1983. *European Court Practice*. London: Sweet & Maxwell.

Valentine, D. 1955. *The Court of Justice of the European Coal and Steel Community*. The Hague: Martinus Nijhoff.

——1965. *The Court of Justice of the European Communities*. London: Stevens and Sons.

Van der Sprenkel, S. 1962. *Legal Institutions in Manchu China: A Sociological Analysis*. London: The Athlone Press.

Van Houtte, A. 1956. La Cour de Justice de la Communauté Européenne du Charbon et de l'Acier. *Annuaire Européen* (II) 183–222.

Van Reepinghen, C. and Orianne, P. 1961. *La procedure devant la Cour de justice des communautés européennes*. Bruxelles: F. Larcier.

Vasiliev, S. 2009. Proofing the ban on 'witness proofing': did the ICC get it right. *CLF* (20) 193–261.

Vogel 2000. *Islamic Law and Legal System*.

Vohrah, L., Pocar, F., Featherstone, Y, Fourmy, O., Graham, C., Hocking, J., and Robosn, N. 2003. *Man's Inhumanity to Man: Essays on International Law in Honour of Antonio Cassese*. The Hague: Kluwer Law International.

Von Mehren, A. 1963. *Law in Japan: The Legal Order in a Changing Society*. Cambridge: Harvard University Press.

Wall, E. 1966. *The Court of Justice of the European Communities: Jurisdiction and Procedure*. London: Butterworths.

Watts, A. 2002. New Practice Directions of the International Court of Justice. *LPICT* (1), 247–56.

Weiss, F. 2001. *Improving WTO dispute settlement procedures: issues and lessons from the practice of other international courts and tribunals*. London: Cameron May.

Werner, J. 2000. When Arbitration Becomes War: Some Reflections on the Frailty of the Arbitral Process in Cases involving Authoritarian States', *Journal of International Arbitration* (17), 97–103.

Wesler, T. and Laird, I. (eds). 2009. *Investment Treaty Arbitration and International Law*. New York: Juris Publishing.

Wetter 1979. *The International Arbitral Process: Public and Private (Vol. III)*.

Whewell, W. 1853. *Hugonis Grotii de jure belli et pacis libri tres*. Cambridge: Cambridge University Press.

Wickremasinghe, C. 2000. *The International Lawyer as Practitioner*. London: British Institute of International and Comparative Law.

Wickremasinghe, C. and Gardner, J. 1997. *The International Court of Justice: Process, Practice and Procedure*. London: British Institute of International and Comparative Law.

Witt, J. 2007. *Patriots and Cosmopolitans: Hidden Histories of American Law*. Cambridge: Harvard University Press.

Wolfrum, R. 2001. *Max Planck Yearbook of United Nations Law*. Leiden: Martinus Nijhoff.

Wolfrum, R. and Gätzschmann, I. (eds). 2013. *International Dispute Settlement: Room for Innovations?* Heidelberg: Springer.

Yannaca-Small, K. (ed.), Arbitration under International Investment Agreements. Oxford: Oxford University Press.

Yarrow, S. and Abrams, P. 1999. Conditional Fees: The Challenge to Ethics. *Legal Ethics* (2), 193–213.

Zappala, S. 2003. *Human Rights in International Criminal Proceedings*. Oxford: Oxford University Press.

Zimmerman, A., Tomuschat, C. and Oellers-Frahm, K. 2006. *The Statute of the International Court of Justice: A Commentary*. Oxford: Oxford University Press.

CONFERENCE PRESENTATIONS

Key, P. 2011. 'Draft Codes of Conduct for Practitioners in Investor-State and International Commercial Arbitration: From Brazil via Brussels to Beyond?', International Law Association British Branch Seminar Presentation;

GOVERNMENT AND INTERNATIONAL RECORDS

1945. *Documents of the United Nations Conference on International Organization*. London: United Nations Information Office.

United Nations General Assembly Official Records. New York: United Nations.

Chernichenko, S. and Treat, W. 1991. The right to a fair trial: Current recognition and measures necessary for its strengthening. UN Commission on Human Rights, UN Doc. E/CN.1/Sub.2/1991/21.

International Court of Justice, *Acts and Documents*. The Hague: International Court of Justice.
International Court of Justice, *Yearbook*. The Hague: International Court of Justice.

INTERVIEWS[1]

Coulon, Emmanuel. 14 October 2010. Luxembourg.
Cot, Jean-Pierre. 13 September 2010. Brussels.
Doherty, Teresa. 20 August 2010. The Hague.
Edward, David. 27 August 2010. Edinburgh.
Forwood, Nicholas. 14 October 2010. Luxembourg.
Fulford, Adrian. 8 July 2011. London.
Fura, Elisabet. 15 October 2010. Strasbourg.
Harhoff, Frederik. 17 August 2010. The Hague.
Higgins, Rosalyn. 30 September 2010. London.
Jaeger, Eric. 14 October 2010. Luxembourg.
Keith, Kenneth. 10 November 2010. London.
Koroma, Abdul. 4 August 2011. Telephone.
Meisenberg, Simon. 20 August 2010. The Hague.
Ovey, Clare. 15 October 2010. Strasbourg.
Pocar, Fausto. 17 August 2010. The Hague.
Sachithanandan, Pubudu. 20 August 2010. The Hague.
Valencia-Ospina, Eduardo. 19 August 2010. The Hague.
Vaughan, David. 22 July 2010. Telephone.
Wisskirchen, C. 7 July 2010. Telephone.

NEWSPAPERS

Isikoff, M. 19 February 2010. Report: Bush Lawyer said President could order civilians to be 'massacred'. *Newsweek*.
Norton-Taylor, R. 26 January 2010. Chilcot inquiry: Lawyers expose pressure to give green light for war. *The Guardian*.
Rodríguez Iglesias, G. 28 April 2000. Réformer la Cour de justice européenne. *Le Monde*.
Rozenberg, J. 3 July 2008. Why the World's Most Powerful Prosecutor Should Resign: Part I. *The Daily Telegraph*.
——14 September 2008. Why the world's most powerful prosecutor should resign: Part 2. *The Daily Telegraph*.
——18 August 2010. ICC prosecutors should not be grandstanding on their own cases. *The Guardian*.

ELECTRONIC SOURCES

American Bar Association. Model Rules of Professional Conduct: Online: <http://www.americanbar.org/groups/professional_responsibility/publications/model_rules_of_professional_conduct.html> (Accessed: 26 November 2011).
Bar Standards Board. Code Guidance: <http://www.barstandardsboard.org.uk/standardsandguidance/codeguidance> (Accessed: 11 November 2011).
Biografiá del Dr José Gustavo Guerrero: <http://www.elsalvadorhistorico.org/biografias/138-dr-gustavo-guerrero.html> and <http://www.rree.gob.sv/index.

[1] Four additional interview subjects spoke on condition of complete anonymity.

php?option=com_content&view= article&id=113&Itemid=202> (Accessed: 10 March 2011).

Bishop, R.D. and Stevens, M. 'The Compelling Need for a Code of Ethics in International Arbitration: Transparency, Integrity and Legitimacy', <> (Accessed: 28 April 2013);

British Broadcasting Corporation. 2004. Jacques Verges: 'The Devil's Advocate': <http://news.bbc.co.uk/1/hi/world/europe/3578421.stm> (Accessed: 10 March 2011).

Council of Europe Committee of Legal Advisers on Public International Law 2006. Item 7: Organisation and Functions of the Office of the Legal Adviser of the Ministry for Foreign Affairs: Document submitted by the Delegation of the UK: <www.coe.int/t/dlapil/cahdi> (Accessed: 10 December 2011).

Centre d'histoire Sciences Po: Pierre Cot. <http://centre-histoire.sciences-po.fr/archives/fonds/pierre_cot.html> (Accessed: 10 March 2011).

Council of Bars and Law Societies of Europe: <http://www.ccbe.org> (Accessed: 20 December 2011).

Encyclopaedia Britannica. 2011: <http://www.britannica.com/EBchecked/topic/557065/sovereignty> (Accessed: 10 May 2011).

Hoffman, L. 2009. The Universality of Human Rights. *Judicial Studies Board Annual Lecture*: <http://www.judiciary.gov.uk/Resources/JCO/Documents/Speeches/Hoffmann_2009_JSB_Annual_Lecture_Universality_of_Human_Rights.pdf> (Accessed: 6 November 2011)

Institut de Droit International, Code of Arbitral Procedure: <http://www.idi-iil.org/idiF/navig_chron1873.html> (Accessed: 10 December 2011).

International Bar Association: <http://www.ibanet.org> (Accessed: 5 July 2011).

International Court of Justice, President Hisashi Owada: <http://www.icj-cij.org/court> (Accessed: 30 November 2011).

International Law Association: <http://www.ila-hq.org> (Accessed: 4 May 2011).

Mayson, S. 2006. After Clementi: The Impending Legal Landscape, *Legal Services Policy Institute*: <http://www.legalservicesinstitute.co.uk> (Accessed: 4 December 2011).

Oxford Dictionary of Law. 2009: <http://www.oxfordreference.com> (Accessed: 9 February 2011).

Oxford Dictionary of National Biography. 2004: <http://www.oxforddnb.com/view/article/31703> (Accessed: 10 March 2011).

Oxford Dictionary of Philosophy. 2008: <ttp://www.oxfordreference.com/views/ENTRY.html?subview=Main&entry=t98.e2230> (Accessed: 28 October 2011).

Oxford English Dictionary.1989: <http://www.oed.com/view/Entry/196665?redirectedFrom=system#eid> (Accessed: 6 June 2011).

Owada, H. 2011. Sir Ian Brownlie, KT, CBE, QC (1932-2010): The Professor as Counsel. *BYIL*: <www.bybil.oxfordjournals.org> (28 October 2011),

Neuberger, D. Working Party on Entry to the Bar: Final Report: <http://www.barstandardsboard.co.uk> (Accessed: 10 December 2011).

Office of Professional Responsibility, 2009. Report: Investigation into the Office of Legal Counsel's Memoranda: <http://www.judiciary.house.gov> (Accessed: 10 December 2011).

Sydney Chinese Consulate. Curriculum vitae of Consul-General Duan Jielong: <http://sydney.chineseconsulate.org/eng/zlszl/t518871.htm> (Accessed: 28 November 2011).

Weismann, J. 2010. Freshfields Sued in International Racketeering Case. *The National Law Journal*: <http://www.law.com/jsp/nlj/PubArticleNLJ.jsp?id=1202446897911&slreturn=1&hbxlogin=1> (Accessed: 3 July 2011).

Wolfrum, R. 2010. *Max Planck Encyclopaedia of Public International Law*: <http://www.mpepil.com> (Accessed: 10 December 2011).

Wood, D. 2008. Bar Standards Board Review of the Bar Vocational Course Report of the Working Group: <http://www.barstandardsboard.org.uk/news/latest/220.html> (Accessed: 10 December 2011).

Wood, 'Legal Adviser', *MPEPIL*: <http://www.mpepil.com> (Accessed: 25 November 2011).

Index